The Restoration
of American
Politics

POLITICS IN THE TWENTIETH CENTURY

VOLUME   I
THE DECLINE OF DEMOCRATIC POLITICS

VOLUME   II
THE IMPASSE OF AMERICAN FOREIGN POLICY

VOLUME III
THE RESTORATION OF AMERICAN POLITICS

The Restoration
of American
Politics

Hans J. Morgenthau

 THE UNIVERSITY OF CHICAGO PRESS

CHICAGO AND LONDON

International Standard Book Number: 0-226-53823-0
Library of Congress Catalog Card Number: 62-18111

THE UNIVERSITY OF CHICAGO PRESS, CHICAGO 60637
The University of Chicago Press, Ltd., London

Preface

  The essays which comprise this volume have been reprinted without change. I gratefully acknowledge the permission of the following publications and publishers to use copyrighted material: Academy of Political Science, *American Political Science Review*, American Society of International Law, *Bulletin of the Atomic Scientists*, *Challenge*, *China Quarterly*, *Commentary*, Committee for Economic Development, *Common Cause*, *Confluence*, *Encounter*, *Encyclopaedia Britannica*, Foreign Policy Association, *New Leader*, *New Republic*, *New York Times*, Public Affairs Conference Center of the University of Chicago–Rand McNally Co., *Review of Metaphysics*, University of Chicago Press, *Washington Post*, *World Politics*, *Worldview*.

Contents

PART IV–B.   *The Restoration of Foreign Policy: The Methods—Old and New—of Foreign Policy*

PART IV–C.   *The Restoration of Foreign Policy: The Specific Issues*

Introduction

Of the tasks political philosophy must perform, that of restoring a defective political order is the most precarious. The great political philosophers, from Plato onward, have been moved by the defects of the existing political order toward thinking about the nature of politics and of the right political order. By so doing, they sought to guide the powers-that-be toward the realization of that order. In that immediate task, most political philosophers have failed. They did not succeed in stemming the political decline of their respective societies; rather their work tends to demonstrate in retrospect the inevitability of that decline. Yet they have not altogether failed. Their continuing ability to teach posterity the truth about politics testifies to their success. Both their failures and their successes are the result of the peculiar relationship that exists between political theory and political practice.

The rules by which political theory proceeds are bound to be different from those by which political reality is formed. Political reality grows from empirical contingencies, but incompletely and inadequately directed by human reason. Theory, on the other hand, must present a rationally consistent system which takes account of the contingencies without allowing them to spoil its rationality. Thus theory of necessity proceeds by way of elimination; it must neglect what does not fit into its rational scheme in order to maintain itself as theory. Theory cannot help being partial in a dual sense: it looks at reality through the blinkers of its rational scheme and leaves out that part of reality that does not fit into it.

Political theory, then, is of necessity more rational than political reality. It is because political reality is bound to fall short of the rationality of political theory that the latter must fail as a blueprint for political action. Thus political philosophy is constantly exposed to two kinds of corruption: either of becoming subservient to the existing political reality by justifying and rationalizing it or of becoming subservient to an anticipated and desired future political reality by justifying and rationalizing it. In other words, political philosophy has an inherent tendency to perform the functions of either an ideology or a utopia.

As the failure of political philosophy results from the contrast between its own rationality and the contingencies that determine the reality of politics, so its chance to succeed is due to the rational element in political reality that is but a blurred and partial reflection of its own. The actor on the stage of politics carries within his mind a political philosophy, however inchoate and fragmentary and un-acknowledged. That philosophy makes him understand the political scene and act with regard to it. Thus up to a certain point, the po-litical philosopher and the political actor are really engaged in the same intellectual processes. They part company when they contem-plate the purpose of those processes: in the case of the philosopher that purpose is theoretical systematization which must abstract from the contingencies of political life; in the case of the actor it is suc-cessful action which must take those contingencies into account.

An argument can, then, be made in favor of a political philosophy which is systematic in substance but takes its form from political life itself. As far as its form is concerned, it is what might be called an issues-oriented political philosophy, which applies the theoretical principles of politics to a succession of political problems as they arise on the political scene. Edmund Burke is the greatest practi-tioner of that type of political philosophy.

The thought processes of the philosopher are here put into mo-tion by a concrete political issue, and they seek to elucidate that is-sue both for the sake of elucidation and for the benefit of the politi-cal actor. Thus the contemporary philosopher is moved by the con-crete issue of nuclear war to reflect on the meaning of death in the atomic age, and that philosophic reflection, carried on for its own sake, can serve to illuminate the actor's mind and, through it, to fash-ion political action. Similarly, the concrete economic issues of the day move the philosophic observer to a theoretical analysis of the rela-tions between the concentrations of private power, on the one hand, and the government and the individual, on the other. The result of such analysis is a restatement of the nature of freedom and its pre-requisites in the modern world, which again has implications for political action through the influence it can exert upon the mind of the actor.

The sum total of such reflections constitutes a political philosophy in substance; for these reflections seek in an issues-oriented form the same kind of coherent theoretical understanding which is the obvious aim of systematic philosophies. They try to compensate for the lack of obvious systematization with their avoidance of at least the more obvious ideological and utopian temptations and with their direct relevance for the political concerns of the times.

PART I

THE REDISCOVERY

OF POLITICS

1 *Love and Power*

The proposition that power and love are organically connected, growing as they do from the same root of loneliness, must appear to the modern mind paradoxical, if not completely absurd. For power as the domination of man by man, pleasurable to one and painful to the other, and love as the voluntary and pleasurable surrender of two human beings to each other, seem not only to have nothing in common but to be mutually exclusive. Where two human beings are in the relation of power, they cannot be, so it seems to the modern mind, in the relation of love. The inability of the modern mind to see this connection between love and power is the measure of its inability to understand the true dimensions of either love or power. As Paul Tillich put it in the introductory chapter to *Love, Power, and Justice*, "It is unusual to take the word 'confusion' into the title of a chapter. But if one has to write about love, power, and justice the unusual becomes natural."

The modern mind, both in its Marxist and non-Marxist expressions, sees in the power of man over man not an ineluctable outgrowth of human nature but only an ephemeral phenomenon, the product of a peculiar historic configuration, bound to disappear with the disappearance of that configuration. According to Marx, the lust for power and its political manifestations are a mere by-product of the class division of society. In the classless society, the domination of man by man will be replaced by the administration of things. In liberal thought, power politics is regarded as a kind of atavism, a residue from the less enlightened and civilized era of autocratic rule, which is destined to be superseded by the institutions and practices of liberal democracy.

While the modern mind denies the intrinsic relation between the lust for power and human nature, transcending all historic configurations, antedating them, as it were, and even determining them, it does not understand the nature of love at all. Love as the reunion of

From *Commentary*, March, 1962.

two souls and bodies which belong together or, in the Platonic mythology, once were united, is reduced in the modern understanding to sex and gregariousness, the togetherness of the sexes on dates, in marriage, and in other associations, tending to be of a more or less fleeting nature. What the modern understanding misses is the totality of the commitment that characterizes the pure phenomenon of love. It is aware only of surface phenomena which may or may not be manifestations of love, because it is unaware of that very element in man on which love is built: his soul. And it is unaware of that quality of human existence which is the root both of the lust for power and the longing for love: loneliness.

Of all creatures, only man is capable of loneliness because only he is in need of not being alone, without being able in the end to escape being alone. It is that striving to escape his loneliness which gives the impetus to both the lust for power and the longing for love, and it is the inability to escape that loneliness, either at all or for more than a moment, that creates the tension between longing and lack of achievement, which is the tragedy of both power and love. In that existential loneliness man's insufficiency manifests itself. He cannot fulfill himself, he cannot become what he is destined to be, by his own effort, in isolation from other beings. The awareness of that insufficiency drives him on in search of love and power. It drives him on to seek the extension of his self in offspring—the work of his body; in the manufacture of material things—the work of his hands; in philosophy and scholarship—the work of his mind; in art and literature—the work of his imagination; in religion—the work of his pure longing toward transcendence.

Love and power both try to overcome loneliness, and the sense of man's insufficiency stemming from this loneliness, through duplication of his individuality. Through love, man seeks another human being like himself, the Platonic other half of his soul, to form a union which will make him whole. Through power, man seeks to impose his will upon another man, so that the will of the object of his power mirrors his own. What love seeks to discover in another man as a gift of nature, power must create through the artifice of psychological manipulation. Love is reunion through spontaneous mutuality, power seeks to create a union through unilateral imposition.

It is the common quality of love and power that each contains an

8

element of the other. Power points toward love as its fulfilment, as love starts from power and is always threatened with corruption by it. Power, in its ultimate consummation, is the same as love, albeit love is corrupted by an irreducible residue of power. Love, in its ultimate corruption, is the same as power, albeit power is redeemed by an irreducible residue of love.

Love is a psychological relationship which in its pure form is marked by complete and spontaneous mutuality. *A* surrenders himself to *B*, as *B* surrenders himself to *A;* and both do so spontaneously, in recognition of their belonging together. Both are lover and beloved; what *A* is, feels, and wants, *B* is, feels, and wants, too. Love is the most perfect union two human beings are capable of, without losing their respective individualities. Aristophanes has given in the *Symposium* the classic description of the nature of pure love:

And when one of them meets with his other half, the actual half of himself . . . the pair are lost in an amazement of love and friendship and intimacy, and one will not be out of the other's sight, as I may say, even for a moment: these are the people who pass their whole lives together; yet they could not explain what they desire of one another. For the intense yearning which each of them has towards the other does not appear to be the desire of lover's intercourse, but of something else which the soul of either evidently desires and cannot tell, and of which she has only a dark and doubtful presentiment . . . this meeting and melting into one another, this becoming one instead of two, was the very expression of his ancient need. And the reason is that human nature was originally one and we were a whole, and the desire and pursuit of the whole is called love.

Love in its purest form is the rarest of experiences. It is given to few men to experience it at all, and those who experience it do so only in fleeting moments of exaltation. What makes love as commonly experienced fall short of its pure form is the element of power with which love begins in triumph and ends in defeat and which corrupts it throughout. Love typically begins with *A* trying to submit *B* to his will, that is, as a relationship of power, and frequently it does not progress beyond it. As Socrates puts it in the *Phaedrus:* "As wolves love lambs so lovers love their loves." And it is significant that Socrates, in his first speech in that dialogue, in parodying Lysias' conception of love, presents a picture of the love relation which is tantamount to what we would call a relationship of power.

What makes the lover behave like a master and the beloved like the object of the master's power, what makes, in other words, the love relationship similar to the power relationship is the inevitable frustration of love. For if love is a reunion of two human beings who belong together, that reunion can never be complete for any length of time. For, except in the *Liebestod*, which destroys the lovers by uniting them, it stops short of the complete merger of the individualities of the lovers. It is the paradox of love that it seeks the reunion of two individuals while leaving their individualities intact. *A* and *B* want to be one, yet they must want to preserve each other's individuality for the sake of their love for each other. So it is their very love that stands in the way of their love's consummation.

That inner contradiction the lovers endeavor to overcome by letting power do what love is unable to do by itself. Power tries to break down the barrier of individuality which love, because it is love, must leave intact. Yet in the measure that power tries to do the work love cannot do, it puts love in jeopardy. An irreducible element of power is requisite to make a stable relationship of love, which without it would be nothing more than a succession of precarious exaltations. Thus without power love cannot persist; but through power it is corrupted and threatened with destruction. That destruction becomes actual when *A* and *B*, by trying to reduce each other to an object of their respective wills, transform the spontaneous mutuality of the love relationship into the unilateral imposition of the relationship of power.

Thus the lust for power is, as it were, the twin of despairing love. Power becomes a substitute for love. What man cannot achieve for any length of time through love he tries to achieve through power: to fulfill himself, to make himself whole by overcoming his loneliness, his isolation. As Shakespeare's Richard III puts it:

> And this word "love," which greybeards call divine,
> Be resident in men like one another
> And not in me: I am myself alone. . . .
> And am I then a man to be belov'd?
> O, monstrous fault, to harbor such a thought!
> Then, since this earth affords no joy to me,
> But to command, to check, to o'erbear such
> As are of better person than myself,
> I'll make my heaven to dream upon the crown. . . .

Yet of what love can at least approximate and in a fleeting moment actually achieve, power can only give the illusion.

Power is a psychological relationship in which one man controls certain actions of another man through the influence he exerts over the latter's will. That influence derives from three sources: the expectation of benefits, the fear of disadvantages, the respect or love for men or institutions. It may be exerted through orders, threats, promises, persuasion, the authority or charisma of a man or of an office, or a combination of any of these.

It is in the very nature of the power relationship that the position of the two actors within it is ambivalent. *A* seeks to exert power over *B; B* tries to resist that power and seeks to exert power over *A*, which *A* resists. Thus the actor on the political stage is always at the same time a prospective master over others and a prospective object of the power of others. While he seeks power over others, others seek power over him. Victory will fall to him who marshals the stronger weapons of influence with greater skill.

Yet a political victory won with the weapons of threats and promises is likely to be precarious; for the power relation thus established depends upon the continuing submissiveness of a recalcitrant will, generated and maintained by the master's continuing influence. The will of the subject reflects the will of the master but incompletely and tenuously as long as the will of the master is imposed upon the will of the subject from without and against the latter's resistance. How to overcome that resistance and make the will of the subject one with the will of the master is one of the crucial issues with which all political orders must come to terms. It is the issue of political stability. The political masters, actual and potential, and on all levels of social interaction from the family to the state, have sought to meet that issue by basing their power upon the spontaneous consent of the subject. If the subject can be made to duplicate spontaneously within himself the master's will so that what the master wills the subject wills, too, not through inducement from without but through spontaneous consent from within, then the will of the master and the will of the subject are one, and the power of the master is founded not upon the master's threats and promises but upon the subject's love for the master.

So it is not by accident that the political philosophies which emphasize the stability of power relationships, such as those of monarchies and autocracies, make a point of appealing to the love of the subject for the ruler. The philosophy and ritual of absolute monarchy, in particular, are full of references to the love of the subject for the monarch as the foundation of the monarch's power. That foundation has perhaps nowhere been more clearly revealed than in a letter which John Durie, Scotch Presbyterian and worker for Protestant unity, wrote in 1632 to the British Ambassador, Thomas Roe, explaining the decline of the power of Gustavus Adolphus of Sweden, then fighting for the Protestant cause in Germany:

> The increase of his authority is the ground of his abode; and love is the ground of his authority; it must be through love; for it cannot be through power; for his power is not in his own subjects but in strangers; not in his money, but in theirs; not in their good will, but in mere necessity as things stand now betwixt him and them; therefore if the necessity be not so urgent as it is; or if any other means be shown by God (who is able to do as much by another man as by him) to avoid this necessity; the money and the power and the assistance which it yieldeth unto him will fall from him and so his authority is lost, and his abode will be no longer: for the love which was at first is gone. . . .

In recent times, the continuous references to "our beloved leader" in the literature and ritual of Naziism and Stalinism point to the same relationship between ruler and subject—in the case of Naziism in good measure as an actual fact, however corrupted by power and hate; in the case of Stalinism as something to be desired but unattainable.

Obviously, this transformation of the unilateral imposition of the power relationship into the mutuality of love is in the political sphere, at least in its modern secular form, an ideal rather than an attainable goal. Thus the great political masters, the Alexanders and Napoleons, while painfully aware of the love that is beyond their reach, seek to compensate for the love they must miss with an ever greater accumulation of power. From the subjection of ever more men to their will, they seem to expect the achievement of that communion which the lack of love withholds from them. Yet the acquisition of power only begets the desire for more; for the more men the master holds bound to his will, the more he is aware of his loneliness. His success in terms of power only serves to illuminate his failure in terms of love.

There is then in the great political masters a demoniac and frantic striving for ever more power—as there is in the misguided lovers, the Don Juans who mistake sex for love, a limitless and ever unsatiated compulsion toward more and more experiences of sex—which will be satisfied only when the last living man has been subjected to the master's will. " 'More! More!' " in the words of William Blake, "is the cry of a mistaken soul; less than all cannot satisfy man." Thus the heights of the master's power signal the depths of his despair. For the world conqueror can subject all inhabitants of the earth to his will, but he cannot compel a single one to love him. The master of all men is also the loneliest of all men; for his loneliness, in spite of the totality of his power, proves that it cannot be cured by power. That fruitless search for love through power leads in the most passionate of the seekers of power from a despair, impotent in the fulness of power, to a hate, destructive of the objects of their successful power and frustrated love. Thus the Genghis Khans, Hitlers, and Stalins lash out with unreasoning fury at their subjects whom they can dominate but whose love they cannot command and, hence, whom they cannot afford to love.

Yet while the subjects may not love the master and the master may impose his will with bloody tyranny, there is even in the crudest of power relationships an irreducible element of love. What both master and subject seek is that union which remedies the awareness of insufficiency born of loneliness and which only love can give. But they have chosen the wrong track of power and are doomed to failure. Thus they—master and subject—must search forever and in vain for that other human being to whom they could say, I love you, to hear the reply, I love you, too.

The power relationship is, then, in the last analysis, a frustrated relationship of love. Those who must use and suffer power would rather be united in love. Master and subject are at the bottom of their souls lovers who have gone astray. The hostility of their relationship carries a trace of that frustrated love which is at the root of a type of hate. Napoleon, in his conversations with De Las Cases on Saint Helena, and Hitler, in his harangues to his generals, have bemoaned their fate that in the fulness of their power they could trust nobody and found nobody worthy of their love. Many of the powerful have throughout history sought the illusion of love in the promiscuous enjoyment of sex. Beneath that artificial community which power builds as a substitute for, and a spite to, love, there remains at least a glimmer of an aspiration which longs for that reunion only love can give. It manifests itself in the sometimes sudden emergence of charity, pity, and forgiveness in the relations between master and subject. Nowhere has that kinship of power and love been expressed with simpler profundity than in the two words which Homer makes Achilles speak when he is about to slay Lykaos: "Die, friend."

The loneliness of man is, then, impervious to both love and power. Power can only unite through the unilateral imposition of subjection, which leaves the master's isolation intact. Behold that master whom the wills of millions obey and who cannot find a single soul with which to unite his own. Love can unite only in the fleeting moments when two souls and bodies merge in spontaneous mutuality. The lovers bear the dual burden of Adam and Eve and of Moses. They see the promised land in their longing's imagination and enter it only to be expelled from it. Behold the lovers who find in their embrace the illusion of complete union and in fleeting moments even its reality, only to awaken alone in the embrace of another lover.

Thus in the end, his wings seared, his heart-blood spent, his projects come to nought—despairing of power and thirsting for, and forsaken by, love—man peoples the heavens with gods and mothers and virgins and saints who love him and whom he can love and to whose power he can subject himself spontaneously because their power is the power of love. Yet whatever he expects of the other world, he must leave this world as he entered it: alone.

2 *The Demands of Prudence*

An unbridgeable gulf separates the demands of Christian ethics from the way man is compelled by his natural aspirations to act. That conflict is foreordained by the nature of Christian ethics and the nature of man. Christian ethics demands love, humility, the abnegation of self; man as a natural creature seeks the aggrandizement of self through pride and power. It is the tragedy of man that he is incapable, by dint of his nature, to do what Christian ethics demands of him.

It is the guilt of man that he is unwilling, by dint of his corruption, to do what he could do to meet the demands of Christian ethics. The best man is capable of is to be guided by the vision of a life lived in compliance with the Christian code and to narrow the gap between his conduct and that code. The closing of that gap through complete harmony between the demands of Christian ethics and man's conduct is not a problem for ethics but for theology. Only divine grace can establish that harmony in another world.

What is true of man in general applies with particular force to political man. For the natural aspirations proper to the political sphere—and there is no difference in kind between domestic and international politics—contravene by definition the demands of Christian ethics. No compromise is possible between the great commandment of Christian ethics, "Love thy neighbor as thyself," and the great commandment of politics, "Use thy neighbor as a means to the ends of thy power." It is a priori impossible for political man to be at the same time a good politician—complying with the rules of political conduct—and to be a good Christian—complying with the demands of Christian ethics. In the measure that he tries to be the one he must cease to be the other.

No politician can accept the truth of that incompatibility, for it is exactly in the appearance of being moral while seeking power that he finds both peace of mind and an element of power itself. Few moralists have found that incompatibility palatable, for the reconcilia-

From *Worldview*, June, 1960.

tion of the irreconcilable is intellectually more attractive and socially more rewarding than the radical postulation of alternatives. To face the conflict between ethics and politics squarely places an intolerable burden upon our actions or our consciences. Thus Western man has endeavored to obliterate the gap between the demands of Christian ethics and the aspirations of human nature by closing his eyes to it. He has reinterpreted the demands of Christian ethics by "liberalizing" them. He has made it appear as though the Christian gospel did not mean what it obviously says, and he has invented ingenious theological devices which make it easier to sin because they make forgiveness easy. He has watered down the demands of Christian ethics, thus making it appear as though human action were complying with these demands. This is the escape of the Pharisees.

The other escape is that of the Sophists. They approach the problem from the side of human action. They try to build a bridge between ethics and politics on the foundation of distorted human action rather than misinterpreted Christian ethics. Man is here presented as naturally good and human action as naturally moral; this is assumed to be true particularly of oneself and one's own action and of the collectivity to which one happens to belong and of its action. Here is the root of political ideology, the most persuasive attempt Western man has undertaken to make its peace with the demands of Christian ethics without having to forego his natural aspirations.

If there be any truth in this necessarily sketchy analysis, then the moral problem of politics resolves itself into the question: Given the existential incompatibility between politics and Christian ethics, how must moral man act in the political sphere? While he is precluded from acting morally, the best he can do is to minimize the intrinsic immorality of the political act. He must choose from among the political actions at his disposal the one which is likely to do the least violence to the commands of Christian ethics. The moral strategy of politics is, then, to try to choose the lesser evil.

This strategy, it should be added, is no more peculiar to politics than is the incompatibility between the demands of Christian ethics and the political aspirations of man. Both are special instances of the human condition; but they are particularly poignant instances because of the poignancy of the moral problem of politics. Yet, as to choose the lesser evil is the best the moral politician can do, so it is also the best moral man at large can do.

It is at the point of choosing the lesser evil that moral evaluation and political calculation merge. For what is more or less morally evil must be determined through anticipation of the probable consequences of different courses of action. Obviously, Father John Courtney Murray finds nuclear weapons "from the moral point of view . . . unshootable" because of the consequences of shooting them (*Morality and Modern War* [New York: Church Peace Union, 1960]). A foreign policy that preserves peace is morally superior to one that leads to limited war, and the latter, in turn, is superior to one which increases the danger of all-out nuclear war. The right moral choice is here obviously identical with the right political choice. A foreign policy which seeks an avoidable limited war is morally inferior to one which actually avoids such a war. On the other hand, a foreign policy which shies away from the risk of limited war and thereby brings on all-out nuclear war is morally inferior to a foreign policy which faces that risk.

No one can be certain before the event which choice is morally right and politically sound. We all act on hunches which the future may or may not prove to have been correct. It is this uncertainty of both moral judgment and political calculation which creates those "ambiguities" and "dilemmas" which Father Murray so dislikes. These ambiguities and dilemmas were not invented by theologians, Protestant or otherwise, but they grow inevitably from the nature of the relationship between Christian ethics and political action. The ambiguities which we find baffling in the character of Hamlet, and the dilemmas with which he was unable to cope, were not peculiar to the prince of Denmark. They are but the ambiguities and the dilemmas which no morally sensitive actor on the political scene can escape.

This being so, recourse to natural law will not free us from these intellectual and moral disabilities. To the contrary, such recourse will only serve to emphasize their inevitability. For the gap between the rational postulates of natural law and the contingencies of the concrete situation within which man must act and judge is just as wide as the gulf which separates the demands of Christian ethics from the rules of political action. In truth, as a more detailed discussion of natural law and its relation to ethics would show, both gaps are identical. Natural law can only provide us with the general principles of right action. It cannot tell us with any degree of certainty which of alternative actions is the right one in a concrete situation. That choice natural law leaves to prudential considerations—strangely enough, there is no reference to prudence in Father Murray's argument—that is, to our intellectually fallible minds and morally weak wills. And those minds and wills put us again in the presence of the ambiguities and dilemmas.

I join Father Murray in deploring the decline of the tradition of natural law in America, the weakening of those objective rational standards which once gave guidance to private and public judgments and actions. However, it is not secular liberalism alone which ought to be blamed for that decline. Defenders of natural law must share in that responsibility. For natural law has been intellectually and politically discredited in good measure because it has been made to bear a burden which it could not carry. The attempts to apply natural law directly, without the intermediary of prudence, to political action were bound to fail. Either they provided no guide to political action because of the generality of natural law to which we have referred, or else they provided a particular political position with an ideological rationalization and justification. Thus the appeal to natural law became either meaningless or suspect.

I should say in passing that Father Murray has failed to do justice to the recent debate which has centered on the problem of morality and foreign policy. This has been by and large a serious and fruitful debate. It has deepened and refined the understanding of both politics and morality. I know of no evidence, with the exception of some offhand remarks by one author, to suggest that "to the political realists or cynics . . . all public issues are simply issues of power in which moral judgments have no place at all." And I must have expressed myself consistently with extreme imprecision if to Father Murray (p. 21) my "basic view . . . seems to be that all moralities are purely 'national'; they cannot be subjected to judgment in terms of universal principles." I have tried to express the exactly opposite view for more than fifteen years. I have particularly pointed to "national moralities" as political ideologies which endeavor to invest the interests of a particular nation with the sanction of universal moral principles.

3 *Death in the Nuclear Age*

It is obvious that the nuclear age has radically changed man's relations to nature and to his fellow men. It has enormously increased man's ability to use the forces of nature for his purposes and has thus concentrated unprecedented destructive powers in the hands of governments. That concentration of power has fundamentally altered the relations which have existed throughout history between government and people and among governments themselves. It has made popular revolution impossible, and it has made war an absurdity. Yet, less obvious and more important, the nuclear age has changed man's relations to himself. It has done so by giving death a new meaning.

Death is the great scandal in the experience of man; for death—as the destruction of the human person after a finite span of time—is the very negation of all man experiences as specifically human in his existence: the consciousness of himself and of his world, the remembrance of things past and the anticipation of things to come, a creativeness in thought and action which aspires to, and approximates, the eternal. Thus man has been compelled, for the sake of his existence as man, to bridge the gap between death and his specifically human attributes by transcending death. He has done so in three different ways: by making himself, within narrow limits, the master of death; by denying the reality of death through the belief in the immortality of his person; by conquering the reality of death through the immortality of the world he leaves behind.

Man can make himself the master of death by putting an end to his biological existence whenever he wishes. While he cannot live as long as he wants to, he can stop living whenever he wants to. While he cannot choose life over death when his life has reached its biological limits, he can choose death over life regardless of these limits. He can commit suicide; or he can commit what Nietzsche has called "suicide with a good conscience" by seeking out death, especially at

From *Commentary*, September, 1961.

the hand of someone else. He is capable of sacrificial death. In his self-chosen death for a cause in particular, on the battlefield or elsewhere, man triumphs over death, however incompletely. He triumphs because he does not wait until his body is ready to die, but he offers his life to death when his chosen purpose demands it. Yet that triumph is incomplete because it cannot overcome the inevitability of death but only controls its coming.

Man also denies the reality of death by believing in the immortality of his person. This belief can take two different forms. It may take the form of the assumption that the finiteness of man's biological existence is but apparent and that his body will live on in another world. It can also take the form of the assumption that what is specifically human in man will survive the destruction of his body and that man's soul will live on forever, either separated from any body or reincarnated in someone else's. This belief in personal immortality, in defiance of the empirical evidence of the finiteness of man's biological existence, is of course peculiar to the religious realm. It presupposes the existence of a world which is not only inaccessible to the senses but also superior to the world of the senses in that what is truly human in man is there preserved forever.

It is a distinctive characteristic of our secular age that it has replaced the belief in the immortality of the human person with the attempt to assure the immortality of the world he leaves behind. Man can transcend the finiteness of his biological existence either in his consciousness or in objective reality by adding to that existence four different dimensions which are in one way or another independent of that finiteness. They are different dimensions of immortality. He can extend his consciousness into the past by remembering it. He can extend his consciousness into the future by anticipating it. As *homo faber*, he imbeds his biological existence within technological and social artifacts which survive that existence. His imagination creates new worlds of religion, art, and reason that live after their creator.

By thus bestowing immortality upon the past, man assures himself of immortality to be granted by future generations who will remember him. As the past lives on in his historic recollection, so will he continue to live in the memory of his successors. The continuity of history gives the individual at least a chance to survive himself in the collective memory of mankind. Those who are eminent, or believe themselves to be so, aspire to posthumous fame which will enable them to live on, perhaps forever.

The ability to remember and the aspiration to be remembered call for deliberate action to assure that remembrance. The assurance of his life after death becomes one of man's main concerns here and now. Man on all levels of civilization is moved to create monuments which testify to his existence and will live after him. He founds a family and lives on in his sons, who bear his name as he bears his father's. He leaves an inheritance of visible things not to be consumed but to be preserved as tangible mementos of past generations. Over his grave he causes a monument of stone to be erected whose durability, as it were, compensates for the impermanence of what lies beneath. Or he may even refuse to accept that impermanence altogether and have his body preserved in the likeness of life. At the very least, he will have pictures made of himself to perpetuate his physical likeness.

This concern with immortality in this world manifests itself on the highest level of consciousness in the preparation of man's fame. He lives in such a way as to make sure that his fame will survive him. All of us, from the peasant and handicraft man to the founders of churches, the architects of empires, the builders of cities, the tamers of the forces of nature, seek to leave behind the works of our wills and hands to testify to our existence. "*Roma eterna,*" "the Reich of a thousand years" are but the most ambitious attempts to perpetuate man in his deeds. The tree that he has planted, the house that he has built, have been given a life likely to last longer than his own. At best, he as a person will live on in his works; at worst, he has the satisfaction of living on anonymously in what he has created.

It is, however, in the works of his imagination that man conquers the mortality of his body in the most specifically human way. The artists and poets, the philosophers and the writers, can point with different degrees of assurance to their work and say, with Horace: "I have finished a monument more lasting than bronze and loftier than the Pyramids' royal pile, one that no wasting rain, no furious north wind can destroy, or the countless chain of years and the ages' flight. I shall not altogether die. . . ." In the works of his mind it is not just his physical existence, the bare fact that he once lived, that is remembered. Rather, what is rememberd is the creative quality that sets him apart from all other creatures, that is peculiar to him as a man. What is remembered is not only the specifically human quality, but also and most importantly the quality in which he lives on as a unique individual, the like of whom has never existed before or since. In the works of his mind, man, the creator, survives.

Yet why are those works a "monument more lasting than bronze," and why can their creator be confident that "on and on shall I grow, ever fresh with the glory of after time"? Because the man endowed with a creative mind knows himself to be a member in an unbroken chain emerging from the past and reaching into the future, which is made of the same stuff his mind is made of and, hence, is capable of participating in, and perpetuating, his mind's creation. He may be mortal, but humanity is not, and so he will be immortal in his works. This is the triumphant message of Horace.

Our life, then, receives one of its meanings from the meaning we give to death. What we make of life is shaped by what we make of death; for we live in the presence of the inevitability of death and we dedicate our lives to the proof of the proposition that death is not what it seems to be: the irrevocable end of our existence. We search for immortality, and the kind of immortality we seek determines the kind of life we lead.

The significance of the possibility of nuclear death is that it radically affects the meaning of death, of immortality, of life itself. It affects that meaning by destroying most of it. Nuclear destruction is mass destruction, both of persons and of things. It signifies the simultaneous destruction of tens of millions of people, of whole families, generations, and societies, of all things that they have inherited and created. It signifies the total destruction of whole societies by killing their members, destroying their visible achievements, and therefore reducing the survivors to barbarism. Thus nuclear destruction destroys the meaning of death by depriving it of its individuality. It destroys the meaning of immortality by making both society and history impossible. It destroys the meaning of life by throwing life back upon itself.

Sacrificial death has meaning only as the outgrowth of an individual decision which chooses death over life. The hero who risks his life or dies for a cause is bound to be one man, an identifiable individual. There is meaning in Leonidas falling at Thermopylae, in Socrates drinking the cup of hemlock, in Jesus nailed to the cross. There can be no meaning in the slaughter of the innocent, the murder of six million Jews, the prospective nuclear destruction of, say, fifty million Americans and an equal number of Russians. There is then, a radical difference in meaning between a man risking death by an act of will and fifty million people simultaneously reduced— by somebody switching a key thousands of miles away—to radioactive ashes, indistinguishable from the ashes of their houses, books, and animals. Horace could say, thinking of the individual soldier ready to die, "It is sweet and honorable to die for one's country." Yet Wilfred Owen, describing the effects of a gas attack in the First World War, could call Horace's famous phrase "The old Lie," and beholding a victim of modern mass destruction, could only bewail the futility of such a death and ask in despair, "Was it for this the clay grew tall? O what made fatuous sunbeams toil to break earth's sleep at all?" The death of the Horatian soldier is the assertion of man's freedom from biological necessity, a limited triumph over death. The death of Owen's soldier and of his prospective successors in the nuclear age is the negation not only of man's freedom but of his life's meaning as well.

Man gives his life and death meaning by his ability to make himself and his works remembered after his death. Patroclus dies to be avenged by Achilles. Hector dies to be mourned by Priam. Yet if Patroclus, Hector, and all those who could remember them were killed simultaneously, what would become of the meaning of Patroclus' and Hector's deaths? Their lives and deaths would lose their meaning. They would die, not like men but like beasts, killed in the mass, and what would be remembered would be the quantity of the killed—six million, twenty million, fifty million—not the quality of one man's death as over against another's.

Of their deeds, nothing would remain but the faint hope of remembrance in distant places. The very concept of fame would disappear, and the historians, the professional immortalizers, would have nothing to report. What had been preserved and created through the mind, will, and hands of man would be dissolved like man himself. Civilization itself would perish. Perhaps in some faraway place some evidence would be preserved of the perished civilization and of the men who created it. Nothing more than that would be left of the immortality man had once been able to achieve through the persistence of his fame and the permanence of his works.

And what would become of life itself? If our age had not replaced the belief in the immortality of the individual person with the immortality of humanity and its civilization, we could take the prospect of nuclear death in our stride. We could even afford to look forward to the day of the great slaughter as a day on which the preparatory and vain life on this earth would come to an end for most of us and the true, eternal life in another world begin. Yet a secular age, which has lost faith in individual immortality in another world and is aware of the impending doom of the world through which it tries to perpetuate itself here and now, is left without a remedy. Once it has become aware of its condition, it must despair. It is the saving grace of our age that it has not yet become aware of its condition.

We think and act as though the possibility of nuclear death had no bearing upon the meaning of life and death. In spite of what some of us know in our reason, we continue to think and act as though the possibility of nuclear death portended only a quantitative extension of the mass destruction of the past and not a qualitative transformation of the meaning of our existence. Thus we talk about defending the freedom of West Berlin as we used to talk about defending the freedom of the American colonies. Thus we talk about defending Western civilization against communism as the ancient Greeks used to talk about defending their civilization against the Persians. Thus we propose to die with honor rather than to live in shame.

Yet the possibility of nuclear death, by destroying the meaning of life and death, has reduced to absurd clichés the noble words of yesterday. To defend freedom and civilization is absurd when to defend them amounts to destroying them. To die with honor is absurd if nobody is left to honor the dead. The very conceptions of honor and shame require a society that knows what honor and shame mean.

It is this contrast between our consciousness and the objective conditions in which we live, the backwardness of our consciousness in view of the possibility of nuclear death, that threatens us with the actuality of nuclear death. It would indeed be the height of thoughtless optimism to assume that something so absurd as a nuclear war cannot happen because it is so absurd. An age whose objective conditions of existence have been radically transformed by the possibility of nuclear death evades the need for a radical transformation of its thought and action by thinking and acting as though nothing of radical import had happened. This refusal to adapt thought and action to radically new conditions has spelled the doom of men and civilizations before. It is likely to do so again.

PART II

THE ATTEMPTS AT
RESTORATION

4 *The Corruption of Liberal Thought:*
Harold Laski

The decline of the political philosophy of liberalism is due to the defects of its general philosophy, which contemporary developments have brought to the fore. What liberalism had to say about the nature of man, society, and politics is at odds with what we have experienced. More specifically, it has been unable to reconcile its original libertarian assumptions and postulates with its latter-day philosophy of the administrative and welfare state. Professor Laski, the most brilliant, erudite, and prolific exponent of the last stage of liberalism, exemplifies the philosophic insufficiency and political confusion of liberal thought. He also exemplifies the intellectual corruption that follows inevitably from an attempt to square the disparate elements of liberalism with each other and with the experiences of the age.

Liberty in the Modern State makes these points in ways quite unintended and unsuspected by its author. The book was first published in 1930; it was republished with a long, new introduction in 1937, then republished again in 1949.[1] The Introduction to this last edition was obviously completed in 1947 and incorporates substantial parts of that of 1937. Shockingly great is the distance between the Introduction and the main body of the book, which is a substantially unchanged reprint of the edition of 1930. That distance concerns philosophy and scholarship, quality of argument and of language, and, above all, intellectual responsibility. In the decline of a once great and exceptionally gifted mind, it demonstrates the initial weakness of the political philosophy of liberalism, the recent decomposition of that philosophy, and the reasons for the decline of liberty itself.

The only substantial deviations from the preceding editions occur in the Introduction, and philosophically they are less significant than the lack of change in the body of the book. The Introduction to the edition of 1937 started with a discussion of the crisis of capitalist

From *Common Cause*, March, 1950.
[1] New York: Viking Press, 1949.

democracy and of its inherent tendencies toward fascism, followed by a sympathetic and optimistic dissertation on the Soviet Union. This dissertation has been substantially retained in the 1949 edition, with only a few significant changes, to one of which we shall return. The other part has been replaced by a new discussion of the ills of capitalist democracy, arriving at the dual conclusion that "private ownership of the means of production is no longer compatible with democratic institutions" (p. 17) and that "the principle of national sovereignty has exhausted its usefulness" (p. 18).

When the body of this book first appeared in 1930 it was received with deserved praise. The nobility of its moral concern for the individual, the cogency of its argument, the sweep of its erudition are indeed impressive. Its strength, no less than its weakness, is in large measure that of John Stuart Mill, and this is high praise indeed. There is, it is true, already in the Laski of 1930 a certain sentimental verbosity and fuzziness in concepts which are happily absent in Mill. Yet the philosophic position of Laski is that of classic liberalism. Professors Hayek and Mises can hardly have found fault with it. In his own words, this is

the essence of [the] argument. I have taken the view that liberty means that there is no restraint upon those conditions which, in modern civilization, are the necessary guarantees of individual happiness. There is no liberty without freedom of speech. There is no liberty if special privilege restricts the franchise to a portion of the community. There is no liberty if a dominant opinion can control the social habits of the rest without persuading the latter that there are reasonable grounds for the control. For, as I have argued, since each man's experience is ultimately unique, he alone can fully appreciate its significance....

But no man, of course, stands alone. He lives with others and in others. His liberty, therefore, is never absolute, since the conflict of experience means the imposition of certain ways of behavior upon all of us lest conflict destroy peace. That imposition, broadly speaking, is essential to liberty, since it makes for peace; and peace is the condition of continuity of liberty [p. 129].

The philosophic weakness of this position is to be found in the weakness of its five basic concepts: liberty, the individual, the individual good, the common good, the identification of the absolute and relative good.

The problem of liberty in relation to the state concerns, in the words of John Stuart Mill, "the nature and limits of the power which can be legitimately exercised by society over the individual." Its perennial theme is "the struggle between Liberty and Authority." A concept of liberty as broad and indefinite as that used by Laski carries within itself the possibility of conclusions destructive of the very antithesis which gives rise to the problem of liberty. This problem is intelligible only under the assumption that man ought to be free from political authority in certain respects and subject to it in others. The assumptions of totalitarianism, destroying the rights of the individual in the face of political authority, and the assumptions of anarchism, denying the claims of political authority, make it altogether impossible to speak of liberty in the political sense. It has often been noticed that a consistent liberalism leads to anarchism. Laski recognizes that connection, too, and approves of it.

The conception of the individual as a unique personality with experiences and judgments all his own may be valid in some systems of art, religion, or psychology, but it certainly is the very negation of political experience. However right the author may be in his strictures against the excesses of the idealistic theory of the state, political authority is founded upon a consensus of all or at least of the majority, that is, upon shared moral and political convictions which are the very negation of that uniqueness and privacy upon which Laski dwells. Such consensus may be the product of a common religion, a secular tradition, the national mores or it may be instilled in the reluctant citizens with fire and sword. Without it there can be no state and no government; for without it there can be no political authority accepted at least by the majority as legitimate, nor that voluntary obedience which the author so rightly stresses. Here again, the conclusion from the premise is anarchy.

Laski conceives of the individual good, which freedom must promote, as happiness, and of happiness as the satisfaction of individual desires. We are here not concerned with the question of whether such a conception of happiness is psychologically valid. Even if it were, it would still have to be admitted that it is a distinctive characteristic of civil society, as it is of individual morality, to approve of certain desires as good and to reject others as bad. As a philosophic conception, happiness has meaning only within the context of a system of selective values which define what happiness is in the first place. In the absence of such a system, happiness will be defined by the accident of implicit valuations, that is, by the preferences of the author or of the group for which he pretends to speak.

Laski is, of course, not oblivious of the inevitability of conflict arising from the incompatibility of unique personalities and their valuations and desires, and he recognizes the consequent need for a mediating force. He finds that force in reason. However, reason in the abstract has nothing to say about the solution of social conflicts. It is only in the concrete, in a specific philosophic and social context, that reason can tell us which interests must be protected and which sacrificed. In other words, no rational solution of a social conflict, in theory or in practice, can dispense with a political philosophy which has developed a concept of the common good, or with an appraisal of the power of the social forces identified with the two sides of the conflict. Yet Laski's conception of the common good is identical with the sum total of the individual desires mediated by reason. That argument begs the question and leaves the problem where we encountered it.

These weaknesses of Laski's philosophic position are intimately connected with the last of the weaknesses that we have proposed to discuss. Political philosophy, to be fruitful, must make the Aristotelian distinction between what is ideally good and what is good under the circumstances. It is one thing to provide an ideal solution for the conflict between liberty and authority, a solution which might well be tantamount to anarchism. It is quite another thing to consider the problem of liberty in the context of what is attainable under the conditions of British society in 1930 or of American society in 1950. To confound both approaches, as Laski does, may lead, if the author is consistent, to the condemnation of all actually possible solutions in view of the unattainable ideal. If the author is inconsistent but is quite naturally moved by strong personal preferences, as Laski is, he will measure some political systems by the ideal, others by the attainable, and thus obtain the political conclusions that he prefers to obtain.

These defects, let us repeat it, are the defects of the intellectual tradition to which Laski belongs. The faults of the Introduction of 1937 and 1947 are all his own. To point all of them out and analyze them would require a book. Let us limit ourselves to four representative ones: one conceptual, one philosophic, and two factual.

On the very first page of the Introduction the conceptual foundation for any rational discussion of the problem of liberty disintegrates with the statement that "the future of liberty depends upon the realization of those four freedoms upon which President Roosevelt laid such eloquent emphasis. . . ." It is fanciful to suggest that the determination of "the nature and limits of the power which can be legitimately exercised by society over the individual" depends upon the realization of such vague and unattainable ideals as freedom from fear and freedom from want. Given this conceptual starting point, no demonstration is needed to show that these ideals, whatever they may mean, are not, and are not likely to be, realized and that, hence, liberty does not exist and is not likely to exist. There is nothing left for us to do but to bewail this sad state of affairs with sentimental rhetoric and to comment on it with the shopworn clichés of progressive journalism.

To turn to an example of philosophic analysis, it is obvious that the phenomenon of fascism has a profound bearing upon the problem of liberty in our time. What, then, is the purpose of fascism in this respect? "The purpose of fascism is to prevent the relations of production from coming into a natural harmony with the forces of production; for that prevention, and increasingly, the method of coercion is inescapable" (p. 30). Can anything be simpler, or more absurd? One must, then, I suppose, assume that the wave of pseudo-religious fanaticism with its worship of violence for its own sake, which swept through Germany long before the industrialists as a class, together with virtually all other social groups, jumped on the bandwagon of naziism, was just an ideological superstructure whirling in the air until it settled down upon its material foundations, discovered as a dialectic afterthought. To call this kind of reasoning by cliché Marxism would be an insult to the memory of Marx and Engels, Kautsky and Luxemburg, Lenin and Trotsky. Call it "Pravdaism" or "Browderism," if you wish.

But let us consider simple matters, matters of fact. On pages 20–21 we read: ". . . and it is still more true of the great corporations today than it was when General Negrier wrote of them nearly forty years ago that '*les sociétés financières estiment que les gouverne-*

ments ont le devoir de faire la guerre pour assurer leurs bénéfices' ['the corporations believe that it is the governments' duty to make war so that they may be assured of their profits'].'' The general, whoever he was, may plead ignorance, for he could not have been acquainted with the empirical studies of Robbins, Schumpeter, Staley, Sulzbach, Viner, and Winslow, which have exploded the Marxist myth of the warmongering capitalists. But what excuses does Laski have?

Laski finds little actual liberty in the Soviet Union but great promise for the future. On page 43 of the edition of 1937 he said: "In the classic sense of absolute liberalism freedom does not exist in the Soviet Union." This is, of course, true of the Soviet Union as of all other political systems past or present, and, hence, the statement is trivial. On page 27 of the edition of 1949 that passage reads as follows: "In the classic sense the Four Freedoms do not exist in the Soviet Union." The truth is that, while we can speak of classic liberalism in contrast to other types, there is no such thing as freedom from want or freedom from fear in the classic or in any other sense. There is freedom from want and freedom from fear, or there is not. Laski must have known that the Four Freedoms are not realized in the Soviet Union; yet his political preferences did not allow him to admit it. Thus he suggested that, while the Four Freedoms in the classic sense do not exist in the Soviet Union, they might well exist in some other sense.

How was such a descent from the comparative heights of 1930 possible? The answer to this question will shed light upon the decline of liberalism as theory and practice of government.

The rise of bolshevism and fascism in the Western world denied the very assumptions upon which the philosophy of nineteenth-century liberalism had been founded. The society of rational individuals, either developing their unique personalities and satisfying their desires in harmony or settling conflicts among them by the appeal to reason, revealed itself as a mirage engendered by the fleeting conditions of a unique historic constellation. Under different historic conditions, such as those of the interwar years, large segments of Western society showed none of the rational qualities of the liberal prototype. Instead, they sought a new consensus either in revealed religion or in the political religions of totalitarianism. In the face of this phenomenon, for the advent of which their political philosophy did not prepare them, the liberals either continue to reassert the laissez-faire principles of 1850 and thus, by standing still while society moves, become the spokesmen for the tories of the 1950's; or they embrace, sometimes without knowing it, one or the other of the totalitarian creeds. Laski, who cannot be a Fascist and can no longer be a liberal in the "classic" sense in which he was one in 1930, becomes a Marxist who tries to interpret the reality of Russian bolshevism in terms of the liberal philosophy. He tries to do for bolshevism what in the thirties so many of his countrymen tried to do for fascism, that is, to prove that totalitarianism is really a kind of advanced liberalism, disfigured by some blemishes of which time will take care.

Yet the Laski of 1930 at least intimated the impossibility of such a task. He showed then that absolute power, far from tending to limit and reform itself, has the innate tendency to increase its hold upon the individual and to become more oppressive as voluntary obedience wanes. He could have added, if his philosophy had not obscured the realities of politics, that this is particularly true of an absolute power which identifies its monopoly of power with a monopoly of truth, whose monopoly of the most effective weapons of warfare makes popular revolution impossible, and whose totalitarian control no private activity can escape. Here lies the real threat to liberty in our time. The Laski of 1930 could see at least part of that truth, the Laski of 1947 cannot. In this respect, it may be said, Professor Laski differs somewhat from the Bourbons of the Restoration. They are said to have learned nothing and to have forgotten nothing. Comparing the Laski of 1947 with the Laski of 1930 one cannot help concluding, with genuine sorrow, that he has learned little and forgotten a great deal.

5 *The Surrender to the Immanence of Power: E. H. Carr*

Of the four books which constitute Mr. Carr's major contribution to political thought, one, *The Twenty Years' Crisis*,[1] is primarily diagnostic and critical; the three others, *Conditions of Peace*,[2] *Nationalism and After*,[3] and *The Soviet Impact on the Western World*,[4] are intended to be primarily constructive and to offer a cure for the disease.

The foundation upon which the critical analysis of *The Twenty Years' Crisis* is built is the juxtaposition of utopianism and realism. In its period of immaturity, all science goes through a utopian stage "in which the element of wish or purpose is overwhelmingly strong, and the inclination to analyze facts and means weak or non-existent" (p. 8). That initial stage is succeeded by a period of realism which is able "to distinguish the analysis of what is from aspiration about what should be" (p. 13). Realism "places its emphasis on the acceptance of facts and on the analysis of their causes and consequences" (p. 14). The experiences of the interwar years revealed the weakness of the utopian approach to international politics and made its realistic analysis both possible and imperative. Yet a mature political science must combine utopian and realistic thought, purpose and analysis, ethics and politics.

According to Mr. Carr, "the exposure by realistic criticism of the hollowness of the utopian edifice is the most urgent task of the moment in international thought" (p. 113). "Clearly all popular postwar theories of international politics are reflections, seen in an America mirror, of nineteenth-century liberal thought" (p. 37). Mr. Carr finds the utopian element in the belief that "nineteenth century liberal democracy was based, not on a balance of forces peculiar to the economic development of the period and of the countries concerned, but on certain *a priori* rational principles which had only to be applied in other contexts to produce similar results" (p. 37).

From *World Politics*, October, 1948.

[1] London: Macmillan & Co., 1940. [3] New York: Macmillan Co., 1945.
[2] New York: Macmillan Co., 1942. [4] New York: Macmillan Co., 1947.

This writer has no quarrel with Mr. Carr's detailed analysis, in the light of these assumptions, of the main modes of international thought and of the institutional devices which were carried from the domestic scene of the nineteenth century to the international scene of the twentieth. The League of Nations, harmony of interests, collective security, and identification of the national interest with the universal good are indeed classic examples of a utopian rationalism which erects limited experiences and interests into absolute principles and deduces from those principles solutions capable of universal application. "What matters is that these supposedly absolute and universal principles were not principles at all, but the unconscious reflections of national policy based on a particular interpretation of national interests at a particular time. . . . The bankruptcy of utopianism resides not in its failure to live up to its principles, but in the exposure of its inability to provide any absolute and disinterested standard for the conduct of international affairs" (p. 111).

Yet while Mr. Carr destroys the nineteenth-century legacy of political thought, he knows that realism is not enough. "Consistent realism excludes four things which appear to be essential ingredients of all effective political thinking: a finite goal, an emotional appeal, a right of moral judgment, and a ground for action" (p. 113). "Having demolished the current utopia with the weapons of realism, we still need to build a new utopia of our own, which will one day fall to the same weapons. The human will, will continue to seek an escape from the logical consequences of realism in the vision of an international order which, as soon as it crystallizes itself into concrete political form, becomes tainted with self-interest and hypocrisy, and must once more be attacked with the instruments of realism" (p. 118).

Thus Mr. Carr, the realist, sets out in search of a new utopia, and all his subsequent thinking becomes the Odyssey of a mind that has discovered the phenomenon of power and longs to transcend it. That search for principles which can give moral meaning, and set normative limits, to the struggle for power on the international scene brings Mr. Carr back to where he started from: to power itself.

That return to power takes on four different aspects in different periods of Mr. Carr's thinking: appeasement of Germany in *The*

Twenty Years' Crisis, the postulate of a strong collectivist state in *Conditions of Peace*, the sacrifice of the small nations to the great powers in *Nationalism and After*, fascination by the Soviet Union in *The Soviet Impact on the Western World*.

In *The Twenty Years' Crisis*, the last word of international morality is the demand for self-sacrifice. That demand is addressed particularly to the beneficiaries of the status quo. They must give up some of their advantages, not only to those who seek adjustments within the framework of the existing status quo, but also and primarily to those who challenge the existence and justice of that status quo itself. "The process of give-and-take must apply to challenges to the existing order. Those who profit most by that order can in the long run only hope to maintain it by making sufficient concessions to make it tolerable to those who profit by it least. And the responsibility for seeing that these changes take place as far as possible in an orderly way rests as much on the defenders as on the challengers" (p. 215). In consequence, "a successful foreign policy must oscillate between the apparently opposite poles of force and appeasement" (p. 284). The Munich settlement of 1938, then, becomes a modern paradigm of a successful foreign policy thus defined, and Neville Chamberlain, the prototype of a statesman combining the elements of realism and utopianism in his thought and action. "The element of power was present" in that settlement. "The element of morality was also present in the form of the common recognition by the powers . . . of a criterion applicable to the dispute: the principle of self-determination. . . . The change in itself was one which corresponded both to a change in the European equilibrium of forces and to accepted canons of international morality" (p. 282).

The Twenty Years' Crisis was in page proof when the Second World War broke out; *Conditions of Peace* was in the press when the attack on Pearl Harbor brought the United States into the war and Germany and Japan were at the summit of their power. *The Twenty Years' Crisis* attacked the application of the nineteenth-century philosophy of liberal democracy to international affairs; *Conditions of Peace* examines that philosophy in all its manifestations and finds it wanting. More determinedly and more seriously than even *The Twenty Years' Crisis*, *Conditions of Peace* is permeated with the conviction that the twentieth century is fundamentally different from the century that preceded it and that there could be a turning-back to the nineteenth-century modes of thought and action only at the risk of catastrophic failure. The democracies were satisfied to defend the domestic and international status quo with the outworn ideas and institutions of the nineteenth century. Thus it fell to bolshevism and fascism to offer the world a new political order. "Soviet Russia, soon to be followed by Fascist Italy and Nazi Germany, found in 'planned economy' the new twentieth-century concept which was to replace nineteenth-century liberalism; and having gained the initiative, these countries at length compelled the conservative Powers to follow slowly and reluctantly in their train" (p. xx). The idealists of the English-speaking world transform themselves into the reactionaries of the twentieth century, "carried away by the last expiring convulsions of a world revolution which set in 150 years ago" and putting themselves "in opposition to the new world revolution which first broke through the crust of the existing order in the Bolshevik revolution of 1917" (p. 7). Hitler, the Napoleon of the twentieth century, "has consummated the work, which Marx and Lenin had begun, of overthrowing the nineteenth-century capitalistic system . . . and in this sense his work, like that of Napoleon, cannot and will not be undone" (pp. 9–10).

The revolution of the twentieth century is directed against liberal democracy, national self-determination, and laissez faire economics. The revolutionary challenge to democracy and national self-determination must be met by redefinition and reinterpretation. The challege to nineteenth-century economics must be met by a planned economy. It is here that the foremost task of revolutionary renewal is to be found. Democratic forms and political rights have been rendered illusory by the overriding force of economic power. "Under existing democratic institutions, the will of the unorganised majority is impotent to assert itself against the domination of organised economic power. It has come to be widely believed today, and with much plausibility, that the attitudes and policies of political parties in most democratic countries are determined only in a minor degree by the opinions of the electorate which they purport to represent, and in a major degree by the vested interests which supply the bulk of the party funds. In other words, national policy on vital issues is really settled, as Marx alleged, not by a democratic counting of votes, but by the result of a perpetual struggle for power between rival economic interests . . ." (pp. 27–28). "Democracy must be redefined as a system of government based on political rights valid not merely against military, but against economic, power" (p. 23). To make planning possible, we must search for a "moral purpose powerful enough to generate self-sacrifice on the scale requisite to enable civilization to survive" (p. 119). Communism, like Christianity, has such a moral purpose. "The cooperation between the Western peoples and Soviet Russia in the war should help to resolve the antithesis, incidental rather than fundamental, between the secular ideals of Christianity and those of Communism" (p. 121). In both the domestic and the international spheres, the traditional emphasis upon rights and benefits must be replaced by stress on obligations and services.

These themes are more fully developed in *Nationalism and After*, published at the end of the Second World War, and in *The Soviet Impact on the Western World*, published in 1947, when the conflict between the Soviet Union and the Western world had reached unprecedented depths. Mr. Carr makes a convincing case for the assertion that twentieth-century nationalism differs profoundly from its nineteenth-century predecessor. This difference is the result of three factors: "the bringing of new social strata within the effective membership of the nation, the visible reunion of economic with political power, and the increase in the number of nations" (p. 18). "The combination of these factors has found expression in two world wars, or two installments of the same world war, in a single generation, and has imparted to them a peculiar quality of embittered exasperation for which it would be difficult to find a precedent in any war in history" (p. 27). "The failure to create an international community of nations on the basis of international treaties and international law marks the final bankruptcy of nationalism in the West" (p. 32).

Mr. Carr detects a retrogression of unbridled nationalism in certain tendencies which have become visible during the Second World War, such as the widespread collaboration with the German conqueror and the acceptance of a new, supranational order. The nation as the final unit of international organization has been made obsolete by modern military and economic developments. The self-sufficient nation can no longer assure to its members military security or economic well-being. National self-determination, in particular, applied without regard to such military and economic considerations, has become an anarchical force destructive of international order. The solution, according to Mr. Carr, lies in the separation of non-political from political authority. The nation may remain the center of certain types of non-political authority and loyalty. Politically, economically, and militarily the nation must yield to multinational units of which the *Grossraum* of Nazi Germany and the Soviet Union are the outstanding examples.

In *The Soviet Impact on the Western World*, the Soviet Union takes the place of the pioneer of the future. As Hitler was saluted as the Napoleon of the twentieth century in *Conditions of Peace*, so now Stalin appears to Mr. Carr as the Wilson of the Second World War. "The missionary role which had been filled in the first World War by American democracy and Woodrow Wilson had passed in the second World War to Soviet democracy and Marshal Stalin" (p. 3). What Mr. Carr calls "Soviet democracy" is, according to him, really an offshoot of Western democracy. In the West, political democracy and social democracy became antagonistic after the middle class had achieved its revolutionary objectives against the feudal order. The bourgeoisie of the West led political democracy to victory. The Russian proletariat achieved social democracy. "The challenge which Soviet democracy presents to the Western world is a challenge to complete the unfinished revolution" (p. 10). In consequence, Mr. Carr equates the Cromwellian, Jacobin, and Bolshevist dictatorships as instruments for achieving democracy. "There is, therefore, no essential incompatibility between democracy and dictatorship" (p. 11). Since in this view the Soviet Union has become the champion of democracy in the mid-twentieth century, it is not surprising to learn that "the cult of the 'common man' now fashionable in English-speaking countries is perhaps a first result of the impact of Soviet democracy" (p. 12). "The broad lines of Soviet policy may be dictated from the center. But the Soviet Union has never ignored the human element, or underestimated the extent to which the execution of any policy depends on the enthusiasm and initiative of the individual citizen; and it has shown itself as well aware as the western world of what Sir Ernest Barker has described as a main function of democracy—to 'enlist the effective thought of the whole community in the operation of discussion.' Here at any rate is a challenge of Soviet democracy to western political institutions about which western democrats will be well advised to ponder" (pp. 18–19). What is true of the cult of the common man and of public discussion is also true of planning: ". . . Lord Keynes' doctrines found such ready acceptance in Great Britain and elsewhere partly because the ground had already been prepared in the minds of his contemporaries by contemplation of the planned economy of the Soviet Union" (p. 34).

In international affairs the Soviet impact has been in the main twofold: the development of propaganda as a normal instrument of foreign policy and the emphasis upon the power factor as against its ideological disguises, practiced by the Western statesmen of the League of Nations period. Fundamentally, however, the Soviet impact on the Western world is moral. "The gravamen of the Marxist revolution is not that it has exposed the failures and shortcomings of western democracy, but that it has called in question the moral authority of the ideals and principles of western democracy by declaring them to be a reflexion of the interests of a privileged class" (p. 94). "The fate of the western world will turn on its ability to meet the Soviet challenge by a successful search for new forms of social and economic action in which what is valid in individualist and democratic tradition can be applied to the problems of mass civilization" (p. 113).

There can be no doubt that Mr. Carr's work constitutes a contribution to political thought of the first order. No contemporary thinker, with the exception of Reinhold Niebuhr, has seen more clearly and exposed with more acute brilliance the essential defects of Western political thought. Even in so monumental a failure as *The Soviet Impact on the Western World*—a failure because it confronts Soviet ideology with democratic practice—there is much critical analysis which Western thinkers might well ponder. Yet, as we have seen, it was Mr. Carr's purpose not only to give a critical analysis of the Western tradition of political thought but also to replace the old and obsolete with a new synthesis of realism and utopianism, theory and practice, ethics and politics; and the main bulk of Mr. Carr's work is dedicated to that purpose. In view of this purpose the over-all impression of Mr. Carr's work is one of failure. What are the reasons for the failure of a work undertaken with so singular an equipment of mind, learning, and honest purpose?

The fundamental reason is philosophic. Mr. Carr sets out to discover a new morality in the political world without a clear notion of what morality is. The philosophically untenable equation of utopia, theory, and morality, which is at the foundation of *The Twenty Years' Crisis*, leads of necessity to a relativistic, instrumentalist conception of morality. Morality, then, becomes "an escape from the logical consequences of realism, which, once it is achieved, must once more be attacked with instruments of realism" (*The Twenty Years' Crisis*, p. 118). In another contribution to the problem, "The Moral Foundations for World Order,"[5] Mr. Carr has nothing better to offer than a "compromise between morality and power," and throughout his work he relies heavily upon Niebuhr's *Moral Man and Immoral Society*, unaware that Mr. Niebuhr has long since given up the juxtaposition which the title indicates.

Consequently, Mr. Carr has no transcendent point of view from which to survey the political scene and to appraise the phenomenon of power. Thus the political moralist transforms himself into a utopian of power. Whoever holds seeming superiority of power becomes of necessity the repository of superior morality as well. Power thus corrupts, not only the actor on the political scene, but even the observer, unfortified by a transcendent standard of ethics. This is the lesson taught by the fate of the political romantics of whom the outstanding representatives are Adam Müller and Carl Schmitt. It is a dangerous thing to be a Machiavelli. It is a disastrous thing to be a Machiavelli without *virtù*.

[5] In *Foundations for World Order* (Denver: Social Science Foundation, University of Denver, 1948).

6 *The Evocation of the Past: Bertrand de Jouvenel*

Bertrand de Jouvenel undertakes to face the problem of power, indeed the central problem of our age, but in truth he does not face it at all. The intended confrontation becomes evasion and escape. It must be borne in mind that theoretical concern with power as a general phenomenon is peculiar to our age. Before Hobbes, no Western political thinker dealt systematically with power as a general phenomenon, and Hobbes himself remained an incident rather than the founder of a tradition. It was only in the historiography and philosophy of history of the nineteenth century that such a tradition was established, and the sociology and political science of the twentieth century have taken up the theme. Yet they have done so only halfheartedly, qualifying and distorting, obscuring and embellishing the reality of power as a general phenomenon. Of this modern tendency to face the problem of power but to face it, as it were, with a squinting eye, M. de Jouvenel's book, *On Power: Its Nature and the History of Its Growth*,[1] is an outstanding example. It is outstanding in its originality and brilliance, its force of argument, and the relevance of its diagnosis. It is also outstanding in the arbitrariness of its argumentation from history and in the partiality with which the central problem is posed and developed.

It is significant—and the significance of it will become fully apparent in the course of the discussion—that the book is not "on power" at all. According to the translator, "the word 'Power,' whenever it begins with a capital letter, denotes the central governmental authority in states or communities—*l'ensemble des éléments gouvernementaux* . . ." (p. xiii). In other words, the book is concerned only with a particular type of power, that is, governmental power, while implicitly assuming in the title and throughout the argument that there is no other power to be concerned about. This substitution of *pars pro toto* gives the book its peculiar focus. The book

From the *Review of Metaphysics*, June, 1950.
[1] New York: Viking Press, 1949.

observes with striking clarity what is within that focus; it sees either not at all or only in dim, distorted outline what is outside the focus. But all the time, by means of a semantic equivocation, the illusion is created that the focus comprises not only Power, that is, government, but also power as such, that is, as a general social phenomenon. It requires a very attentive reader to keep in mind that in the terminology of the author Power is sometimes quite different from power, different as object of scientific analysis and different as object of moral evaluation.

The central theme of the book is the enormous power of the modern state. The modern state has become a "Minotaur," and the continuous increase in the power of the state for almost a thousand years is concomitant with the incessant advance of warfare toward total war. "Therefore the extension of Power, which means its ability to control ever more completely a nation's activities, is responsible for the extension of war" (p. 7). Democracy, in turn, is responsible for the extension of Power. "Democracy, then, in the centralizing, pattern-making, absolutist shape which we have given to it is, it is clear, the time of tyranny's incubation" (p. 11). It is the purpose of the book "to examine the reasons why, and the way in which, Power grows in society" (p. 13).

At the core of the author's argument lies the contrast between aristocratic and monarchical government, on the one hand, and democracy, on the other. The bad and dangerous effects of Power are connected with the latter; what is beneficial and harmless in Power derives from the former. The modern history of the Western world is generally conceived as a progression toward liberty and, in turn, toward limitation on government, liberty becoming greater and government growing weaker as we approach the twentieth century. According to the author, the exact opposite is true. "The idea that Power is of God buttressed, so it is said, a monarchy that was both arbitrary and unlimited right through the Dark Ages. . . . There is not a word of truth in all this. Let us remember . . . that Power in medieval times was shared . . . , limited . . . , and that, above all, it was not sovereign. . . . In fact, so far from having been a cause of greatness in Power, the conception of divine sovereignty was for many centuries the companion of its weakness" (p. 28).

"The consecrated king of the Middle Ages was a Power as tied down and as little arbitrary as we can conceive. He was simultaneously constrained by standing human law, i.e., custom, and by the Divine Law, and could hardly trust his own reading of his duty about anything. The court of peers was there to compel his respect for custom, and the Church took care that he continued as the assiduous viceregent of the heavenly king, whose instructions in their every point he must obey" (p. 30).

The common belief in the progressive liberation of the individual is an illusion. "The reason [for this illusion] is that there are in society, in addition to the state and the individual, social authorities as well, which also claim from the human being their due of obedience and services. And the diminution or disappearance of his obligations to a social authority may affect his life and stir his interest more than the aggravation of his obligations to the political authority" (p. 158).

A revolution, prepared by Marsilius of Padua and by the Reformation, was needed to substitute for the sovereignty of God the sovereignty of the people. With the weakening of the Church, God was transformed from an ally of the people against Power into an ally of Power against the people. With that transformation the absolute monarchy came into existence. Yet at the same time there arose the doctrine that Power is conferred by the people, thus barring the road to absolutism. That, according to the author, is "the great illusion" (p. 33). By quoting extensively from Hobbes, Spinoza, and Rousseau, the author reaches the conclusion that the unlimited character of Power is the inevitable result of popular sovereignty. "What a contrast is here," he exclaims by juxtaposing Spinoza and St. Augustine, "between a Power which is held to the execution of the divine law and one which, after subsuming every individual right, has become a law to itself!" (p. 35).

Popular sovereignty and divine sovereignty seem to be rather similar in their relation to Power. "Both allow a right of command which, though it is unlimited, is not inherent in the governors. The right belongs to a superior power—whether it be God or the people —which cannot by its nature exercise the right itself. Therefore they have to confer a mandate on a Power which can exercise it. Both state more or less explicitly that the mandatories will be tied by rules: in other words, Power's behaviour is subject to either the

Divine Will or the general will" (p. 39). Yet the holders of Power tend to usurp the sovereignty which in theory they exercise by delegation. "They will in the end give themselves out as resuming in their own persons the Divine Will or the general will, as the case may be; Louis XIV, for instance, claimed the rights of God, and Napoleon those of the people" (p. 39). Control of Power, either through the Church or through parliament, is bound to remain ineffective; for sovereignty, being "in essence one and indivisible" (p. 40), cannot be shared by two different sets of agents. Thus the monarchy wins over the Church at the end of the Middle Ages, as in our age either the executive or the legislature comes to dominate the people.

This despotism of our age, however, is likely to be more formidable than that of divine sovereignty for two reasons. Popular sovereignty dispenses with "the Divine Will, which shows itself to men under the forms of a Law Eternal, to command whatever he pleases" (p. 42). Further, popular sovereignty justifies itself primarily in terms of its origin, so that whatever the people want is good because they want it. Medieval Power is limited by the conception of its end, which must be just for Power to be legitimate. When the conception of the end of government reappears in the political thought of the nineteenth century, it is no longer connected with individuals as such but with the state as an organism, which has an existence of its own transcending that of its individual members and is an end in itself, to which the individuals are subservient. This is the heritage of Hegel. In it democracy takes on a new meaning. "In the sense of individualist social philosophy it is the rule of the Rights of Man; in a political philosophy divorced from social individualism it is the absolutism of a government which draws its title from the masses" (p. 47). Here, then, the end is no longer, as it was in the Middle Ages, justice in the sense that each individual must obtain his due. Justice, now, becomes a postulate of society, and to realize this end the limitless expansion of Power is justified.

Underlying this discussion is the conception that Power, that is, the state and its government, are not "the natural product of human sociability" (p. 99). They owe their existence to the instinct of domination, that is, the lust for power (with a small p). "The monarch is not in the least the creature of his people, set up to satisfy their wants. He is rather a parasitic and dominating growth which has detached itself from the dominating group of parasitic conquerors. But the need to establish his authority, to maintain it and keep it supplied, binds him to a course of conduct which profits the vast majority of his subjects. To suppose that majority rule functions only in democracy is a fantastic illusion. The king, who is but one solitary individual, stands far more in need of the general support of society than any other form of government. And, since it is human nature for habit to engender affection, the king, though acting at first only from concern for authority, comes to act with affection as well and in the end to be motivated by affection. The mystical principle of the *rex* has come again" (p. 106).

This duality and inner contradiction of Power is of its essence; it must be egoist and social at the same time. To prepare for Power which has rid itself of its egoism and has become completely virtuous is the worst of illusions; "it has become the fruitful cause of the great disturbances which desolate our age and threaten the very existence of civilization" (p. 117). "It is a noteworthy fact that all the greatest political mistakes stem from defective appraisals of the common good—mistakes from which egoism, had it been called into consultation, would have warned Power off" (p. 124). Similarly, it is not surprising that the philosopher constructing a simple and rigid system of thought finds himself in alliance with the tyrant who endeavors to translate such a system of thought into action. To accomplish what the philosopher demands, Power must grow to enormous dimensions, and Power grows in proportion to the moral sublimity and comprehensiveness of the utopian scheme.

The growth of Power manifests itself in history in three different respects: in the ever increasing quantity of human and material resources which Power marshals for its own purposes, especially for the purposes of war; in the ability of Power to make the laws, and any kind of them, instead of, as in the Middle Ages, being subject to an unchangeable set of rules of conduct; and in the leveling process by which all intermediate social authorities are eliminated. In this last capacity Power plays a revolutionary role. As the king destroys the feudal aristocracy, so the modern state undermines the capitalist authorities. In these revolutions, Power is always the ally of the

common people. "The passion for absolutism is, inevitably, in conspiracy with the passion for equality" (p. 177).

"Where will it end? In the destruction of all other commands for
the benefit of one alone—that of the state. In each man's absolute
freedom from every family and social authority, a freedom the price
of which is complete submission to the state. In the complete equality as between themselves of all citizens, paid for by their equal
abasement before the power of their absolute master—the state. In
the disappearance of every constraint which does not emanate from
the state, and in the denial of every pre-eminence which is not
approved by the state. In a word, it ends in the atomization of
society, and in the rupture of every private tie linking man and
man, whose only bond is now their common bondage to the state.
The extremes of individualism and socialism meet: that was their
predestined course" (p. 172). Yet this is not the end. "Conqueror
though it is of the aristocracy which took shape in society, the state
will in the end be dismembered by the statocracy which it itself has
borne. The beneficiaries of the state leave it, taking with them a
veritable dowry of wealth and authority, leaving the state impover-
ished and powerless. Then it becomes the turn of the state to break
down these new social molecules, containing as they do the human
energies which it needs. And so the process of the state's expansion
starts all over again.

"Such is the spectacle which history presents to us. Now we see
an aggressive state pulling down what other authorities have built
up, now we see an omnipotent and distended state bursting like a
ripe spore and releasing from its midst a new feudalism which robs
it of its substance" (p. 176). And each popular revolution, undertaken in the name of liberty, is but a milestone in the growth of
Power. "In the final analysis revolutions are made, not for man,
but for Power" (p. 235).

Of this development, democracy is the prime example. "Conceived as the foundation of liberty, it paves the way for tyranny.
Born for the purpose of standing as a bulwark against Power, it
ends by providing Power with the finest soil it has ever had in which
to spread itself over the social field" (p. 238). It amounts to "the
substitution of the arbitrary will of a body or of a crowd for the
arbitrary will of a monarch as the principle of rule" (p. 252). This

development is particularly obvious in modern parliamentary institutions. "What had been a body for the protection of private citizens is now one for the advancement of the public interest, and has been clothed with the formidable power of legislation. . . . In the end, therefore, the principle of legality, intended as the absolute guarantee of each man's liberty, was to come to justify the absolute commission of that liberty to the discretion of a parliamentary aristocracy" (pp. 242–43).

Here again, monarchy gains by comparison. "The royal will was, and was known to be, that of a crowned head, his favourite, or his minister; it was in that respect as human and *personal* as that of anyone else. The will of democratic Power goes by the name of *general*. It crushes each individual beneath the weight of the sum of the individuals represented by it; it oppresses each private interest in the name of a general interest which is incarnate in itself. The democratic fiction confers on the rulers the authority of the whole. It is the whole that both wills and acts" (p. 257). "It comes to this: that the 'Power of the people,' so called, is in fact linked to the people only by an extremely slack umbilical cord—general elections; it is, to all intents and purposes, a 'Power over the people,' a Power which is all the greater for getting its authorization from this cord" (p. 280).

Ultimately, sovereignty passes "from parliament to the victorious machine, and elections are now no more than a plebiscite by which a whole people puts itself in the power of a small gang" (p. 275). The end is inevitably a totalitarianism which promises security and destroys liberty. Power, erecting the fragments of its knowledge into a dogma to bring happiness to mankind, transforms itself into a theocracy whose beneficence and, hence, whose authority have no limits. Thus totalitarian democracy unites, for the first time in Western civilization, the spiritual and temporal powers. "From not having known how to preserve, and from not knowing how to restore, the delicate and living harmony of a highly civilized society, we are returning to the form of cohesion which is that of the primitive tribe" (p. 377).

The great merit of this book lies in a penetrating and subtle analysis of the growth of governmental power in our time and of the pitfalls that modern mass democracy encounters. In this analysis the book is incomparably superior to anything that goes with us by the name of academic political philosophy. As a systematic philosophic system, however, it suffers from four major weaknesses, weaknesses so major as to vitiate its claim altogether to be a valid political philosophy.

We have already pointed to the semantic distortion resulting from the use of the term "Power" with a capital "*P*" as a synonym of government. This distortion, however, is but a symptom of the use of Power as a metaphysical abstraction which has an essence, a life, a behavior of its own. Thus we read for instance that "it is of Power's essence not to be weak" (p. 11). Power (with a small *p*) can obviously be conceived as a quality of a certain individual in his relations with another individual. In this sense we can say that A has power over B or that B fears the power of A. It is also possible to abstract from certain individuals as points of reference for power and refer to certain offices and a certain status regardless of the individuals connected with them. Thus we can say that the President of the United States, whoever he may be, has a certain kind of power with regard to the members of the cabinet, whoever they may be. It is also possible to attribute to such power certain qualities which it has in common with, or in which it differs from, power in general or certain other types of power.

What M. de Jouvenel does is bad metaphysics in that Hegelian tradition which has rendered useless so much of German social philosophy. The method of that metaphysics consists in endowing a metaphor, such as Power or Leviathan or Minotaur, or a legal abstraction, such as the government or the state, with certain qualities which are meaningful only when they are attributed to real persons. From the hypostatized qualities of such a metaphysical entity theoretical and practical conclusions are drawn, and the nature of the conclusions is limited only by the imagination of the author who has endowed the metaphysical entity with certain qualities in the first place.

Bad metaphysics leads of necessity to bad political philosophy. The metaphysics of Power distorts, if it does not blot out, the reality of power. What validity is there in the assertion that Power in the Middle Ages, that is, the authority of the prince, was limited and beneficial and that liberty flourished under it, without any con-

sideration of the power of the Church and of the feudal lords because they had only power and not Power? The test of the author's
assertion, which, as we have seen, is at the core of his philosophy,
can be provided, not by this kind of metaphysical juggling, but only
by raising the question: what was the status of the common man
vis-à-vis the public authorities, say, in the twelfth and eighteenth
centuries in comparison with what it is in the Western world today?
Is M. de Jouvenel prepared to defend the proposition that the
common man enjoyed greater freedom—moral, intellectual, social—
in those past centuries than he is enjoying today? To put that question is to answer it. It is a fundamental objection to the author's
philosophic method that it incapacitates him even to put that question in empirical terms.

M. de Jouvenel achieves the same result of the glorification of
medieval monarchy and of the damnation of modern democracy
by yet another, more common and also more vulgar device. He
rightly stresses the enormous increase in the power of the state in
our time and the concomitant threat to individual liberty. He con-
trasts with this sad state of affairs the constitutional principles and
arrangements of times past. The juxtaposition of the political practices of one society with the constitutional theory and law of another, however, is not philosophy but demagogy. By this device
Communist writers prove to their satisfaction that true democracy
exists only in the Soviet Union and that what the Western world
calls democracy is but a fraud. And there can indeed be no doubt
that the provisions of the Soviet constitution are more democratic
than the political practices of the United States. Is it any more convincing to tell us that the medieval state, in contrast to modern
democracy, was limited by the divine law without telling us to what
political uses that divine law was put? Or that in medieval times
Power, that is, the royal authority, was limited by the power of the
feudal barons without asking whose will regularly prevailed in case
of conflict, the king's or the barons'?

Finally, many of the author's strictures against modern democracy
are vitiated by his failure to distinguish between the general evils
which flow from the ubiquity of the lust for power and, hence, are
beyond remedy by human effort, and the specific evils which result
from concrete historic circumstances and, hence, are subject to cor-
rection by the processes of history, supported by conscious human

effort. All power, however spelled, negates the freedom of the individuals over whom it is exercised, and the concentrated, monopolistic power of the modern state is particularly dangerous to individual liberty. That danger does not stem from the innate metaphysical qualities of Power, nor from the disappearance of intermediate social authorities, nor from the enfeeblement of the belief in divine law as a limiting factor on government. Its causes are fivefold: intellectual, moral, political, economic, and technological.

The secularization of thought, as it manifests itself in the spirit of science, has given the modern mind an unprecedented confidence in its own efforts, unaided by supernatural powers and virtually unlimited by the obstacles of nature, a confidence which, under the conditions of modern technology, is transferred to the government as an agency of central planning. A mass civilization, under the impact of the scientific spirit and largely oblivious of the heritage of Western civilization and catering to the lowest instincts of the greatest number, is destroying in those responsible for government, that is, in all, the sense of moral discrimination which is the prerequisite of good government. The participation of the broad masses of the population in the political processes under democratic conditions has led to an unprecedented centralization of the processes of government. The modern conditions of economic activity have brought about an unprecedented centralization of economic power which, in turn, has called into being, as a corrective, the centralized powers of the state. This centralization is in good measure the result of the character of modern technology which, by giving the state a monopoly of the most destructive weapons of warfare, has made popular revolutions impossible. Of this phenomenon, which bears so heavily upon his central theme, the learned author has, strangely enough, nothing to say.

To call attention to and illuminate the evils of centralized power, in the face of the prevailing thoughtless optimism, is a great merit indeed. The modern state, by solving some problems, raises others which must be solved in turn. That the mechanical repetition of democratic incantations will not solve them is certain. It is no less certain that they will not be solved by a backward-looking romantic aristocratism which follows in the footpaths of Bonald, De Maistre, De Tocqueville, and Taine and shares in their brilliance and insights as well as in their aberrations.

7 *The Rediscovery of Imagination and Religion: Arnold Toynbee*

The reaction against philosophic relativism, methodological dogmatism, and positivist scientism has been most sweeping not in the field of political science but in that of history. Arnold Toynbee's work, by virtue of its very existence, is a frontal attack against the mood prevailing in all the social sciences. In *A Study of History* Mr. Toynbee tries to restore the claims of historic imagination and spirituality. Yet by doing so, he raises anew and more profoundly the dilemma of truth in matters political. He does so in three spheres: historiography, philosophy of history, and religion.

Mr. Toynbee's work poses anew, by implication, the problem of historiography. If what Mr. Toynbee is doing is a valid writing of history, then most of what is going by the name of academic history is, at worst, irrelevant or, at best, mere preparation. On the other hand, if the writing of history is a science with all that the word "science" connotes in terms of the use of documentary evidence and the renunciation of judgments of value, then certainly Mr. Toynbee is not a historian. This conflict between two conceptions of history is not likely to be resolved through methodological argument; for within that argument the philosophic assumption predetermines the conclusion. Method being a means to an end, achievement is the only valid test of method. What, then, is it that we expect history to achieve?

Burckhardt has told us that it is the purpose of history "to make us not clever for one day, but wise forever." History imparts its wisdom by giving a meaningful account of the life and deeds of men who came before us. This account receives its meaning from the connection which the selective and appraising mind of the historian establishes between the data of history and the perennial concerns of man.

If this be the standard by which history must be judged, then Mr. Toynbee's contribution dwarfs scientific historiography, not in this or that of its manifestations, but as a category of historic thinking.

From *Encounter*, March, 1955.

The great achievement of Mr. Toynbee as a historian lies in that very subjectivity which is the horror of scientific historiography. Mr. Toynbee has recovered the courage, which the scientific dogma had put to sleep, to ask from history questions which are meaningful for him and, through him as a man, for other men as well and to force history to answer him. Never mind that history may have no answer to some of the questions Mr. Toynbee asks, that the facts are sometimes arranged to produce the answers expected, and that not all the "facts" are facts in the scientific sense. Mr. Toynbee has awakened the historic imagination from its dogmatic slumber; he has communicated his own wonderment about the ways of man to his readers, and through innumerable flashes of insight, suggestive reinterpretations, and fertile hypotheses he has demonstrated by his own example the worth of historiography in the classic manner.

Compare with the richness and infectious dynamics of his historic imagination the unproblematic poverty of scientific historiography! The "science" of history leaves nothing to the imagination. What cannot be proved by the documents not only is not true but can have no meaning to be communicated by the historian. To have demonstrated, not through argument but through example, the richness of philosophic historiography, however problematical in detail, as against the self-impoverishment of "scientific" history, unproblematic in detail but a problem in its very conception of history, is the great merit of Mr. Toynbee's work. What in our time had become a mere historic recollection, Mr. Toynbee has again made a living reality: the creativeness of the historic imagination.

This historic imagination is not at the service of history, properly speaking. It is not Mr. Toynbee's purpose to give a coherent account of the historic process. His purpose is philosophic rather than historical. He searches for the laws which determine the rise and fall of civilizations.

On the face of it, such an undertaking appears to be sociological rather than philosophic. For it appears to require, not the philosophic assessment of the different civilizations from an over-all world view, but rather the empirical analysis of the morphology of civilizations, proceeding from empirically verifiable similarities to ever broadening generalizations. The main categories Mr. Toynbee employs, such as challenge and response, contacts in space and contacts in time, point to such a sociological intent. And in page after page the work reads like a gigantic collection of sociological essays and aphorisms, of illuminating similarities and analogies across the accustomed barriers of historic time, but loosely held together by the work's general plan. Still, the general plan is philosophic and could have been no other. For what Mr. Toynbee sets out to do is beyond the ken of empirical verification.

The possibility of all empirical verification resides in the shared perspective of all actual and potential observers. Astronomy as empirical science is possible because observers with the same perceptive and rational faculties look at the same object from the same planetary perspective. The deeper we move from the world of nature into the world of man as the subject and object of valuations, the more we find the objectivity of empirical science qualified by the ever narrowing limits of common perspective. For astronomy these limits are for all practical purposes irrelevant, since they coincide with the confines of the earth. In the sciences of man the rational core, common to all science, is diminished, obscured, and distorted by the inevitably partial perspective of the observer.

That impairment is minimized when both the object and the perspective of observation are identical with the confines of a particular civilization. A parochial civilization, looking at itself from the perspective of its own values, can achieve a high degree of empirical objectivity, given the limits of that perspective. Impairment is maximized when the perspectives of one civilization are applied to an object lying beyond its confines. For, in order to do justice to such an object, the observer would have to transcend the confines of his own civilization and apply to that object categories that transcend the confines of any particular civilization and, hence, are applicable to all. This, however, is an epistemological impossibility. It is this impossibility which Mr. Toynbee has endeavored to achieve.

The examination of but a few of Mr. Toynbee's basic concepts will show that it is impossible to verify them empirically but that they must be validated philosophically if they are to be validated at all. The very concept of civilization lacks empirical precision, once we leave behind the two extremes of primitivity and such generalizations as Western and Eastern civilization and share Mr. Toynbee's concern with the major historic civilizations. At what point can we say that a civilization is autonomous, that it is a derivative "offshoot" of another, or that it has no autonomy of its own, being a mere variety of a dominant one? Obviously American civilization is both distinct from, and similar to, British civilization. An Englishman might well try to comprehend American civilization in the terms of his own, or at best regard it as a mere "offshoot" of his own, while the American might assume its autonomy; for the Chinese observer, on the other hand, the differences between the two civilizations, obvious to both Englishman and American, might be hardly worth noting. From the point of view of imperial Rome, Roman civilization was the culmination of the civilization of Greece; for Hellenism it might very well have looked like Greek civilization in a state of decay; and Western Christian civilization has seen the civilization of Greece and Rome as a mere preparation for itself. Can one speak of one Chinese civilization as a continuum extending through the whole history of the Chinese state, or is it possible and necessary to speak of a number of civilizations following each other within the geographic and political space called China? Here again, the answer will differ according to the observer's perspective. There is no need to multiply examples in order to show that judgments about a civilization are mere reflections of the valuations of a particular one. It is not by accident that there has been a tendency for history to be written in terms of political or geographic units rather than of civilizations; for the former lend themselves more readily to empirical verification than do the latter.

What is true of the very concept of civilization applies also to the specific concepts referring to its alleged life cycle. What are the verifiable characteristics of the birth and death of a civilization, when does it flower, when break down and disintegrate? Did the Greek, Roman, and Jewish civilizations ever die or were they but transferred by political circumstances from one geographic locale to another? If we should assume that Greek civilization actually died, did it die through the degeneration of its inner life-substance, or was it killed, as it were, by military assassination, which in view of its own inner potentialities was a mere accident? If Western civilization should dissolve tomorrow into radioactive rubble, would it have died a "natural" death because of inner exhaustion or would it have committed suicide in an isolated act of intellectual and moral degeneracy, or would it have been killed by an atomic assassin? If Western civilization should be spared atomic destruction and if it should move into an age of material abundance, who is to prove scientifically that such a civilization would be inferior, or for that matter superior, to, say, the thirteenth or eighteenth or nineteenth centuries of Western civilization? The answers to all these questions obviously depend upon what we mean by civilization. To speak again of Western civilization only, there are those who see nothing but decay from the fifteenth century onward; there are others who see nothing but darkness before the fifteenth century and nothing but decay from the seventeenth century onward. For still others, Western civilization culminates at the turn of the nineteenth century, while there are those for whom all history preceding Marx is a mere prescientific preparation for the self-emancipation of man.

The concept of civilization and of its different stages, then, which we apply to other civilizations, cannot but be a function of the valuations of our own. The very simile of life and death has an objective, empirically verifiable meaning for biological units and is still susceptible of a high degree of empirical precision in the political sphere: a state or a party can be said to live and die. However, when we speak of the life and death of a nation as a cultural entity, we sacrifice, in a measure which will change with differing historic situations, empirical precision for a philosophic metaphor. That substitution of philosophic valuation for empirical science is bound to become total when we enter the realm of civilization, which as a concept is a kind of synthesis of the valuations of a member of a particular civilization. The appraisal of civilizations other than one's own is possible only through the erection of a partial world view into a philosophic system claiming universal validity. From Vico through Hegel and Comte to Marx, philosophy had the self-confidence to sit in judgment over all history and to assign to its different periods what appeared to be their rightful place. Our age has transferred its confidence from philosophy to science. Thus it must endeavor to prove scientifically what other ages have tried to demonstrate through philosophy.

This is the tragic paradox which Marx was still able to overcome by identifying philosophy and science, but before which Spengler and Toynbee could not but founder. For, unlike Marx, they have no philosophic system to fall back on which would lend their valuations at least an element of rational objectivity. In this respect Mr. Toynbee is philosophically more sophisticated than Spengler. He is aware of the dilemma without being able to overcome it. Spengler, with that Hegelian consistency which takes absurd conclusions in its stride as long as they follow logically from premises, forces the history of civilizations into the biological straitjacket and, again not unlike Hegel, finds in the apparent trends of the contemporary scene experimental proof for the pseudoscientific premise of biological necessity.

Mr. Toynbee, with an intention as sweeping as any of the system-builders before him, has too much common sense to sacrifice the evidence of history on the altar of logical consistency. He allows for human creativity to modify, if not stop altogether, the life cycle of all civilizations, and particularly of our own. Yet this concession to the unpredictability of history, which is a function of human freedom, confronts Mr. Toynbee with still another dilemma. If a civilization can escape its life cycle by an act of human will, if, in other words, it can refuse to die if it so wills and knows how to live for ever, what, then, is the cognitive value of the biological scheme? Is there a tendency in civilizations to die, which tendency can be reversed? Or were other civilizations bound to die while ours—faint echo of *Roma eterna*—might live for ever. Obviously, what Mr. Toynbee's concession to common sense has gained for history it has lost for philosophy.

It is a measure of Mr. Toynbee's philosophic sophistication that he not only allows human freedom to qualify, if not disrupt, the determinism of the biological life cycle but he is also aware of the need for standards of evaluation which transcend the empirical sequence of biological phases. He does not, and cannot, find these standards in philosophy; for our age has lost the rational boldness and self-reliance which still allowed a Comte and a Marx to build a philosophic system which pretended to explain the laws by which history proceeds. Instead Mr. Toynbee turns to religion. By doing so, Mr. Toynbee raises three issues: the meaning of the return to religion, the value for civilization of a return to religion, the ability of a civilization to return to religion by an act of will.

Mr. Toynbee's claim that only religion can save Western civilization coincides with a popular movement, especially strong in the United States, which also seeks in religion salvation from the evils and dangers of the times. Church membership is rising; prominent intellectuals are converted or return to the fold of their church; politicians justify themselves and their policies in religious terms; and the display of religious observances has begun to become standard practice for public men. Much of Mr. Toynbee's popularity in the United States can be attributed to the apparent convergence of his call for the renewal of religious faith with these popular tendencies. He is in danger of becoming the prophet of a new cult, a kind of Billy Graham of the eggheads.

This popularity is unjust to Mr. Toynbee's intent, but it illuminates the weakness of his achievement. Mr. Toynbee has no illusions about the impossibility of reviving a lost religious faith by joining or rejoining an established church. He calls not so much for a return to a particular established religion as for a revival of religious faith which might find confirmation in any established religion or a combination of elements of them. Mr. Toynbee's personal preference, if I understand him aright, seems to be a kind of intellectual and aesthetic eclecticism which open-mindedly accepts and receives all that is congenial in the different historic religions.

However, this stress upon a new syncretic religion tends to obscure a distinction which is vital for the understanding of the religious problem and, in turn, has strengthened the popular misunderstanding of Mr. Toynbee's position to which we have just referred. This confusion concerns the distinction between religion and religiosity. It can well be argued—and I would support the argument—that most of the failures of the modern age and many of its accomplishments stem from one single source: the lack of religiosity. Modern man, as he sees himself, has become a self-sufficient entity who knows what he sees and can do what he wills. He has lost the awareness of his dependence upon a will and a power which are beyond his understanding and control. To warn modern man against the irreligious self-glorification, which in a sense is his self-mutilation, for it deprives human experience of mystery, tragedy, and guilt, is one thing; to advocate a kind of religious eclecticism is quite another.

This distinction between religiosity and religion has a direct bearing upon the question which is central to Mr. Toynbee's concern and for the sake of which he has raised the issue of religion in the first place: What makes a civilization live and what will enable our civilization in particular to survive? Mr. Toynbee answers: Return to religion by reviving your religious faith. Yet this answer is open to serious doubt. The doubt arises not from metaphysical speculation but from the experience of history itself. Is there any historic evidence to show that religious ages are monopolistically or even especially productive of the values of civilization, as commonly understood? And is there not rather overwhelming historic evidence in support of the proposition that the weakening of religious faith coincides with the flowering of civilizations, as commonly understood?

We are using the term "commonly understood" on purpose; for here the observer's subjective preference, as pointed out above, is bound to color his judgment. If we assume that only religious civilization is worthy of the name, it cannot be hard to demonstrate that the flowering of civilization depends upon religious faith. Yet if we give to civilization its common secular meaning, it can hardly be open to doubt that from Plato to Kant, from Sophocles to Dostoevski, from Michelangelo to Rodin, the weakening of religious faith and the flowering of civilization not only coincide in time but also are organically interconnected. It is true that these great achievements of civilization owe their greatness to the religious experience of mystery, tragedy, and guilt. Yet it must further be allowed that the achievements of material civilization, in terms of rational control of nature and society, owe much, if not everything, to the modern denial of both religious faith and religiosity, which assumes the limitless powers of man and demonstrates them within self-chosen limits.

But even if it were true that the return to religious faith can save Western civilization, can a civilization recover its religious faith by an act of will? Here it is necessary, paradoxical as it may seem, to invoke the very spirit of religion against its most learned advocate. It requires nothing but an act of will to join a church and to perform its rituals. To have religious faith demands an act of grace, for which, however, man may well prepare himself through rational instruction. Religiosity, in turn, is the fruit of experience, more particularly of suffering, transformed into intellectual and moral awareness by mind and conscience.

The clarion calling a civilization to return to religion, en masse as it were, finds, and must find, its response in a eclectic idolatry, often blasphemous in man's self-identification with the deity, which popularizes the trappings of religion without reviving the dormant substance of its religiosity. To restore man to the fulness of his stature and thus give his civilization a new lease on life requires indeed the teaching of men like Mr. Toynbee. Yet their teaching must seek to illuminate a mysterious, tragic, and sinful experience common to all men in terms of a religiosity likewise common to all men. Neither a teacher nor a whole civilization can by an act of will create the symbolic and ritualistic expressions of religiosity thus restored; least of all can they create them out of the fragments of religions, whose decline has made the restoration of religiosity necessary in the first place. What religions will grow from this new religiosity man must leave to fate. He must be content to be ready, and to make others ready, to see the signs and to read them aright when they appear.

What Mr. Toynbee has been trying to do as a philosopher of history could no longer be done in an age which tries to reduce truth to science. What Mr. Toynbee has been trying to do as a herald of religious faith no man could have achieved in any age. One hundred years ago he might have been the last of the great philosophers of history. Four hundred years ago he might have been the last of the great scholastics—or mystics. Such achievements are not for this age. Yet Mr. Toynbee's Icarian effort does for our age what the great representative works of the mind have done for others. It both presents its spirit and attempts to transcend it in the search for the perennial truths by which all ages must be judged. His achievement belongs to all ages; his failure belongs to his own and, hence, is ours as well as his.

8 *The Revival of Objective Standards:* *Walter Lippmann*

"And where are the political theorists of democracy today?" Professor Alfred Cobban of University College, London, asks and answers this question in an important article, "The Decline of Political Theory," published in the *Political Science Quarterly* of September, 1953:

Democracy, for lack of thought, has ceased to be a live political idea. . . . For the most part it has ceased to be discussed seriously and in relation to the concrete problems of practical politics. It has largely become a meaningless formula. Politicians, like the princes in the fairy tale condemned to the oracular utterances of frogs, seem scarcely able to open their mouths without some platitude flopping out, wet and flappy, and slightly repulsive, but is this political theory? If it is, no wonder that practical men prefer to ignore it. Coins can remain valid currency even when they are worn quite smooth. Political ideas need periodical recoining if they are to retain their value.

It is the great contribution, one is almost tempted to say the historic contribution, of Walter Lippmann's *The Public Philosophy*,[1] that it poses the fundamental problems of democracy again in terms relevant to the concrete political problems of the day. All great contributions to political theory, from the biblical prophets and Plato to Laski—and I grant that the span in both time and quality is considerable—have reflected not upon the theories of others, let alone upon theories about theories—an innocuous and, hence, popular academic pastime—but upon the concrete, burning, "controversial" political problems of their times. To do this requires a peculiar combination of detachment and absorption, a commitment both to a society and to a truth transcending it. It also requires a philosophy that is not merely the reflection of popular preferences but is grounded in a rational perception of the true order of things. Finally, it requires the moral courage to pit one's independent knowledge of what is true in matters political and of what needs to be done against what the crowd believes and wants. If these qualities

From the *New Republic*, February 21, 1955.
[1] Boston: Little, Brown & Co., 1955.

make the authentic political philosopher, Walter Lippmann has again proved that he is one.

The decisive experience which in this book has moved Mr. Lippmann's thinking on its course, is the derangement of the relationships which ought to exist in a democracy between the government and the people: "The people have acquired power which they are incapable of exercising, and the governments they elect have lost powers which they must recover if they are to govern. . . . Where mass opinion dominates the government, there is a morbid derangement of the true functions of power. The derangement brings about the enfeeblement, verging on paralysis, of the capacity to govern. This breakdown in the constitutional order is the cause of the precipitate and catastrophic decline of Western society" (pp. 14–15). More particularly, legislative assemblies have usurped the powers which rightfully belong to the executive branch and which they are unable to exercise properly. Representative government tends to become paralyzed government. The people, then, must choose between freedom and authority: "They will choose authority, which promises to be paternal, in preference to freedom which threatens to be fratricidal. . . . No ideal of freedom and of democracy will long be allowed to stand in the way of their being governed" (p. 61). In this fashion the very weakness of democracy as a viable political order has given birth to totalitarianism as an antidote.

Democracy which has thus perished and which is threatened today is of the Jacobin type. It equates good policy with the will of a legislative or popular majority and, hence, is forced to the conclusion that a proposition is good because it is popular. By making the will of the people its ultimate standard, it seeks the solution of all problems and the elimination of evil itself from a continuous onslaught against all traditions and all objective standards. In this it is a Christian heresy which seeks a religious end without having to undergo the religious experience.

To this degenerate and doomed type of democracy, Mr. Lippmann opposes another type which is represented by the English political system. The English type of democracy presumes an objective order within which the political process takes place. Majority rule cannot overthrow that order; it presupposes it. The principles of that order have been codified in documents such as Magna Carta, the

Declaration of Independence, the Bill of Rights of 1689, and the first ten amendments of our Constitution. Yet the better part of that order was never committed to writing. It lives on in what Lippmann calls "the traditions of civility" and has been formulated and applied in "the public philosophy." It is identical with that rational order which has been traditionally called natural law and upon whose principles all men once agreed, and can agree again, by virtue of their rational nature.

How can the belief in natural law and its effectiveness as a standard for political action be renewed? "In order to repair the capacity to believe in the public philosophy," answers Mr. Lippmann, "it will be necessary to demonstrate the practical relevance and the productivity of the public philosophy. It is almost impossible to deny its high and broad generalities. The difficulty is to see how they are to be applied in the practical affairs of a modern state . . ." (p. 115) applied in such a way that only the "wilfully irrational" can deny their validity and only the "wilfully subversive" can reject the obligations deriving from them.

The difficulty of restoring the public philosophy results from the positivist climate of opinion which cannot but be hostile to the assumption of objective standards not subject to the conditions of time and place. The modern age is no longer satisfied with ordering the political sphere by the standards of the public philosophy and thus establishing an uneasy and ever precarious balance between the good and the possible. Instead, "it promises, not the good life of this world, but the perfect life of heaven." It confuses the two realms of man's existence, that of this world with its contingencies and that of the transcendent world of the spirit. That combination of relativistic positivism and utopian perfectionism has destroyed the public philosophy and has rendered modern man powerless to order his political world by transcendent objective standards.

Since Mr. Lippmann sees the root of the evil primarily in the prevailing philosophy, the main remedy he suggests consists in the restoration of the philosophy which the prevailing one replaced: "I do not contend, though I hope, that the decline of Western society will be arrested if the teachers in our schools and universities come back to the great tradition of the public philosophy. But I do contend that the decline . . . cannot be arrested if the prevailing philosophers oppose this restoration and revival . . ." (p. 178). With this last word of Mr. Lippmann, I can have no quarrel. Yet I must doubt that it can be the last word.

This book is animated by a noble and moving faith, reminiscent of the rationalistic idealism of the eighteenth century, in the self-sustaining power of reason to transform the philosophy by which men live and, through it, their very lives. Mr. Lippmann believes that men in their political thoughts and actions can be "sincerely and lucidly rational," and he considers this rationality the very foundation of the public philosophy. Yet Herbert Butterfield, Reinhold Niebuhr, myself, and others have tried to show how much more ambiguous and involved the relations between reason and politics are than is suggested by this simple rationalistic faith. It must suffice here to point out that the public philosophy was not destroyed by its own rational deficiencies or by the hostility of the intellectuals, but—and Mr. Lippmann says as much—by the modern conditions and problems of life which the public philosophy, as it has come down to us, is unable to reflect and solve.

First of all, natural law, the form in which the public philosophy has been transmitted to us, has not only been the reflection of the objective standards of politics, but it has also always been a political ideology and predominantly an ideology of the status quo. In other words, the existing political order was identified with the objective and rational order. Yet when the existing political order lost its viability, natural law, through its intimate connection with it, lost its plausibility. It became a mere ideological tool by which partial interests and subjective opinions tried to establish their universality and objectivity. We cannot forget that experience, and no self-contained intellectual movement can obliterate its philosophic effects.

All political philosophy is concerned with the burning political problems of the day and is in turn a reflection, in the light of a truth which all ages have in common, upon the political experiences of the day before. The task of political philosophy in our age, then, is to apply the perennial truths of politics to the political world for the dual purpose of understanding it and of solving its problems. To this task Mr. Lippmann applies himself with outstanding success. Yet the restoration of a viable democratic order is not coterminous with that success being approved and shared by all rational men. As that order has been weakened and in places destroyed by its own defects, so its health can be restored only by political action remedying its defects. Political philosophy can hold up to society the mirror of its ills and contrast it with the ideal picture of health, hoping to mold thought and inspire action. Thus it is uneasily suspended between the consummated action of the past, which it reflects, and the hoped-for action of the future, which it propounds. It is its dilemma that it knows in a general way what ought to be done but cannot do it. There is its strength and its weakness, its victory and its defeat, and it should claim no more.

On the other hand, it is the dilemma of political action that it must act without being certain that what it does ought to be done. Political action without philosophy is blind; and even with philosophy it cannot help being shortsighted. For the gap between the general propositions of political philosophy and the concrete measures of political action must be bridged not by the logical deductions of a utopian rationalism but by the trial and error of political experience. The philosopher-king in whom the tension between philosophy and action is dissolved is an ideal which reality approaches only in the greatest of statesmen. In reality, the philosopher, that is, the political thinker, knows more than the king, that is, the political actor, and cannot act according to his knowledge. The king, even if he knew all the philosopher knows, would still not know for certain what action the concrete situation requires. No theoretical knowledge but only the experience of acting can teach him that. Yet even that experience will teach him only how to avoid the repetition of yesterday's blunder, not how not to commit a new one tomorrow.

Here, in this inescapable tension between reason and experience, between theoretical and practical knowledge, between the light of political philosophy and the twilight of political action, is indeed the ultimate dilemma of politics.

PART III

THE RESTORATION OF

DOMESTIC POLITICS

9 *Freedom*

During the Civil War, which was a war for freedom in a truer sense than most of the wars which have been so called, Abraham Lincoln laid bare the essentials of the dilemma which has baffled the philosophic understanding of freedom and which has made it appear that there was always something left to be desired in its political realization. On April 18, 1864, Lincoln gave a brief and unpretentious address to the crowd assembled at the Sanitary Fair in Baltimore.

"The world has never had a good definition of the word liberty," he said,

and the American people, just now, are much in want of one. We all declare for liberty; but in using the same *word* we do not all mean the same *thing*. With some the word liberty may mean for each man to do as he pleases with himself, and the product of his labor; while with others the same word may mean for some men to do as they please with other men, and the product of other men's labor. Here are two, not only different, but incompatible things, called by the same name—liberty. And it follows that each of the things is, by the respective parties, called by two different and incompatible names—liberty and tyranny.

The shepherd drives the wolf from the sheep's throat, for which the sheep thanks the shepherd as a *liberator*, while the wolf denounces him for the same act as the destroyer of liberty, especially as the sheep was a black one. Plainly the sheep and the wolf are not agreed upon a definition of the word liberty; and precisely the same difference prevails today among us human creatures, even in the North, and all professing to love liberty. Hence we behold the processes by which thousands are daily passing from under the yoke of bondage, hailed by some as the advance of liberty, and bewailed by others as the destruction of all liberty.

Political freedom, then, has two different and incompatible meanings according to whether we think of the holder or the subject of political power. Freedom for the holder of political power signifies the opportunity to exercise political domination; freedom for the subject means the absence of such domination. Not only are these two conceptions of freedom mutually exclusive in logic, but they are also incapable of coexisting in fact within any particular sphere of action. One can only be realized at the expense of the other, and the more there is of the one the less there is bound to be of the other.

From the *American Political Science Review*, September, 1957.

The concept of freedom is contradictory as seen from the vantage point of the political master and his subject. It is also ambivalent in that most members of society are not simply one or the other, master or subject, but both at the same time. B is the master of C and also the subject of A, and C, in turn, is the master of D, and so on. Most men play a dual role with regard to political power, subjecting some to it and being subjected to it by others. When they claim freedom for themselves, what do they mean: their freedom to dominate others or their freedom from domination by others? Perhaps they mean one; perhaps they mean the other; perhaps they mean both. This ambivalence makes inevitably for continuous confusion, manifesting itself typically in ideologies which rationalize and justify the freedom to dominate in terms of the freedom from domination.

It follows that universal and absolute freedom is a contradiction in terms. In the political realm, the freedom of one is always paid for by the lack of freedom of somebody else. The political master can have his freedom only at the price of the freedom of those who are subject to him; the latter can be free only if the master is made to sacrifice his freedom as a master.

What applies to the freedom to exercise political power also reveals itself in the profession and application of the political truth which justifies and informs the exercise of political power. He who believes that he has a monopoly of truth in matters political is free to propound his "truth," which to him appears to be all the truth there is, and to act upon it only if the non-believers are not free to oppose their "truths" to his; for freedom for error to corrupt thought and action is incompatible with the freedom of *the* truth to prevail. On the other hand, the freedom of the many to compete in the market place for acceptance of their different truths requires the abrogation of the freedom of the one to impose his conception of truth upon all.

In any given society not everyone can be as free as everyone else. Every society must decide for itself who shall have what freedom. The kind of freedom a particular society is able to realize in a particular period of its history, then, depends upon the kind of political order under which it lives. The nature of that particular order, in turn, is determined by the fundamental values with which that society identifies itself and which it attempts to realize through the medium of politics. In short, the kind of liberty a society enjoys is determined by the kind of political justice it seeks. Liberty cannot be defined without justice, and it can only be realized by a particular political order informed by a particular sense of justice.

All attempts at realizing freedom have throughout history derived from one of two incompatible conceptions of justice: one, minoritarian; the other, equalitarian.

The minoritarian conception of justice assumes that only a minority, determined by birth, supernatural charisma, or qualifications of achievement, is capable of finding and understanding the truth about matters political and of acting successfully on it. The majority, not so endowed, is subject to the will of the minority, both for its own sake and for the sake of the whole commonwealth. From Plato and Aristotle to the modern justifications of aristocratic and totalitarian government, the denial of political freedom for the majority has derived from a conception of political justice which limits to a minority the ability and, hence, the right to enjoy political freedom.

This conception determines not only the over-all character of political society but also the specific nature of its institutions. It claims for these institutions the attribute of freedom, if not in good faith, at least in good logic. To what Lincoln experienced in the controversies over slavery we can add our experiences with totalitarian arguments.

Communist theory claims that the government monopoly of information and control over the mass media of communication means freedom of the press and the only freedom of the press there is, while what we call freedom of the press is but a sham. The absurdity of the argument does not lie in the claim itself but in the underlying assumption of a government monopoly of political truth, from which the claim follows with logical necessity. For since we have all the political truth there is, so the Communist argument runs, how can we allow freedom of expression to those who refuse to recognize the political truth and, hence, are by definition enemies of the truth, that is, criminals, saboteurs, or foreign agents? And what you in the West call freedom of the press is nothing but the license to sow confusion by propounding error as truth.

The decisive argument against the Communist idea of freedom

and against all political philosophies reserving political freedom to a minority, however defined, must come to terms with the philosophic assumption from which those political philosophies derive. That argument is two-pronged.

It opposes the monistic assumption of a monopoly of political truth vested in a minority with the pluralistic assumption that, while no member of society has a monopoly of political truth or can even be certain what action political truth requires in a given situation, all members of society as rational beings have access to a measure of political truth, however dimly seen. From this equalitarian political ontology and anthropology evolves an equalitarian conception of political justice which postulates equality of political rights and equal treatment of equal situations. Since no conception of political truth, or any political philosophy and program of action derived from it, is necessarily and demonstrably superior to any other, they must all have an equal chance to prevail, but none of them must be given an a priori chance to prevail once and for all. The mechanism through which this equal chance materializes is the periodical majority vote, which decides the issue temporarily either through popular elections or through the enactments of legislative assemblies.

Equalitarianism, then, attacks the minoritarian conception of political justice on the grounds that no minority can be politically so wise in comparison with the majority as to possess a monopoly of political wisdom. No minority can be trusted with absolute power on the assumption that it possesses absolute wisdom. When Cromwell appeals to the representatives of the Church of Scotland, "I beseech you, in the bowels of Christ, to think it possible you may be mistaken," he expresses in the religious sphere the equalitarian mood.

Yet equalitarianism not only refuses to accept the explicit minoritarian claim of infallibility but also rejects its implicit claim to incorruptibility. Here is the other prong of the equalitarian argument. The minoritarian claim to a monopoly of political freedom derives from the overt assumption of a monopoly of political wisdom and of necessity implies a monopoly of political goodness. For the minoritarian claim can be defended by the minority and accepted by the majority only on the assumption that the minority will not abuse its absolute power. The nature of man, as it reveals itself to introspection and through the evidence of history, militates against the correctness of that assumption. The inevitable corruptiveness of power is the political manifestation of the inevitability of sin. Equalitarianism attempts to limit the opportunities for the abuse of power by limiting the political freedom of the holders of power. Western constitutionalism is an elaborate device to subject the political freedom of the holders of political power to institutional limitations and legal controls.

The decisive safeguard, however, against the abuse of political power is the institution of periodical popular elections. The very fact that political power is subject to recall and can be taken for granted only for limited periods of time limits the duration of political power with mechanical sharpness. But it also limits the freedom with which political power can be used as long as it lasts. For since the holders of political power have a natural tendency to keep themselves in power by having themselves re-elected, they must use their political freedom in view of winning the ever impending elections. Thus the preferences of the electorate, real or fancied, are an ever present limitation on the freedom of the holders of political power to use that power as they would like to. The absolute ruler is free to govern as he sees fit, subject only to the limits of physical nature. The freedom of constitutional government is hemmed in not only by institutional devices and, in so far as it is democratic, by the mechanical limits of popular elections but also by the political dynamics of the democratic process. It is this contrast between the complete freedom of the absolute ruler to exercise the authority of government at his discretion and the limits within which constitutional government must operate which Theodore Roosevelt had in mind when he expressed the wish to be for twenty-four hours President, Congress, and Supreme Court at the same time.

The democratic processes, in order to be able to delimit the freedom of the rulers to govern, must themselves be free to bring the will of the majority to bear upon the personnel and policies of the government. The freedom of the governed to control and replace the rulers and the limitations upon the rulers' freedom to govern are the two sides of the same coin, the latter being a function of the former. Without that freedom of the governed, democracy loses its substance; for it no longer provides the people with the freedom of choosing rulers and, through them, policies. A democracy that loses that freedom can survive only as the periodical plebiscitarian approval of the personnel and the policies of the government. This is the totalitarian type of democracy.

One would misunderstand the nature of democracy and of totalitarianism as well as their relationship were one to suggest that totalitarian elections are necessarily and always a sham and that they never reflect the true will of the people. They may well reflect that will, as elections in Nazi Germany and Fascist Italy undoubtedly did, expressing a consensus between the popular will and the government. Here lies the decisive difference between traditional autocracy and modern totalitarianism. Autocracy imposes its will upon an indifferent or hostile people; totalitarianism aims at, and may succeed in, governing with the consent of the governed.

However, what sets totalitarianism apart from genuine democracy is the manner in which the government attains the consent of the governed. Totalitarianism creates that consent through the monopolistic manipulation of the mass media of communication; the consent of the people does not set limits for the government but is a function of its unlimited freedom. In a genuine democracy, on the other hand, the consent of the governed is the temporary result of the interplay of antagonistic forces, competing freely with each other for popular support. The government enters this contest essentially as an equal; whatever advantages it may have by virtue of prestige, influence, and information do not substantially affect the principle of free competition. Thus a genuinely democratic government can never be certain whether it will survive the next election to be replaced by another which, in turn, must subject its personnel and policies to the popular judgment in still another election to come.

Genuine democracy must forever guard against the temptation to transform itself into an imperfect type and then to degenerate into totalitarianism. While democracy requires that the will of the people limit the freedom of the government, it also requires that the freedom of the popular will be limited. A popular will not so limited becomes the tyranny of the majority which destroys the freedom of political competition and thus uses the powers of the government to prevent a new majority from forming and to intrench itself permanently in the seat of power. There is only a small step from the destruction of the freedom of competition, that is, imperfect democracy, to the destruction of competition itself, that is, totalitarianism.

The freedom of political competition essential to democracy can be impaired in two different ways. The people are being deprived of their freedom of choosing among alternative policies by choosing among different candidates for office if the different candidates for office are not identified with different policies but compete for power as an end in itself, not as a means for a particular policy. The people may still be able to choose in terms of the personal qualities of the candidates, such as competence and trustworthiness; their choice has no meaning for the substance of the policies to be pursued. The people, if they do not vote for the person of a candidate as such, will then vote out of habit or not at all, and in the measure in which this happens democratic elections will have lost their ability to protect the freedom of the people by limiting the freedom of action of the government.

The other—and more insidious—threat to freedom of political competition stems from the tendency of all majorities to act upon the assumption that they are more—at best—than temporary approximations to political truth, that is, the repositories of all the political truth there is. They tend to think and act, as long as they last as majorities, as though their will provided the ultimate standard of thought and action and as though there were no higher law to limit their freedom. The majority, as long as it lasts, tends to become the absolute master, the tyrant, of the body politic, stifling in that body the vital spirit of questioning and initiative and evoking instead the submissiveness of conformity. Yet since there is no higher standard for thought and action than the will of the majority, in theory at least each successive majority may produce a new tyrant with a political truth of its own. One political orthodoxy may be succeeded by another, calling forth a new conformity, and the very relativism which is the philosophic mainspring of the supremacy of the majority will produce not only the tyranny of the majority but also a succession of tyrannies, all justified by the will of the majority.

While this is possible in theory, it is, however, not likely to occur for any length of time in practice. For the majority, by making itself the supreme arbiter of matters political, must at least implicitly deny to the minority the right to make itself the majority of tomorrow. Since the majority of today tends to claim a monopoly of political truth, it must also tend to claim a monopoly of political power, freezing the existing distribution of power. In one word, the majority of today tends to transform itself into a permanent majority and, by the same token, to reduce the minority of today to a permanent one.

This development not only reduces the minority to a permanent one but also deprives it of its democratic reason to exist. That reason is its ability, equal in principle to that of the majority, to have access to political truth and act upon it; hence its claim to compete freely for becoming the majority tomorrow. The assumption that the majority has a monopoly of political truth destroys the minority's political function and gives the respect for its existence an anachronistic quality. Since its continuing existence implicitly challenges the majority's monopolistic claims, is a living reminder of alternative rulers and policies, and may, by virtue of these attributes, become a political nuisance to the majority, the minority cannot for long survive the destruction of its philosophic justification and political function. With its destruction, democracy itself comes to an end. The unlimited freedom, that is, the tyranny, of the rulers corresponds to the unlimited lack of freedom of the ruled.

Thus decadent democracy goes through three stages before it transforms itself into its opposite: totalitarian tyranny. It starts out by emptying itself of part of its substance: it destroys the freedom of choosing policies by choosing men. Then it substitutes for the spirit of free political competition, which derives from a pluralistic conception of political truth, the monistic assumption that only the majority possesses that truth. Then it subjects the minority to restrictions which put it at a decisive disadvantage in the competition for intellectual influence and political power, thus transforming the majority into a permanent one, existing side by side with a permanent minority. The process of degeneration is consummated with the majority becoming the sole legitimate political organization, which combines the claim to a monopoly of political truth with a monopoly of political power.

Against these tendencies toward self-destruction, inherent in the dynamics of democracy, the institutions and the spirit of liberalism stand guard. Liberalism has erected two kinds of safeguards: one in the realm of philosophic principle, the other in the sphere of political action.

Liberalism holds certain truths to be self-evident, which no majority has the right to abrogate and from which, in turn, the legitimacy of majority rule derives. These truths, however formulated in a particular historic epoch, can be subsumed under the proposition that the individual—his integrity, happiness, and self-development—is the ultimate point of reference for the political order and, as such, owes nothing to any secular order or human institution.

It is on this absolute and transcendent foundation that the philosophy of genuine democracy rests, and it is within this immutable framework that the processes of genuine democracy take place. The pluralism of these processes is subordinated to, and oriented toward, those absolute and transcendent truths. It is this subordination and orientation that distinguishes the pluralism of the genuine type of democracy from the relativism of its corrupted types. For in the latter the will of the majority is the ultimate point of reference of the political order and the ultimate test of what is politically true. Whatever group gains the support of the majority for its point of view gains thereby also the attributes of political truth, and the content of political truth changes with every change in the majority. Out of this relativism which makes political truth a function of political power develops, as we have seen, first the tyranny, and then the totalitarianism, of the majority, unlimited as it is by an absolute, transcendent conception of political truth. Thus the relativism of majority rule, denying the existence of absolute, transcendent truth independent of the majority will, tends toward the immanent absolutism of a tyrannical or totalitarian majority, while the pluralism of genuine democracy assumes as its corollary the existence of such truth limiting the will of the majority.

As a matter of philosophic principle, the political order is oriented toward the individual; the political order is the means to the individual's end. Yet as a matter of political fact, as we have seen, it is the very earmark of politics that men use other men as means to their ends. That this cannot be otherwise is one of the paradoxes of the politics of liberalism; for political reality disavows, and does so continuously and drastically, the postulates of liberal philosophy. Liberalism believes in the truth of man's freedom, but it finds man everywhere a slave. Thus it adds another paradox—more shocking than the first for being the result of liberalism's own efforts—by creating political institutions which limit the freedom of some in order to preserve the freedom of others. Constitutional guaranties of civil rights and their legislative and judicial implementation are the liberal defenses of freedom of political competition. While the will of the majority decides how these guaranties are to be implemented, the existence of the guaranties themselves is not subject to that will. Quite to the contrary, these guaranties set the conditions under which the will of the majority is to be formed and exercised. They establish the framework of democratic legitimacy for the rule of the majority.

Yet the very need for these safeguards limiting the freedom of the majority points up the dilemma that liberalism faces. If the majority could be trusted with its power, the liberal safeguards would be unnecessary. Since it cannot be so trusted, its freedom must be curtailed for the very sake of freedom. The dilemma which concerned Lincoln in the individual relations between the wolf and the lamb reappears in the collective relations between majority and minority. It manifests itself here typically in the concrete terms of the antinomy between individual rights and some collective good, such as general welfare, administrative efficiency, national security. The liberal concern for individual rights may stand in the way of the maximization of such a collective good, and the greater the need for the full realization of a collective good appears to be, the greater is the temptation to sacrifice individual rights for its sake. Is individual freedom more important than national security, without which there will be no freedom at all? What benefits does a man draw from the Bill of Rights if, in the absence of measures of general welfare, it guarantees him the right to sleep under bridges and sell apples in the street?

This dilemma lies outside the purview of liberal philosophy, which inclined to identify itself in the nineteenth century with the individualistic prong of the dilemma and shifted in the twentieth to the other, collectivist, one. Thus the philosophy of liberalism can provide no intellectual tools with which to master this dilemma. The decline, in our time, of liberalism as theory and practice is the result.

Liberalism conceived of the problem of freedom in terms of a simple juxtaposition between society and the state. It saw the sole threat to individual freedom in the state, conceived either as an aristocratic minority or a democratic majority. Liberal policy, then, had a twofold aim: to erect a wall between the government and the people, behind which the citizens would be secure, and to confine the government behind that wall in as narrow a space as possible. The smaller the sphere of the state, the larger the sphere of individual freedom was bound to be.

However, the aspirations for power, and the struggle for power resulting from them, could not be so neatly confined; for these aspirations are not the exclusive property of any group but common to all men, ruler and ruled, oligarchs and democrats. The autonomous forces of society, left to themselves, engendered new accumulations of power as dangerous to the freedom of the individual as the power of the government had ever been. And while liberalism had assumed that the weakness of the government assured the freedom of the individual, it now became obvious that it also assured the unhindered growth of private power, destructive of individual freedom. Against these concentrations of private power, which derived primarily from economic controls, the state was called back from the corner in which it had been confined to do battle. The state, which had just been relegated to the inconspicuous and relatively innocuous role of a night watchman by a society fearful of its power, was now restored to power as the protector of individual rights. Thus the modern state bears a Janus head: one face that of a monster lusting for power over the individual, the other with the benevolent mien of the individual's defender against his fellows' infringements of his freedom.

The struggle for freedom in the modern state has thus become a three-cornered fight, and the old dilemma reappears in a new and intricate configuration. A new feudalism of giant concentrations of economic power in the form of corporations and labor unions vies with the old tyranny of the state for limiting the freedom of the individual, subjecting ever new spheres of formerly free individual action to ever more stringent restrictions. That new feudalism calls into being the "new despotism" of the administrative state, which, for the sake of individual freedom, superimposes its restrictions upon those of the concentrations of economic power. From the latter's vantage point, this is but the old tyranny in modern garb. Yet the mass of individual citizens welcomes the administrative state as the champion of freedom.

It is the measure of the inadequacy of the simple juxtapositions of nineteenth-century liberal philosophy and the measure of the inner contradictions and ambivalences of freedom as it actually operates in the modern state that both sides have a point. The administrative state can become a new despot to some and a new liberator to others, as majority rule can be both the nearest approximation to freedom in a mass society and a many-headed and, hence, unassailable destroyer of freedom.

10 *The New Despotism and the New Feudalism*

This precarious state of freedom in the modern age is most obvious in the economic sphere. It is the result of two factors: the denial of freedom from within the economic sphere itself through the accumulation of uncontrolled power in the hands of economic organizations, such as corporations and labor unions, and the denial of freedom in consequence of the intervention of the state in the economic sphere, in good measure in order to restore its freedom threatened from within. Thus the economic sphere has lost whatever autonomy it has had in the past: it is subject to political control as it, in turn, tries to control political decisions. We are in the presence of the revival of a truly political economy, and the major economic problems are political in nature.

This interconnectedness of the political and economic spheres is not peculiar to our age. Even in the heyday of nineteenth-century liberalism, the strict separation of the two spheres was in the nature of a political ideal rather than the reflection of observable reality. The monetary, tax, and tariff policies of the government had then, as they have now, a direct bearing upon the economic life—and so had the outlawry of the association of working men as criminal conspiracy. Yet the ideal of strict separation served the political purpose of protecting the economic forces from political control without impeding their influence in the political sphere.

What is peculiar to our age is not the interconnectedness of politics and economics but its positive philosophic justification and its all-persuasiveness. The state is no longer looked upon solely as the umpire who sees to it that the rules of the game are observed and who intervenes actively only if, as in the case of the railroads, the rules of the game favor one player to excess and thereby threaten to disrupt the game itself. In our age, aside from still being the umpire, the state has also become the most powerful player, who, in order to make sure of the outcome, in good measure rewrites the rules of the game as he goes along. No longer does the government or soci-

Committee for Economic Development, *Problems of United States Economic Development*, 1958.

ety at large rely exclusively upon the mechanisms of the market to insure that the game keeps going. Both deem it the continuing duty of the government to see to it that it does.

In the United States, the state pursues three main purposes in the economic sphere: observance of the rules of the game, maintenance of economic stability, and national defense.

The rules of the game are oriented toward the pluralistic objectives of American society. Thus they seek to prevent any sector of the economy from gaining absolute power vis-à-vis other sectors of the economy, competitors, or the individuals as such, by controlling and limiting its power. Regulatory commissions, legislation controlling and limiting the strong and supporting the weak, tariff and monetary policies serve this purpose.

While the state started to assume responsibility for the rules of the game in the last decades of the nineteenth century, it made itself responsible for economic stability in the 1930's. Economic stability, in this context, signifies the mitigation, if not the elimination in certain sectors, of the business cycle. Its main positive characteristics, as conceived by the government of the United States, are stability of employment, stability of the value of the dollar, and stability of agricultural prices. A plethora of legislative and administrative devices serves this purpose.

Since the end of the Second World War, technological research and industrial production have become to an ever increasing extent the backbone of military defense. The regular annual expenditure by the government of close to forty billion dollars on national defense, its decrease or increase from year to year, its shift from one sector of the economy to another, all exert a sometimes drastic influence upon the economic life of the nation. They have made the government the most important single customer for the products of the national economy. In addition, many tax and monetary policies and price and wage policies are determined by considerations of national defense.

With the government thus exerting an enormous controlling, limiting, and stimulating influence upon the economic life, the ability to influence the economic decisions of the government becomes an indispensable element in the competition for economic advantage. Economic competition manifests itself inevitably in competition for political influence. This political influence is exerted through two channels: control of, and pressure upon, government personnel.

The most effective political influence is exerted by the direct control of government personnel. The economic organization which has its representatives elected to the legislature or appointed to the relevant administrative and executive positions exerts its political influence as far as the political influence of its representatives reaches. In so far as the representatives of these economic organizations cannot decide the issue by themselves, the competition for political influence and, through it, economic advantage will be fought out within the collective bodies of the government by the representatives of different economic interests. While this relationship of direct control is typical in Europe, it is by no means unknown in the United States. State legislatures have been controlled by mining companies, public utilities, and railroads, and many individual members of Congress represent specific economic interests. Independent administrative agencies have come under the sway of the economic forces which they were intended to control. The large-scale interchange of top personnel between business and the executive branch of the government cannot help but influence, however subtly and intangibly, decisions of the government relevant to the economic sphere.

However, in the United States the most important political influence is exerted through the influence of pressure groups. The decision of the government agent—legislator, independent administrator, member of the executive branch—is here not a foregone conclusion by virtue of the economic control to which he is subject. His decision is in doubt, for he is still open to divergent economic pressures. The competition for determining the decisions of the government takes place not among the government agents themselves but between the government agent, on the one hand, and several economic pressure groups, on the other. Only after this competition among several pressure groups has been settled one way or another will the government agents compete with each other, provided the issue is still in doubt.

The political struggle, ostensibly fought for victory in periodical elections by political parties, reveals itself in good measure as a contest of economic forces for the control of government action. In consequence, the decision of the government, and more particularly of legislatures, ostensibly rendered "on the merits of the case," tends to reflect the weight of economic influence and, at worst, to give political sanction to decisions taken elsewhere. Legislators and administrators tend to transform themselves into ambassadors of economic forces, defending and promoting the interests of their mandatories in dealing with each other on behalf of them. The result is a new feudalism which, like that of the Middle Ages, diminishes the authority of the civil government and threatens it with extinction by parceling out its several functions among economic organizations to be appropriated and used as private property. And just like the feudalism of the Middle Ages, these new concentrations of private power tend to command the primary loyalties of the individual citizens who owe them their livelihood and security. In the end, the constitutionally established government tends to become, in the words of Chief Justice Marshall, a "solemn mockery," glossing over the loss of political vitality with the performance of political rituals.

If giant concentrations of economic power, in the form of corporations and labor unions, were thus to become laws unto themselves, deciding with finality the matters vital to them and using the government only for the purpose of ratifying these decisions, they would not only have drained the lifeblood from the body politic but also have destroyed the vital energies of the economic system. For the vitality of the American economic system has resided in its ability to renew itself on new technological opportunities, unfettered by the interests identified with an obsolescent technology. Seen from the vantage point of the individual enterprise, this is what we call freedom of competition. This freedom of competition has been a function of the rules of the economic game, as formulated and enforced by the state.

Yet the new feudalism, if it is not controlled and restrained, must inevitably tend to abrogate these rules of the game in order to assure the survival of the economic giants which, in turn, tend to take over the functions of the state. The consummation of this development, possible but not inevitable, would be a state of affairs in which for those giants the rule of life would not be freedom of competition, which might jeopardize their survival, but freedom from competition in order to secure their survival. The dynamics of the capitalistic system, especially in the United States, continually destroying and creating as life itself, would then give way to a gigantic system of vested interests in which the established giants would use the state to make themselves secure from competitive displacement, only to die the slow death of attrition.

It is the measure of the quandary which modern society faces in this problem that the most obvious cure raises issues as grave as the disease. That cure is a state strong enough to hold its own against the concentrations of private power. In good measure, such a state already exists. It is the state whose importance for the economic life of the nation we have discussed above. In so far as this state is able to act as an independent political force, controlling, restraining, and redirecting economic activities, it is indeed the strong state, capable of keeping the concentrations of private power in check. Yet such a state, by being strong enough for this task, cannot fail to be also strong enough to control, restrain, and redirect the economic activities of everybody. In other words, as the liberal tradition correctly assumes, a strong government, whatever else it may be able to accomplish, threatens the liberties of the individual, especially in the economic sphere.

Thus modern society is faced with a real dilemma: a government which is too weak to threaten the freedom of the individual is also too weak to hold its own against the new feudalism; and a government which is strong enough to keep the new feudalism in check in order to protect the freedom of the many is also strong enough to destroy the freedom of all. What, then, must it be: the new feudalism of private power or the new despotism of the public power? The problem thus posed cannot be solved by any simple formula which endeavors to restore the juxtaposition of society and state from which the philosophy of nineteenth-century liberalism evolved. Rather, the solution of the problem must start from the terms in which it poses itself in the twentieth century.

A fruitful approach to this dilemma is suggested by the principles underlying the constitutional devices, institutional arrangements, and political dynamics of the American system of government by which *The Federalist* successfully tried to combine, in the simple relations between society as a whole and the state, a strong government with a pluralistic society. The same combination, in the complex conditions of the contemporary, three-cornered contest, must rest upon the same foundation of the intricate interplay of multiple systems of checks and balances. These systems, if they work perfectly, limit on all levels of social interaction, private and governmental, the freedom of all for the sake of everybody's freedom. They do so in two different respects, through their internal structure and through their relations with each other. The classic analysis of these two functions is provided by Number 51 of *The Federalist*. As concerns the function of the internal structure of a particular system:

This policy of supplying by opposite and rival interests, the defect of better motives, might be traced through the whole system of human affairs, private as well as public. We see it particularly displayed in all the subordinate distributions of power; where the constant aim is, to divide and arrange the several offices in such a manner, as that each may be a check on the other; that the private interest of every individual, may be a sentinel over the public rights.

And for the relations among different systems:

It is of great importance in a republic, not only to guard the society against the oppression of its rulers; but to guard one part of the society against the injustice of the other part. Different interests necessarily exist in different classes of citizens. If a majority be united by a common interest, the rights of the minority will be insecure. There are but two methods of providing against this evil: The one by creating a will in the community independent of the majority, that is, of the society itself; the other by comprehending in the society so many separate descriptions of citizens, as will render an unjust combination of a majority of the whole very improbable, if not impracticable. . . . The second method will be exemplified in the federal republic of the United States. Whilst all authority in it will be derived from, and dependent on the society, the society itself will be broken into so many parts, interests, and classes of citizens, that the rights of individuals, or of the minority, will be in little danger from interested combinations of the majority. In a free government, the security of civil rights must be the same as that for religious rights. It consists in the one case in the multiplicity of interests, and in the other, in the multiplicity of sects. The degree of security in both cases will depend on the number of interests and sects. . . .

In the end, the freedom—economic and political—of the individual in the modern state is not the result of one specific constitutional device or institutional arrangement, although such a device or arrangement may well make freedom more secure. Freedom rather reposes upon the social order as a whole, the distribution of concrete values to which society is committed. It is not enough for society to recognize the inalienable right of the lambs to life, liberty, and the pursuit of happiness and to have on the statute books provisions against the activities of wolves detrimental to the lambs. The freedom of both the wolves and the lambs will in the end depend upon the values which society attributes, not in the abstract but in the carving out of concrete spheres of action, to the freedom of the wolves and the lambs. What is their due? How far can they be allowed to go? Since neither, and especially not the wolves, can be allowed to go as far as they would like and would be able to go, society must intervene, deciding the value it wishes to put upon their respective capabilities and interests and assigning to each a sphere and mode of action. That intervention may take the form of an explicit decision settling the issue once and for all. More likely and more typically, it will result from the interplay of the totality of social forces, opposing, checking, supporting each other, as the case may be, in ever changing configurations, forming an intricate web of horizontal and vertical connections. It is upon that complex and shifting ground that freedom rests in the modern world.

11 *The Decline of Democratic Government*

Democratic government in the United States has declined by virtue of three basic misunderstandings: misunderstanding of the nature of politics, of the purposes of government in a revolutionary age, of the function of government in a democracy. These misunderstandings have corrupted our political judgment and perverted our actions with a subtle yet well-nigh irresistible logic.

Under the impact of nineteenth-century liberalism, Anglo-American society has been strongly influenced, and at times dominated, by a philosophy that denies politics a prominent and honorable place in the order of things. Politics as a conflict of interests decided through a struggle for power is here regarded as an ephemeral phenomenon, a kind of residue of either aristocratic or capitalistic society, for the time being to be pushed into a corner fenced off by constitutional safeguards and ultimately to be abolished altogether. The corollary to this conception of politics as a passing and inferior phase of social life is the erection of the private virtues as the sole standard by which the qualities of both private and public action and the qualifications of both private and public persons are to be judged. This philosophy necessarily destroys the tension between the private and the public sphere, between man per se and man as a citizen, which has been a perennial theme of Western political thought. For that philosophy, Aristotle's question of whether the virtue of a good man is identical with the virtue of a good citizen is meaningless, for here the virtue of a good man and of a good citizen are by definition identical.

This philosophy is translated into the folklore of American politics as the conviction that the main qualification for a political career is personal honesty. A politician may be wrongheaded in judgment, weak in decision, unsuccessful in action. "But don't you see how sincere he is," people will say. "He is at least an honest man." "He means well." The man in the street transfers the values he cherishes in his private life to the political stage and judges the actors by the

From the *New Republic*, December 16, 1957.

same standards he applies to himself and his fellows in their private spheres.

The values of the Eisenhower administration, both in verbal expression and in the character of its most prominent members, conform to these popular standards, and its virtually unshakable popularity owes much to this identity of political standards. The President, with characteristic frankness and consistency, has time and again measured his public actions by the yardstick of private values and expressed his conviction that since he did not find these public actions wanting, when tested by the values of private life, they had passed the political test as well. He summarized his philosophy in his news conference of August 8, 1957, in these terms: "I, as you know, never employ threats. I never try to hold up clubs of any kind, I just say, 'this is what I believe to be best for the United States,' and I try to convince people by the logic of my position. If that is wrong politically, well then I suppose you will just have to say I am wrong, but that is my method, and that is what I try to do." The public sphere appears here as a mere extension of private life, devoid of those conflicts of interests to be settled by contests of power, by employing threats and holding up clubs—methods which are traditionally associated with politics—and subject to the same rational rules of conduct which are supposed to make the private sphere orderly, peaceful, and harmonious.

When President Eisenhower was asked at his news conference of July 31, 1957, about the circumstances under which Mr. Gluck was appointed ambassador to Ceylon, he replied with indignation, ". . . in the first place, if anybody is ever recommended to me on the basis of any contribution he has ever made to any political party, that man will never be considered. I never heard it mentioned to me as a consideration, and I don't take it very kindly as suggesting I would be influenced by such things." Here again, the issue was seen in strictly private terms. The issue for the President hinged exclusively upon his personal knowledge of a campaign contribution, and since he had no such knowledge there was no issue. In this philosophy there is no room for the recognition of an objective conflict of interests to which the state of the conscience of any single individual may well be irrelevant.

It stands to reason that Mr. George Humphrey's philosophy of government is simply the application of the alleged principles of private business to the political sphere. And for Mr. Charles Wilson national defense was a problem of production and organization within the limits of sound finance as defined by Mr. Humphrey, completely divorced from any meaningful political context. Of the many of Mr. Wilson's statements showing a complete unawareness of this political context, none is perhaps more revealing than the one he made June 29, 1956, as a witness before the Senate Armed Services Subcommittee on Air Power:

> The Russian people, the ones that I have known through the years, have a great many qualities that Americans have. As a matter of fact, basically I think that the Russian people rather like Americans.
>
> It is too bad that we have got this conflict of ideology and that they have got a dictatorship on their hands. They wanted to get rid of the czar and they got something that is just as bad or worse, temporarily.
>
> It is very interesting. One of the troubles, they think of our type of free competitive society as the same thing they had under the czars, and of course it is not that thing at all. They have replaced in what you might call their point of hate.
>
> It is too bad they did away with the czars completely. If some of them were still left in one piece of Russia so they could hate the czars, they would not be hating our people so much.

A defense establishment which is intended to cope with an international situation thus conceived in terms of private emotions is likely to be different from one that seeks to defend the national interest in a world of conflicting interests and competing power.

Not only have the dominant members of the Eisenhower administration expressed themselves and acted in terms of a philosophy alien to politics, but many of them have also been selected in view of their excellence as private citizens, on the assumption that the qualities which go into the making of a good man and, more particularly, of a good businessman, go also into the making of a good statesman. Indeed, many selections have been excellent within the limits of the standards applied. Certainly, men like Eisenhower, Benson, Humphrey, and Wilson are superior in private excellence to many of their respective predecessors. But these excellent men have in all innocence done greater damage to the political life and the political interests of the nation than many of their less worthy predecessors; for they have brought to their public offices nothing but personal excellence, no understanding of political life, let alone ability to cope with the processes of politics.

The experience of this contrast between personal excellence and, more particularly, success in business and failure in politics is by no means limited to this administration nor even to this country. Look at the records of Baldwin and Chamberlain in Great Britain, of Cuno and Bruning in Germany! They were all good men, and how ruinous their governments were for their respective nations! In this country it is particularly illuminating to compare the virtually uniform political failure of the production geniuses with the spectacular political successes of the investment bankers. Why is it that the Knudsens and the Wilsons have failed and the Forrestals, the Lovetts, the Nitzes have succeeded? Because the excellence of the investment banker is, as it were, akin to that of the statesman while the excellence of the production genius is alien to it.

A good man who becomes an actor on the political scene without knowing anything about the rules of politics is like a good man who goes into business without knowing anything about it or who drives a car while being ignorant of driving. Yet while it is well recognized that society must protect itself against the latter, it feels no need for protection against the former. The virtuous political dilettante has for it even a well-nigh irresistible fascination. It is as though society were anxious to atone for the sacrifices of private virtue which the political sphere demands and to take out insurance against the moral risks of political action by identifying itself with political leaders who sacrifice the public good on the altar of their private virtue.

Society has learned to take the bad men in its stride and even to protect itself against those who know the rules of the political game only too well and use them to the detriment of society. Society will have to learn, if it wants to survive, that it needs protection also from the good men who are too good even to take note of the rules of the political game. And it must reconcile itself to the uncomfortable paradox that bad men who put their knowledge of those rules at the service of society are to be preferred to good men whose ignorance and moral selfishness put the very survival of society in jeopardy. In short, it must learn what Henry Taylor taught more than a century ago when he wrote in the *Statesman:* "It sometimes happens that he who would not hurt a fly will hurt a nation."

From the soil of this misunderstanding of what politics is all about two intellectual and political weeds have grown: utopian liberalism and utopian conservatism. This country has had its share of the former; it is now being taught the political lessons of the latter. Conservatism has become a modish word, which has been made to provide respectable cover for a multitude of intellectual and political sins. As the nihilists of the Left call themselves democratic, while disavowing with their very being the tenets of democracy, so the nihilists of the Right, who used in the twenties and thirties to proclaim their adherence to "true" democracy, now try to monopolize conservatism for themselves. Yet the iron test of the authenticity of a professed conservatism is its attitude to civil liberties, that is, restraints upon the powers of government on behalf of the individual. By this test, Hegel, at the beginning of the nineteenth century, could deny Haller the right to call himself conservative, and the German resistance to Naziism was as authentically conservative as McCarthyism, in spite of its claim, was not.

Authentic conservatism concerns either the philosophy and methods of politics or its purposes. The confusion between these two types is likely to do more damage to American politics in the long run than political nihilism, pretending to be conservative, has done. Conservatism of philosophy and method is indeed part and parcel of the American political tradition. *The Federalist* is its greatest literary monument, Alexander Hamilton is its greatest theoretician, John Quincy Adams and Abraham Lincoln are in different ways its greatest practitioners, and Woodrow Wilson is its greatest antithesis in theory and practice. That conservatism holds—as we saw the realist philosophy of international relations to hold—that the world, imperfect as it is from the rational point of view, is the result of forces inherent in human nature. To improve the world one must work with those forces, not against them. This being inherently a world of opposing interests and of conflict among them, moral principles can never be fully realized, but must at best be approximated through the ever temporary balancing of interests and the ever

94

precarious settlement of conflicts. Conservatism, then, sees in a system of checks and balances a universal principle for all pluralist societies. It appeals to historic precedent rather than abstract principles and aims at the realization of the lesser evil rather than of the absolute good.

A good case can be made, it seems to me, in favor of the proposition that this conservatism of philosophy and method presents political reality as it ought to be presented and deals with it as it ought to be dealt with. I have argued that case more than a decade ago in *Scientific Man vs. Power Politics,* when, I might say in passing, it was not fashionable but most unwelcome to argue the conservative side of political philosophy and method.

On the other hand, the conservative view of the purposes of politics endows the status quo with a special dignity and seeks to maintain and improve it. This conservatism lives in the best of all possible worlds, and, if it can conceive of a different world at all, it finds that world not in the future but in the past, a golden age to be restored. That conservatism has its natural political environment in Europe; it has no place in the American tradition of politics. Europe, in contrast to America, has known classes, determined by heredity or otherwise sharply and permanently defined in composition and social status, which have had a stake in defending the present status quo or restoring an actual or fictitious status quo of the past. But for the defense or restoration of what status quo could the American conservative fight? For private power, state's rights, the abolition of the income tax, exclusive male suffrage, nullification, slavery, or perhaps the British monarchy? The absurdity of this rhetorical question illustrates the absurdity of the conservative position in terms of purposes within the context of American politics.

The great issues of American politics concern neither the preservation of the present nor the restoration of the past but the creation, without reference to either, of the future. American politics does not defend the past and present against the future but one kind of future against another kind of future. While in philosophy and method conservatism is the most potent single influence in American politics, the purposes of our politics from the very beginning were unique and revolutionary, not only in the narrow political sense, but also in the more general terms of being oblivious to tradition. They have so remained throughout, only temporarily disfigured by periods which were dominated by a conservatism of purpose and, hence, in the context of American politics spelled stagnation. In other words, the point of reference of American politics has never been the present, and only in a historically inconsequential way has it been the past.

In the past, the United States could afford such intermittent periods of stagnation; for the world around it, relatively speaking, stagnated too, and, more importantly, when the United States moved forward again it set the pace for the world and in many respects left it behind. Today it is the world that moves ahead and the United States which is being left behind. All around us the world is in violent transformation. The political revolution has destroyed the state system, which for half a millennium had provided the political girders for Western civilization, and has brought to the fore two superpowers threatening each other and the world with destruction. At the same time it has dissolved the old order of empire into the anarchy of scores of feeble sovereignties, whose uncontrolled frictions may well provide the sparks for the ultimate conflagration. A succession of technological revolutions has virtually eliminated the elements of time and space from this globe and, by adding to the numerical superiority of the so-called backward peoples the social and military potential of modern industry, challenges Western civilization from still another quarter. Finally, the moral revolution of totalitarianism denies the basic values upon which Western civilization has been built and, as bolshevism, attracts millions of people throughout the world to its militant support.

How have we reacted to this triple challenge? We have reacted by a conservatism of stagnation, which is not only oblivious of the revolutionary dynamism of our national tradition but also self-defeating as a weapon in the international contest in which the nation is engaged. We have projected the antirevolutionary and conservative image of our national task and destiny onto the international scene, seeing in the political, technological, and moral ferment of the world but the evil effects of the cunning obstinacy of the doomed leaders of bolshevism. Unwilling to adjust the comforting and flattering picture we have formed of our national life to the national realities, we proceeded to adjust the international realities to that picture. Thus we are looking at a world which appears in need of improvement, adjustment, and reform, but not of radical, unheard-of change. The world cries out for transformations commensurate in their revolutionary novelty with the revolutions that threaten it; it cries out for political imagination, audacity, and the risky experiment. What we are offering it is nothing but stagnation, masquerading in the garb of a utopian conservatism. Faced with the moral and virtually certain danger that soon a great number of nations will have atomic weapons, we continue the old game of disarmament negotiations, which is no longer good even for purposes of propaganda. Our policies in Europe and Asia are stagnant; we continue unwilling either to change the status quo of which we disapprove or to recognize it. Latin America has become our forgotten back yard which we think we can take for granted. Asia, the Middle East, and Africa are for us primarily opportunities for the conclusion of military alliances and the expenditure of money for ill-defined purposes.

In consequence of underestimating the revolutionary tradition of our society and the revolutionary nature of the world with which we must come to terms, we have made underestimation of the Soviet Union a national habit of mind. All the evidence of the Russian capabilities, from General Guillaume's "Soviet Arms and Soviet Power," published in 1949 by the *Infantry Journal*, to our own intelligence reports, made no impression upon the official mind; for if it had, we would have had to discard a whole philosophy which we are mistaking for our way of life.

This retreat into a stagnant conservatism has been accompanied by a retreat from government itself. This is not surprising, since the conservative commitment to holding the line, to keeping things as they are in domestic and foreign policy, required less of an expenditure of energy and of ideas than dynamic and imaginative policies do. That this atrophy of government, inevitably resulting from the atrophy of its purposes, has been acutely aggravated by the lapse of leadership at the top is too obvious to require elaboration; but it might be pointed out that that lapse of leadership was, in turn, made possible and perhaps even temporarily tolerable by that decline in purpose.

When we speak of the atrophy of government, we obviously do not refer to the quantity of institutions and their activities which go by the name of government; for there has been no decline of those. What we have in mind is a subtle quality which is vital to a democratic government: its quality as a teacher and leader. In its absence the government cannot govern in a truly democratic fashion, that is, with the freely given consent of the governed. Modern government—democratic or non-democratic—is not merely the formulation and execution of policies. It is also and necessarily the creation of public consent for the policies formulated and to be executed. In non-democratic societies this consent is created by the government's monopolistic manipulation of the mass media of communication. Democracies create it ideally through the free interplay of plural opinions and interests, out of which the consensus of the majority emerges.

From these different conceptions of consent two different attitudes toward secrecy and truth follow. A non-democratic government can afford to conceal and misrepresent because there are no autonomous social forces which could expose it to scrutiny and propose factual and political alternatives. Under certain conditions, it will even be compelled to conceal and misrepresent because it will have no other way to create consent for its policy. A democratic government, while having an obvious advantage in the contest of opinion, ideally at least cannot afford nor does it need to conceal and misrepresent. A responsible parliament and an alert public opinion force it to lay its cards on the table or at the very least check the government version of the truth against their own. And the assumption of democratic pluralism that neither the government nor anybody else has a monopoly of truth in matters political minimizes the temptation for the government to impose its version upon society by concealment and misrepresentation.

It is the measure of the decline of democratic government in the United States that the administration has—not on occasion but consistently—concealed from the people and its elected representatives information in both the most vital and the most trivial matters and misrepresented the truth known to it. While the administration was aware of the deterioration of American power in comparison with that of the Soviet Union, its most eminent spokesmen assured us time and again that our strength vis-à-vis the Soviet Union was unimpaired if not actually increased. What we were told officially was, at best, but a hint of the actual state of affairs. To speak of very trivial things in passing, the American people have not been allowed to learn what present the king of Saudi Arabia gave the President on his visit in January, 1957.

Secrecy and misrepresentation, not as occasional aberrations but as a system of government, are in our case intimately related to the atrophy of government of which we have spoken earlier. The administration, philosophically and politically committed to stagnation and, hence, unable to lead and educate, has put appearance in the place of substance. Thus it is not by accident that the techniques of advertising have so thoroughly replaced the processes of free discussion in the relations between government and people. Judged by the standards of advertising, the result has been gratifying. The administration has been popular, and the people have been happy. Yet judged by the standards of the American destiny and survival, the result has been disquieting in the extreme. We witness the beginning of a crisis of confidence in the administration, and we must beware lest it turn into a crisis of confidence in the democratic processes themselves.

Before men want to be governed well, they want to be governed. Before they choose between good and bad policies, they want some policies to choose from. Regardless of the course they want the ship of state to take, they want to be sure that a strong hand is at the helm. The great revolutions of the modern age—from the French Revolution of 1789 through the two Russian revolutions of 1917 and the Fascist revolutions in Italy and Germany to the Chinese revolution of the forties—were carried forward by men who were dismayed, not only at being governed badly, but also and more importantly at not being governed enough. These revolutions owed their success to the determination and ability of their leaders to seize power, to hold it, and to use it to govern perhaps badly but firmly. The modern masses have risen in despair and fury not against some particular policy but against the weakness of government, reflected in spectacular failures.

Of the failures which are likely to be in store for us, we have had only a first and very partial glimpse. We are but at the beginning of our disillusions, frustrations, and tribulations. Faced with this crisis in its fortunes, as taxing as any it has experienced, the nation certainly stands in need of sound policies. What it needs more is a government that restores its sense of mission, that galvanizes its latent energies by giving them a purpose, that, in short, acts as the guardian of the nation's past and an earnest of its future. The nation has no such government now.

12 *The Difference between the Politician and the Statesman*

On September 30, 1961, the eminent French sociologist and columnist Raymond Aron addressed in *Le Figaro* an open letter to President Kennedy. This letter is both a moving and an important document. It is moving because it is written with sympathy and concern by a man who calls himself an "enthusiastic partisan" of the President. It is important because it raises one of the two great issues of government which will ruin the Kennedy administration and perhaps the country if the President does not meet them successfully.

Mr. Aron addresses himself to the President's method of deciding issues of foreign policy, taking as his point of departure the invasion of Cuba. The President had to choose between two incompatible courses of action suggested by his advisers: to stage an invasion of Cuba, with American military support if necessary, or not to intervene. In order to avoid the risks which either course of action, consistently pursued, would have entailed, the President tried to steer a middle course, intervening just a little bit but not enough to assure success. Confronted with a choice between black and white, he chose gray. "Yet in foreign policy," as Mr. Aron puts it, "the half-measure, the compromise ordinarily combines the disadvantages of the two possible policies."

Mr. Aron was, and perhaps still is, afraid that the President might repeat this error in his approach to the Berlin crisis. For here again, the President must choose between counsels recommending diametrically opposed courses of action: a negotiated settlement which is bound to weaken the American position in West Berlin and West Germany, and an intransigent position which, at the very least for the immediate future, increases the risks of war. As Mr. Aron sees it, the President has chosen, at least in theory, the "hard" line; yet in his style, method, and language he has committed himself also to

From *Commentary*, January, 1962.

"flexibility." In consequence, nobody can be sure whether Mr. Kennedy intends to play the role of Churchill or of Chamberlain. Nobody—the American people, our allies, probably Mr. Khrushchev himself—knows what our negotiating position is, assuming we have one.

Mr. Aron did not answer the question, What has been the matter with Kennedy? For the indecisiveness of the Cuban intervention and the apparent indecisiveness of Mr. Kennedy's approach to the Berlin crisis are but the manifestations of a deficiency which is deeply embedded in the President's experience and personality. To put it bluntly: the President does not know what the statesman's task is while he knows only too well the politician's, and thus he endeavors to accomplish the task of the statesman with the tools of the politician. Yet the virtues of the politician can easily become vices when they are brought to bear upon the statesman's task.

The decision of the statesman has three distinctive qualities. It is a commitment to action. It is a commitment to a particular action that precludes all other courses of action. It is a decision taken in the face of the unknown and the unknowable.

The politician can take words for deeds, and in so far as his words seek to influence people to vote for him or for his measures, his words actually are deeds. He can make promises without keeping them, and his promises may not even be expected to be kept. He can run on a platform every two or four years and take his stand on quite different ground in between. He can equivocate between different courses of action and bridge the chasm between incompatible positions by embracing them both. He can vote one way today and another way tomorrow, and if he can't make up his mind he can abstain from voting. He can try to reduce to a minimum the uncertainties of the future by preparing his action with proper attention to the facts, organization, and planning.

The statesman, especially in his dealings with other nations, can hardly ever afford to do any of these things. His rhetoric is verbalized action, an explanation of deeds done or a foretaste of deeds to come. What still moves us today in the recorded oratory of a Churchill or a Roosevelt is not so much the literary quality per se as the organic connection between the words and the deeds. Listening to those words, we remember the deeds, and we are moved.

The statesman must commit himself to a particular course of action to the exclusion of all others. He must cross the Rubicon or refrain from crossing it, but he cannot have it both ways. If he goes forward he takes certain risks, and if he stands still he takes other risks. There is no riskless middle ground. Nor can he, recoiling before the risks of one course of action, retrace his steps and try some other tack that promises risks different and fewer. He has crossed the Rubicon and cannot undo that crossing.

The statesman must cross the Rubicon not knowing how deep and turbulent the river is, or what he will find on the other side. He must commit himself to a particular course of action in ignorance of its consequences, and he must be capable of acting decisively in spite of that ignorance. He must be capable of staking the fate of the nation upon a hunch. He must face the impenetrable darkness of the future and still not flinch from walking into it, drawing the nation behind him. Rather than seeking unattainable knowledge, he must reconcile himself to ineluctable ignorance. His is the leading part in a tragedy, and he must act the part.

The extent to which the style of the Kennedy administration resembles the politician's rather than the statesman's is revealed not only by the policies it has pursued but more particularly by its mode of operation. Rhetoric has been divorced from action and has tended to be taken as a substitute for it. To give only one glaring example: in July, 1961, the President committed himself in a speech to a program of fallout shelters, without having a policy. Ever since, his aides have searched for a sensible policy which would not be too much at variance with the President's words.

Yet the President cannot help making decisions and the method by which he has reached them suffers from three defects. It is informal to the point of being haphazard. It tends to lose sight of the distinction between what is paramount and must be decided by the President and nobody else, and what is only important enough to be decided not by the President but by somebody else. It has the quality of indecisiveness because it vainly seeks a certainty that is beyond its reach.

The President has wisely discarded the committee system through which his predecessor governed, shielding him from direct contact with the issues in all their complexity. Yet he has unwisely replaced this system with another one that threatens to overwhelm him with an unmanageable variety of issues and opinions.

The President exposes himself deliberately to advice from a great variety of sources. These sources are generally individuals who talk to him at length in his office or over the phone. This system, or lack of it, has the virtue of making the President familiar with all shades of opinion. It has the double vice of making it either too easy or too difficult for the President to make up his mind.

The President may well be swayed by a particular counsel, especially when it is presented with that subjective self-assurance which some mistake for objective certainty, and with that facility for expression and brilliance of formulation which some mistake for depth. Impressed with these qualities of form, he may commit himself to the substance of the advice without being fully aware of the meaning of that commitment. It has been reported on good authority that the President was once presented with advice concerning a policy of capital importance. He approved of that policy orally and asked the individual concerned to instruct the head of the department within whose jurisdiction the policy fell to put it into operation. This was done. When the head of the department some weeks later informed the President of the progress made in the execution of that policy, the President questioned its wisdom, obviously unaware that he had approved it and ordered its execution.

This casualness of policy formation puts two obstacles in the way of the President's making up his mind. Counseling on the spur of the moment with all kinds of people on all kinds of issues, the President is overwhelmed with issues to be decided and advice to be weighed. In consequence, his mind can no longer perceive clearly the vital distinction between the paramount issues he alone must settle and the merely important ones which others may decide with or without his guidance. The President has lost sight of the natural relationship that exists between the gravity of the issue to be decided and the level of authority that decides it. Thus some paramount issues will remain unattended or will be ineffectually attended to by officials lacking sufficient authority, while the President will concern himself with secondary issues which could be more effectively disposed of by subordinate authorities.

Thus it has come about after many months of deliberations by a great many officials that if we have a policy with regard to Berlin, neither the American public nor the allies of the United States are aware of it. The *New York Times* could publish on October 21 a report from Washington under the headline "Allied Confusion Stalls Thompson. Envoy Unable To Get Clear Stand for Moscow Talks." The result is not only confusion but also the surrender of the determination of policy to some other nation whose interests may or may not coincide with those of the United States. Thus, again, the *Times* reported on October 26 as the official position of the United States government that "the United States could not get nearer to war than the West Germans wish to go, and could not get nearer to peace than they were willing to go." Many months of contingency planning did not prepare the administration for the possibility that the East Germans might effectively seal East Berlin off by erecting a wall. Hence the administration did not know what to do when the wall went up in August, and did nothing. The show of force through which the United States in October tried to maintain the status quo concerning the access of its military personnel to East Berlin ended in confused retreat.

The President must overcome the indecisiveness of his own mind. That mind seeks the predictability to which it is accustomed from domestic politics. There meticulous ascertainment of the facts, precise planning, and elaborate organization years in advance paid off in victory in the primaries, the nominating convention, and the elections. To be sure, a margin of uncertainty remained, but it was small compared with what one knew and had prepared and planned for.

The President searches for the same kind of certainty in his conduct of foreign policy. He tries to eliminate the darkness of ignorance and to probe the depth of uncertainty that even so astute a mind as his cannot penetrate by drawing upon the most luminous and knowledgeable minds he can find and by making use of all the information he can lay his hands on. Yet those dark spots on the landscape of foreign policy are impervious to the most brilliant intelligence, and factual knowledge cannot prevail against them. Thus the President's mind hestitates and his will falters when he seeks the answer to the riddle in more advice and additional information.

The frantic search for advice and information performs for the

President the same function the employment of astrologers and soothsayers did for the princes of old: to create the illusion of certainty where there can be no certainty. The more facile the President's advisers are with words and the more self-assured they are in their convictions, the more adept they are in encouraging the President in such futile search. They cannot give him what he needs more than anything else: the tragic sense of politics. In view of that need, he could do worse than add to the ranks of his advisers a philosopher who would remind him at regular intervals that there are more questions than answers and that the great decisions must be made in ignorance and without certitude. The President, who knows his history, will remember that the princes of old reserved a place among their advisers for a man who called their attention to the limits of their power, beyond which there is the realm of Providence and fate.

This particular issue of government stems from the President's personal approach to his task. He has created it; it has never before in American history appeared in this way and is not likely to appear so again. The other issue of government with which the President must come to terms is inherent in the American system. All Presidents have had to face it and live with it one way or another. It concerns the relationship between domestic politics and foreign policy.

The issue is posed by the incompatibility between the rational requirements of sound foreign policy and the emotional preferences of a democratically controlled public opinion. As Tocqueville put it with special reference to the United States:

Foreign politics demand scarcely any of those qualities which are peculiar to a democracy; they require, on the contrary, the perfect use of almost all those in which it is deficient. Democracy is favorable to the increase of the internal resources of a state; it diffuses wealth and comfort, promotes public spirit, and fortifies the respect for law in all classes of society: all these are advantages which have only an indirect influence over the relations which one people bears to another. But a democracy can only with great difficulty regulate the details of an important undertaking, persevere in a fixed design, and work out its execution in spite of serious obstacles. It cannot combine its measures with secrecy or await their consequences with patience. . . .

The propensity that induces democracies to obey impulse rather than prudence, and to abandon mature design for the gratification of momentary passion, was clearly seen in America on the breaking-out of the French Revolution.

Confronted with this dilemma between the requirements of good foreign policy and the preferences of public opinion, the President has the supreme task of reconciling the two. The dilemma is tragic because it can never be fully resolved. If the President pursues uncompromisingly the foreign policy he regards to be sound, as Woodrow Wilson did, he risks losing the support of opinion at home; if he accommodates himself to that opinion at the expense of what sound foreign policy requires, he risks jeopardizing the interests of the country. In order to be able to avoid these two extremes—the one fatal to his personal power, the other fatal to the power of the nation—the President must perform the two historic functions of his office: to be the educator of the people and the conciliator of seemingly irreconcilable positions. The President must impress upon the people the requirements of sound foreign policy by telling them the facts of political life and what they require of the nation, and then strike a compromise which leaves the essence of sound foreign policy intact while assuaging domestic opinion.

It is the measure of Mr. Kennedy's failure that he has performed neither task. Instead, substituting again the politician's concerns for the statesman's, he has tended to subordinate the requirements of sound foreign policy to the requirement of winning elections in 1962 and 1964. The President knows that our Far Eastern policy has so far failed to result in catastrophe, not because it is sound, but because of circumstances which are likely to change drastically to our disadvantage. The President knows that what we call our German policy has been for fifteen years a verbal commitment to the illusion of unification rather than a policy. But the great mass of the American people know nothing of this because the President has not dared to tell them. To return to the fallout shelters: not only did the President commit himself in words to a fallout shelter program before he had a policy, but he now has committed himself to a policy in order to be able to compete in 1962 and 1964 with Mr. Rockefeller who has developed such a policy for the state of New York.

Yet the President, with his sense and knowledge of history, and groping as he does for his proper place in the scheme of things, cannot but feel where his true mission lies.

It is for the President to reassert his historic role as both the initiator of policy and the awakener of public opinion. It is true that only a strong, wise, and shrewd President can marshal to the support of wise policies the strength and wisdom latent in that slumbering giant—American public opinion. Yet while it is true that great men have rarely been elected President of the United States, it is upon that greatness, which is the greatness of its people personified, that the United States, from Washington to Franklin D. Roosevelt, has had to rely in the conduct of its foreign affairs. It is upon that greatness that Western Civilization must rely for its survival.

These words I addressed in 1949 to Mr. Truman and in 1956 to Mr. Eisenhower. It is the measure of the chronic weakness of Presidential leadership that the same words must be addressed to Mr. Kennedy in 1962, at the beginning of his second year in office.

13 *The Perils of Empiricism*

American foreign policy has in the past suffered from one great defect: the belief that a great power could somehow escape the risks and liabilities of foreign policy. It could escape them, so it was believed, by isolating itself from the affairs of the world; if it abstained from pursuing active foreign policies vis-à-vis other nations, other nations would reciprocate. It could escape them by promoting a grand design, such as the League of Nations or the United Nations, which, in the words of Franklin D. Roosevelt, would make an end to "the system of unilateral action and exclusive alliances and spheres of influence and balances of power and all the other expedients which have been tried for centuries—and have failed." In other words, the United Nations was expected to put an end to foreign policy itself.

We have learned the lesson that a great nation cannot escape the risks and liabilities of foreign policy by an act of will, by choosing either to retreat from it or to soar above it. Yet we are now in the process of going to the other extreme of surrendering piecemeal to the facts of foreign policy, of allowing ourselves to be sucked in by them, of thinking and acting as though there were nothing else to foreign policy but this particular set of empirical facts, say, of Laos or of Cuba. The President has admonished us to "look at things as they are," and we are following his advice. We are doing so in the name of pragmatism or empiricism. Nowadays these terms are used in Washington with pride. They are used as though to be pragmatic and empirical when faced with a political problem were to be rational almost by definition. The idea which the pragmatists and empiricists want to convey is that they are not escapists or utopians, that they have no illusions about the facts as they are or any grand design to change them; they have the courage to look the facts in the face and the willingness and ability to deal with each issue on its own terms. There is more truth in their claim than merit.

From *Commentary*, July, 1962.

This new attitude toward foreign policy stems from an intellectual disposition which is deeply imbedded in the American folklore of social action. That disposition shuns elaborate philosophies and consistent theories. It bows to the facts which are supposed to "tell their own story" and "not to lie." It accepts only one test of the truth of a proposition: that it works. It expects the problems of the social world to yield to a series of piecemeal empirical attacks, unencumbered by preconceived notions and comprehensive planning. If a social problem proves obstinate, it must be made to yield to a new empirical attack, armed with more facts more thoroughly understood.

That theory of social action, however persuasive it may sound to our ears by virtue of apparently being supported by our domestic experience, is in truth without foundation. Facts have no social meaning in themselves. It is the significance we attribute to certain facts of our sensual experience, in terms of our hopes and fears, our memories, intentions, and expectations, that create them as social facts. The social world itself, then, is but an artifact of man's mind as the reflection of his thoughts and the creation of his actions.

Every social act and even our awareness of empirical data as social facts presuppose a theory of society, however unacknowledged, inchoate, and fragmentary. It is not given to us to choose between a social philosophy and the unconditional surrender to the facts as they are. Rather we must choose between a philosophy consistent within itself and founded on experience which can serve as a guide to understanding and as an instrument for successful action and an implicit and untested philosophy which is likely to blur understanding and mislead action. The Wilsonian grand design and the isolationist abstentionism missed the mark in their refusal, each in its own way, to take account of the concrete facts of the political situation. On the other hand, the empiricism of our day has been led astray by its absorption with the empirical facts of particular situations. It endeavors to manipulate the trees without concern for the shape of the forest.

Thus we deal with Laos on its own terms; we deal with Vietnam on its own terms; we deal with Taiwan on its own terms. And we deal with Communist China on its own terms. We want to neutralize Laos, even at the risk of partial or complete Communist domination. We want to win the civil war in Vietnam, even at the risk of a full military commitment on the part of the United States. We want to maintain the status quo in the Taiwan Strait, even at the risk of war with China. And we want to contain Chinese power within its present territorial limits by committing ourselves to the defense of military positions scattered around the periphery of the Chinese empire, regardless of the over-all distribution of military power between China and the rest of the world.

It stands to reason that all these issues are interconnected and that their connection is of a hierarchical nature. The paramount issue in the long run is, at the very least, the peripheral containment of China. Will it be possible, once China has become a first-rate military power and, more particularly, has acquired an arsenal of nuclear weapons, to contain her within the present territorial limits of her power by continuing to commit American military strength to the support of her neighbors? Or will it then be necessary to strike at the heart of Chinese power? If this should prove to be necessary, as I indeed think it will, if—in other words—our present policy of peripheral containment will either fail or involve us sooner or later in an all-out war with China, it is necessary to ask now, not five or ten years from now when circumstances may have given the answer and left us no choice, two fundamental questions. What is the place of the containment of China within the hierarchy of the objectives of our foreign policy, especially in view of our relations with the Soviet Union? And if we assign to the containment of China a very high priority, worth the risk of all-out war, must we wait to fight this inevitable war until China feels strong enough to wage it on terms favorable to herself, or ought we not to fight it under conditions most favorable to ourselves?

These are indeed unpleasant and, hence, unpopular questions, and since they became acute twelve years ago in consequence of the Korean War, no administration has seen fit to raise them in public. Nor has any administration come to terms with them in its secret councils, if the actions of successive administrations give any clue to the over-all conception which has guided our Asian policies. The conduct of the Korean War and the origin of the Laotian crisis are cases in point. The Chinese intervention in the Korean War, being the inevitable response to our advance to the Yalu, could take us by surprise only because it did not occur to us to consider our Korean policy as an integral part of our relations with China. Similarly, our decision to replace the neutralist government of Laos with a pro-Western one, initiated in 1960 against the advice of our ambassador and the CIA agents in Laos, was predicated upon the unrealistic assumption that such an attempt to change the status quo in favor of the West might not call forth from the Communist neighbors of Laos a counterattempt, more likely to succeed in view of the distribution of local power.

As our policies in southeast Asia and the Taiwan Strait must be seen in the context of our over-all relations with China, so our policies in the different nations of southeast Asia are organically interconnected. Since we are committed to the military defense of South Vietnam, a commitment the soundness of which we have questioned before in this magazine (see below, chapter 46 [in this book]), we cannot reconcile ourselves at the same time to the communization at the very least of those parts of Laos adjacent to South Vietnam; for our Vietnamese policy, questionable on other grounds, is doomed to failure by our Laotian policy, which provides the Vietnamese guerillas with a supply and staging area beyond the borders of Vietnam. The Greek and Algerian civil wars have shown in different ways that guerillas who have the support of the indigenous population cannot be defeated as long as they can be supplied from, and retreat to, areas beyond the borders of their native country.

What ails our Asian policy is its fragmentation, its compartmentalization into localized policies, independent of each other and of an over-all conception which would assign them their proper place in the total scheme of things. That ailment, however, is not limited to our Asian policy. It impedes our policies elsewhere and cramps the very style of our foreign policy. Berlin and the relations with our allies are cases in point.

It is of course obvious that the issue of the Western presence in West Berlin can no more be dealt with as a local problem, isolated from the over-all relations between the United States and the Soviet Union, than the issue of Taiwan can be considered in isolation from the over-all relations between the United States and China. Khrushchev raised the issue of Berlin in order to compel the United States to settle on Soviet terms the issue which has been the main concern of Soviet foreign policy since the end of the Second World War and to which the very origin of the Cold War can be traced: American recognition of the Western boundaries of the Soviet empire.

With regard to this issue, the United States can pursue one of two alternative policies. It can continue its present policy of non-recognition of the territorial status quo in Central Europe as a matter of law while implicitly recognizing it as a matter of political and military fact unchangeable short of a victorious war. This policy becomes increasingly precarious in the measure that the independent military power of West Germany provides support for a revisionist policy. The other alternative is for the United States to embark upon a new policy of at least edging toward the reconciliation of its explicit policy of non-recognition with its implicit recognition of the territorial status quo in Central Europe.

Our Berlin policy, soundly conceived, is a symbolic manifestation of our over-all German policy and of our over-all relations with the Soviet Union. Yet unwilling to face the realities of the German problem, we have either endeavored to manipulate the modalities of our presence in West Berlin in isolation from the underlying issue, or we have refused to engage in serious negotiations altogether, committing ourselves to the defense of the status quo in Berlin without really intending thereby to put into question the territorial status quo in Central Europe. In consequence, the Berlin issue is at the moment of this writing as unresolved as it was when it was first raised by Khrushchev in November, 1958, and our position with regard to the territorial status quo in Central Europe remains as ambiguous as it was fifteen years ago.

This refusal to face the problem of Germany and this tendency to approach the Berlin issue as though it could be dealt with in isolation from the German problem are in good measure due to the virtual veto with which the government of West Germany has been able to paralyze our Germany policy and stalemate our relations with the Soviet Union. Our relations with West Germany are duplicated by our relations with many of our other allies, such as Taiwan, South Vietnam, Laos, Pakistan, and France. These allies either prevent us from pursuing the policies we would want to pursue, or else pursue policies of their own which run counter to our own interests and expressed preferences.

Chiang Kai-shek has put some of his best troops on the offshore islands, and we have been unable to persuade him to desist from that folly. President Diem of South Vietnam bears the major share of responsibility for the disintegration of his regime and the advances of communism, but we have been unable to make him change his policies. The policies which Pakistan has been pursuing toward its neighbors Afghanistan and India have been a continuous irritant to our relations with those nations, but we have been unable to do anything about them. The policies of France have only by coincidence any relation to our interests and preferences. The policies Great Britain and Canada are pursuing vis-à-vis China run counter to our own and reduce their effectiveness; and so do the policies which Canada and some of our European allies pursue toward Cuba. While in theory we intend to give economic aid only to nations which through political and economic reform have at least cleared the path toward economic development, in practice the threat of a recipient government to collapse or go Communist is generally sufficient for us to give without conditions.

We have tried to manipulate the acute manifestations of this endemic crisis of our alliances in two different ways: through ineffective persuasion or through enthusiastic surrender. We have made the subversion of our interests and the frustration of our policies by our allies tolerable by investing the interests and policies of our allies with a peculiar virtue. We have done so through the intermediary of our emotional commitment to certain rulers, such as Chiang Kai-shek, Diem, Ayub, and Franco. Some of our ambassadors have been emotionally committed to one or the other of these rulers to such a scandalous extent that, instead of representing the interests and policies of the United States abroad, they have become the advocates in Washington of the policies and interests of the governments to which they are accredited.

These are not isolated acts of misguided individuals, to be remedied by changes in personnel. We are here in the presence of a persistent pattern which points to a flaw in our conception of what an alliance is about, of the interconnectedness of different alliances, such as our alliances with France and Germany, and, more particularly, of the relationship which ought to exist between members of an alliance differing drastically in power. Again the remedy must be sought not in the manipulation of individual situations but in a revision of the modes of thought and action which we have brought to bear upon our alliances throughout the world. We could do worse than remember the warning of Washington's Farewell Address:

So likewise, a passionate attachment of one Nation for another produces a variety of evils. Sympathy for the favorite Nation, facilitating the illusion of an imaginary common interest, in cases where no real common interest exists, and infusing into one the enmities of the other, betrays the former into a participation in the quarrels and wars of the latter, without adequate inducement or justification. . . . And it gives to ambitious, corrupted, or deluded citizens (who devote themselves to the favorite nation) facility to betray, or sacrifice the interests of their own country, without odium, sometimes even with popularity; gilding with the appearances of a virtuous sense of obligations, a commendable deference for public opinion, or a laudable zeal for public good, the base or foolish compliances of ambition, corruption, or infatuation.

Our foreign policy, then, has disintegrated into a series of disconnected operations whose extent is determined by the facts of a particular crisis situation, be it Vietnam, Laos, or Berlin. It must be said in passing that this disintegration of substantive foreign policy is paralleled and accentuated by the *modus operandi* of the administration, which tends—through what I have called elsewhere (see below, chapter 37 [in this book]) "the equalitarian diffusion of the advisory function"—to dissolve the powers of decision-making into a series of disconnected acts. Trying to escape the Scylla of utopianism and isolationism, we have come dangerously close to being swallowed by the Charybdis of empiricism. There is no middle ground; in order to escape this dilemma, we must—like Odysseus—sail ahead and leave it behind.

Historic experience indicates what our course must be. The statesmen who became masters of events and thus conscious creators of history—the Washingtons and the Lincolns, the Richelieus and the Bismarcks—had one quality in common: they combined a conscious general conception of foreign policy, of its direction and aim, with the ability to manipulate concrete circumstances in the light of that conception. In other words, Wilson had a point which Kennedy has missed, and vice versa. Without the grand design, informed by historic experience and seeking what is politically possible, foreign policy is blind; it moves without knowing where it is going. Without respect for facts and the ability to change them, foreign policy is lame; it cannot move in the direction the grand design has charted.

THE RESTORATION OF

FOREIGN POLICY

The Overriding Issue—Nuclear War

14 *The H-Bomb and After*

The public discussion of the H-bomb has centered around three problems: its technological feasibility and advisability, its moral justification, its politico-military neutralization by way of disarmament.

On the first issue the layman has very little to say. He may ask a few questions. He can ask whether the attempt to build an H-bomb is likely to succeed; whether we have the resources to combine the production of H-bombs with the preparation of atomic defenses; whether a comparison of this weapon's usefulness with other available instruments of war justifies the commitment of the resources necessary for the production of H-bombs; whether, in particular, the character of the probable targets against which the H-bomb might be used makes it the most effective available weapon; whether the psychological effects upon friend and foe alike of the decision to produce it, and the political developments therefrom, might not outweigh the direct military advantage. It is one of the peculiarities of the technological character of modern war that the layman may at best be able to formulate a few relevant questions, but that he is unable to answer them. It is for the technological experts to answer them, and the layman must accept the answers.

The question of the moral justification cannot fail to be answered in the affirmative. The moral dilemma with which the H-bomb confronts the United States is different only in magnitude, but not in kind, from the dilemmas with which all the modern instruments of mass destruction, from the machine gun onward, have confronted the conscience of the Western world. The problem is insoluble on the technological level, for, short of a universal moratorium on scientific progress, there is no way of preventing the inner logic of scientific development from presenting us with ever greater opportunities for either betterment or destruction. Nor is the problem soluble on the level of pure morality. On all levels of technology the

From the *Bulletin of the Atomic Scientists*, March, 1950.

means of retaliation are bound to be commensurate with the means of attack. Hence, the modern state can no more afford to be without all the weapons which modern technology puts at its disposal than could the medieval knight afford to be without a sword since his potential adversary was thus armed. In June 11, 1938, Secretary of State Hull declared with reference to the aerial bombardment of Canton by Japan that the administration disapproved of the sale of aircraft and aircraft armaments to countries which engaged in the bombing of civilian populations; on December 2, 1939, President Roosevelt declared a similar moral embargo against the Soviet Union in view of the bombing of Finnish civilians. A few years later the ruins of bombed cities on either side of the battle lines gave eloquent testimony to the impotence of moral scruples in the face of generally available and generally recognized technological opportunities.

It is this awareness of the ineluctable ascendancy of technology over morality in times of war which, ever since Hiroshima, has given rise to the cry for international control of atomic energy, that is, atomic disarmament. Thus, once the inevitability of the H-bomb was conceded, the virtually unanimous reaction of public opinion was: Let us have another try at international control. Let us atone, as it were, for our atomic sins, past and future, by trying to devise a mechanism which will restrain us, who are unable to restrain ourselves. Even if we should continue to fail in our endeavors—and there is little real expectation that atomic disarmament can succeed under present conditions—we shall then have at least the moral satisfaction of having done everything humanly possible to stave off the calamity of a war fought with H-bombs. Undismayed by almost uniform failure, the Western world has, since the end of the Napoleonic Wars, been fascinated by the hope that the threat of war can be met by disarmament. It remains only consistent, while dooming itself to renewed failure, when it seems to be able to think of only one answer to the threat of the H-bomb: disarmament.

Yet while one must sympathize with the psychological compulsion to break out of the vicious circle of the armaments race, one cannot but recognize the grievous error in the means employed and the objectives sought. First of all, even if atomic disarmament were possible, it would not mean peace but only the elimination of certain types of weapons. Second, and most important, disarmament can succeed only as the by-product of a political settlement not as a substitute for it. Both historic experience and political analysis bear out these propositions.

The advocates of disarmament start with the assumption that men fight because they have arms. It follows from this assumption that men would stop fighting if they were deprived of arms. Actually, the relation between the possession of arms and the issue of war and peace is the exact opposite from that which the advocates of disarmament assume it to be. Men do not fight because they have arms. They have arms because they deem it necessary to be prepared to fight. The cause of war must be sought in the social conditions which make it inevitable that the struggle for power be fought with threats of violence, and which may make war appear to be the lesser of two evils. In these conditions must be sought the disease of which the desire for, and the possession of, arms is but a symptom.

The elimination of certain types of weapons, such as atomic bombs, would in itself have no influence upon the incidence of war; it could only affect the technology of warfare and, through it, the conduct of hostilities. The effective prohibition of atomic bombs would simply tend to stabilize the technology of war in the field of high explosives at the level on which it operated on the morning of July 16, 1945, when the first atomic bomb was exploded. Under the conditions prevailing at present in the society of nations, the nations adhering to the prohibition of atomic bombs would then be free to employ their resources for the development of weapons other than atomic bombs. Whether this would be a gain for humanity in view, for instance, of the potentialities of guided missiles and bacteriological warfare is an open question. In any event, the effective prohibition of atomic bombs by itself would leave the incidence of war exactly where it was before.

Furthermore, the effective prohibition of atomic bombs would in all probability reduce the technology of warfare to the pre-atomic level only at the beginning of the war, for while it is legally possible to outlaw the atomic bomb, it is impossible to outlaw the technological skill to produce atomic bombs. This has been the reason why the prohibition of particular weapons has generally not been effective in war, e.g., the prohibition of the use of lightweight projectiles charged with explosive or inflammable substances, of the bombing of civilians from airplanes, and of unlimited submarine warfare.

From 1816, when the tsar of Russia proposed to the British government the "simultaneous reduction of the armed forces of every kind," to the present, there have been more than a score of major attempts at disarmament. Of these only two resulted in genuine disarmament: the Rush-Bagot Convention of 1817 and the Washington Treaty for the Limitation of Naval Armaments of 1922. Both were the technical manifestations of political settlements, and their results in the field of disarmament lasted as long as the political settlements to which they owed their existence. The Rush-Bagot agreement, providing for naval disarmament on the Great Lakes, is predicated upon the absence of a competition for power between the United States and Canada which might transform itself into an armed quest for each other's territory. It is upon this permanent absence of political conflict between the two nations that the permanence of the naval disarmament, agreed upon in 1817, depends.

The Washington Treaty of 1922 established approximate equality of capital ships between the United States and the British Empire, with the strength of Japan, France, and Italy trailing the English-speaking countries in this order. In consequence, the United States, the British Empire, and Japan scrapped about 40 per cent of their strength in capital ships. It was furthermore stipulated that replacements, to begin in 1931, should establish by 1942 a 5:5:3:1.67:1.67 ratio for the capital ships of the British Empire, the United States, Japan, France, and Italy. Here again, it was the absence of political conflict or the settlement of outstanding political issues which made at least partial disarmament possible; and with the revival of political conflict, disarmament yielded to a renewed armaments race issuing in war.

The United States sought parity with Great Britain in battleship strength. She was bound to achieve that parity because of her superior and militarily uncommitted industrial resources. The only question was whether she would achieve parity by way of bitter and costly competition or by way of mutual agreement. Since there was no political conflict between the two countries which would have justified such competition, the two countries agreed upon a practically identical maximum tonnage for the battleships of both.

Furthermore, the First World War had made Japan the preponderant naval power in the Far East, thus threatening the interests of the United States and Great Britain in that region and inviting them to a naval armaments race. Such a race, however, the United States, for financial and psychological reasons, was anxious to avoid. Great Britain, on the other hand, was tied to Japan by a military alliance. More particularly, the British dominions dreaded the possibility of finding themselves on the Japanese side in the event of a conflict between Japan and the United States. Thus, Great Britain and the United States not only were not separated by political conflicts which might lead to war; they had also an identical interest in avoiding an armaments race with Japan. By dissolving the alliance with Japan and agreeing to parity with the United States on a level she could afford, Great Britain solved her politico-military problems in the field of naval armaments. By separating Great Britain from Japan and reaching parity with Great Britain cheaply, the United States, too, obtained what she wanted in that field.

This understanding between the United States and Great Britain not only isolated Japan but placed her at the same time in a position of hopeless inferiority with regard to heavy naval armaments. Instead of embarking upon a ruinous armaments race, which she had no chance of winning, Japan made the best of an unfavorable and humiliating situation: she accepted her status of inferiority for the time being and agreed upon stabilizing this inferiority at the ratio mentioned above. When the Anglo-American reaction to Japan's invasion of China at the beginning of the thirties showed that the united front of Great Britain and the United States with regard to the Far East, which had made the Washington Treaty of 1922 possible, no longer existed, Japan at once freed herself from the shackles of that treaty. As far as the Japanese position vis-à-vis the Anglo-American naval supremacy was concerned, the disarmament provisions of the Washington Treaty were the product of a peculiar political situation. These provisions could not survive the political conditions which had created them.

The conflict between the United States and the Soviet Union over atomic disarmament, enacted on the stage of the United Nations Atomic Energy Commission, reveals itself, too, as a mere reflection of the underlying struggle for power. This conflict was essentially a new production of the play which was staged at the World Disarmament Conference in the early thirties. The United States played the role which France played after the First World War, and the Soviet Union recited the text which Germany made familiar to the world. The issue, in the language of disarmament, was again security *vs.* equality. The monopoly of the atomic bomb gave the United States a military advantage over the Soviet Union which the United States was willing to give up only in return for adequate guarantees against any other nation's being able to produce atomic weapons. During the period of transition from an atomic armament race to the abolition of all atomic arms, guaranteed by international safeguards, the United States would have retained her superiority. This superiority would have been fully and definitely relinquished only at the end of that period when the system of international guarantees would have proved to be in working order.

The Russian conception of atomic disarmament reversed the sequence which the American plan envisaged. Instead of security first, equality later, the Russian conception postulated the immediate establishment of equality, the creation of guarantees against the production of atomic arms to be left to later negotiations, which might or might not succeed. If this state of affairs could actually have been brought about, it would have given the Soviet Union two military advantages. On the one hand, it would have wiped out with one stroke the superiority of the United States over the Soviet Union in atomic weapons. On the other hand, it would have given the Soviet Union her only opportunity of gaining superiority in atomic weapons over the United States. The Soviet Union would also have obtained equality in atomic weapons under the American plan, that is, the equality of zero, even though only in the future and with the proviso that this equality could never be transformed into superiority. The Russian plan would have given the Soviet Union the equality of zero right away and with it her only chance to become superior to the United States sometime in the future.

The two fundamental facts which determined the policies of the two nations during that period were the temporary American monopoly of the atomic bomb and the military preponderance of the Soviet Union on the continents of Europe and Asia. The paramount interest of the Soviet Union was to make the period of American supremacy in atomic weapons as short as possible while perpetuating this preponderance. The United States was vitally interested in maintaining her monopoly of atomic weapons as long as possible and in reducing the Russian superiority on the two continents. The policies of both countries regarding disarmament were the true reflection of those facts and interests.

The conflict between the United States and the Soviet Union, then, like that between France and Germany of the early thirties, was fought on two levels: on the superficial level of disarmament and on the fundamental level of the struggle for power. On the level of disarmament the conflict resolved itself into a controversy between two theoretical conceptions: security first, equality later *vs.* equality first, security later. On the level of the struggle for power, the conflict is posed in terms of two antagonistic policies: defense of the status quo *vs.* overthrow of the status quo. The American insistence upon security is the equivalent, in terms of atomic disarmament, of the American policy of the status quo, as the Russian emphasis upon equality is the expression, in terms of atomic weapons, of the Russian policy of expanding and making unassailable the ascendancy of the Soviet Union in Europe and Asia.

Such is the nature of the power conflict between the United States and the Soviet Union. Of this conflict the controversy on atomic disarmament is but an outward expression, following the contours of the conflict as the cast of clay follows the shape of the form into which it is molded. As the cast can only be changed by changing the mold, so the problem of atomic disarmament can only be solved through a settlement of the power conflict from which it has arisen.

The political factors which have obviated the attempts at atomic disarmament will inevitably militate against disarmament with regard to the H-bomb. As long as the struggle for power between the United States and the Soviet Union rages unabated and unsettled, the impasse with regard to disarmament will continue whatever type of weapon may be chosen as an object and however ingenious a legal formula and institutional device may be contrived to make disarmament effective, could it be agreed upon. Shall we then persist in an error which led the United Nations Atomic Energy Commission into an impasse, which condemned the World Disarmament

Conference of the thirties to futility, and which for more than a century and a half has strewn the road of humanity with disappointed hopes and ever more frequent and destructive wars? Are we to continue trying to doctor the symptoms and let the disease, unattended, take its deadly course?

Peace through competitive armaments is indeed an illusion. As Lord Grey put it in melancholy retrospect upon the origins of the First World War, in which he had so prominent a part:

> More than one true thing may be said about the causes of the war, but the statement that comprises most truth is that militarism and armaments inseparable from it made war inevitable. Armaments were intended to produce a sense of security in each nation—that was the justification put forward in defence of them. What they really did was to produce fear in everybody. Fear causes suspicion and hatred; it is hardly too much to say that, between nations, it stimulates all that is bad, and depresses all that is good.
>
> One nation increases its army and makes strategical railways towards the frontiers of neighbouring countries. The second nation makes counter-strategical railways and increases its army in reply. This first nation says this is very reasonable, because its own military preparations were only precautions; the second nation says that its preparations also were only precautions, and points out with some cogency, that the first nation began the competition; and so it goes on, till the whole Continent is an armed camp covered by strategical railways.
>
> After 1870 Germany had no reason to be afraid, but she fortified herself with armaments and the Triple Alliance in order that she might never have reason to be afraid in the future. France naturally was afraid after 1870, and she made her military preparations and the Dual Alliance (with Russia). Britain, with a very small Army and a very large Empire, became first uncomfortable and then (particularly when Germany began a big-fleet programme) afraid of isolation. She made the Anglo-Japanese Alliance, made up her quarrels with France and Russia, and entered into the Entente. Finally, Germany became afraid that she would presently be afraid, and struck the blow, while she believed her power to be still invincible. . . .[1]

But it is no answer to the illusion of competitive armaments to counter it with the illusion of disarmament. Both are symptoms of the underlying political relations—either of a raging political conflict or of a political conflict peacefully settled. Disarmament is in-

[1] Viscount Grey of Fallodon, *Twenty-five Years, 1892–1916* (New York: Frederic A. Stokes Co., 1925), II, 53, 54.

deed an indispensable step toward pacification, but it cannot be the first step. It is the result of political settlement, never its precondition. As long as the United States and the Soviet Union advance contradictory claims for the domination of Europe, of which the focus at present is Germany, it is idle for them to talk about disarmament, for they are forced by the very logic of this power contest to compete for armaments. The threat of atomic destruction can be met only on the level from which it arises, that is, the political level. If we cannot settle the political conflicts which threaten to involve us in war with the Soviet Union regardless of the prevailing technological conditions, we must face, as we must threaten, destruction with the latest technological means of destruction available to men. If the United States and the Soviet Union can settle these conflicts peacefully by safeguarding their vital interests and compromising on secondary issues, the technological progress of mankind will, by that very fact, have lost its threat. They can then afford to agree upon limitation of their armaments. Disarmament, in turn, will contribute to the general pacification, for the degree of the disarmament agreed upon will be the measure of the political understanding achieved.

There are only three ways by which international conflicts can be settled: overwhelming power, war, negotiations. Since overwhelming power is no longer at our disposal and beyond our grasp for the foreseeable future, the choice is between war and negotiations. Consequently, Mr. Churchill and the Vatican, not to mention some of the wisest and most experienced American observers, have called for direct negotiations between the United States and the Soviet Union. It is indeed in the success of such negotiations that the sole hope for peace resides. If we do not dare to face the realities of the power conflict in which we are engaged, and if we cannot hope to settle it peacefully on its own level, we cannot hope for peace. The concentration of our efforts upon illusory disarmament, then, becomes a mere evasion of the issue of life and death, the indulgence in primitive "concrete" thinking which confounds appearance with substance, symptom with cause, the pastime of political children at the rim of the abyss, a wasted effort on the eve of universal disaster.

15 *Massive Retaliation*

The "instant retaliation" speech of Secretary Dulles, delivered on January 12, 1954, was presented as a major re-definition of United States policy for the decade to come. Its importance, if not its meaning, was confirmed by the debate it has provoked. Lester Pearson has questioned it; Adlai Stevenson has criticized it; Vice-President Nixon has defended it; Sir John Slessor has amplified it; Secretary Wilson has minimized it; Admiral Radford and his colleagues have set out to "explain" it and ended by explaining it away; President Eisenhower has stated that the new doctrine is not a new doctrine at all; Secretary Dulles has reaffirmed its newness in a somewhat more modest form.

Through the confusion of these conflicting statements certain clear lines of argument can be seen. Congress and our allies have asked who will decide on "instant retaliation" and have been assured that their "consent and acquiescence" is necessary. Army and navy spokesmen have stressed that conventional weapons are still needed and this also is conceded. Objections have been advanced to the rigidity of the Dulles formula and in turn the Secretary of State acknowledges that its application in any given situation will turn on the facts. For all these modifications and qualifications, however, the doctrine itself has not been questioned by those in power. The January 12 speech stands in its essentials as the expression of a major step by the National Security Council. It outlines a fundamental change that has taken place in United States strategy and that is affirmed day by day in important decisions such as those to eliminate three active army divisions, to reduce naval personnel by one hundred thousand men, to extend the use of atomic weapons, and at the same time to warn our opponents that, in the event of new aggression in Korea, our counteraction will not stop short at that nation's northern frontier.

With this in mind, let us start over by re-examining the January

From the *New Republic*, March 29, 1954.

12 address, setting aside interpretations of Secretary Dulles' address by his colleagues and assuming that he meant precisely what he said. Mr. Dulles makes essentially five points which serve as the keystones of the new policy.

First, "emergency action, imposed on us by our enemies" and exemplified by the Korean War and the Marshall Plan, must be replaced by a long-term plan which provides a "maximum deterrent at a bearable cost."

Second, we shall—and this is "the basic decision" made by the President and the National Security Council—"depend primarily upon a great capacity to retaliate, instantly, by means and at places of our choosing."

Third, as a corollary to "placing more reliance on deterrent power," we shall depend less on "local defensive power."

Fourth, "broadly speaking, foreign budgetary aid is being limited to situations where it clearly contributes to military strength."

Fifth, "if we can deter such aggression as would mean general war . . . then we can let time and fundamentals work for us. . . . The fundamental, on our side, is the richness—spiritual, intellectual and material—that freedom can produce and the irresistible attraction it then sets up." Thus "we shall confront dictatorship with a task that is, in the long run, beyond its strength."

In order to understand the nature and value of this policy it is necessary to visualize the five contingencies for which the United States must prepare: (1) prevention of atomic war; (2) victory in atomic war; (3) local resistance to local aggression; (4) resistance to local aggression by striking at its source; (5) revolutionary changes without open Soviet intervention. The new policy can hardly hope for (2), it depreciates (3), and obviously has no relevance at all to (5). Its relevance is limited to (1) and (4).

The new policy assumes that the threat to the United States will take the form of open military aggression to be prevented by the threat, or answered by the reality, of atomic retaliation. With this assumption, the new policy reverts to the pattern of the forties when the American monopoly of the atomic bomb or at least of a stockpile of atomic bombs sufficient to wage successful atomic war stabilized the line of demarcation of 1945 between East and West. The virtual certainty that any step taken by the Soviet Union beyond that line would lead to the outbreak of a third world war, fought only by the United States with atomic weapons, may have prevented such a step from being taken. It may seem trite, but in view of the somnambulistic quality of much official argumentation it is not superfluous, to point out that a policy of atomic retaliation is a sure deterrent only if the retaliatory power has a monopoly or at least a vast superiority in the retaliatory weapon. But what if the power to be retaliated against is in a position to retaliate against the retaliation or to make retaliation impossible by prevention?

The new policy is intended in the future to make local aggression, Korea-style, impossible, for no government in its senses will embark upon local aggression in the knowledge that its industrial and population centers will be reduced to rubble in retaliation. In other words, the policy of atomic retaliation, by the very fact of its announcement, removes the need for its implementation. However, this is not the end of the story. It is easy to imagine situations where local aggression will not be deterred by the threat of atomic retaliation but will be regarded by the aggressor nation of such vital importance to itself that it must be undertaken in spite of the risk of an atomic war. One can well imagine a situation arising in Central Europe which will induce the Soviet Union to take military measures which come under the heading of local aggression.

The advocates of the new policy foresee such a contingency and think they have an answer to it. "In a situation like, say, the Czech crisis of 1938," declares Air Marshal Sir John Cotesworth Slessor, "the first step would be a clear warning in secret that any attempt at a solution by force would bring the guarantee into operation. If that did not work . . . the people concerned should be told clearly—by radio and pamphlets dropped from the air—what will happen if their government uses force and warned to evacuate a specified list of cities. . . . At the same time we should move the bomber forces to war stations and publish the fact that we were doing so." Splendid strategy indeed for 1950, but nothing short of absurd in 1954! For what does the Air Marshal expect the aggressor nation to do in the face of such a threat? Once things have gone so far as the Air Marshal anticipates they might, the aggressor nation has only one choice: to start a war of atomic prevention against the threat of a war of atomic retaliation. A new Korean or Czechoslovakian crisis, then, will not start with ground troops marching into Korean or Czech territory but with the aggressor dropping atomic bombs on the military and industrial installations of the nations committed to atomic retaliation.

This being so, the policy of atomic retaliation requires by its very logic an effective policy of defense, for the defenseless installations of a nation committed to a policy of atomic retaliation offer a temptation to an aggressor, which under certain circumstances might well-nigh be irresistible, to make retaliation impossible through an atomic war of prevention. Yet the administration has committed itself to atomic retaliation without seemingly having either an adequate policy of military defense against atomic attack or a policy of civilian defense which would make atomic attack less attractive through the dispersal and, hence, multiplication of targets.

Yet, even if the new policy were implemented by civilian and military defense, in order to be successful, it would have to guard against two drawbacks. Mr. Dulles, speaking on January 12 before the Council on Foreign Relations in New York, could speak bravely about what we would do with our atomic bombs. In contrast, no President would give an order to start an atomic war without much soul-searching, hesitation, and doubt. Yet a policy of atomic retaliation will prevent an atomic war rather than provoke it only if there is not the shadow of a doubt in the minds of friend and foe alike about what will happen in the case of local aggression. If the prospective aggressor is reasonably certain that local aggression will be met with atomic retaliation, either there will be no local aggression at all or there will be atomic prevention. But if we leave the prospective aggressor in doubt, the policy will invite that kind of miscalculation that has so often in the past led to the outbreak of a general war which nobody wanted and which would not have broken out had the potential aggressor known in advance how the other side was likely to react.

The new policy shifts the emphasis from the conventional weapons to the new instruments of atomic power. By doing so, it recognizes what, at least in theory, has not always been recognized before, namely, that the United States has not the resources to oppose more than one local aggression at a time by local means. The United States would not have been able to fight two Korean Wars at the same time. By recognizing these limits of American strength, the new policy also recognizes that there may be local aggressions to which we have no answer at all, e.g., Indochina, or against which our only answer is the atomic bomb. The shift from the traditional weapons of local defense to atomic weapons, then, on the one hand, limits our ability to meet local aggression by local means, as we did in Korea, and, on the other, increases the temptation to use the atomic bomb against local aggression where under the old strategy we might have used traditional weapons. In other words, the new policy tends to limit our choices. Formerly, we could have met local aggression by doing nothing, by resisting it locally, or by striking at its source with atomic bombs. The new policy contracts the sphere within which the second alternative can operate. Confronted with a choice between doing nothing at all or dropping an atomic bomb, the new policy increases the incentive for doing the latter. In the words of William Graham Sumner: "For what we prepare for is what we shall get."

Yet the chances that any of these contingencies will actually come to pass may well be small, for the immediate threat to the security of the West arises not from local aggression, Soviet inspired or otherwise, nor from atomic war deliberately embarked upon by the Soviet Union, but from the revolutionary fire which is sweeping through much of Asia, Africa, Western Europe, and Latin America. Atomic retaliation can only be an answer to open military aggression. It stands to reason that to drop atomic bombs on Moscow or Peking is no answer to the threat of Communist revolution in Italy or Indochina. The crucial problem of national and social revolutions, that Moscow did not create but which it exploits, Mr. Dulles fails to face. The generalities of freedom are offered, of course; it is the specifics of freedom that concern the nations whose futures are now in doubt.

Nothing in the January 12 address shows more clearly the new policy's lack of political sensitivity and imagination and its predominant concern with military matters than Mr. Dulles' assurance that "foreign budgetary aid is being limited to situations where it clearly contributes to military strength." This is a far cry indeed from the promise of Point Four. Yet the full measure of the reduction of American political and military strategy to the threat of atomic retaliation and of its moral, political, and even military impoverishment

is revealed only if one compares Mr. Dulles' speech with the one
Dean Acheson gave exactly four years earlier, painting a vivid picture of the Asiatic revolution and of the role America must play in
it.

Perhaps, however, the key to the new policy is to be sought not
in such considerations of high political and military policy, but in
the fact that in a speech of about thirty-five hundred words there are
no less than fifteen references to the comparative cost of alternative
policies and to the cheapness of the new one. Perhaps it is all a matter of saving money. Perhaps the London *Times* is right in saying:
"It is indeed hard to see where and how the great strategic change
has taken place, though it is not hard to recognize the economic reason why it has become politically desirable to assume that it has done
so." If the economic interpretation of the new policy is correct, and
much in the recent statements of the President and of Mr. Dulles
point to its correctness, it may again seem trite, but it is not superfluous, to remind the money-savers that a Korean War, even one
fought in perpetuity, is cheaper in every respect than an atomic war.
The President no doubt would agree, and some observers feel that in
his press conference of March 17 he rubbed all the newness off the
"new look." The doubts remain, however, and extemporaneous remarks and speeches by subordinates cannot suffice. The President
owes it to the nation and the world to make clear in a speech as formal and momentous as the January 12 address just what the administration has in mind.

16 *Has Atomic War Really Become Impossible?*

The spirit which the Geneva Conference of July, 1955, generated was not so much an intangible quality of the soul as an intoxicant rendering the mind euphoric while stifling its reasoning powers. The uncritical alacrity with which both our leaders and public opinion at large saluted the spirit of Geneva as the swallow heralding the advent of a healthier and more pleasant political season revealed a political immaturity which astounded and disquieted those who had been proud of the speed and thoroughness with which the American people appeared to have learned the most important political lessons of the past decade, for the enthusiasm over the spirit of Geneva stemmed from the assumption—belonging to that political nursery school which some of us thought we had outgrown—that the intractability of the political conflicts between East and West and the Cold War are the result of manners and individual attitudes rather than of the objective conditions under which the protagonists in that power struggle must pursue their respective national interests. If that assumption were correct, then, indeed, unsolved political problems might yield to a change in manners from bad to good and to a transformation of hostile and suspicious individual attitudes into friendly and trusting ones. As it is, these changes and transformations are indispensable prerequisites for a negotiated settlement of the Cold War, for there can be no negotiation, diplomatic or otherwise, without at least a modicum of civilized intercourse and mutual trust. However, the settlement itself depends upon the possibility of reconciling conflicting and apparently incompatible interests.

Russian policy has cured us of most of the illusions which the Geneva Conference engendered. Nobody will find today, as President Eisenhower did on his return from the Geneva Conference, "evidence of a new friendliness in the world." Nobody can think today that the Geneva Conference has brought closer to solution the problems of Germany, of European security, of disarmament, or of any

From the *Bulletin of the Atomic Scientists*, January, 1956.

of the other outstanding international problems. If it has achieved anything, it has made it for the time being somewhat easier for persons and ideas to make contact across the Iron Curtain.

However, in one respect the spirit of Geneva lingers on, perpetuating a misconception which threatens to become a basic assumption of our political and military policies. This is the idea that at the Geneva Conference of July, 1955, the United States and the Soviet Union agreed, at least implicitly, not to resort to all-out atomic war in support of their respective interests. Even the few sober observers who were not at the time taken in by the other illusions of Geneva have continued to maintain that the Geneva Conference has made atomic war "unthinkable" and has for all practical purposes outlawed it as an instrument of national policy. Yet whatever element of truth there is in these assertions has not been created, but only restated and re-emphasized, by the Geneva Conference. Furthermore, that element of truth is but a part of the whole truth of the situation and, hence, if taken as the whole, will confound rather than aid our understanding, impair our position, and weaken our policies.

All-out atomic war has not become unthinkable. Nor has it been agreed upon at Geneva or anywhere else that it would not be resorted to as an instrument of national policy. Rather, the certainty that under present conditions neither the United States nor the Soviet Union can win such a war has also made it certain that neither side will deliberately start such a war. The "present conditions" from which these two certainties derive are the atomic stalemate, which, for all practical purposes, equalizes the power of destruction of the United States and the Soviet Union. It is to this atomic stalemate and not to the Geneva Conference that the credit must go for the certainty that neither the United States nor the Soviet Union will deliberately start an all-out atomic war.

It will be noted that, when speaking of this certainty, we have made two qualifications, the importance of which it is the purpose of this paper to elucidate. We have spoken of the "present conditions" of the atomic stalemate, implying that there might be conditions under which there would be no atomic stalemate, and we have referred to the "deliberate" starting of an all-out atomic war, implying that there might be other ways for an all-out atomic war to begin than by deliberate action by either the United States or the Soviet Union.

The present atomic stalemate is composed of four main factors: the —for all practical purposes—evenly matched atomic capabilities; the similarly matched capabilities for defense; the similarly matched availability of vital targets; and the monopoly, vested in the United States and the Soviet Union, of the capability to wage all-out atomic war. Only as long as these four factors persist together will the atomic stalemate itself persist and continue to assert its restraining influence upon the United States and the Soviet Union. Yet as the present atomic stalemate is the result of the dynamics of modern technology, so is its permanence threatened by the very same dynamics. While some of the four factors of which it is composed appear to be more permanent than others, the permanence of none can be taken for granted.

It is certainly possible from the technological point of view for one or the other side to gain—however temporarily—superiority in aggressive or defensive capabilities, which it might be tempted to use in order to remove the threat of atomic destruction once and for all. One can also imagine an accentuation of the already existing discrepancy in the availability of vital targets to such a point as to present to one or the other side the apparent opportunity for a decisive blow without incurring the risk of receiving one. It must also be borne in mind, in view of both the dynamics of technological developments and the uncertainty of their actual effects, that either side's subjective estimate—however erroneous the test of actual performance may reveal it to be—of a decisive advantage in the atomic race may be as instrumental for the deliberate starting of an all-out atomic war as the actual demonstrable advantage itself. In other words, a nation may be tempted to launch such a war because it is convinced that it has broken the atomic stalemate; and in view of the prospect of the outbreak of such a war, it does not matter whether or not this conviction is unfounded.

While thus far we have engaged in a kind of speculation which may well have but a very remote relation to the actual developments of the future, we turn now to a much less speculative development: the forthcoming disappearance of the American and Russian monopoly of the ability to wage all-out atomic war. When atomic power was first used for purposes of destruction, its potentialities for evil were considered to be so great as to warrant a government monopoly of the production and possession of fissionable material. In the meantime, impressed with the opportunities for the peaceful use of atomic energy, the government has moved toward relinquishing its monopoly both with regard to its own citizens and other nations. Yet the same atomic technology which has made feasible the peaceful uses of atomic energy has thereby also opened the door for its destructive uses. The same fissionable material may be used for driving a power plant and for triggering an H-bomb. Technologically speaking, fissionable material is neutral as to the uses to which it may be put.

It is this technological neutrality of atomic energy, no longer monopolistically controlled by two frightened and, hence, responsible governments, which opens political vistas, appalling in their revolutionary implications, for what will be left of the atomic stalemate between the United States and the Soviet Union if a number of other nations should have the capability perhaps not of waging all-out atomic war, but at least of blowing up some of the industrial and population centers of their neighbors and, for that matter, of the two superpowers themselves. Atomic power, monopolistically controlled by the United States and the Soviet Union and keeping each other's destructive capability in check, is a force for peace, however precarious. Atomic power, haphazardly distributed among a number of nations, is bound to be a source of unprecedented insecurity, if not of panic.

It is certainly not necessary here to dwell upon all the possible contingencies which one can visualize. It will be sufficient to point out that any nation not operating under the restraint of certain destruction through atomic retaliation is likely to use atomic weapons in pursuit of its national interests, either openly or surreptitiously. To illustrate the latter possibility: under the condition of the existing bipolarity of atomic capabilities, an anonymous atomic explosion in the United States would necessarily be attributed to the Soviet Union, calling forth atomic retribution. Under the condition of dispersion of atomic capabilities among, say, six or ten different nations, such an anonymous explosion could with certainty be attributed to nobody, however much suspicion might point to a particular nation. The constant threat of at least partial atomic destruction, under which all nations will then live, will put a premium on preventive and retaliatory action, and never mind which suspect it will hit. Compared with the anarchy and limitless violence which then will reign, the first decade of the atomic era might well appear in retrospect as a kind of golden age in which the atomic stalemate between two nations guaranteed an uneasy atomic peace. Yet perhaps even more disquieting than these dire prospects of dispersion of atomic power is the apparent unconcern with them on the part of a government and public alike, both of which seem to be satisfied that all-out atomic war has become impossible.

The atomic stalemate is a function of the two-nation monopoly of atomic power; the former cannot survive with the disappearance of the latter. Yet even under the assumption that it will survive for the immediate future, a threat to atomic peace is likely to arise from two interconnected quarters: the new Cold War of maneuver, the really important change which the Geneva Conference of July, 1955, has brought to the international scene, and the possibility of limited atomic war. We are here in the presence of the other qualification we made at the outset about the impossibility of all-out atomic war when we referred to an all-out atomic war being started through other than the deliberate action on the part of either the United States or the Soviet Union.

It is trivial but not superfluous to point out that the atomic stalemate has not altered the intrinsic nature of the political interests with which the great powers are identified and of the political problems to which the antagonism of those interests give rise. It has only modified, as long as it lasts, the means by which they pursue these interests and try to solve these problems. In the shadow of the threat of all-out atomic war and of the universal destruction it would bring in its wake, the age-old problems of foreign policy still occupy the chanceries of the great powers, which, however, shy away from any step which might bring the materialization of this threat measurably closer. And what is true of the chanceries applies to the general staffs: they, too, plan for military support of national policies in the conventional strategic framework and with the conventional tactical means, to which atomic weaons have been added.

The period of the Cold War which the Geneva Conference of July, 1955, seems to have brought to a close offered little opportunity for using the traditional methods of either diplomacy or warfare. During that period, the main task of the political and military policies of both sides was to hold the line of military demarcation established at the end of the Second World War. Policy consisted, in the main, in the warning, supported by actual preparedness, that a step taken by the other side beyond that line would necessarily lead to all-out atomic war. In short, a general political and military stalemate corresponded to the stalemate with respect to all-out atomic war.

If indications do not deceive, the Geneva Conference of July, 1955, marks the end of the political stalemate of the first postwar decade. The new era in international relations is likely to be characterized by greater flexibility within the two power blocs, tending toward a loosening of their inner coherence if not their dissolution, and, consequently, by greater flexibility between the two power blocs as well. Four facts are in the main responsible for this fundamental change in international relations: the decrease in the dependence of the great powers of second rank upon the superpowers; the impending rise of Germany and Japan to great power status; the impending dispersion of atomic power among a multitude of nations, some of which, by virtue of their possession of atomic power, will gain or regain the status of great powers; and finally, the spread and sharpening of the colonial revolutions in Asia, Africa, and Latin America. These new developments will force the United States and the Soviet Union to embark upon policies of vigorous competition. The problem which their foreign policies must solve is no longer to hold a certain predetermined line, but to establish a new line by gaining the allegiance of powerful uncommitted nations and by weaning committed nations away from the other camp.

It would be surprising if the diplomacy of maneuver which this new situation calls for did not find its counterpart in a new military policy of maneuver, thus ending the military stalemate as well. How will the United States and the Soviet Union meet the military challenge of the new political situation? Committed as they are to foregoing the deliberate resort to all-out atomic war, they must limit themselves to the use of conventional forces and tactical atomic weapons. Yet these two types of weapons are unequally distributed between them. The Soviet Union can rely upon its superiority in conventional forces, unchallengeable in their own terms and restrained only by the threat of all-out atomic retaliation. The United States, on the other hand, must counter this Russian superiority with tactical atomic weapons, sufficient for this purpose but falling far short of all-out atomic retaliation. It is this misproportion of military means and its inner logic which for the immediate future constitutes perhaps the greatest risk of an unintended all-out atomic war.

The United States cannot afford to wage an all-out atomic war because it cannot win such a war. Nor can it afford to wage a conventional war, for, in view of its weakness in conventional forces, it cannot win such a war either. Rather, the United States must prepare for, and fight if necessary, a limited atomic war, with the atomic ingredient carefully adapted to the challenge to be met—strong enough, at the very least, to avoid defeat, but not so strong as to provoke all-out atomic retaliation. It must be willing to defend its vital interests to the very limits where the risk of all-out atomic war becomes acute, yet it must forego pushing its advantage if victory can be had only at such a risk.

The very idea of such a war—ever precariously balanced between defeat and suicide—poses two grave and interrelated questions: Can it be controlled, and will it deter? The successful conduct of such a graduated atomic war, a war with just the right atomic dosage, depends upon the continuous presence of two indispensable factors. On the one hand, the political and military leaders of the United States must bring to their tasks a blend of self-restraint and daring, which very few leaders in history have proven themselves to be capable of for any length of time. Similarly, these leaders must apply to the problem of limited atomic war good political and military judgment to such an extraordinary degree of excellence as to border on the unfailing. On the other hand, the Soviet Union must match these qualities of will and mind.

If one side were to push the other into defeat, in reliance upon the latter's resolution not to start an all-out atomic war, it might provoke that very war. If one side were to declare that under no circumstances would it resort to all-out atomic war, it would condemn itself to a policy of appeasement, inviting defeat after defeat and issuing either in impotence or an all-out atomic war fought in desperation under the most unfavorable conditions. The United States and the Soviet Union must face the paradox that their chance to avoid all-out atomic war resides in their willingness and ability to fight it. They can master this dilemma only if they deprive each other of the incentive to resort to all-out atomic war by creating and preserving political and military conditions which do not call for such a war. Yet what, if one or the other side loosens the reins of self-restraint, taking a risk or an advantage which should not have been taken, or commits an error of judgment, overestimating or underrating intentions and capabilities? These are ominous questions to which there is no good answer.

In any event, the assumption that all-out atomic war has become impossible is not the answer. Nothing in the actual facts warrants this assumption. Quite to the contrary, it is the very essence of the paradox to which we have referred that to the extent that we assume the impossibility of all-out atomic war and act on the assumption, we increase the very possibility of such a war.

17 *Disarmament*

Let me first make a distinction which it seems to me is basic to the whole problem of disarmament. That is the distinction between disarmament concerning weapons for all-out atomic war and disarmament with regard to weapons for what is generally called conventional war. I assume under the term "weapons of conventional war" also tactical atomic weapons.

Now, with regard to weapons for all-out atomic war, it seems to me to be impossible to talk realistically about disarmament. From all points of view—political, technical—inspection, for instance, seems to me to be obvious, and that is always true since the Acheson-Baruch-Lilienthal proposals were published, that effective over-all disarmament is tantamount to the establishment of a world government. That is to say, without a supranational authority which is able to inspect, control, and direct the whole economic life of the nation, it is impossible to conceive of disarmament in that field. I would also say that while over-all atomic disarmament would be extremely desirable, as long as only two or three nations mortally afraid of each other and able to destroy each completely in the process of atomic war have atomic weapons, there seems to me to be very little chance for an all-out atomic war breaking out through the deliberate action of either the United States or Soviet government. There is, of course, the possibility of an all-out atomic war breaking out in connection with a local war out of circumstances which nobody is able to control. But this is, I think, a risk with which we must live for the time being, and I shall say in a moment a few words about how I think this risk can be minimized.

There is, however, one problem with regard to all-out atomic war which is not yet acute, but which is likely to become acute in a few years' time and which will arise when more than two or three nations will have the ability to wage all-out atomic war, for if I am cor-

Statement before a subcommittee of the Senate Committee on Foreign Relations, January 10, 1957.

rectly informed by scientists, it will be possible within five years or a decade for six or eight or ten or twelve or perhaps fifteen nations who have fissionable material to use the by-products of fissionable material for the purpose of manufacturing atomic weapons. Once this contingency has occurred, it seems to me we will then be confronted with a situation infinitely more serious and infinitely less susceptible to control by self-restraint than the one which exists today.

Today if an atomic bomb explodes in the port of New York, we know who only could have planted it and could use atomic retaliation in order to operate against it; and the very fact that we know it and the very fact that we can use that atomic retaliation prevents such an atomic bomb from being exploded by the Soviet Union. But what is going to happen if in ten years' time an atomic bomb explodes in the port of New York? Against whom are we going to use atomic retaliation? Against whom are we going to drop atomic bombs? Nobody will know or nobody needs to know at least who planted that bomb. I dare say in comparison with the insecurity, perhaps even the panic, which will exist then in the relations among nations, the first decade of the atomic age may well appear as a kind of golden atomic age.

I think there is urgent need today before this contingency has materialized to reflect upon ways and means by which this contingency can be forestalled; and while I regard many of the disarmament proposals which have been suggested in recent times and in the last one hundred fifty years or so as utopian, as not susceptible to realization, I think here is one area of disarmament where the vital interests of the United States and the Soviet Union coincide. And it seems to me there is urgent need on the part of the government of the United States to think about ways and means to forestall this contingency and to control strictly the use of fissionable material for peaceful purposes.

SENATOR HUMPHREY: Yesterday Mr. Kennan said there are times when you can find an identity of interest between even alleged enemies; therefore the agreement becomes self-enforceable because of the need of both countries to have the agreement working.

You are saying here that it may very well be that the United States and the U.S.S.R. may finally have some identity of interest in controlling fissionable materials, the production and the distribution and processing, simply because if they don't do it now while the field is limited, they may never be able to do it at all when the field gets enlarged. Thereby both would become the victims of insecurity and the ultimate victims of an unknown attack.

MR. MORGENTHAU: Destruction, because the U.S.S.R. will be in the same boat as the United States.

SENATOR HUMPHREY: Wouldn't this be particularly true if a major power outside the United States—Germany, for instance—becomes an atomic power. Let's say the Argentine becomes one. Let's say that Japan becomes one. Let's say that China becomes one. Let's add Indonesia and India.

MR. MORGENTHAU: France.

SENATOR HUMPHREY: These are all big nations. All of them have certain problems with their neighbors or someone else. It is entirely possible, is it not, under your thesis that if you woke up some day to learn that an attack had taken place—you would have to be somewhere else to learn that it happened—the question confronting you is where did the attack come from, particularly with the intercontinental ballistic missiles and other means of delivery. Is that what you are saying?

MR. MORGENTHAU: Exactly.

SENATOR HUMPHREY: Therefore, the time may be more propitious now than later on.

MR. MORGENTHAU: Exactly. The whole mechanism of mutual deterrence will not operate when more than two nations are able to stage an atomic attack. The very foundation for the peace of the world, however precarious it is, will have disappeared under the impact of this dispersion of the ability to wage atomic war.

SENATOR PASTORE: May I ask a question on this point?

I concede the desirability of that happening. We are living in a realistic world. What is it that America can do to stop nations that do have fissionable material from developing it, as we have or as Russia has? Portugal, for instance, has the source material. If it desired to develop it, what would we, or what could we, do to stop it?

MR. MORGENTHAU: Portugal does not have the industrial establishment necessary for the transformation of raw uranium into fissionable material and into atomic power.

SENATOR PASTORE: She doesn't have it today. It doesn't mean she might not have it ten years from today. She can develop the industrial productive capacity.

How would you write that into a disarmament agreement? That is the practical question I would like to ask. Maybe it would have been a wonderful thing if this tremendous power had not been discovered at all. It may prove to be a boon. On the other hand, it may bring about chaos. It could be used for good, but it has been used for bad. Now realizing the fact that it is here and all the nations of the world know it is here, realizing the fact that all the nations of the world will be dealing with this tremendous power even for peaceful uses and the transition between using it for a war and using it for peace is so small and so slight—as a matter of fact, a distinguished gentleman said here this morning it is like remolding some soap—realizing that this plutonium which is a by-product of your reactor can be used for the purpose of making a bomb, and most of the nations in the world will be dealing with reactors in time to come and may be producing plutonium that could be made into bombs, how could two nations write an agreement that would stop the wheels of progress?

MR. MORGENTHAU: Senator, I appreciate your question and I confess I have no satisfactory answer to it. This is in fact part a technical question whether there are the technical devices available or possible of development by which one may be able to control the use of atomic energy.

Furthermore, it is a political problem, for if the United States and the Soviet Union are equally interested in stopping a development which if it is not stopped is likely to destroy mankind, then one can envisage some kind of world government which will be established for the purpose of preventing this contingency from occurring.

SENATOR HUMPHREY: Dr. Morgenthau, I didn't understand you to say that this agreement would be just between the United States and the U.S.S.R. I understood you to say there should be a multilateral international agreement.

MR. MORGENTHAU: Yes.

SENATOR HUMPHREY: Now—before it reaches a point where you can't get it.

MR. MORGENTHAU: That is correct. If you get it. The international atomic energy statute which probably will soon be before the Congress for consideration contains provisions for control which in my opinion are very weak. Whether they could be strengthened and by what means they could be strengthened is in my opinion an open question. But what I want to point to is the enormous importance of this problem and the very little discussion in public which has taken account of that very importance.

SENATOR HUMPHREY: Take, for example, the control of production of weapons. I understand that the Republic of France, for example, says "Not until we produce our weapon." The French are right at the point now of being able to produce nuclear weapons. They have had their fissionable material and their peacetime use for some time, but the most recent report is that they are unwilling to enter into a particular kind of settlement until they have produced a stockpile of bombs.

MR. MORGENTHAU: Especially under the impact of their weakness which has been revealed recently in the venture in Egypt. The question then is what should the United States do if such agreement is not obtainable, and it is very unlikely that it will be obtainable for the very reasons you have just outlined. A country such as France, which realizes that it cannot be regarded as a great power without atomic weapons, will hardly agree to see such a self-limitation which will forever ratify its status as a second- or third-rate power.

Let me then, if I may, turn to the other area of problems which it seems to me must be distinguished from the first and which concern the weapons useful for conventional war, within which I include tactical atomic weapons.

Now, it seems to me that here exists a wide field of possible measures which could be proposed and might be taken and which are all related to the political problems which await settlement. I think there exists not only an intimate relation between unsolved political problems and the armaments race; there exists also a priority which clearly points to the paramount importance of political problems.

Why is it, for instance, that of all the many disarmament proposals which have been made, only two have succeeded—one permanently and the other temporarily—and they both have followed a previous political settlement. I am referring to disarmament between the United States and Canada, which was a result, you may say a by-product, of the settlement of the outstanding political issues. And the other one was the Washington Treaty of 1922 limiting naval armaments between the United States, Great Britain, Japan, France, and Italy, which also followed, especially in the relation between the United States and Great Britain on the one hand and Japan on the other, a political settlement. As long as this political settlement lasted, the disarmament treaty was observed. At the very moment when Japan thought it was able to revoke the political settlement by invading Manchuria, it also revoked the clauses of the Washington Treaty of 1922 limiting its freedom of action in the field of disarmament. And I think one can make another test in order to show that a political settlement must have priority over disarmament. Why is it, for instance, that we are afraid of Russian arms and the Russians are afraid of American arms but we are not afraid of British arms? Nobody thinks of the danger coming from Great Britain of an atomic attack, I think, for the obvious reason that there exists no political issue between the United States and Great Britain which would make it appear convenient or advantageous for Great Britain to stage such an attack.

And so I think it is imperative that we realize the priority which political settlements must have over the technical aspects of disarmament. It seems to me especially that the interwar period is highly instructive in this respect. The enormous intellectual energies and time spent in devising ingenious formulas for the relation between France and Germany, for instance, all came to naught because the basic political problem separating France and Germany had not been solved—had hardly been faced.

There is great danger that we get absorbed in the technicalities of disarmament without realizing that the outstanding political issue, the unsolved political issues, such as the question of Red China or the unification of Germany, are the issues which threaten war and not the fact that nations happen to have arms. If we can imagine for a moment that all the outstanding political issues were settled, nobody need worry about the fact that nations have arms because there would be no incentive, no issue for which those nations might want to use those arms. I suppose this is all I wanted to say in this context.

SENATOR HUMPHREY: In other words you are placing your emphasis upon the importance of the settlement of the political issues as a priority to proposals relating to disarmament, Doctor?

MR. MORGENTHAU: Yes, indeed.

SENATOR HUMPHREY: You heard Mr. Cohen speak before you. He felt there was a kind of simultaneous or concurrent reaction between the political and the disarmament proposals.

MR. MORGENTHAU: That is true, of course, to a certain extent. If you could induce both parties to withdraw troops from the center of Europe, you would thereby have contributed to the alleviation of tension. The question, however, arises whether you can do that without having first tackled the political problem. So you are really here facing the old problem of the chicken and the egg. Certainly, there exists a relationship, but I would still say that disarmament itself, meaningful disarmament, becomes impossible as long as there exist unsolved political issues which the participating nations regard as vital to themselves.

SENATOR HUMPHREY: Mr. Morgenthau, we have noted of late that there has been an increased role for the Secretary General of the United Nations, and that he has been called upon to serve in the midst of crises, as an agent of the U.N., seeking to settle the dispute at issue. He often must perform this role with little instruction or policy to guide him. I recall that he had very little policy to guide him on some of the Egyptian matters. Do you believe that, within the limits of his office and under the kinds of resolutions by which he has been called upon to act, the Secretary General could properly make recommendations for various kinds of disarmament devices, such as demilitarized zones and control over the arms traffic; and should such recommendations cover specific geographic areas as well as recommendations which would apply generally?

MR. MORGENTHAU: I would regard this proposal as extremely daring and dangerous for the U.N. itself. We should not forget that what the Secretary General was able to do in the Suez Canal crisis was not to contribute anything to the substantive solution of the outstanding issues, but simply to provide modes by which it was made easier for the nations concerned to stop the fighting and to contribute to the restoration of the status quo ante bellum.

What your statement refers to is part of the substance of the political settlement itself. You could well isolate the creation of a neutralized zone or the withdrawal of troops from a certain region of the earth from the over-all political problem, and certainly the Secretary General of the U.N., as it is at present constituted, has no possibility to substitute a solution of its own—a political substantive solution of its own—for those of the nations concerned. The Secretary General can help in effectuating such a solution, but I think the substantive solution itself must come from the nations concerned. And I think the recent crisis and our attitude toward the recent crisis has tended to obscure this essential relationship between the national policies of the members of the U.N. and the functions which the U.N. is able to perform with regard to them.

SENATOR HUMPHREY: This is a very important observation that you have made, Doctor, and I want to say that this is one that bears a good deal of study from here on out on the part of our foreign policy and its direction. It is one thing to work through the U.N. or to place your problems in the U.N.; it is another thing to be able to follow through with the detail, the lines of demarcation in which the U.N. is to work, the policy directives that are to come. And I think when you study the role of the Secretary-General—and this is not to criticize him because I think he has taken on almost a superhuman and inhuman task in recent efforts—you see that there has been all too little real policy guidance. He has been left more or less to find his way. This is one of the pitfalls, it seems to me, of U.N. activity or of working through the U.N. that we have not faced up to.

I also think it may result in a weakness in our own national foreign policy because after all the U.N. is a mechanism through which we work and unless our road map is pretty well designed as to the objective of our journey, we can get into the mechanism but have no idea where we are going.

MR. MORGENTHAU: In other words, the U.N. is not a substitute for national policies. It is simply a channel through which——

SENATOR HUMPHREY: It is a new channel or instrumentality for the utilization or direction of national policies.

MR. MORGENTHAU: Yes, indeed.

SENATOR HUMPHREY: I don't think this has been able to sink home yet. The U.N. is really but a structure. As such it does not have spirit and direction and purpose except in so far as the member states give it that direction, spirit, and purpose. I think it is very important, as we get into disarmament discussions and utilize the U.N., that we understand—unless the instructions are quite specific and the lines are quite carefully drawn—that we may well turn over to agents in the U.N. responsibilities which we wouldn't even entrust to our own nationals and which may vitally affect the national security.

MR. MORGENTHAU: And you might get results at variance with your national objective.

SENATOR HUMPHREY: Exactly. Once you put the process in motion, it is pretty difficult to call it off—particularly for a nation who abides by the charter—even though it may get out of hand. . . .

SENATOR HUMPHREY: I want to ask Dr. Morgenthau just a word about arms traffic. Do you think that in certain areas—I asked this question of Mr. Cohen—the problem of arms traffic is acute; and secondly, should some attempt be made to control it through international agreement?

MR. MORGENTHAU: I answer your first question in the affirmative, and I would answer your second question with a shrug of the shoulder. I must say that I doubt, at least on the basis of all precedents, that the control of arms traffic can be successful when one great power is interested in that very traffic. And I think the real problem does not lie in the traffic of arms, but in the unsettled political situation. I would again find that if one would concentrate too much attention upon such a technical problem as the arms traffic, one would deal with a symptom and not with the cause of the disease.

SENATOR HUMPHREY: Deal with the symptom?

MR. MORGENTHAU: Yes; I think this is really a minor issue in the over-all situation. Let me suppose you were able, which you probably will never be able, to control all traffic of arms in the Middle East; what you would then have is exactly the same incentive to war you will have with the arms traffic going on, only that it would be fought on a lower level of weaponry, either with obsolescent weapons or with fewer weapons, but the danger of war arising out of the unsettled political situation would remain exactly as it was.

SENATOR HUMPHREY: One of your contemporaries in an article in the *Foreign Affairs* magazine, I speak of Mr. James E. King, propounded the theory that if we were to reach an agreement that nuclear weapons were not to be used in any future war, the United States would have an advantage over the conventional forces of the Communist bloc because it is precisely in the ability to develop and utilize modern weapons, or modern weapons systems of conventional warfare, that the United States has an advantage. Therefore, do you believe that consideration should be given to negotiating agreement on the kind of weapons that should not be utilized in war, such as an agreement not to use nuclear weapons? Do you believe that without any agreement limiting the kind of weapons, there is danger that the threat of all-out nuclear war might result in a reluctance to use force or threaten the use of force at the time when the international situation may require such action? . . .

The first part [of the question] is, do you believe that consideration should be given to negotiating agreement on kinds of weapons that could, or may, or should be utilized in case of arms conflict?

MR. MORGENTHAU: I doubt that such a proposal is feasible at all. First of all, I would question the assumption upon which this proposal is based, to wit, that the United States has an advantage, would have an advantage if the use of atomic weapons were outlawed. The whole evidence of our new—or the latest—military look is against it, because we are trying to make up for our inferior manpower by the use of tactical atomic weapons. Our whole strategy in Europe is based upon that conception. Furthermore, I don't believe for a moment—and again I think history bears me out on that—that you can make such an agreement stick.

When it comes to war, that is to say, to victory or defeat or survival or destruction, all nations will use all the weapons which they deem to be serving their interests, with or without agreement. They will refrain from using certain weapons which might become self-defeating or useless, such as was poison gas in the Second World War, or they may use other weapons only in a limited way. But legal agreements, I think, are virtually useless when it comes to such questions of survival.

Take, for instance, the international treaties which have been concluded concerning the limitation of submarine warfare, which you may safely say were not worth the paper on which they were written, because they were violated wholesale in the first war under protest and in the second war they were violated without any protesting.

SENATOR HUMPHREY: Dr. Morgenthau, there is just this one observation I would like to get from you. Do you feel that we have made more policy or more security commitments with other nations in areas of the world than is in the capacity of our military to fulfil?

Do you so understand?

MR. MORGENTHAU: Yes, I am just trying to phrase my answer in such a way as to make myself clear. If you consider those different security agreements, the different alliances, in terms of the different local situations, the different areas to which they apply, it is certainly beyond the imagination that we have the manpower to defend those different areas physically within those areas.

Certainly it is inconceivable, and I think no military man, no military planner, would conceive of it, that we could send armies around the globe to all of our allies defending them against aggression. However, I think this has not really been the purpose of those agreements, even though their phrasing and their whole appearance lends itself to such an interpretation. The actual purpose has been rather unilateral—a declaration that we will resort to either atomic retaliation or whatever military measures may be necessary beyond local defense if and when one of those countries should become the victim of outside aggression.

I personally believe that this purpose would have been much better served by some kind of unilateral declaration on the part of the United States, such as is now before the Congress with regard to the Middle East, which declares the interest of the United States in a certain region and its willingness to use military force to defend it. I think this unilateral method would have been less ambiguous and less burdensome in its legal stipulations for the United States than the present multilateral arrangements all over the globe.

SENATOR HUMPHREY: Now, speaking of the Middle East, there is the Baghdad Pact there. I was looking at the map the other day as we were listening to some of the preliminary discussions on the present proposal relating to the Middle East, and the only country which has any immediate geographical relationship to the Soviet Union that is not covered in a security treaty with the United States is Iran.

MR. MORGENTHAU: Is Iran not covered by security arrangements?

SENATOR HUMPHREY: Iran may have some kind of a mutual assistance pact with our government. I don't recall.

MR. MORGENTHAU: I would say those technicalities are really not very important.

SENATOR HUMPHREY: I agree.

MR. MORGENTHAU: For if war breaks out nobody is going to look up the different treaties and compare one provision with the other. Everybody will ask, as in the case of Korea, should we do anything, and if so, what? And it will be done within a couple of hours.

SENATOR HUMPHREY: What I am getting at is the President now asks for participation by the Congress in a statement to the effect that we authorize the President to use the armed forces to resist Communist aggression. I am of the opinion that we already made that commitment in so far as NATO is concerned. I am confident we made it in so far as SEATO is concerned. What I am saying is, there was one country—Iran—to which I wasn't sure we had made it openly and publicly. What is the need of a unilateral declaration here? Isn't it understood that if the Soviet moves into a vital area where American interests are at stake, that it is to be presumed that we have been spending these millions of dollars to do something, namely, to defend ourselves?

MR. MORGENTHAU: But under certain circumstances it may be necessary to say something twice. We have already said it before under entirely different circumstances. But now British power, which was the only stabilizing factor in the Middle East until recently, has disappeared, and it has disappeared in good measure because of our own policy. So there is a vacuum which has been partly filled by the Soviet Union, as in the case of Egypt and Syria, and I think a demonstration is needed in view of the difficulty that foreign statesmen have in understanding the processes of American policy— sometimes Americans have such difficulties, too—to say in unmistaken terms that we are vitally interested in that area and that we replace the British power which has disappeared.

I personally find the phraseology of the President's message unfortunate. I think this declaration is in truth not directed against Russian aggression. I cannot imagine where the Russians can attack in open military aggression in the Middle East, and I have difficulty in understanding how you define subversion, Communist subversion or Russian subversion, in such a way as to make a clear-cut case for military intervention.

I regret this and I have some ideas why this has been done. I think that it primarily has been done because the executive branch, as often before, has underestimated the willingness of Congress to agree to do what is necessary on a clear-cut, straightforward presentation of the fact. In actuality, this resolution is not directed primarily against Communist aggression but against general disorder. That is to say, we commit ourselves to see to it, if necessary with military force, that some semblance of order is maintained or if need be restored in the Middle East. . . .

18 *Atomic Force and Foreign Policy*

The actions and pronouncements of the government of the United States since the great international crises of November, 1956, the British white paper on defense of April 4, 1957, and the private warnings addressed by Bulganin to the British and French governments in the fall of 1956, all agree on one point: rejection of the use of force, except in self-defense, as an instrument of national policy. When Bulganin wrote to Eden on September 11, 1956, that "it is no longer possible to threaten and brandish weapons . . . [and] any military measures directed against sovereignty and territorial integrity . . . can end only in failure"; when he wrote to Mollet on the same date that "in the age of atomic weapons, one must not threaten to use arms or brandish arms," he anticipated Eisenhower's statement of November 1: "I, as your President am proud—and I trust that you are proud—that the United States declared itself against the use of force in, not one, but both of these cases [Egypt and Hungary]." The British white paper draws the practical conclusion from these statements by asking for a military establishment which is geared to preventing wars rather than fighting them.

What the Kellogg-Briand Pact envisaged in 1929 as a legal obligation and a moral postulate appears to have become reality in 1957. Swords are to be beaten, it is true, into guided missiles rather than plowshares, yet the result still appears as the achievement of the biblical vision of eternal peace. Contemporary Western society, profoundly pacifist except in the face of patent provocation, is easily tempted to accept this conclusion without examination, especially since not accepting it would necessitate a great moral and intellectual effort without promising to produce so clear-cut and satisfying a result. However, the popularity of the argument that war is no longer possible calls for, rather than allows us to dispense with, a critical analysis of its logic and assumptions.

From *Commentary*, June, 1957.

The new pacifism, as expressed in the consensus of our quotations, differs fundamentally from the traditional pacifism of which the Kellogg-Briand Pact is the most notable modern manifestation. Traditional pacifism, aside from its moral revulsion from violence, argued that any war was an irrational way of settling international disputes. War does not solve anything. War does not pay. Nobody has ever won a war. War is the "Great Illusion." "There never was," Benjamin Franklin wrote to Josiah Quincy on September 17, 1773, "a good war or a bad peace."

Nevertheless, while statesmen paid lip service to the pacifist arguments against war, especially in the interwar period, their actions belied their protestations. War continued to be regarded, as it had been throughout history, as a rational instrument of national policies. Statesmen continuously weighed the advantages and risks of employing the peaceful means of diplomatic pressure and negotiation against those of the threat and use of force. They might be mistaken in choosing force if they could obtain their goals by peaceful means or if they lost the war. Yet even then their choice was a rational one because the risks they took were not out of proportion to the objectives sought. By and large, statesmen acted like gamblers who commit only as much of their resources as they can afford to lose. If they win, the gain justifies the risk taken; if they lose, the loss sets them back—but not necessarily beyond possible recovery. Even the Second World War conformed to this pattern: the risks taken were commensurate with the objectives sought.

The feasibility of all-out atomic war has completely destroyed this rational relation between force and foreign policy. All-out atomic war, being an instrument of universal destruction, obliterates not only the traditional distinction between victor and vanquished, but also the material objective of the war itself. In the pre-atomic age, it would have been perfectly rational for the United States to go to war in order to liberate the nations of Eastern Europe, provided that liberation had a sufficiently high priority among American national objectives and that American power appeared sufficiently strong in relation to the opposing power to have a chance of success. In the atomic age, however, the United States has emphatically ruled out the use of force to liberate the satellite countries; she was afraid, rightly or wrongly, that the threat of force in Eastern Europe might lead to all-out atomic war. The Soviet Union has for the very same reasons denied herself the use of force with regard to Western Europe, which cannot be defended against the Red Army. In the Korean War, both sides refrained from committing, qualitatively and quantitatively, more than a fraction of their resources and from exploiting their strategic opportunities to the full and thus granted "privileged sanctuaries" to each other, fearful as each was lest one provoke the other into an all-out atomic war,

All-out atomic war, no longer being considered an instrument of national policy, has taken on a function which is novel at least in its exclusiveness. Traditional force is an instrument for breaking the will of the opponent either through successful defense or attack; it is in the effectiveness of its physical application that its primary function lies. But the primary function of all-out atomic force lies in making its physical application superfluous by deterring the prospective opponent from using it. While traditional force operates psychologically through the intermediary of actual physical employment, all-out atomic force has a psychological function pure and simple. The prospective opponents are kept constantly aware of the inevitability of their own destruction should they resort to all-out atomic force, and this awareness prevents them from resorting to it.

It is worth noting that in the pre-atomic age the threat and the counterthreat of force could always be, and frequently were, put to the test of actual performance, and either the threat or the counterthreat was then proved to be empty. In the atomic age, the very purpose of threat and counterthreat is to prevent the test of actual performance from taking place. The appearance of possessing both the ability and the resolution to make good threat and counterthreat becomes, then, of paramount importance as a condition for the success of mutual deterrence.

The nature of this condition, it will be noted, is political rather than military, for what is essential is the *appearance* of possessing the ability and resolution to make good threat and counterthreat, not the reality of such possession. In order to make mutual deterrence work, two nations need only to create the mutual belief that they are willing and able to destroy each other in all-out atomic war. As long as this belief exists, it is irrelevant whether or not the reality corresponds to it. In other words, the mechanics of mutual deterrence require an element of bluff, either real or suspect.

At this point, the mechanics of mutual deterrence raise a most serious political dilemma. No nation can afford to yield to a threat of all-out atomic war that is only a bluff; nor can it afford to stand up to a threat that turns out not to be a bluff. Miscalculation is bound to be fatal either to the interests of the nation concerned, if it yields to the bluff, or to its existence, if it stands up to an atomic threat that is not a bluff. And the trouble is that a nation cannot determine when the other side is bluffing without the test of actual performance—a test which it is the very purpose of mutual deterrence to avoid.

Is there any issue at all, short of self-defense, for the sake of which either the United States or the Soviet Union would be willing to blow up the world? Is the Soviet Union justified in believing that the United States will really blow up the world in defense of Western Europe? Was the United States correct in assuming in November, 1956, that the Soviet Union would be willing to blow up the world in defense of Hungary? And would the Soviet Union in November, 1956, really have taken the chance of an all-out atomic war by sending volunteers to the Middle East and attacking Great Britain and France in defense of Egypt?

The philosophy of mutual deterrence answers these questions in the negative, for it assumes that no nation will resort to all-out atomic war on any conceivable issue short of all-out atomic attack against itself. That is, no nation will ever start an all-out atomic war; hence, all-out atomic war has really become "impossible." However, neither the United States nor the Soviet Union has pretended to act on that assumption. The United States has refrained from certain actions because she feared the Soviet Union might reply to them with all-out atomic war, and the Soviet Union has threatened certain actions which at least implied the possibility of all-out atomic war. Thus the pacifist confidence of the official pronouncements is belied by the—positive or negative—concern with all-out atomic war reflected in official actions.

The new pacifism, consistent within itself but not with the political attitudes of governments in so far as all-out atomic war is concerned, raises another fundamental problem for the day-to-day conduct of foreign policy without providing a satisfactory answer. It proposes to eliminate the use of force *of any kind* by the same means it has thus far successfully employed in staving off all-out atomic war: deterrence.

The deterrence to be exercised against the use of force which falls short of all-out atomic war and may be called conventional is supposed to be "graduated," that is, commensurate with the force threatened. The use of force is to be prevented by the threat of counterforce sufficient to deter the prospective user. But is graduatd deterrence with conventional force likely to operate with the same degree of reliability that has thus far enabled all-out atomic deterrence to prevent all-out atomic war? That the certainty of complete atomic destruction constitutes an absolute deterrent to all but madmen stands to reason. But what are the conventional weapons in the arsenal of the Western powers by which they hope to deter prospective opponents from using conventional force? They are two: a rudimentary conventional military establishment partially armed with tactical atomic weapons and what has been called "moral suasion."

The unilateral partial disarmament of the Western nations as regards conventional forces, coupled with their primary reliance upon tactical atomic weapons, casts doubt on the feasibility of graduated deterrence. It does so for two reasons. First of all, tactical atomic weapons are obviously not of the same broad, well-nigh universal applicability as are bullets, shells, and bombs. In street fighting, guerrila war, and night operations in jungles and mountains—to mention only a few contingencies—atomic weapons may be of little if any avail. To the degree that atomic weapons are recognized by the nation to be deterred as being blunt weapons or weapons impossible to use at all under the circumstances, the nation that threatens their use will be considered to be bluffing, and the threat will not deter. Furthermore, and most important, the element of bluff, actual or suspect, is bound to figure much more prominently here than with respect to the all-out atomic deterrent. What tactical atomic weapons can do in actual warfare is still largely a matter of conjecture. No nation will lightly employ such an untried weapon, especially in view of the choices before it should tactical atomic weapons prove to be ineffective.

These choices are three, all of them unsatisfactory in different ways. The nation can accept defeat and give up the fight. Or it can continue fighting with non-atomic conventional armed forces, running the risk of its unpreparedness in this respect. Or it can resort to ever more powerful atomic weapons until in the end it finds itself face to face with that unacceptable contingency which all its policies were intended to obviate: all-out atomic war. We should not have to remind ourselves, though the prevailing complacency makes it necessary to do so, that these uncertainties and risks are magnified by the possibility that the nation to be deterred may also be provided with atomic weapons, tactical and strategic. In other words, "graduated deterrence" is a two-way street.

That under such conditions a nation would follow up its threat with actual atomic warfare, however limited initially, is possible but certainly cannot be taken for granted. Yet, to the degree in which it is not taken for granted by the nation to be deterred, the threat must lose its deterrent effect. The Secretary of State of the United States has let it be known that he takes pride in his "brinkmanship," which three times—in Korea, Indochina, and Formosa—led him to the brink of war but not over it. Regardless of the actual historical circumstances under which the use of force was here averted, there can be little doubt that "brinkmanship" cannot be practiced indefinitely without challenge, and that this must be even more true of what might be called "open brinkmanship, openly arrived at"—that is, "brinkmanship" whose deterrent effect is counteracted by retrospective boasts as well as by the official rhetoric of pacifism. Sooner or later someone will want to know whether the statesman approaching the brink is serious or bluffing, whether he will jump or pull back. Then the alternative will be war, or peace by appeasement. Let us not forget that Germany attacked Belgium in 1914 and Poland in 1939 on the assumption that Great Britain was bluffing and would not fight, an assumption derived primarily from Great Britain's reputation for pacifism.

However, the new pacifism claims to provide still another alternative to the alternative of war or appeasement: "moral suasion." Little need be said to show that "moral suasion" is a euphemism for impotence. There are only two ways in which men, acting for their nation, can be dissuaded from taking a certain course of action: the promise of benefits and the threat of disadvantages. No man has ever been thus dissuaded by abstract references to the moral law or by entreaties to be good. Religions have had to rely upon promises of heaven and threats of hell in order to influence the behavior of their adherents. More particularly, a statesman who has resolved to use force in support of a certain policy cannot be expected to yield to "moral suasion" unless it is backed up by promises or threats.

The dilemma that confronts the Western world today as it contemplates the use of force is only partly the consequence of the unacceptable horror of all-out atomic war. In good part, too, it is the consequence of the "new look" of Western military policy, for what makes it so difficult for the West to contemplate the use of force is its own tendency, created by its new military policy, to identify force with atomic force. Yet the use of atomic force, however narrowly circumscribed by the initial intent, entails the enormous and unbearable risk that it may develop, imperceptibly but ineluctably, into the use of all-out atomic force.

The nations of the Western world could have avoided this dilemma if they had continued to maintain a non-atomic military establishment sufficient to support their foreign policies. They have said that they cannot afford to maintain two military establishments —one designed to deter all-out atomic war, the other to wage nonatomic conventional war. To say this is tantamount to saying that— in contrast to the Soviet Union, which continues to support two military establishments—the richest, politically and technologically most advanced, and still most powerful combination of nations on earth cannot afford to protect their interests without running the risk of universal destruction. Which is another way of saying that they cannot protect their interests at all, in so far as that protection requires the use of force. The truth is that financially, economically, and technologically they can well afford two military establishments. What their leaders think they cannot afford is the political courage to demand of their peoples the sacrifices necessary to protect and promote their national interests under the condition of atomic peace. In a word: the deficit is political and moral, not economic and financial.

With the decision to scrap traditional military establishments and arm its remnants with atomic weapons, the Western world may well have passed the point of no return. At the end of the road that the new pacifism has begun to travel there may indeed lie peace, either the peace of appeasement and ultimate surrender or else the peace of Babylon and Carthage—the peace of total destruction.

19 *The Nuclear Test-Ban Negotiations*

The Soviet Union has just made another concession in the Geneva negotiations on the cessation of atomic tests. It has declared its willingness to allow international inspection of a limited number of underground disturbances whose nature cannot be identified with the presently available seismographic equipment. This concession follows a number of others concerning international inspection and control on Russian territory, which together constitute a radical departure from past Soviet attitudes. Speculation is of course rife about the reasons why the Russians are taking this unprecedented attitude, which has been explained primarily in terms of propagandistic and military tactics.

I have been consistently suspicious of Soviet intentions and have raised my pen against the spirit of Geneva of 1955 and the spirit of Camp David of 1959 as soon as they transpired. But I have always credited the leaders of the Soviet Union with a sense of reality.

A realistic evaluation of the world scene has convinced me since 1955 that if the nuclear armaments race cannot be brought under control before any number of nations will have nuclear weapons, only a miracle will save mankind. The controlled cessation of atomic tests is a first small step in the direction of the control of the atomic armaments race itself. If the United States and the Soviet Union cannot agree on this, they will not be able to agree on anything else in this field. We are standing, therefore, at a turning point in the history of the world. If we fail here, we have in all likelihood sealed our and mankind's doom, and the only issue remaining to be settled will be how and when we shall be doomed.

Is it farfetched to assume that the Russian leaders are aware of what most knowledgeable observers outside the Soviet Union know, and that they have radically changed their position with regard to international control and inspection on their territory because they want to survive?

Letter to the *New York Times*, February 17, 1960.

This explanation, I admit, is simple and lacks in that elaborate and improbable sophistication with which some Soviet experts like to make things complicated and, hence, unmanageable. But it may well be worthy of some consideration by that unfortunate interdepartmental committee which, for lack of guidance from above, must hammer out as best it can our policy on this momentous issue.

THE RESTORATION OF

FOREIGN POLICY

The Methods—Old and New—of Foreign Policy

20 *International Relations*

In its broadest, literal meaning, this term denotes relations among the autonomous political units which today we call nations, or among individual members of such units. On the collective level, such relations can be political, military, economic, or cultural; they can comprise all kinds of individual relations involving members of different nations. Yet when we refer to international relations as a distinct object of human action and understanding, we have in mind only those collective or individual relations, transcending national boundaries, which affect the position of nations vis-à-vis each other. International relations in this sense are political relations; they comprise, aside from the foreign policy of nations, all collective and individual relations which impinge upon the political position of a nation vis-à-vis other nations. The term in this sense is a synonym for foreign relations, as used, for instance, in the name "senate foreign relations committee."

International relations are as old as political history itself and have shown throughout the ages constant patterns of relationships and policies, whether entered into by hereditary monarchs or elective governments, cities or nation-states, continental empires or tiny principalities, ecclesiastic or secular rulers. The consistency of patterns beneath the variety of historic manifestations makes both historic understanding and theoretical analysis of international relations possible. Thus we are able to understand the international relations of the Greek city-states that Thucydides describes, the international relations of the Indian states of the fourth century B.C. from which Kautilya derived his philosophy, the international relations of the ancient near east of which the Old Testament tells, as well as those of the more recent past. By detecting in the international relations of different cultures and historic periods identical responses to identical challenges, we are able to develop certain theoretical propositions about international relations that are true regardless of time and place.

From *Encyclopaedia Britannica*, 1961.

The dynamic force that molds international relations is to be found in the aspirations for power of autonomous political units. These aspirations crystallize into three basic patterns: to keep one's power, to increase one's power, to demonstrate one's power. From these patterns three basic types of policy ensue: the policy of the status quo, the policy of imperialism, and the policy of prestige. The clash of these policies—A trying to maintain the status quo, B trying to change it at the expense of A—leads to an unending struggle for power which characterizes all international relations. This struggle for power can be fought by two different means: diplomacy and military force. It leads of necessity to the balance of power through which nation A, either alone or in conjunction with other nations similarly threatened, tries to maintain itself against B. When A and B pursue their goals in conjunction with other nations, they embark upon a policy of alliances. When nations carry on the struggle for power by military means, they engage in an armaments race or war. When they try to justify and rationalize their positions in the power struggle by reference to universal values, typically of a moral nature, they develop political ideologies. Continuous peaceful contacts among them lead to the development of an institutionalized diplomacy.

Throughout the better part of history, several systems of international relations have existed side by side with little or no contact among them. Until the discovery of America, the American system or systems of international relations led a completely separate existence. The Chinese and Indian systems had only intermittent contacts with others.

Three different patterns of international relations can be distinguished according to the distribution of power within them: multiple, bipolar, and imperial systems. The multiple system is distinguished by a number of units of approximately equal strength which combine and oppose each other in ever changing alignments. Its main characteristics are flexibility, uncertainty as to the relative strength and future policies of its members, and the propensity for limited, inconclusive wars. The European state system, from the end of the Thirty Years' War in 1648 to the beginning of the First World War in 1914, with the exception of the period of the Napoleonic Wars, conformed to this pattern.

The bipolar system is characterized by the predominance of two major powers of approximately equal strength, around which the other members are grouped in different degrees of closeness. This system is rigid and stable as long as the approximately equal distribution of power between its two predominant members persists. Any marked shift in that distribution threatens the system with destruction. The structure of international relations that emerged from the Second World War exemplifies this pattern.

The imperial system consists of one predominant nation with a number of subordinate members clustered around it. The stability of such a system is great, and conflicts within it tend to be marginal. Its existence can be threatened by the disintegration of the predominant member, the rise of a number of subordinate members to a position from which they can challenge the predominant one, or by a challenge from outside the system. The system of international relations dominated by the Roman empire is the classic example of this pattern.

International relations have undergone in modern times four drastic changes: the formerly separate systems of international relations have merged into one world-wide system; the predominance of the European system has disappeared; the possibility and actuality of total war have come to dominate the international scene; the feasibility of universal destruction with nuclear weapons has radically altered the function of force as a means to the ends of foreign policy. While the first three changes do not affect the dynamics and structure of international relations as we have known them since the beginning of history, the last constitutes a veritable revolution, the only one in recorded history, in the structure of international relations.

The expansion of the European state system into the other continents by means of colonial empires, starting early in the sixteenth century, broke down the barriers which had separated the different systems of international relations. They were all brought into contact with, and into some form of dependence upon, the European state system, and through it they came into contact with each other. The two world wars of the twentieth century, in which most nations of the world participated, point in their very name to the transformation of a number of separate systems of international relations into one world-wide system. That process of political unification was greatly advanced and expanded to the individual sphere through the development of the technology of transportation and communications. This development started with the great voyages at the end of the fifteenth century and culminated in the drastic reduction of geographic distances for transportation and the virtual obliteration of the limits of time and space for communications.

The last phase of this transformation of international relations into a world-wide system, covering roughly the period from the end of the First World War to the aftermath of the Second, coincides with a radical change in the distribution of power within the system. From the beginning of the sixteenth century to the First World War the European system provided the dynamics and the preponderant power for this transformation; now two nations, either completely or predominantly non-European — the United States and the Soviet Union — have taken its place. This decline of Europe as the political center of the world may be said to have started with the Monroe Doctrine of 1823, declaring the mutual political independence of Europe and the Western Hemisphere. This declaration foreshadowed the fragmentation of the European empires which was virtually consummated after the Second World War in the colonial revolutions sweeping Africa and Asia. Most of the colonial possessions of European nations, one after the other, have gained their national independence, and many of them have either withdrawn their political support from the European nations or joined their enemies. The outstanding examples of these two different forms of political emancipation are India and China.

The decline of Europe resulting from the colonial revolutions coincided with the rise to predominance of formerly backward nations such as Russia and China. The technological unification of the world gave these nations the tools to transform their superior potential in geography, population, and natural resources into the actuality of national power.

The decisive factors in the decline of Europe as the political center of the world were the two world wars of the twentieth century. At the same time that they weakened the main European nations in their human and material resources, these conflicts brought non-European nations to the fore — the United States and Japan in consequence of the First World War, the United States and the Soviet Union in consequence of the Second World War. These two world wars differed not only in their consequences but also in their intrinsic character from other wars fought in the Western world in modern times. Most of the latter were limited wars in that only a fraction of the total human and material resources of the belligerents was committed to them. Only a fraction of the total population was morally identified with these wars and suffered from them, and each war was waged only for limited objectives. The two world wars, and those for which the most powerful nations have continued to prepare, were total in all these four respects. The actuality and threat of total war have been, indeed, the most important distinctive characteristics of international relations in the mid-twentieth century. They have been due to an unprecedented accumulation of destructive power in the hands of the most powerful nations and to the incentive to use that power for national purposes. The accumulation of power has resulted from drastic changes in the distribution of political and technological power in the world; the incentive has been presented by the closing of the colonial frontier and the ascendancy of a universalistic nationalism.

Throughout the modern period, with the exception of the wars of religion of the sixteenth and seventeenth centuries and of the Napoleonic Wars, wars were limited in every respect. Power was so widely dispersed among a great number of sovereign states that no single state or possible combination of states was strong enough to gain more than limited objectives against its adversaries. The drastic reduction in the number of sovereign states and the resulting concentration of power in the hands of a few nations of the first rank, which occurred between the end of the Thirty Years' War and the end of the Second World War, created one precondition for total war. The treaty of Westphalia of 1648, for instance, reduced the number of sovereign states of which the German empire was composed from 900 to 355. The diet of Regensburg of 1803 eliminated 200 more. When the German confederation was founded in 1815, only 36 sovereign states were left to join it. The unification of Italy in 1861 and that of Germany in 1871 eliminated 31 additional sovereign states.

At the end of the Napoleonic Wars in 1815, only five nations of the first rank were left—Austria, France, Great Britain, Russia, and

Prussia. In the 1860's Italy and the United States joined them, followed toward the end of the century by Japan. At the beginning of the First World War in 1914, eight nations were of the first rank, with Germany having replaced Prussia. After the First World War the trend toward reduction of the number of sovereign states was reversed; their number almost doubled because the Ottoman, Austro-Hungarian, British, and French empires were broken up. Yet the trend toward concentration of more and more power in the hands of fewer and fewer states continued. At the end of the Second World War the number of nations of the first rank was reduced to two: the United States and the Soviet Union.

It is not by accident that the two most powerful nations capable of threatening each other with total war are also most advanced technologically and industrially. The mechanization of warfare in terms of weapons, supplies, transportation, and communications requires, in case of actual hostilities, the virtually total commitment of the industrial productivity of the nation. This total commitment has been made possible by the enormous increase in economic productivity brought about by a series of technological and industrial revolutions starting in the eighteenth century. By contrast, in earlier periods of history, economic productivity was so low that after it had barely provided for the needs of the population, little was left for military purposes. Thus premodern technology could support only limited war, while modern industry is productive enough to allow the commitment of the lion's share of its products for military purposes.

One incentive for the great nations to use this enormous productive power for the purposes of mutual destruction was provided by a change in international relations which can be called the disappearance of the colonial frontier. The generally limited character of the means and ends of foreign policy from the end of the middle ages to the First World War was in good measure due to the opportunity for the great European nations to seek satisfaction for their aspirations for power not in all-out contests with each other but through competitive expansion into Africa, the Americas, and the part of Asia bordering on the eastern oceans. Colonial competition and conflict during that period provided outlets through which the European nations could compete for power without endangering their existence. But by the beginning of the twentieth century the colonial frontier was, for all practical purposes, closed. Virtually all politically weak or empty spaces around the globe had been transformed into colonies or spheres of influence by one or another of the European nations. From then on, as the two world wars showed, the great European powers, deprived of the colonial safety valve, fought each other not for limited advantage but for total stakes, and they could do so with the instruments of total war.

These stakes have become total, not only in that total war threatens the belligerents with total destruction, but also in that the issue over which nations compete and fight has become total. That issue is no longer a limited military or territorial advantage but the universal triumph or defeat of a particular philosophy and way of life, which is supposed to be incarnate in a particular nation. While traditionally the international relations of the Western world have been carried on within the framework of common moral principles and a common way of life, which imposed effective limitations upon the struggle for power, international relations in the mid-twentieth century have been dominated by the conflict between democracy and communism, each putting forth a universal message of salvation, each trying—with different intensity—to extend its dominion to all mankind, and each identified with one of the two great powers left in the world. Thus international relations have come to be characterized not only by the traditional threat and use of military force on behalf of the aspirations of individual nations but also by a struggle for the minds of men. The proponents of the two antagonistic philosophies and ways of life, using the instruments of propaganda, foreign aid and foreign trade, have endeavored to gain the allegiance of uncommitted nations. By the same token, the traditional methods of diplomacy have been in eclipse. Nations can negotiate and bargain about their interests and conclude compromises concerning them, but they feel that they cannot yield an inch where their philosophies and ways of life are at stake.

While similar situations have existed before, temporarily and on a limited scale, especially in periods of religious conflicts and wars, international relations after the First and Second World Wars have been marked by a change in structure unprecedented in recorded history. Throughout history, there has existed a rational relationship between the threat and use of military force and the ends of foreign policy. It was rational for a nation to ask itself whether it could achieve its ends vis-à-vis another nation by peaceful means or whether it had to resort to military force to achieve them, for the risks involved in the resort to military force were generally not out of proportion to the ends sought. Great ends justified great risks, since the risks were generally not so great as to obviate the ends. Yet all-out nuclear war, likely to destroy all belligerents and thus to eliminate the very distinction between victor and vanquished, is a completely irrational undertaking. No possible end can justify it; it is an instrument of mass murder and mass suicide.

International relations, then, are faced with two interconnected dilemmas upon the solution of which depends the survival of Western civilization and perhaps of mankind itself. The first dilemma consists in the contrast between the technological unification of the world and the parochial moral commitments and political institutions of the age. Moral commitments and political institutions, dating from an age which modern technology has left behind, have not kept pace with technological achievements and, hence, are incapable of controlling their destructive potentialities. The second dilemma consists in the contrast between the need of nations to support their interests by resort to violence and the irrationality of resort to nuclear arms. If a nation cannot resort to nuclear weapons without risking its own destruction, how can it support its interests in a world of sovereign nations which is ruled by violence as the last resort?

These two dilemmas put into question the very survival of the existing system of international relations. The first dilemma suggests a higher principle of international organization, transcending the nation-state, in the form either of a universal organization, such as the United Nations, which would minimize threats to international peace, or of regional organizations, such as the European communities or a projected Atlantic union, which would eliminate local threats to peace and facilitate the rational use of regional resources. The second dilemma suggests the abolition of international relations itself through the merger of all national sovereignties into one world state which would have a monopoly of the most destructive instruments of violence. Both kinds of solutions are supported by the awareness of the unity of mankind underlying the inevitable fragmentation of international relations. However inarticulate and submerged, this awareness has never completely disappeared even in the heyday of nationalism, and it has been sharpened by the threat of nuclear destruction facing all mankind. These solutions are also supported by the longing to give that unity a viable political form, a longing which has time and again endeavored through theoretical schemes and practical measures to transform international relations into a supranational political order. This longing, in times past mainly a spiritual or humanitarian impulse, in the nuclear age has been greatly strengthened by the desire, innate in all men, for self-preservation.

21 *Alliances*

Alliances are a necessary function of the balance of power operating within a multiple state system. Nations A and B, competing with each other, have three choices in maintaining and improving their relative power positions. They can increase their own power, they can add to their own power the power of other nations, or they can withhold the power of other nations from the adversary. When they make the first choice, they embark upon an armaments race. When they choose the second and third alternatives, they pursue a policy of alliances.

Whether or not a nation shall pursue a policy of alliances is, then, not a matter of principle but of expediency. A nation will shun alliances if it believes that it is strong enough to hold its own unaided or that the burden of the commitments resulting from the alliance is likely to outweigh the advantages to be expected. It is for one or the other or both of these reasons that, throughout the better part of their history, Great Britain and the United States have refrained from entering into peacetime alliances with other nations.

Yet Great Britain and the United States have also refrained from concluding an alliance with each other even though, from the proclamation of the Monroe Doctrine in 1823 to the attack on Pearl Harbor in 1941, they have acted, at least in relation to the other European nations, as if they were allied. Their relationship during that period provides another instance of a situation in which nations dispense with an alliance. It occurs when their interests so obviously call for concerted policies and actions that an explicit formulation of these interests, policies, and actions in the form of a treaty of alliance appears to be redundant.

Both Great Britain and the United States have had with regard to the continent of Europe one interest in common: the preservation of the European balance of power. Thus when Great Britain went to war in 1914 and 1939 in order to protect the European balance of

From *Confluence*, Winter, 1958.

power, the United States first supported Great Britain with a conspicuous lack of that impartiality befitting a neutral and then joined her on the battlefield. Had the United States been tied to Great Britain by a formal treaty of alliance in 1914 and 1939, it might have declared war earlier, but its general policies and concrete actions would not have been materially different than they actually were.

Not every community of interests calling for common policies and actions also calls for legal codification in an explicit alliance. On the other hand, an alliance requires a community of interests for its foundation. Under what conditions, then, does an existing community of interests require the explicit formulation of an alliance? What is it that an alliance adds to the existing community of interests?

An alliance adds precision, especially in the form of limitation, to an existing community of interests and to the general policies and concrete measures serving them.[1] The interests nations have in common are not typically so precise and limited as to geographic region, objectives, and appropriate policies as has been the American and British interest in the preservation of the European balance of power. Nor are they so incapable of precision and limitation as concerns the prospective common enemy, for while a typical alliance is directed against a specific nation or group of nations, the enemy of the Anglo-American community of interests could in the nature of things not be specified beforehand. As Jefferson shifted his sympathies back and forth between Napoleon and Great Britain according to who seemed to threaten the balance of power at the time, so during the century following the Napoleonic Wars Great Britain and the United States had to decide in the light of circumstances ever liable to change who posed at the moment the greatest threat. This blanket character of the enemy, determined not individually but by the function he performs, brings to mind a similar characteristic of collective security, which is directed against the abstractly designed aggressor, whoever he may be.

The typical interests which unite two nations against a third are both more definite as concerns the determination of the enemy and

[1] Glancing through the treaties of alliance of the seventeenth and eighteenth centuries, one is struck by the meticulous precision with which obligations to furnish troops, equipment, logistic support, food, money, and the like were defined.

less precise as concerns the objectives to be sought and the policies to be pursued. In the last decades of the nineteenth century, France was opposed to Germany and Russia was opposed to Austria, while Austria was allied with Germany against France and Russia. How could the interests of France and Russia be brought to a common denominator, determining policy and guiding action? How could, in other words, the *casus foederis* be defined so that both friend and foe would know what to expect in certain contingencies affecting their respective interests? It was for the treaty of alliances of 1894 to perform these functions. Had the objectives and policies of the Franco-Russian alliance of 1894 been as clear as are the objectives and policies of Anglo-American co-operation in Europe, no alliance treaty would have been necessary. Had the enemy been as indeterminate, no alliance treaty would have been feasible.

Not every community of interests calling for co-operation between two or more nations, then, requires that the terms of this co-operation be specified through the legal stipulations of a treaty of alliance. It is only when the common interests are inchoate in terms of policy and action that a treaty of alliance is required to make them explicit and operative. These interests, as well as the alliances expressing them and the policies serving them, can be distinguished in five different ways: according to their intrinsic nature and relationship, the distribution of benefits and power, their coverage in relation to the total interests of the nations concerned, their coverage in terms of time, and their effectiveness in terms of common policies and actions. In consequence, we can distinguish alliances serving identical, complementary, and ideological interests and policies. We can further distinguish mutual and one-sided, general and limited, temporary and permanent, operative and inoperative alliances.[2]

The Anglo-American alliance with regard to Europe provides the classic example of an alliance serving identical interests. The alliance between the United States and Pakistan is one of many contemporary instances of an alliance serving complementary interests. For the United States it serves the primary purpose of expanding the scope of the policy of containment; for Pakistan it serves primarily

[2] Sanskrit has sixteen words for different types of alliances.

the purpose of increasing her political, military, and economic potential vis-à-vis her neighbors.

The pure type of an ideological alliance is presented by the Treaty of the Holy Alliance of 1815 and the Atlantic Charter of 1941. Both documents laid down general moral principles to which the signatories pledged their adherence and general objectives whose realization they pledged themselves to seek. Much more typical is the addition of ideological commitments to material ones in one and the same treaty of alliance.[3] Thus the Three Emperors' League of 1873 provided for military assistance among Austria, Germany, and Russia in case of attack on any of the three and at the same time emphasized the solidarity of the three monarchies against republican subversion. In our times, the ideological commitment against Communist subversion, inserted in treaties of alliance, performs a similar function. The ideological factor also manifests itself in the official interpretation of an alliance, in terms of an ideological solidarity transcending the limitations of material interests. The conception of the Anglo-American alliance, common before the British invasion of Egypt in 1956, as all-inclusive and world-embracing, based upon common culture, political institutions, and ideals, is a case in point.

As concerns the political effect of this ideological factor upon an alliance, three possibilities must be distinguished. A purely ideological alliance, unrelated to material interests, cannot but be stillborn; it is unable to determine policies or guide actions, and misleads by giving the appearance of political solidarity where there is none. The ideological factor, when it is superimposed upon an actual community of interests, can lend strength to the alliance by marshaling moral convictions and emotional preferences to its support. It can also weaken it by obscuring the nature and limits of the common interests which the alliance was supposed to make precise and by raising expectations, bound to be disappointed, concerning the extent of concerted policies and actions. For both these last possibilities, the Anglo-American alliance can again serve as an example.

Ideally, the distribution of benefits within an alliance should be one of complete mutuality. This ideal is most likely to be approxi-

[3] It ought to be pointed out that both the Holy Alliance and the Atlantic Charter actually supplement material commitments contained in separate legal instruments.

mated in an alliance concluded among equals in power and serving identical interests; here the equal resources of all, responding to equal incentives, serve one single interest. The other extreme in the distribution of benefits is one-sidedness, in which one party receives the lion's share of benefits while the other bears the main bulk of burdens. In so far as the object of such an alliance is the preservation of the territorial and political integrity of the receiving party, such an alliance is indistinguishable from a treaty of guarantee. Complementary interests lend themselves most easily to this kind of disproportion since they are by definition different in substance and their comparative assessment is likely to be distorted by subjective interpretation.

The distribution of benefits and determination of policies is thus likely to reflect the distribution of power within an alliance. It is for this reason that Machiavelli warned weak nations against making alliances with strong ones except by necessity.[4] However, this correlation between benefits, policies, and power is by no means inevitable. A weak nation may well possess an asset which is of such great value for its strong ally as to be irreplaceable. Here the unique benefit the former is able to grant or withhold may give it a status within the alliance completely out of keeping with the actual distribution of material power. The relationships between the United States and Iceland with regard to bases and between Great Britain and Iraq with regard to oil can serve as examples.

The misinterpretation of the Anglo-American alliance, mentioned before, is also a case in point for the confusion between limited and general alliances. In the age of total war, wartime alliances tend to be general in that they comprise the total interests of the contracting parties both with regard to the waging of the war and the peace settlement. On the other hand, peacetime alliances tend to be limited to a fraction of the total interests and objectives of the signatories. A nation will conclude a multitude of alliances with different nations which may overlap and contradict each other on specific points.

A typical alliance attempts to transform a small fraction of the total interests of the contracting parties into common policies and measures. Some of these interests are irrelevant to the purposes of

[4] *The Prince*, chap. xxi.

the alliance, others support them, others diverge from them, and others still are incompatible with them. Whether and for how long an alliance will remain operative depends upon the strength of the interests underlying it as over against the strength of the other interests of the nations concerned. The value and the chances of an alliance, however limited in scope, must be considered within the context of the over-all policies within which it is expected to operate.

General alliances are usually of temporary duration and most prevalent in wartime. The overriding common interest in winning the war and securing through the peace settlement the interests for which the war was waged is bound to yield, once victory is won and the peace treaties are signed, to the traditionally separate and frequently incompatible interests of the individual nations. On the other hand, there exists a correlation between the permanency of an alliance and the limited character of the interests it serves, for only such a specific, limited interest is likely to last long enough to provide the foundation for a durable alliance. The alliance between Great Britain and Portugal, concluded in 1703, has survived the centuries because Portugal's interest in the protection of her ports by the British fleet and the British interest in the control of the Atlantic approaches to Portugal have endured. Yet it can be stated as a general historical observation that while alliance treaties have frequently assumed permanent validity by being concluded "in perpetuity" or for periods of ten or twenty years, they could not have been more durable than the generally precarious and fleeting configurations of common interests which they were intended to serve.

The dependence of alliances upon the underlying community of interests also accounts for the distinction between operative and inoperative alliances. For an alliance to be operative, its members must agree not only on general objectives but on policies and measures as well. Many alliances have remained scraps of paper because no such agreement was forthcoming, and it was not forthcoming because the community of interests did not extend beyond general objectives to concrete policies and measures. The Franco-Russian alliances of 1935 and 1944 and the Anglo-Russian alliance of 1942 are cases in point.

The examination of contemporary alliances in the light of these categories will be divided under three headings: the Atlantic alliance, the Western alliances outside Europe, the Communist alliances.

The vital interest of the United States in the protection of the nations of Western Europe against Russian domination is identical with the interest of these nations in preserving their national independence. Yet this foundation of the Atlantic alliance has undergone a change both subtle and drastic. The Atlantic alliance is beset by a crisis which the events of November, 1956, made obvious but did not create.

Seen from the perspective of the nations of Western Europe, three factors sustained the Atlantic alliance in the decade following the Second World War: the atomic monopoly of the United States, the economic weakness of the nations of Western Europe, and the intransigence of Stalinist policies. The conjunction of these factors confronted the nations of Western Europe with the choice between suicide and the acceptance of the political, economic, and military support of the United States. In other words, the Atlantic alliance was for the nations of Western Europe a prerequisite for national survival.

This connection between national survival and the Atlantic alliance is no longer as close nor as obvious as it used to be. The atomic monopoly of the United States provided the nations of Western Europe with absolute protection against Russian conquest. With the Soviet Union having become an atomic power equal, if not superior, to the United States, the Atlantic alliance is no longer solely a protection for the nations of Western Europe, but has also become a liability. The atomic stalemate threatens not only the two superpowers but also their allies with total destruction. Paradoxical as it may seem, the drastically increased threat of Soviet power has drastically weakened the Western alliance. The Soviet Union has not been slow to point out, and the man in the street in Western Europe has not been slow to understand, that if there is a chance for the nations of Western Europe to survive in an atomic war, it may lie in not being too closely identified, or perhaps not being identified at all, with the United States. Thus a latent neutralism has had a slowly corrosive influence upon the Atlantic alliance. The rise of this neutralism in Western Europe as a popular mass movement is not primarily the result of Communist propaganda, or of faintness of heart, but of the new objective conditions under which the nations of Western Europe must live in the age of the atomic stalemate.

Secondly, the economic recovery of the nations of Western Europe has greatly diminished their dependence upon the United States. The Coal and Steel Community, Euratom, the Common Market, and the development of East-West trade are likely to decrease it still more. Thus while the nations of Western Europe are still in need of American economic aid, that aid is no longer a question of life and death, as it was ten years ago. Today they have, or at least have evidence that they soon will have, an alternative. They can stand on their own feet again and look beyond the wall of containment for new outlets for their energies and products.

These factors affect West Germany's attitude toward the Atlantic alliance with particular intensity. Their effect is strengthened by the political issue which has the widest, and is likely to have an ever deepening, emotional appeal: unification. The Western alliance has been presented to West Germany, both by American and German official spokesmen, as the instrument through which unification would be achieved. While this view was from the outset open to serious doubts, the historic experience of its failure has led to a crisis of confidence which is likely to deepen as time goes on. The Atlantic alliance, far from being supported as the instrument of unification, is ever more loudly and widely blamed as the main obstacle to it.

The Soviet Union has been eager to use these new political, military, and economic conditions under which the nations of Western Europe live for the purpose of weakening and ultimately destroying the Atlantic alliance. What has been called the "new look" of Soviet foreign policy is essentially a new flexibility which has taken the place of the monotony of the Stalinist threats. In the face of these threats, no nation which wanted to survive as a nation had any choice; thus Stalin was really the architect of the Atlantic alliance. The new Soviet foreign policy alternately threatens and tempts, as the occasion seems to require, but always seeks to hold before the eyes of Western Europe an acceptable or even preferable alternative to the Atlantic alliance. In consequence, the Atlantic alliance has lost much of its urgency and vitality. Great Britain and France, for instance, no longer feel that they have to subordinate their separate national interests to the common defense against the Soviet Union; and they have begun, in different degrees, to pursue those interests regardless, and sometimes at the expense, of the common interests of the alliance. They have also begun to vent openly their resentment at their lack of great-power status and to allow their policies to be influenced by it. The rise of Germany to a position of political, military, and economic eminence cannot but add to the opportunities of the new Soviet foreign policy.

As viewed from the vantage point of the United States, the Atlantic alliance is also in the process of undergoing a subtle change, which in the end is bound to be drastic. For the United States, the Atlantic alliance is the political and military implementation of its perennial interest in the maintenance of the European balance of power. However, the military implementation of this interest is likely to change under the impact of a new technology of warfare. As long as the main deterrent to Russian aggression remains the atomic bomb delivered by plane, the military strategy of the United States requires military installations in Western Europe; and the nations of Western Europe have a corresponding interest in providing them. To the extent that the intercontinental guided missile will replace airplanes as a means of delivering atomic attack, the interest in American military installations in Western Europe will diminish on both sides of the Atlantic. This interest will decrease still further when some of the nations of Western Europe have atomic installations of their own. When this day comes, the Atlantic alliance will take on a new complexion, probably losing some of its specific military aspects and tending to revert to an implicit community of interests like that which tied the United States to Great Britain from 1823 to 1941.

However, the interests of the United States and the nations of Western Europe are not limited to that continent. Those of the United States and Great Britain are world-wide, and France is engaged in Africa. And whatever the community interests within the Atlantic alliance in Europe, these interests do not necessarily coincide elsewhere. The coincidence or divergence of these non-European interests has had a strengthening or debilitating, as the case might be, effect upon the Atlantic alliance itself; and the vital interest of all members of the alliance has, in turn, limited their freedom of action outside Europe.

The United States in particular, in dealing with the colonial revolutions which are directed primarily against Great Britain and France, has been continuously confronted with a painful and inherently insoluble dilemma. The horns of that dilemma are the interest of the United States in the continuing strength of Great Britain and France as her principal allies and the American interest in preventing the colonial revolutions from falling under the sway of communism. If the United States underwrites the colonial position of Great Britain or France, as it did in Indochina, it may strengthen its principal European allies, but will impair its standing with the anticolonial peoples of Asia and Africa. If the United States sides unreservedly with the Afro-Asian bloc, as it did in the United Nations on the occasion of the Suez Canal crisis of autumn, 1956, it weakens Great Britain and France and, in consequence, the Atlantic alliance. Faced with this dilemma, which can only be solved at the price of impairing the vital interests of the United States in one or the other respect, the United States has inevitably been reduced to straddling the fence by halfheartedly supporting one side on one occasion and the other side on another, or else keeping hands off altogether. Algeria and Cyprus exemplify at present the dilemma and its evasion. In such situations, then, the Atlantic alliance does not operate at all, for there are no common interests which could support its operation.

That such divergencies of interest and policy have not imposed greater stresses upon the Atlantic alliance and have left it essentially unimpaired testifies to its inherent strength. But that strength cannot be taken for granted. The common interests underlying the Atlantic alliance have thus far prevailed over the divergent ones only because of the conviction of the members of the alliance that they have a greater stake in their common than in their divergent interests. But in recent years the latter have grown stronger, and the former weaker. If this trend should continue unchecked, it would indeed put in jeopardy the very survival of the Atlantic alliance.

Common interests are the rock on which all alliances are built. Yet upon this rock all kinds of structures may be erected, some solid and spacious, others crumbling and confining. In other words, there are good and bad alliances: some work smoothly and are enthusiastically supported, others are cumbersome and are grudgingly accepted as a lesser evil. While the existence of the alliance depends upon a community of interests, the quality of the alliance is determined by the manner in which common interests are translated into concrete policies and day-by-day measures. It is in this latter respect that there is cause for concern about the Atlantic alliance. Here, too, the crisis of November, 1956, has made obvious defects which antedate that crisis. Three such defects have continuously and to an ever increasing degree impaired the operation of the Atlantic alliance: its organizational structure; the policies, domestic and international, of its leading members; and the prestige enjoyed by some of its leading statesmen.

The common interest of the members of the Atlantic alliance in the military protection of their independence has found its organizational expression in the North Atlantic Treaty Organization. The strategic conception which underlies NATO is the assumption that the European members of the Atlantic alliance are able to defend themselves through a co-operative effort against a military attack by the Soviet Union. But NATO has never developed a convincing philosophy of purpose. All members of NATO are agreed upon one objective: to defend their independence without having to fight for it. But how is this purpose to be achieved? Is primary reliance to be placed upon atomic retaliation with the local forces of NATO performing the function of the "plate glass" or "trip wire," or is a prospective aggressor to be deterred by the inherent military strength of local forces? The members of NATO have not seen eye to eye on this fundamental question, and NATO itself in its official proclamations and policies has not seemed to be of one mind either. More particularly, the declared purposes of NATO have been consistently at variance with the measures requested of its members for implementation of these purposes; and the measures requested, in turn, have been invariably at variance with the measures actually taken. Furthermore, declared purposes, requested measures, and the measures actually taken have been subjected to a number of drastic and confusing changes which cannot be explained exclusively by the revolutionary transformation which military technology is in the process of undergoing.

This confusion in policy, itself conducive to political disunity and friction in day-by-day operations, has been magnified by the elaborate organizational superstructure which is intended to put the policies of NATO into practice. This superstructure, which encompasses a plethora of committees charged with co-ordinating a variety of political, military, and economic policies of the member states, must make for friction and inefficiency even under the best of circumstances. It magnifies defects because it is much too ambitious in purpose and elaborate in operation for the agreed purpose of NATO. In the absence of agreement on philosophy and basic policy, an elaborate organizational superstructure can be a source of weakness rather than of strength.

Since an alliance, in its day-by-day operations, rests in good measure upon mutual confidence, the character and ability of its leading statesmen and the policies they pursue become of critical concern. In both respects, the Atlantic alliance has shown itself deficient. There can be no doubt that the prestige of the United States as leader of the Atlantic alliance has drastically declined. Rightly or wrongly, the United States is no longer looked upon by its allies, as it was during the period immediately following the Second World War, as the leader whose strength and resolution can be relied upon to keep the Atlantic alliance on an even course. Three factors are in the main responsible for this crisis of confidence.

In foreign policy it is sometime useful to keep the enemy guessing. But to keep allies guessing is bound to erode the foundations of confidence upon which an alliance must rest. The allies of the United States have noted discrepancies between the policy pronouncements of our leaders and the actual policies pursued, which appear to them to have evolved into a consistent pattern of unreliability.

This slow accumulation of loss of confidence reached a critical stage in the Suez Canal crisis, for here unreliability in policy appeared to be joined by indifference, if not hostility, to the vital interests of America's principal allies. For the vital interests of the United States and her allies to coincide in Europe and diverge elsewhere is one thing; but for the vital interests of her principal allies elsewhere to be actively opposed by the United States is quite another. To the former, the allies of the United States could reconcile themselves with relative equanimity; the latter could not help but raise for them the crucial question as to whether the Atlantic alliance was worth so high a price. That they answered the question in the affirmative testifies to the vitality of the alliance. Their resentment was kindled by the demonstration of their inability to pursue active foreign policies of their own without the support and against the opposition of one or the other of the superpowers. Thus, under the dramatic impact of the experience which saw the interests and power of our allies destroyed in a region vital to themselves, with the approval and active participation of the United States, the Atlantic alliance has tended to transform itself for them from an association of like-minded nations into a burden grudgingly borne.

As far as long-range policies are concerned, the relations among nations must be conceived in terms of interests. As concerns their day-by-day relations, we must also think in terms of personalities. We say that the United States and Great Britain have agreed on a certain policy, but tend to forget that Great Britain and the United States are abstractions and that in actuality the President and Secretary of State of the United States and the Prime Minister and Secretary for Foreign Affairs of Great Britain, speaking in the name of their respective nations, have agreed with each other. The smooth and effective operation of an alliance, then, depends in good measure upon the maintenance of trust and respect among its principal statesmen. There is no gainsaying the fact that the absence of such relations has become a great handicap in the day-by-day operations of the Atlantic alliance. Regardless of the objective merits of the case, there can be no doubt that the leaders of our European allies no longer have the same confidence in the judgment and the authority of the President of the United States they had in times past, and that they dislike and mistrust the Secretary of State with varying degrees of intensity but with virtual unanimity. These reactions have increased the strains under which the Atlantic alliance operates at present.

Our reactions, similarly negative, cannot help but add to the strain. The instability of French governments, the collapse of the Eden cabinet, the seeming futility of British and French policies in Cyprus and Algeria, the failure of their intervention in Egypt, all have produced some doubt regarding both the power of our principal allies and the wisdom of their leadership.

The traditional political rhetoric on both side of the Atlantic has tended to gloss over all these stresses and strains and has made it appear as though the Atlantic alliance were something broader and smoother and also something more diffuse than it actually is. It is indeed built upon a rock of common interests, but the rock is of limited dimensions and its surfaces are sometimes rough. In spite of the great damage which the crisis of November, 1956, has done to the Atlantic alliance, it has been useful in circumscribing more closely its limits and demonstrating for all to see its still considerable strength.

While the Atlantic alliance reposes upon the firm foundation of identical interests, no such general and reassuring statement can be made about the Western alliances outside Europe. Considering Asia and the Middle East, it can be said that of the American alliances only those with Formosa, South Korea, South Vietnam, and Japan are based upon identical interests. These nations, with the exception of Japan, owe their very existence as nations to the interests and power of the United States. Yet only their complete dependence upon the United States has prevented some, if not all, of these nations from pursuing policies at variance with those of the United States. Thus the stability of these alliances rests both upon identical interests and extreme discrepancy of power.

Our alliance with Japan, like that with Germany, was, during the first decade following the Second World War, likewise based upon the dual foundation of identical interests and overwhelming American power. Yet neither foundation can be any longer taken for granted. Three factors have combined to restore Japan's freedom of choice. First, Japan has again become the strongest power in Asia, leaving even China a considerable distance behind. If the wartime memories of Japan's imperialism were not still alive in the rest of Asia, Japan would be the favorite candidate for taking over the economic and political leadership of Asia. Second, the atomic stalemate has had the same psychological effect on Japan as on Western Europe; the American alliance has become for Japan a mixed blessing, if not a liability. Finally, to the degree that the aggressiveness of Stalinist and Chinese Korean War policies is replaced by a new flexibility which stresses the complementary character of Russian, Chinese, and Japanese interests, Japan may find a practical alternative to its identification with the United States.

The other Asian alliances, of which SEATO and the Baghdad Pact provide the outstanding examples, are of an entirely different type. They have three characteristics in common: complementary interests tending toward transformation into incompatible ones, a radically unequal distribution of benefits, and an ideological emphasis.

These alliances, on the face of them, were conceived in terms of common action on behalf of common interests. However, in view of the remoteness of the apparent *casus foederis*, that is, Communist attack upon a member, and of the virtual impossibility in case of such an attack for most members to act in common, commitment to common action has receded into the background and been distilled into an anti-Communist ideological commitment. Of the Asian members, this commitment requires nothing more than membership in the alliance; it requires no common objective, policy, or action—beyond anticommunism at home and abroad. Yet of the Western members, especially the United States, it requires specific policies and actions on behalf of the Asian members.

The Asian members are interested in these alliances primarily because of the economic, military, and political support they receive from the United States. Many of them consider their membership in the alliance to constitute a special claim upon the American treasury, American weapons, and American political support for their special national aspirations. However valuable the United States judges this membership to be, in terms of actual policies and measures it bears a unilateral burden. The United States is under continuous pressure to act as an ally, while the Asian allies, once they have signed the treaty of alliance, preserve virtually complete freedom of action. Their foreign policies, for instance, vis-à-vis China, could hardly be more different if they were not members of the alliance. In order to show the irrelevance of the alliance in terms of common objectives, policies, and actions, the prime minister of one Asian nation has gone so far as to equate his country's membership in SEATO with membership in the United Nations.

In so far as the West wants the maximum number of Asian allies and the Asian allies want the maximum amount of Western support, the interests of the two parties can be said to complement each other.

This compatibility is bound to disintegrate whenever a latent conflict of interests between two allies or an ally and another nation becomes acute. The conflicts between Pakistan and India over Kashmir, between Great Britain and Greece, and Turkey and Greece, over Cyprus, and between Iraq and Israel are cases in point. It is only because these alliances limit a commitment to common action to the very unlikely event of Communist aggression that they have survived such incompatibilities. The United States, in particular, is frequently forced into the uncomfortable position of having either to straddle the fence, as between Great Britain and Greece, or else to sacrifice its interests to its alliance, as between India and Pakistan.

Thus, by virtue of its alliance, the United States increases the armed strength of Pakistan and thereby forces India to increase its expenditures for armaments from thirty million pounds in 1955 to ninety million pounds in 1957. This diversion of scarce funds from economic development to armaments threatens India with economic and political disaster, which the United States has a vital interest in staving off through financial aid. In consequence, the United States engages, as it were, in an armaments race with itself by proxy, its left hand supporting Pakistan by virtue of the alliance, its right hand aiding India by virtue of its vital interests.

As for the alliance among the nations of the Western Hemisphere, appearances are deceptive. As long as the supremacy of the United States within the Western Hemisphere provided unchallengeable protection for the independence of the American nations, these alliances could indeed be taken for granted. For the United States, these alliances provided complete safety since, in view of its unchallengeable supremacy within the hemisphere and of the protection of two oceans, its security could be endangered only by a non-American nation acting in concert with an American one. For the other American nations, these alliances provided complete security from great-power domination since the United States would use its superior power only for the protection and not for the subversion of their national independence.

This identity of interests and the ability of the United States to implement it have provided the rationale and lifeblood of the American state system from the proclamation of the Monroe Doctrine to this day. The intercontinental guided missile confronts this system with a challenge never before experienced, for the supremacy of the United States within the Western Hemisphere, as unchallengeable as ever from within, is of no avail as protection against these novel weapons of tomorrow. The United States can no more protect its American allies against these weapons than it can protect itself. The American allies will come to view the alliance with the United States with the same misgivings with which the European allies and Japan view it already. They may no longer regard their interests as identical with those of the United States and may conclude that safety lies not in closeness to, but rather in distance from, the United States. While these considerations are admittedly speculative from the vantage point of 1957, they may well reflect the actuality of 1960.

The Communist alliances present three different types, which must be sharply distinguished: the alliances of the Soviet Union and China, on the one hand, with North Korea and North Vietnam, on the other; the alliances between the Soviet Union and the nations of Eastern Europe; the alliances of the Soviet Union, on the one hand, with China, Egypt, Syria, and probably Yemen, on the other.

The position of North Korea and North Vietnam within the Communist alliances is identical—in the particulars which interest us here—with the position of South Korea and South Vietnam within their alliances with the United States. There is complete identity of interests and extreme disparity of power.

The alliances between the Soviet Union and the nations of Eastern Europe, codified in the Warsaw Pact of 1955, are in a class by themselves. They are not true alliances in that they do not transform a pre-existing community of interests into legal obligations. It is their distinctive quality that a community of interests is irrelevant for their existence and operation and that they are founded on nothing but unchallengeable superiority of power. Power is here not superimposed upon common interests but becomes a substitute for them. Such so-called treaties of alliance are in truth in the nature of treaties establishing a modern version of protectorates, and the nations subjected to them are correctly called satellites rather than allies.

The nature of this relationship has not been affected, although it might well be in the future, by the development of a community of interests between the Soviet Union and certain satellites, such as Poland and Czechoslovakia, resulting from the emergence of Germany as the predominant power in Europe. Poland and Czechoslovakia, situated as they are between two nations of superior strength, have had to seek protection either from one neighbor against the other or from Western Europe against both. Their present relationship to the Soviet Union provides this protection. Given a change in both Russian and German policies, this protective function might well form the basis for a future genuine alliance.

While this development is purely speculative, the relations between the Soviet Union and the satellites have in recent years undergone an actual transformation similar to that which has affected the Atlantic alliance, and for similar reasons. The emergence of an atomic stalemate between the United States and the Soviet Union has loosened the ties of the satellite relationship. The threat of mutual atomic destruction has stimulated both the desire for self-preservation in the form of neutralism and the aspirations for national independence which had lain dormant under the yoke of the Red Army.

These latent tendencies were brought to the fore by the "new look" in Russian policy following the death of Stalin. In response to it, the spirit of national independence started to push against the lid of Russian oppression, and the Russian proconsuls yielded to the pressure. They rehabilitated most of the national leaders who had tried to combine communism and at least a measure of national independence and relaxed the authoritarian controls over the economic and intellectual life of the satellite. Yet popular reaction went beyond domestic reforms to a striving for national independence, that is, the end of the satellite relationship itself. At this point, the Soviet Union called a halt, reasserting the paramountcy of its interests by the supremacy of its power.

The exact nature of the community of interests between the Soviet Union and China is a matter for speculation. Russian and Chinese interests appear to be identical in so far as their common objective is the strengthening and expansion of the Communist and the weakening and retraction of the anti-Communist camps. They appear to be complementary in so far as the alliance serves the Chinese interest in economic and military development and the Russian interest in keeping the United States militarily engaged and politically handicapped in the Far East.

The alliances between the Soviet Union and the Middle Eastern nations clearly serve complementary interests. The Middle Eastern nations allied with the Soviet Union are enabled by the military support they receive to pursue actively their specific interests, all with regard to Israel, some with regard to Jordan, Saudi Arabia, Turkey, and the remaining British possessions and spheres of influence. The Soviet Union, on the other hand, has no stake in these specific interests except in so far as their active pursuit serves to maintain a state of tension which keeps the Western nations engaged and handicapped in still another region and threatens them with economic stress.

Considering the over-all picture of the alliances as it emerges from the foregoing analysis, one is impressed by the similarity of the changes which have occurred in the structure of the European alliances on both sides of the Iron Curtain. The seemingly irreversible trend toward a two-bloc system which marked the immediate postwar era has been arrested, if not reversed. The uncommitted nations not only want to remain uncommitted but also have, with a few exceptions, shown the ability to do so. On the other hand, many of the European nations which are committed as allies of one or the other of the superpowers would like to join the ranks of the uncommitted nations but have, with the exception of Yugoslavia, been unable to do so. They have at best been able to move to the outer confines of the blocs to which they belong. In consequence, the two-bloc system is in the process of loosening but not of breaking up.

The satellites may become even more unwilling and unreliable partners of the Soviet Union than they are already. Short of outside intervention, which is unlikely, they cannot move out of the Soviet orbit as long as Russian interest—backed by Russian power—requires their submission. And the interest of Russia in the domination of Eastern Europe has been perennial, despite drastic changes in the personnel, philosophy, and structure of government. The weakening of that interest cannot be foreseen short of a revolution in military technology which would make the control of outlying territory irrelevant.

The fate that may be in store for the Atlantic alliance is similarly not its formal dissolution but rather its slow erosion to the point of becoming inoperative. The common fear of communism, either as a subversive force from within or an aggresive one from without, and the common dedication to the values of Western civilization are likely to remain stronger than the disruptive tendencies of divergent and incompatible interests and thus keep the common framework of the Atlantic alliance intact. The demonstrated inability of even Great Britain and France to pursue positive foreign policies against the opposition of the United States adds to this outward stability of the Atlantic alliance. The real danger lies in this common framework becoming an empty shell, drained of its vitality. History abounds with legal compacts, constitutional devices, and institutional forms which have, sometimes—as in the case of the Holy Roman Empire—for centuries, survived as ritualistic observances, or in the words of Chief Justice Marshall, "a solemn mockery," without any longer being capable of directing the interests of men into the channels of common policies and actions.

The danger with which the German situation threatens the Atlantic alliance is, however, far more serious. The tension between the German commitment to the Atlantic alliance and the national goal of unification, which can be achieved only on Russian terms, inevitably raises in German minds the question of whether that commitment and this objective are truly compatible and whether the former must not be sacrificed in order to achieve the latter. This conclusion can be prevented from being translated into actual policy only by the intransigence of Russian and the wisdom of American policies. The danger of German defection from the Atlantic alliance, then, raises in specific terms the general issue of the merits of our alliance policy and of our response to the structural changes which the alliances have undergone in recent times.

Our alliance policy partakes of the doctrinaire, legalistic, and mechanical character of much of American foreign policy. These perennial vices reappear in it in a new form. Instead of recognizing that alliances can be useful, harmful, or superfluous depending on the circumstances and therefore discriminating among them in view of the interests to be served and the policies to be pursued, we have followed what might be called the collector's approach to alliances: the more nations to sign a legal document declaring their support for our policies, the better. While once we were, on principle, against all "entangling alliances," now we are, again on principle, in favor of all alliances.

This emphasis upon the quantity of alliances and, more particularly, upon their military advantages—actual or illusory—has tended to jeopardize our political interests. Frequently our allies have turned our interest in the alliance per se to their political advantage, without any corresponding political advantage accruing to us or, at worst, at the expense of our political interests. In consequence, the weak members of the alliance, knowing what they want to get out of it, have tended to convert the alliance into an instrument of their policies, with the United States paying the political and economic cost.

This tendency to see intrinsic merit in any alliance has been most pronounced in Asia. SEATO, originating in an indiscriminate invitation by the United States to join, is the classic example. Its membership was determined not by the United States in view of its interests but by the other members in view of theirs. Nor has the issue of the mutuality of benefits and liabilities been correlated to our over-all Asian interests, which—except for Formosa, South Korea, and South Vietnam—are political rather than military.

SEATO is for the United States a useless alliance from the military point of view and a harmful one politically and economically in that it alienates the broad masses of Asians. NATO, on the other hand, especially in view of its elaborate organizational superstructure, may well prove to be a superfluous alliance—a view held by a minority within and outside the government when NATO was created in 1949. It may well be asked again—as it was then—whether the obvious identity of interests between the United States and the nations of Western Europe could not have been adequately served by a unilateral guarantee on the part of the United States, fashioned after the model of the Monroe Doctrine. While the very existence of NATO has made this question obviously academic, the rationale underlying it could still be put into practice by dismantling what is useless and harmful in NATO and strengthening what is useful, essential, and lasting.

These speculations culminate in the observation that the problem of alliances must be considered in the context of the over-all character of world politics. If the task facing a nation is primarily military, not to be mastered by its isolated strength alone, a policy of alliances is the answer; and this answer is still the correct one in Europe and in certain exposed regions of Asia. In so far as the task is political, requiring a variety of means to be applied with subtlety, discrimination, and imagination, a policy of alliances will be useless, if not harmful; and this is indeed the situation which confronts the United States in most of the world today where the issue is political allegiance and not military defense. A policy of alliances, in its doctrinaire insistence upon joining the club, in its legalistic concern with signatures and stipulations, in its mechanical counting of heads, serves as but a substitute for political creativeness, the lack of which it may temporarily conceal. What it can neither conceal nor stave off is the failure which attends upon wrong policies as punishment follows the crime.

22 *Diplomacy*

The traditional methods of diplomacy have been under continuous attack since the First World War and have to a considerable extent been discarded in practice since the end of the Second World War. Three main arguments have been directed against them. First, they have been held responsible for the political catastrophes which have befallen mankind in the last four decades or so; methods that appear to have been so unsuccessful must be replaced by better ones. Second, traditional diplomacy has been held to run counter to the principles of democracy, and from the assumption that democracy makes for peace—and autocracy, for war —it has been concluded that diplomacy must be "open," that is, exposed to public scrutiny in all its processes. Finally, the traditional diplomatic practices with their seemingly useless and wasteful formalities, horse-trading, and compromises have seemed to violate moral principles with which democratic nations have felt themselves identified; in other words, the age-old conflict between political realism and idealism has been transferred to the sphere of diplomacy.

These arguments against traditional diplomacy arise from the basic philosophic position, prevalent in our time, that political practices are the result of subjective preferences, to be changed at will. In truth, however, the traditional methods of diplomacy have not been invented by stupid and evil or, for that matter, wise and good men —even though they have certainly been used and abused by such men—but have grown ineluctably from the objective nature of things political. In their essence, they are the reflections of that objective nature, to be disregarded only at the risk of political failure. Whenever two autonomous social entities, anxious to maintain their autonomy, engage in political relations with each other, they cannot but resort to what we call the traditional methods of diplomacy. And it does not matter in this respect whether these diplomatic relations are carried on between two members of a family, two businessmen, two baseball clubs, two political parties, or two sovereign nations. On all levels of such relations, secrecy of negotiation—to

From *The State of the Social Sciences,* edited by Leonard D. White, 1956.

mention only the most prominent and controversial aspect—is not an arbitrary procedural device to be used or dispensed with at will but grows from the objective nature of negotiations. No negotiations of any kind—be they for the contraction of a marriage, the sale of a piece of property, a deal for baseball players, or an international treaty—can be carried out in public without defeating their very purpose: the transformation of conflicting or inchoate interests into a common purpose of the contracting parties.

The specific arguments against the traditional methods of diplomacy are as untenable as is the basic philosophic position from which they stem. If it is true that the traditional practices of diplomacy constitute the method by which the business of foreign policy must be transacted, the failure of a particular foreign policy or of a whole era to bring peace and order to the world cannot be attributed to these practices per se but, at worst, to their incorrect use. This logical deduction is borne out by the experiences of recent history. For the disorganization of international society since the First World War has indeed been concomitant with the neglect, misunderstanding, and abuse of the traditional practices of diplomacy. While it would be far-fetched to suggest that the decline of diplomacy is responsible for the catastrophes that have befallen the world in recent times, it cannot be doubted that that decline has contributed to international disorder, being itself an outgrowth of a deep-seated disorder in the intellectual sphere.

Both the arguments—that democracy means peace and that diplomacy is immoral and therefore undemocratic—have grown from an intellectual attitude hostile to the very idea of foreign policy as an independent sphere of thought and action. They assume that the kind of foreign policy a nation pursues is determined by the kind of domestic institutions it possesses and the kind of political philosophy to which it adheres. All of recorded history militates against that assumption. The national interest of great powers and, in good measure, the methods by which it is to be secured are impervious to ideological or institutional changes. As far back as April 30, 1823, George Canning warned that "the general acquisition of free institutions is not necessarily a security for general peace." Our experience of total wars, waged by democracies for democratic tenets, gives substance to that warning.

The argument that diplomacy is particularly immoral and, hence, incompatible with democratic government similarly assumes that one can escape from the moral dilemmas of foreign policy by forswearing foreign policy itself. At the bottom of this argument there is a dual illusion: the illusion of the moral superiority of domestic politics over foreign policy and the illusion of the possibility of escaping foreign policy altogether. Both philosophic analysis and historic experience show that the moral problems that foreign policy raises are but a peculiar—and particularly drastic—manifestation of the moral problem of politics as such. Taking a wider view, one can even say that the moral problem of politics is but a peculiar instance of the moral problem which man encounters whenever he acts with reference to his fellow men. What distinguishes in this respect foreign policy from domestic politics and from the human situation in general is not the substance of the problem, which is identical on all levels of human interaction, but the social conditions under which the problem arises on the international plane.

There is, then, no way to escape the moral problem of politics, domestic or international; we can only endeavor to smooth down its sharp edges and to mitigate its practical consequences by changing not its substance but the social environment within which it is bound to arise in one form or another. It is not by accident that those who have tried to do more have taken a negative attitude toward foreign policy; for in the traditional methods of diplomacy they could not help seeing the outward manifestations of the political risks and moral liabilities of foreign policy itself. Opposition to the traditional methods of diplomacy is everywhere intimately connected with either an isolationist or universalistic attitude toward international relations. Both consider the traditional methods of diplomacy at best superfluous and at worst pernicious, for they so regard foreign policy itself. In the isolationist view, a country can afford to dispense with an active foreign policy and, hence, with diplomacy. In the universalistic view, foreign policy, carried on through diplomatic methods by sovereign nations, belongs to a dying age and is a stumbling block to the establishment of a more peaceful and orderly organization of the world.

This thought reveals itself in the recent attempts to set up the procedures of the United Nations as an alternative to the traditional methods of diplomacy. Here again, we are in the presence of the assumption that nations have a choice between the traditional methods of diplomacy and some other way of dealing with each other, a way that somehow leads to freedom from the risks and liabilities of foreign policy. In truth, of course, the procedures of the United Nations, as they have emerged in the practice of the organization, do not differ in substance from the traditional practices of diplomacy. What distinguishes the former from the latter is nothing but the social setting and the legal requirements which influence the way in which the traditional business of diplomacy is carried on within the agencies of the United Nations. The United Nations and traditional diplomacy are not mutually exclusive alternatives between which nations must choose. Rather, they supplement each other, serving identical purposes and partaking of the same qualities and characteristics. The secretary-general of the United Nations, in his *Annual Report on the Work of the Organization for July 1, 1954 through June 15, 1955,* has called attention to this relationship in these words:

We have only begun to make use of the real possibilities of the United Nations as the most representative instrument for the relaxation of tensions, for the lessening of distrust and misunderstanding, and for the discovery and delineation of new areas of common ground and interest. . . . Conference diplomacy may usefully be supplemented by more quiet diplomacy within the United Nations, whether directly between representatives of Member Governments or in contacts between the Secretary-General and Member Governments. The obligations of the Charter, the environment of institutions dedicated to seeking out the common ground among the national interests of Member States, the wide representation from all continents and cultures, the presence of the Secretariat established as a principal organ of the United Nations for the purpose of upholding and serving the international interest—all these can provide help not to be found elsewhere, if they are rightly applied and used.

Within the framework of the Charter there are many possibilities, as yet largely unexplored, for variation of practices. . . . It is my hope that solid progress can be made in the coming years in developing new forms of contact, new methods of deliberation and new techniques of reconciliation. With only slight adjustments, discussions of major issues of a kind that have occurred outside the United Nations could often be fitted into its framework, thus at the same time adding to the strength of the world organization and drawing strength from it.

With these considerations we are entering into the positive task of ascertaining the functions of traditional diplomacy and its permanent value. A nation, existing as it does as an equal among other nations, can deal with the outside world in one of three different ways. It can deny the importance of the other nations for itself and its own importance for them and retreat into the impotence of isolation. Or it can deny the equality of the other nations and try to impose its own will upon them by force of arms. In either case, at least in its pure, extreme realization, a nation can afford to dispense with diplomacy. Or a nation can want to pursue its interests in active contact and on the basis of equality with other nations, assuming the universality of that desire. In that case it cannot do without the constant redefinition and adjustment of its interests for the purpose of accommodating the interests of other nations.

Conflict of interests—actual, seeming, or potential—is the overriding fact of international society, as it is one of the overriding facts of all societies, even those most highly integrated and centralized. Diplomacy in all its diverse historic and social manifestations is the technique of accommodating such conflicting interests. That technique proceeds in two stages: the ascertainment of the facts of conflict and the formulation of the terms of settlement.

Nation A pursues certain interests and so does nation B, and the interests of A and B are on the face of them in conflict. Both nations want to settle this conflict peacefully. How can they go about it? They have to define their respective interests and ascertain the point of conflict. That investigation may lead them to one of three possible conclusions.

If what A wants and finds vital to itself B cannot cede without endangering its vital interests or its very existence, because of the intrinsic importance of the territory, frontier, port, or air base at issue, diplomatic accommodation is impossible. When Francis I of France was asked why he always made war against Charles V of Austria, he is reported to have answered: "Because we both want the same thing: Italy." As long as both kings wanted Italy badly enough, they could either go to war over it or else leave the issue unsettled, hoping for future developments to deflect the energies of both sides toward less contentious objectives. Often in history nations have indeed avoided war over their vital interests by allowing time to take the sting out of their conflicts. Yet in such cases it is to the restraint of warlike passions and the renunciation of quick and radical solutions rather than to the practices of diplomacy that the credit for the preservation of peace must go.

Nation A may again pursue an objective vital to itself which nation B could cede only at the price of a vital interest of its own. Yet, in contrast to the type of conflict just discussed, the importance of the objective to both sides is here not intrinsic to the objective itself but rather the result of a peculiar configuration of interests which are subject to manipulation. For instance, the Soviet Union has a vital interest in preventing a united Germany from joining the Western alliance, and the United States has a similarly vital interest in preventing such a Germany from being absorbed by the Soviet bloc. Taken by themselves, these positions are obviously incompatible and, as the history of East-West negotiations has thus far shown, not subject to diplomatic accommodation. Yet one can well imagine, without committing one's self to its practical feasibility in the immediate future, an over-all European or world-wide settlement of which a German settlement would form an organic part, satisfactory to the interests of both sides which could not be reconciled to the unification of Germany considered in isolation. In situations such as this, it is the task of diplomacy to redefine the seemingly incompatible, vital interests of the nations concerned in order to make them compatible.

This task of diplomacy is, as it were, strategic in nature and truly creative, not often attempted and rarely successful. It yields in practical importance to that function with which diplomacy is typically associated in the popular mind: the function of bargaining issuing in a compromise. In conflicts to which this function applies, nation A seeks an objective which nation B either is willing to grant only in part or refuses to grant at all without compensation. Conflicts of this kind concern non-vital interests of which nations are willing to dispose by way of negotiations. The technique of diplomacy consists here in ascertaining the interests of both sides and in allocating the objective at issue in view of these interests and of the power available for their support.

The same diplomatic technique serves not only the peaceful settlement of conflicts among nations but also the delineation and codification of common interests. In this respect it performs its classic function for the negotiation of treaties serving a common purpose of the contracting parties. Called upon to settle a conflict between two nations, diplomacy must create out of the conflicting interests a community of interests, a compromise, which cannot satisfy all parties completely but with which no party will be completely dissatisfied. When the representatives of two nations meet to negotiate a treaty, say, of commerce or alliance, they must discover and make precise an already existing community of interests. This community of interests, before it is crystallized in legal stipulations, is amorphous and inchoate, obscured and distorted by seeming and real conflicts. It is the task of diplomacy to define the area of that pre-existing community of interests and to express it in terms sufficiently precise to serve as a reliable foundation for future action. It need only be mentioned in passing that this function of diplomacy is identical with that of contractual negotiations on all levels of social interaction.

It must be obvious from what has been said thus far that the traditional methods of diplomacy are of vital importance to a nation that seeks to pursue its interests successfully and peaceably. A nation that is unwilling or unable to use diplomacy for that end is of necessity compelled either to forsake its interests or to pursue them by war. As pointed out before, nations have always had a choice among three alternatives: diplomacy, war, renunciation. Which one of these alternatives a nation chose in a concrete situation was a matter of rational calculation; none of them was excluded a priori on rational grounds.

Modern technology, especially in the form of all-out atomic war, has destroyed this rational equality among diplomacy, war, and renunciation and has greatly enhanced the importance of diplomacy. In view of that technology, there is no longer safety in renunciation or in victory in war. From the beginning of history to the Second World War the risks inherent in these three choices were commensurate with the advantages to be expected. Nations would miscalculate and suffer unexpected losses; but it was never rationally foreordained that they could not win. War, in particular, was a rational means to a rational end; victory would justify the risks and losses incurred, and the consequences of defeat were not from the outset out of all proportion to the gains to be expected from victory.

The possibility of all-out atomic war has destroyed these rational relationships. When universal destruction is the result of victory and defeat alike, war itself is no longer a matter of rational choice but becomes an instrument of suicidal despair. The pursuit of a nation's interests short of all-out atomic war, then, becomes a matter of self-preservation. Even on the assumption—at present a moot one—that limited wars can and will still be safely waged, the risk of such a limited war developing into an all-out atomic one will always be present. Hence, the imperative of the avoidance of all-out atomic war gives, at the very least, unprecedented urgency to the pursuit of a nation's interests by peaceful means. Such peaceful pursuit, as we know, spells diplomacy. Neither diplomacy nor all-out atomic war is today one among several rational choices available to a nation. As all-out atomic war is tantamount to suicide, so successful diplomacy provides the only certain chance for survival. A nation which under present conditions is either unwilling or unable to take full advantage of the traditional methods of diplomacy condemns itself either to the slow death of attrition or the sudden death of atomic destruction.

The vital importance that the traditional methods of diplomacy receive from the possibility of all-out atomic war is underlined by the more specific political developments which may well mark the end of the first postwar decade as the beginning of a new era in international relations. The first decade following the Second World War was characterized on the international scene by three basic political phenomena: the bipolarity of international politics, the tendency of this bipolar political system to transform itself into a two-bloc system, and the policy of containment. These three basic facts combined in minimizing the traditional methods of diplomacy, both as a matter of fact and in terms of the objective opportunities available.

During that decade, effective power for purposes of foreign policy was concentrated in Washington and Moscow, and these two power poles tended to attract like magnets most of the other centers of power. Whatever they might have preferred had they been free to choose, Great Britain and France, Poland and China had to lean upon one or the other of the superpowers for political, military, and economic support. Such countries could not have remained neutral, let alone have changed sides, in the East-West conflict, short of a domestic revolution of radical dimensions. In such a situation, rigid in its alignments and inflexible in either side's conception of the interests involved, the main task of both sides is not to make and receive concessions but, at the very least, to hold the line and, at the very best, to advance it unilaterally. Since the balance of power made the latter alternative unfeasible short of a general war, both sides were of necessity reduced to a policy of containment which for all practical purposes forsook advancement at the expense of the other side while at the same time preventing the other side from advancing.

Such a situation of "cold war" offered little opportunity for the use of diplomatic methods either within the two power blocs or between them. The inner coherence of the two blocs resulted primarily from the ineluctable necessity which made their members seek shelter under the roof of one or the other of the superpowers. During that period, the discrepancy of strength between the two superpowers, on the one hand, and their respective allies, on the other, was so obviously extreme and the consequences for those who would dare step out of line so obviously dire that there was very little need for diplomacy to crystallize so obvious a community of interests.

The relations between the two blocs were no less clearly defined by the objective situation. The essence of the policy of containment was military rather than political. It consisted in the main in the warning, supported by actual preparedness, that a step taken by the other side beyond the line of military demarcation of 1945 would of necessity lead to a general war.

The services diplomacy was able to perform for this policy of containment were hardly different from those diplomacy has traditionally performed for the conduct of real war. It could announce the conditions for the settlement of the Cold War and use such and similar announcements for purposes of psychological warfare. The very modalities of the Cold War, then, inevitably transformed diplomacy into a mere auxiliary of a war waged against the enemy, not for the purpose of accommodating conflicting interests, but for the triumph, however verbal, of one nation over the other. Thus it is not by accident that during the first decade following the Second World War the traditional methods of diplomacy virtually ceased to operate in the relations between East and West and that the moves carried on under the labels and with the personnel of diplomacy at the many East-West conferences and within the United Nations served purposes not only far removed from but often diametrically opposed to those of traditional diplomacy.

This period of postwar history has come to a close. It is being replaced by an era marked by greater flexibility within the two power blocs—a tendency toward the loosening of their inner coherence if not toward their dissolution—and, consequently, by greater flexibility in the relationship between the two power blocs as well. To meet the problems of this new era the methods of the Cold War are inadequate. As the conditions of the Cold War led necessarily to the disuse and misuse of the practices of diplomacy, so the new era of international relations with equal necessity calls for the restoration of these practices.

Four facts are in the main responsible for this change in international relations: the decrease in the dependence of the powers of second rank upon the superpowers; the impending rise of Germany and Japan to great-power status; the impending dispersion of atomic power among a multitude of nations, some of which, by virtue of their possession of atomic power, will gain or regain the status of great powers; finally, the spread and sharpening of the colonial revolutions in Asia, Africa, and Latin America.

Viewed from the vantage point of the United States, each of these new facts requires the vigorous application of the traditional practices of diplomacy. Since neither the American atomic monopoly nor extreme dependence upon American support can any longer be relied upon to secure the coherence of the Western alliance, the United States must again resort to the time-honored diplomatic method of fashioning a legally and politically viable community of interests out of the one that exists objectively in an inchoate and ill-defined form. Germany and Japan, no longer the object of the victor's dispositions, must be persuaded by the same methods to see in association with the West the best chance for pursuing their interests. It is hardly necessary to emphasize that a similar approach to the colonial revolutions has been long overdue.

Thus the situation that confronts the United States at the moment of this writing poses the perennial problem of diplomacy with renewed urgency. The objections to the use of diplomacy are without merit. Its indispensability for a successful and peaceful foreign policy grows from the very nature of things political. The possibility of all-out atomic war has made its successful use the condition of survival. The new era of international relations has made its restoration of vital concern for the foreign policy of the United States.

23 *The Qualifications of an Ambassador*

I have been both elated and depressed by Mr. Dulles' definition of an ambassador's qualifications made at his press conference of August 6, 1957.

I am elated because if anybody who has "integrity of character . . . a sharp and quick intelligence" and is "genuinely devoted to the public service" is qualified to be an ambassador of the United States, there must be tens of millions of American citizens who so qualify. Napoleon said that every one of his soldiers carried a marshal's baton in his knapsack. If one takes Mr. Dulles seriously, one can now say that almost every American keeps an ambassador's cutaway and spats in his closet.

I am also depressed because for a quarter of a century I have tried to impress upon my students how exacting the qualifications of an ambassador are. I have told them how much knowledge he must have of history, of current events, of foreign countries, of men. How profound a judgment he must have of men and situations. And how he must be able to cope with, and transform, situations on behalf of the policies of his government. I have quoted the statesmen and diplomatists of the past who stood in awe of what an ambassador must be, know, and do, men like Richelieu, Callières, Mably, John Quincy Adams, Cambon, Jusserand, Harold Nicolson, and many others. I have been particularly fond of quoting the reference of Mr. Dulles' own grandfather, John W. Foster, to "the baneful influence of political favoritism" on diplomatic appointments and his approving quotation from a Senate committee report of 1868 to the effect that "no man can pass from other pursuits directly into the higher grades of diplomatic and consular service and comprehend clearly the nature and scope of his duties."[1] If I take Mr. Dulles seriously, the only thing I need to tell my students now is: "Boys,

Letters to the *New York Times*, August 13, 1957, and *Washington Post*, August 6, 1957.

[1] John W. Foster, *The Practice of Diplomacy* (Boston: Houghton Mifflin Co., 1906), pp. 10–11.

be of good character, intelligent, and devoted to public duty. Class dismissed."

It is obvious that Mr. Dulles cannot be taken seriously. In order to defend an indefensible appointment, Mr. Dulles has laid down a principle which is absurdly at variance with what Mr. Dulles and all men versed in diplomacy know. Yet by doing so, Mr. Dulles has done great harm to the morale of the Foreign Service and to the public understanding of foreign policy. For he has given authoritative support to those still lingering popular prejudices which have proven to be such a formidable handicap to the rational conduct of American foreign policy, his own included. Citizens who have integrity of character, are intelligent, and are devoted to public duty may well wonder whether such a fleeting forensic triumph, if such it is, is not too highly paid for by the lasting damage done to the interests of the United States.

You have performed a public service in giving in your issue of July 28, 1957, prominent place to the interchange between Senator Fulbright and Mr. Gluck on the occasion of the latter's confirmation as United States Ambassador to Ceylon. This episode makes sad and disquieting reading. It puts into sharp focus three issues vital to the United States.

The first issue is the sale of public office, for this is what the appointment of campaign contributors, regardless of qualifications, to positions of responsibility actually amounts to. Within limits and in so far as it affects positions of secondary importance, such a system may be tolerated as part of the price which we must pay for democracy.

When as a general system of government it is applied to the most vital concerns of the country, it becomes indeed intolerable, for the system is bound to operate in an utterly haphazard fashion, since the considerations which determine the appointment have no bearing upon the qualifications necessary for the successful discharge of the official duties.

The episode also raises in concrete form the issue of the consequences of the system for the quality of our representation abroad. The interrogation by Senator Fulbright makes it perfectly clear that

Mr. Gluck not only is completely ignorant of contemporary foreign affairs but also knows as much about what foreign policy is all about as I know about the operation of a chain of stores (which is nothing).

While I am confident that he will learn how to pronounce the name of the Prime Minister of Ceylon, I doubt that he will ever know what an ambassador is supposed to do.

The most serious issue of all, however, is the complete indifference of the Senate, with the exception of Senator Fulbright, not only to the nefarious results of the system in general, but also to the demerits of this particular appointment. Of the fifteen members of the Foreign Relations Committee, only four were present when Mr. Gluck was interrogated, and only one, Senator Fulbright, voted against confirmation.

The plenum of the Senate did not find it worthwhile even to debate the appointment and confirmed it as a matter of course. If the appointment of a postmaster is disposed of in such cavalier fashion, one can shrug it off in view of the limited demands of the office and the limited consequences of failure. Yet an ambassador of the United States is a general who commands a sector of the ramparts of the Free World, and his ability to discharge his duties is one of the factors upon which the survival of the United States and of Western civilization depends.

Mr. Gluck, knowing nothing about Asia, about Ceylon, about what an ambassador has to do, about the very nature of foreign policy, is incapable of performing these functions. While he might well have done a great deal of good in a position for which his experience qualifies him, as Ambassador to Ceylon, with the best of intentions and in complete innocence, he is bound to do a great deal of harm.

This is an injustice to the man, to the country, and to Ceylon; for Ceylon, which has sent one of its most brilliant sons to Washington, deserves better than that and must resent the implicit slight.

When we must try to repair the consequences of such folly by appropriating millions for propaganda and foreign aid, the Senate is very much interested. Would it not be wiser and cheaper for the Senate to interest itself in the quality of our ambassadors, infinitely more important than either propaganda or foreign aid?

In this matter the majority party has a special responsibility to bear, not only because it is the majority party, but also because it is represented in the Foreign Relations Committee by a galaxy of extraordinarily able, knowledgeable, and conscientious men.

These men cannot plead ignorance or lack of judgment. What can they plead?

24 *The New Atlantic Community*

The tasks America as the leader of the Atlantic community faces today result from the need, long felt and only now being met, to adapt its foreign policies to the new circumstances of the hour; to revise the pattern of foreign policy which was established in 1947 in the form of containment—the Truman Doctrine—and the Marshall Plan; to renew that foreign policy through innovations commensurate with the novel problems which the Western world faces today.

In what respects is the situation which confronts us today on the international scene fundamentally different from that which existed immediately after the Second World War and which persisted approximately for a decade? Four fundamental changes have occurred.

First of all, the balance of military power had radically changed. In the aftermath of the Second World War, the United States was unquestionably the most powerful nation on earth. Under the umbrella of its atomic monopoly the United States formed the Atlantic alliance, implementing the policy of containment. The atomic monopoly of the United States provided a virtually absolute protection for the nations which felt themselves threatened by Communist aggression. This protection has disappeared. It has been replaced by an atomic stalemate or by what Sir Winston Churchill has called a "balance of terror," that is to say, the United States is able to destroy the Soviet Union and the Soviet Union is able to destroy the United States in an all-out nuclear war.

In view of this stark and simple situation, an alliance with the United States is no longer being regarded by the allies of the United States as an unmixed blessing. It still provides a certain protection, but it also implies a certain liability. Can the United States be relied upon to come to the aid of an ally if by doing so it risks its own destruction? And would not such aid, even if it should be provided, seal the doom of the ally, since it would in all likelihood be in the

Report to the Fifth Congress of *Il Mulino*, Bologna, April, 1961.

nature of nuclear war to be countered in kind by the enemy? The allies of the United States are raising questions such as these, and they answer them by seeking safety in greater independence from the United States. Either they try to develop foreign and military policies of their own, especially in the nuclear field, or else they tend to move away from the United States into a neutral, or at least a more detached, position.

The second great transformation which has occurred in the political world in recent years is the restoration of the economic and, to a certain extent, the political health of most of the nations of Western Europe. Fifteen and even ten years ago, the alliance with the United States was for nations such as Italy, France, and Great Britain a matter not of choice but of life and death. Without the economic, political, and military support of the United States, those nations could not have survived as independent national entities and would have been in great danger of being subverted by communism or swallowed up by the Soviet Union. Today, this dependence upon the United States has to a great extent disappeared, especially in the economic field; it has become rather ineffective in the political field; and in the military field, as we have seen, its ambivalence has become obvious.

Furthermore, and most importantly, the foreign policy of the Soviet Union has fundamentally changed. Ten years ago, the greatest asset upon which the foreign policies of the nations of the Atlantic community could bank was the foreign policy of Stalin. Whenever there was a slackening in the Western effort, whenever there appeared cracks in the fabric of the Atlantic alliance, Stalin could be counted upon to make a drastic move which demonstrated to everybody concerned how necessary for survival the American connection was.

The foreign policy of Khrushchev is of an entirely different nature. His is not, at least for the time being, a policy of direct military aggression or of direct military threats. Even the Berlin threat is quite different from the threats which Stalin would have uttered under similar circumstances or would even have followed up by action, as he did in the case of the Berlin blockade in 1948. Khrushchev's policies are aimed not so much at the conquest of territories contiguous to the Soviet empire by diplomatic pressure or military threats as at the subversion of the whole non-Communist world through the impact which the power and the technological and economic accomplishments of the Soviet Union make upon that world. This is obviously a much more insidious and subtle way of undermining the Western position than were Stalin's crude challenges.

To these three fundamental changes which have occurred in the world during the last ten years must be added a fourth one, the rise of the former colonial nations in Africa and Asia. These enormous masses of land and populations are no longer under the control of any of the great powers but they will have to seek the support of stronger nations and to fashion their political, economic, and social life in the image of one or the other of the great systems competing for their allegiance. Hence, they have become the great prize in the struggle between East and West. Whoever can attract the loyalties of these so-called uncommitted nations, whoever can impress them with the excellence and superiority of his form of government, of his social and economic system, will in all probability win the struggle for the world. And Mr. Khrushchev has proclaimed that the Soviet Union, through the attractiveness and achievements of communism, will conquer the minds of the uncommitted peoples and thereby inherit the earth.

It is against the background of these great transformations that we must consider the tasks the Atlantic community faces. The crisis of the Atlantic community and, more particularly, of American foreign policy lies in the inadequacy of their responses to those great transformations. In a sense, the great handicap of recent American foreign policy has been the success of the original policy of containment. That is to say, the policy of containment, which has been widely criticized as being ineffective, negative, and static, has not only been sound as a minimal foreign policy—containment of the Soviet Union and of communism being the very minimum objectives to which American foreign policy had to be committed—it has also been eminently successful.

It was this success of the policy of containment which led the United States to transform it into a general principle of American foreign policy, especially as applied to Asia. The United States thought that what had worked so well in Europe was bound to work as well at the periphery of the Soviet and Chinese empires in Asia. It did not work as well. It could not work as well for the simple reason that the threat which the United States had to meet in Asia was essentially different from the threat with which it was faced in Europe. The threat in Europe was primarily the threat of military aggression. It was constituted by the fact that the Russian armies stood in the heart of Europe one hundred miles east of the Rhine. It is this stark fact which still constitutes the major threat to Europe today, and against this threat Europe has to be protected.

The primary threat outside Europe, that is, to Asia, to the Middle East, and also increasingly to Africa and to Latin America, is not military; it is the much more subtle threat of psychological penetration, of political subversion, of economic conquest, of the use of foreign aid and foreign trade for political purposes. And against this subtle and insidious threat the policy of containment, of military alliances, of military barriers, is entirely ineffective. One has only to look at the Middle East in order to see this most clearly. The Baghdad Pact was established by Great Britain and some of the Middle Eastern countries at the instigation of the United States in order to create a military barrier against Communist penetration. But this barrier did not prevent the Soviet Union from gaining a foothold in Egypt. It did not prevent the Iraqi revolution and the Communist gains attendant upon it, for the Communist gains were not due to any threat of military aggression emanating from the Soviet Union. Yet even if there had been such a threat, the military measures taken by the West would have been insufficient to meet it.

Not only has this policy—of which more examples could be cited —been ineffective in its own terms, it has also been counterproductive, for it brought about the very evils which it was intended to prevent. It alienated many nations and many groups within many nations in Asia, the Middle East, and Africa which tended to look upon the United States as a nation primarily interested in gaining, as it were, mercenaries among the indigenous peoples for its own military purposes. The United States was suspected of wanting to bring war to those regions, while the Soviet Union could pose as the champion of peace and the nation interested only in ending the Cold War.

The classic example of the counterproductivity of the policy of containment and of alliances, as it was conceived in recent years, is the case of Pakistan. The United States has an alliance with Pakistan.

It is difficult, if you take a look at the map, to know against whom this alliance could possibly be directed except against India. But obviously the United States has no interest in supporting Pakistan against India. While the United States supports Pakistan against some imaginary enemy, it forces India to divert a considerable amount of its scarce resources to military purposes in order to match the military preparations of Pakistan. Since, of course, the United States realizes that India is infinitely more important than Pakistan in terms of the over-all world situation, it must support India in order to make up the difference between the latter's resources available for economic development and those which had to be diverted for military purposes. So the United States is really engaged in an armaments race with itself. With the left hand the United States supports Pakistan militarily, while with the right hand it supports India economically in order to help it bear up under the weight of the armaments which American support of Pakistan has forced upon it.

The United States has been led to this disregard of its own interest by what amounts to a kind of obsession with military alliances. The Baghdad Pact, the Eisenhower Doctrine, and, more particularly, SEATO were all what one might call open-ended alliances. That is to say, they were based on unilateral declarations on the part of the United States, inviting whoever wanted to join to come in and join. Of necessity, the nations which joined did so not on behalf of the interests of the United States, but on behalf of their own interests. I remember vividly a discussion I had a couple of years ago with the foreign minister of an ally of the United States. He made no bones about the fact that for him the main purpose of the American alliance was to establish a special claim for his country upon the American treasury.

It is also worthy of note that quite a number of allies of the United States have turned out to be handicaps in political as well as in financial terms. They have been able to dictate to the United States the policies it is supposed to pursue with regard to them. Where they have not been able to do that, they have, in many instances, been able to impose a veto upon the foreign policies of the United States. What has been generally noted in recent years as the sterility of American foreign policy—the lack of initiative and determination, the mechanical continuation of old and safe routines—is in good measure the result of the limitations which the alliances impose upon the United States. Wherever there is need for a new departure, there is also an ally pulling at the American coattails and saying, "No. If you want to keep me as your ally, you can't do that." Or, like the lady who uses fainting spells as a weapon, the ally will simply threaten to collapse.

Thus the relations between the United States and its allies and among the allies themselves, especially those of the Atlantic community, are in urgent need of being rethought and revised. The rethinking and revision must aim at coming to terms with four fundamental issues.

What kind of relationship ought to exist among the members of the Atlantic community which will reflect both the community of interests and the dominant position of the United States within it? We must create a viable international order that would translate common interests into a common purpose, fuse the power of individual nations, and assign to them responsibilities commensurate with their interests and power.

Second, how can we bring about a relationship between the Atlantic community and the Soviet Union which will minimize friction by stabilizing the status quo? The answer to that question is enclosed in the German problem, especially in its acute manifestation in Berlin.

Third, how can we establish a relationship, conducive both to peace and freedom, between the Atlantic community and the nations of Eastern Europe that are unwilling objects of Communist domination. The satellites of the Soviet Union cannot be liberated from the outside, but they can be strengthened in their awareness of their membership in Western civilization, which they have in common with the Atlantic community.

Fourth, how do we create a relationship between the Atlantic community and the uncommitted new nations of Africa and Asia which would further the latter's domestic and international stability? The Atlantic community has the collective task of helping the former colonial powers among its members to establish a new relationship of co-operation with their former colonies.

The Atlantic community as a unified social force derives from common interests which can be safeguarded and advanced only through co-operation between the nations of Western Europe and the United States. Its paramount power imposes upon the United States a particular responsibility to initiate policies and to lead in their execution. The interests underlying the Atlantic community are of two kinds: temporary and acute ones, such as those which arose in the aftermath of the Second World War and were, as we have seen, successfully met by the initiative of the United States, and permanent and deep-seated ones which reflect a common membership in Western civilization. The values of that civilization can no longer be left to the care of individual nations. Three new factors dominating the international scene have made this impossible: the reduction of the nations of Western Europe from world powers to strictly European ones; the obsolescence of the nation-state as a principle of political organization, in view of the technologies of communication, transportation, and warfare; and the pressure which communism exerts from within and without upon Western civilization.

It is the great failing of the Atlantic community that it has been unable to create institutions and develop patterns of co-operation commensurate with the extent and depth of the common interests of its members. It is the great failing of the United States that it has been unwilling to lead the Atlantic community toward the creation of such institutions and the development of such patterns of co-operation. Thus the Atlantic community has been capable of expressing only the most elemental of its common interests, that of military defense, in common institutions and modes of action. Its other common interests either have been left unattended or else have received but sporadic attention.

Had the institutions and modes of action of the Atlantic community been commensurate with the comprehensiveness and intensity of its common interests and had the influence exerted by the United States been commensurate with its power, the Atlantic community would have fallen very little short of, if it had not amounted to, a confederation of states merging their most vital activities in the fields of foreign policy, defense, finance, and economics. Nothing of the kind evolved. For the United States proved incapable of playing the role it should have played as the paramount member of the Atlantic community. Three inherited patterns of thought and action are responsible for this failure: the limitation of the direct exercise of

American power to the Western Hemisphere, the principle of equality, and the military approach to foreign policy.

The two previous occasions that carried American power beyond the limits of the Western Hemisphere were peculiar in that they allowed American power to retreat into its traditional limits after it had failed to establish itself firmly beyond them. The liquidation of the conquests of the Spanish-American War began virtually as soon as the conquests had been made. The failure of Wilson's attempt to make the world safe for democracy rendered pointless the presence of American power in Europe. The nature of the Russian threat after the Second World War left the United States no rational choice but to establish its power in permanence at the circumference of the Russian empire. But on what terms was that power to be established? Should it be the supremacy of American power, which in its consistent application would reduce America's allies to the status of satellites, or was it to be the equality of all members of the alliance, which, in its ideal realization, would issue in the harmonious co-operation of like-minded nations? These alternatives confronted the United States with a dilemma.

American power had to operate not in conquered territory where the conqueror could rule as he saw fit, but in the territory of friendly nations whose consent, if not desire, provided the sole title for the American presence. The purpose of that presence was the defense of the freedom and territorial integrity of the allies. The United States, in reducing its allies to the status of satellites, would have defeated the very purpose for the sake of which the European nations had become its allies. On the other hand, the establishment of the alliance on the basis of complete equality was feasible only on the unreal assumption that the identity of interests among the allies and their awareness of it was so complete that they would be capable of pursuing common ends with common measures through free and equal co-operation.

Of these two alternatives, the United States chose the latter. It refused to bring its superior power to bear on the alliance on behalf of common interests that were naturally inchoate and were competing with divergent ones. Thus it forewent the creation of a common framework of permanent and organic co-operation among allies who would relinquish their equal status in return for the common protection of their essential interests. When the United States left the Western Hemisphere, it carried with it its military and economic power but not its creative imagination or its constructive will. Significantly enough, this imagination and will were applied—and rather abortively at that—in the one sphere which is closest to the American tradition in foreign affairs: that is, in the military sphere; and NATO is presently its rather forlorn and brittle monument.

The United States emerged from the Second World War as the most powerful nation on earth by chance, and it assumed the leadership of the Atlantic community by virtue of necessity. In consequence, its will and mind were not equal to its power, responsibility, and opportunity. Had these attributes of America been the result of conscious choice and deliberate aspiration, America would have been intellectually and morally prepared when what it had chosen and aspired to came to pass. Since it was not prepared, it approached the tasks incumbent upon the paramount power of the Atlantic community with unbecoming humility and unwarranted self-restraint. It refused to lead where nobody else could.

Thus the Atlantic community remained an inchoate social fact incapable of becoming a political reality, and its solitary concrete manifestation, NATO, declined. The principle of equality among its fifteen members, applied to the political operations and over-all military planning of NATO, put a virtually insurmountable obstacle in the way of new policies to be pursued by the fifteen allies in response to new opportunities or new threats. The principle of equality would have been compatible with new departures in policy only if all members of the alliance had an equal interest in such departures, were equally aware of these interests, and agreed completely on the means to be used in support of these interests. Short of an open threat of military conquest or revolution, such as confronted the members of NATO in the late 1940's, these conditions cannot be expected to be present at the same time. In the absence of one or another of them, the best an alliance thus constituted can achieve is to translate the lowest common denominator of agreed interests into common action. That denominator is likely to tend toward the irreducible minimum of common policies without which the alliance itself would cease to exist as an operating agency. Thus, while the objective conditions under which the fifteen allies live require a degree of unity in purpose and action far transcending that of a traditional alliance and while NATO was designed at its inception to be the instrument of that kind of unity, in actual performance NATO has become less and less distinguishable from a traditional alliance, and a rather loosely knit and stagnating one at that.

This situation is a far cry from the new order through which the United States was expected to lead in the realization the common purpose of the nations of Western civilization in the atomic age. The factors that brought about this relationship are also responsible for America's failure to project the purpose of the Atlantic community into the areas of the world which are either uncommitted or unwillingly committed to communism. The United States was not able to free itself from the pattern of thought and action established both by its tradition and by its successful reaction to the threat of Russian power in the aftermath of the Second World War—that is, to conceive of its relations to the outside world primarily in military terms. Thus it saw itself surrounded by allies, by uncommitted nations that thus far had refused to become allies, and by satellites that Russian power prevented from becoming its allies. From this picture of the world, three militarily oriented policies ensued. The allies had to be kept in the American orbit, the uncommitted nations had to be drawn into it, and the satellites had to be liberated so that they could join it.

These policies were unsuccessful outside Europe because the picture of the world from which they derived was at odds both with the facts of experience and with the interests of the United States and of the Atlantic community. However, the militarily oriented policy of the Atlantic community remained effective with regard to the one issue, outstanding between East and West, which is of a quasimilitary nature: the issue of Germany. Yet that policy has been effective only in its military aspects: the Soviet Union has indeed been contained. Politically, Western policy has been without results: unification is as distant as ever, and the Oder-Neisse line is firmly established as the eastern boundary of a divided Germany. Yet the very unsettled state of the Germany problem opens up a political opportunity for the West.

The nations of Eastern Europe support the German policies of the Soviet Union primarily because they fear Germany's new military strength. President de Gaulle alone of all the Western statesmen has seen this opportunity by declaring himself in favor of the Oder-Neisse line as the permanent eastern frontier of Germany. If all nations would make such a declaration—in other words, if all nations would make it appear a hopeless undertaking for any German government ever to recover the regions east of the Oder-Neisse line—the present community of interests between the Soviet Union and the nations of Eastern Europe would thereby be weakened, if not destroyed, in so far as their policies toward Germany are concerned. And, I think, the nations of the West would also greatly contribute to the stabilization of order in all of Europe and to the promotion of freedom in Eastern Europe.

These considerations have, of course, but an indirect and negative bearing upon the unification of Germany. They deal with policies and conditions which would make the continuing division of Germany bearable for all concerned, for unification cannot be brought about in the foreseeable future by diplomatic negotiations. Given the continuation of the present balance of military power, it cannot be brought about by force. This is obviously, in terms of German unification, a hopeless outlook. But it is not necessarily a hopeless outlook in terms of the objective interests of all concerned, for the recognition of the legitimacy of the Oder-Neisse line and of the inevitability of the division of Germany reflects the objective interests of all concerned. Once the territorial status quo has been stabilized by virtue of that recognition, the symbol of the Western presence in Berlin will have changed its meaning. From a symbol of irredenta and territorial revision, it will have been transformed into a symbol of the cultural unity of all of Europe. Thus the Western presence in Berlin will be the symbolic manifestation of the policy of the Atlantic community toward the European nations east of the Iron Curtain.

The policies which the Atlantic community, with the United States as its most eminent spokesman, has pursued toward the satellites of the Soviet Union have failed. They have failed because those policies have been unaware of both their limitations and opportunities. The policy of liberation and the explicit inaction on the occasion of the Hungarian revolution of 1956 have been the outward manifestations of this failure. The policy of liberation manifested unconcern with the limitations; inaction on the occasion of the Hungarian revolution demonstrated unawareness of the opportunities.

The policy of liberation must be seen both as a logical extension of the policy of containment and as the positive implementation of the Western refusal to recognize the legitimacy of the European conquests of the Soviet Union. The United States could let it go at that, satisfied with containing Russian power within the limits reached in 1945, and that is essentially what it did up to the beginning of 1953. But once America yielded to the impulse to go beyond this negative, static policy of containment and non-recognition and to give it a positive, dynamic implementation, it had to face the problem of what kind of positive policy it should pursue. Consistent with its general conception of foreign policy, the United States conceived of liberation essentially in military terms—that is, as the evacuation of Eastern Europe by the Red Army. Such evacuation could be brought about only through military pressure carrying with it the risk of war. As the London *Economist* put it on August 30, 1952, when the policy of liberation was first proclaimed: "Unhappily 'liberation' applied to Eastern Europe—and Asia—means either the risk of war or it means nothing. . . . 'Liberation' entails no risk of war only when it means nothing." Since, according to repeated official statements, liberation was to be achieved without resort to war, it could not be achieved.

Thus, what pretended to be a new dynamic policy turned out to be no policy at all, nothing more than a verbal commitment that could not be implemented by action. However, that commitment was taken as a threat by the Soviet Union and as a promise by the satellites. As such, far from contributing anything to the liberation of the satellites, it served, on the one hand, as a pretext for the Soviet Union to maintain its military rule in Eastern Europe and, on the other, as an incentive for the satellites to entertain illusions about what the United States might do and to be disillusioned with American policy and reconciled to their fate when no action was forthcoming.

The unreality of this policy of liberation encountered the ultimate test in the Hungarian revolution of 1956, for here the Atlantic community was faced not with the impossible task of liberating without resort to war but with the opportunity to support a liberation already achieved. If it remained inactive under these most favorable circumstances, it would demonstrate that there was no such thing as a policy of liberation but only verbal pronouncements designed to give the appearance that there was one. This is indeed what happened. The United States declared from the outset through its most authoritative spokesman, the President, that it would abstain from active interference. While it is a moot question as to how much the United States could have done, there can be no doubt—especially in view of the dissension within the Soviet government over the use of force revealed in the meantime by Khrushchev—that it could have done more than nothing.

The United States failed utterly to relate the commitment of the Atlantic community to its unity with the nations of Eastern Europe to the political situations with regard to which it was called upon to act. Its words gave the appearance of novelty and daring to policies that were at best routine and at worst out of tune with what the times demanded. But its failure revealed both the nature and the innate strength of its purpose. In spite of what it said and did, the facts of its life, past and present, spoke louder than its purposeful words and deeds. The words and deeds had by and large been ineffectual and even counterproductive. Yet they were overshadowed and in rare moments obliterated by the universal awareness that equality in freedom still had a home in America. As the Hungarian revolution illuminated like a stroke of lightning the nature of man, showing the urge for freedom to be as elemental a human quality as the lust for power or the desire for wealth, so did the awareness of the freedom achieved within the American borders act as a corrective for words and deeds seemingly oblivious of the American purpose.

When the Vice-President of the United States visited Poland in the spring of 1959 and when the President in the fall of that year visited India, the major uncommitted nation, they were greeted with a popular enthusiasm that was meant not for themselves but for the nation they represented. They were greeted, as Woodrow Wilson and Franklin D. Roosevelt had been before them, as living symbols of what the nation was thought to stand for; and the enthusiasm that the nation evoked in the persons of its representatives was due, it is safe to assume, not to its wealth and power but to the purpose that sets it apart from all other nations and makes it a model for other nations to emulate. When these living symbols of America ventured abroad, they carried with them, as it were, the purpose of America and of the Atlantic community of expanding the area of freedom. They came as symbols not only of what America has achieved at home, but also of what it was to achieve abroad. Thus an ironic twist of historic development made the outside world appear to understand the American purpose better than did America itself, and through a paradoxical reversal of roles the outside world had to recall the American message to an America that was incapable of making clear to the world what it was about. America, in ineffectual perplexity, tried to give the world its message, relating its traditional purpose to the contemporary world. Yet what it could not do for itself through the conscious effort of words and deeds, its very existence did for it. The living presence of its achievements carried the promise of further achievements to the world, and the hope of the world carried that message back to America.

The most important task before the Atlantic community, second only to that of internal cohesion and purpose, is the establishment of confiding and productive relations with the uncommitted nations. With the negative task of liquidating the colonial empires nearing completion, that positive task, to be accomplished in competition with the Communist bloc, takes on special urgency. Its primary instrument is foreign aid.

Thus far, the members of the Atlantic community have extended foreign aid both on an individual and haphazard basis. There have only been the bare beginnings of a collective endeavor, founded upon a well-thought-out philosophy which would apply the common values and purposes of the Atlantic community to foreign aid. In particular the American theory and practice of foreign aid has derived by and large from certain unexamined assumptions that are part of the American folklore of politics. The popular mind has established a number of simple and highly doubtful correlations between foreign aid, on the one hand, and a rising standard of living, social and political stability, democratic institutions and practices, and a peaceful foreign policy, on the other. The simplicity of these correlations is so reassuring and so reminiscent of the Wilsonian correlation between democratic institutions and domestic and international order and peace that the general philosophic proposition has in the past hardly ever been questioned in public, however much the contrary empirical evidence in specific cases forces drastic changes in practice.

Such fundamental questions as the following, concerning the results of foreign aid, have hardly ever been asked explicitly: What are the social, political, and moral effects of foreign aid likely to be in various circumstances? Does successful foreign aid require a particular intellectual, political, and moral climate, or will the injection of capital and technological capability from the outside create this climate? To what extent and under what conditions is it possible for one nation to transform through outside intervention the economic and technological life of another nation? More specifically, in terms of the political objective of keeping the uncommitted nations uncommitted, how is one to create in the mind of the recipient the positive relationship between the aid and its beneficial results, on the one hand, and the political philosophy, system, and objectives of the giver, on the other? As long as the recipient disapproves of the politics of the giver, despite the aid he has received, the political effects of the aid are lost. These effects are similarly lost as long as the recipient remains unconvinced that the aid is but a natural, if not inevitable, manifestation of the politics of the giver. Foreign aid, then, remains politically ineffective as long as the recipient says either "Aid is good, but the politics of the giver is bad," or "Aid is good, but the politics of the giver—good, bad, or indifferent—has nothing to do with it."

Questions such as these require for answers policies of extraordinary subtlety and intricacy. Policies based on a simple correlation between foreign aid and what the giver desires in the uncommitted nations do not suffice. That correlation is a projection of the domestic experience of the industrial nations of the West onto the international scene. Capital formation and investment and technological innovation created the wealth and prosperity of these nations, and, so it was assumed, the export of Western capital and technology to the underdeveloped nations would bring forth similar results there. Yet these results are not forthcoming in those uncommitted nations which are lacking in the cultural preconditions for economic development, especially a rational attitude toward production and a moral code governing production, distribution, and administration. It is here that the Atlantic community, following the example of the British Commonwealth of Nations, must bring the values of Western civilization collectively to bear upon the political, cultural, and economic development of the uncommitted nations.

It is especially in the political field that the uncommitted nations present the Atlantic community with a truly creative opportunity. It is not enough that we have left behind unqualified opposition to neutralism, of which the indiscriminate search for allies—the collector's approach to alliances—was a logical consequence. Having recognized that political non-commitment is the only policy many of the new nations can afford to pursue, we must find a positive relationship to these neutralist nations. A number of uncommitted nations are weak to the point of lack of viability, and their weakness together with the Balkanization of vast areas of the globe, especially of Africa, has greatly increased the sources of disorder in the world. That Balkanization runs counter to the technological requirements of the age, which call for political units larger than even the traditional nation-states of Europe. What is required is a "new order" to replace the defunct order of empire. Communism offers such a new order, adapted to the wants of neutralism. There are all kinds and degrees of political non-commitment, and the uncommitted nations may well incline toward one or the other side in their moral preferences, political sympathies, economic interests, and even, when the chips are down, military support. International communism seeks exactly this implicit kind of alignment without formal explicit commitment.

We have tended to counter this Communist attempt at establishing a new order among the uncommitted nations by offering them protection against communism. Yet while as a matter of fact these nations need such protection, they refuse to recognize that need, for dedication to neutralism makes them afraid that if they did they would thereby be drawn into the Cold War on the side of the West. For them the paramount issue is not communism but colonialism. The invocation of anticommunism pure and simple, then, is a self-defeating policy toward the uncommitted nations. What is needed is a positive alternative to, rather than a negative polemic against, the Communist "new order." It goes without saying that the new order to be promoted and supported by the Atlantic community must be unequivocally anticolonist and must meet the material aspirations and requirements of the uncommitted nations. Yet that new order must also be a political order which has room for all kinds and degrees of political non-commitment. The uncommitted nations may well incline toward one or the other side in their moral preferences, political sympathies, economic interests, and even limited military support. The reconciliation of these different shades of neutralism with the interests of the Atlantic community, without compelling the neutralists to enter into an explicit commitment, will put Western statesmanship to its supreme test.

Even so, resentment against Western power is likely to persist among neutralist nations and with it the tendency to play the East off against the West. To counteract this psychological predisposition, it will avail the Atlantic community little if it tries, as a matter of principle, to curry favor with the neutralists by trimming the sails of its policies to the wind of their preferences, for that kind of neutralism feeds on this kind of weakness. Rather we must pursue clearly defined, strongly executed, and ably presented policies to a successful conclusion, thereby demonstrating to all concerned that we know what we are about and that it does not pay to cross us. Only so will we gain the respect of the neutralists and have a chance to win their support as well. And we might well remind the uncommitted nations at appropriate occasions, tactfully but firmly, that their neutralism is but a function of the power of the Atlantic community. Were that power not committed to containing the Communist bloc, neutralism could not exist as a policy and would at best survive as an impotent desire and a vain hope, for neutralism in the cold war, like neutrality in a shooting war, depends upon the operations of the balance of power. It is a luxury which certain nations can afford because the power of one antagonist cancels out the power of the other. Weaken the power of one or the other and the neutral nations are at the mercy of the stronger power.

The foregoing discussion issues in five general conclusions. First, the interests that tie the members of the Atlantic community together are not only and not even primarily of a military nature. They are first of all a common concern for the survival and expansion of the values of Western civilization. Second, these interests cannot be pursued by individual nations in separation. The pursuit of these interests requires a collective effort under the leadership of the United States, supported by common institutions and policies. Third, the stabilization of the territorial status quo in Europe is a precondition for the successful pursuit of these interests. Fourth, the Atlantic community must keep the awareness of a common membership in Western civilization alive in the European nations behind the Iron Curtain by impressing upon them the vitality of that civilization. Fifth, the Atlantic community must enter into a positive relationship with the uncommitted nations by respecting their uncommitted status and conveying to them the benefits of its political, economic, and cultural experiences.

25 *Building a European Federation*

I shall approach my topic, "The Schuman Plan and European Federation," in the spirit of the balance of power, the national interest, and what is now called old-fashioned diplomacy. That is to say, I shall pay less attention to the literal content of the rules of law contained in the statute of the Coal and Steel Community, and I shall pay more attention to the underlying political, social, and economic forces with which the future of the Schuman Plan stands or falls.

Some well-meaning members of this society have referred to this approach as neo-Machiavellian, a term which implies at once moral depravity and intellectual obsolescence. I shall not defend myself against the accusation of moral depravity, an obviously hopeless task, but I shall make just one remark about the alleged intellectual obsolescence of this approach to problems of international law and international politics.

Less than twenty years ago the leading treatise on international law, that of Oppenheim, contained a very brilliant and extensive chapter on the relations between the balance of power and international law, trying to show—and I think successfully—that the legal rules governing the international community depend for their existence and efficacy upon a working system of balance of power. Professor Lauterpacht, the editor of Oppenheim's treatise, took this chapter on the balance of power out, and it has not reappeared since. Perhaps soon it will reappear again.

Let me take my cue for the approach to the problem of the Schuman Plan from two speeches which most of you have heard. One is from the Secretary of State's speech of last night, in which he said:

Organization, whether national or international, is merely an instrument and must be used by skillful craftsmen. The existence of an instrument does not eliminate the need for craftsmanship, nor does the existence of international organization eliminate the need for statesmanship.

From the *Proceedings of the American Society of International Law*, 1952.

The other remark to which I want to refer is contained in the closing passage of the paper by the Assistant Secretary of State for Far Eastern Affairs. The Assistant Secretary of State made the point, quoting with approval a statement I had made on another occasion, that the Japanese peace treaty, as all international treaties, depends for its efficacy and very existence as a legal instrument upon the identity or concurrence of the interests of the contracting parties.

This is exactly the point which one must not lose sight of in discussing the Schuman Plan. The Schuman Plan is a legal instrument, a blueprint for an international organization. While it is interesting to know what the legal structure of that instrument is and what has gone into its making, it seems to me of infinitely greater importance to know to what social uses it is likely to be put. In other words, an international organization such as the Schuman Plan organization is like a knife which may be used for cutting sausages, but it may also be used for cutting throats, or it may not be used at all. No description of the inherent qualities of that knife will tell you for what purposes it is likely to be used.

The Schuman Plan constitutes indeed a revolutionary attempt at solving an age-old political problem. That problem is characterized, it seems to me, by two basic facts. One is the natural superiority of Germany among the nations of Europe; the other fact is the unwillingness of the other European nations to accept that fact. Since 1870 the great convulsions and the diplomatic moves preceding those convulsions on the European continent were all dominated by those two facts. France tried before and after the First World War to solve this problem, to meet those two facts, by the methods which were suggested by the balance of power as it was practiced in previous centuries. That is to say, it tried to make up for its own inherent weakness by a system of alliances which would be able to counterbalance the natural superiority of Germany. In those attempts, as we know, France failed. In both world wars, France was saved neither by its own strength nor by the strength of its Continental allies but by the intervention of Great Britain and, more particularly, of the United States. This is another fact which we must keep in mind if we want to assess the chances of the Schuman Plan.

The Schuman Plan, I have said, constitutes a revolutionary departure from those traditional methods of countering superior power on the part of an inferior power; for instead of countering that potentially superior power by a system of alliances, what France is now trying to do is, as it were, to draw Germany into its own arms in order to disarm it and to make the superior strength of Germany innocuous. It is, in other words, an attempt at fusing a superior power with an inferior one for the purpose of creating a common control of the pooled power. Thus France hopes to be able to forestall the possibility that that power may be used for hostile purposes or for the purpose of recreating a German hegemony on the European continent.

The Schuman Plan is equally revolutionary in view of the way in which France tries to realize this objective. In former times, and especially in the interwar period, the unification of Europe was attempted, as it were, from the top. That is to say, an all-comprehensive legal organization was proposed or established; a legal framework for an over-all government was the goal of those attempts. The Council of Europe today moves in that tradition. The Schuman Plan starts from the opposite end of the envisaged structure. It starts from the bottom rather than from the top. It tries to create a functional unity within a limited sphere of action, expecting that the operations of that unity within that limited sphere will lead, first of all, to a community of interest within that particular sphere, and that this example will then spread to other functional fields, such as agriculture, transport, electricity, and military forces. For all those fields the French foreign office has already developed schemes of unification. Finally, so it is hoped, out of that series of functional unities, political unity will grow organically, for national sovereignty will have been transferred to a series of functional governments without the individual nations really being aware of it. Once all those functional organizations have been established, sovereignty in fact will have been transferred to a common European government.

It seems to me that the success of this scheme depends upon four fundamental factors, all having to do with the national interests of the individual nations and with the distribution of power among them. The first question one must ask in this respect is, What is the internal distribution of power to be within and among the different agencies of the Coal and Steel Community? Second, What is the distribution of power to be between the agencies of the Coal and Steel Community and the member governments? Third, What is the degree of unity going to be in the economic, military, and political fields among the member nations? And finally, What is the distribution of power going to be between the members of the Coal and Steel Community, on the one hand, and the other main coal and steel-producing nations—that is to say, Great Britain and the United States—on the other?

In the few minutes left I must limit myself to elaborating these questions rather than try to answer them. To give an example concerning the first question: What is the composition of the High Authority of the Coal and Steel Community going to be? Is it going to be composed of technicians following an independent course on the basis of their technical convictions as to the best techniques of coal and steel production and distribution, or are they going to be the representatives of the member governments, perhaps not taking orders from the member governments, but being unable to banish from their minds the national interests of the member nations and their own dedication to them?

What is the relation going to be between the High Authority and the Assembly, the pseudoparliamentary representation of the six member nations? What is the relation going to be between the High Authority and the Council of Ministers, the representatives of the governments concerned? What kind of use is the Court going to make of its enormous powers, at least on paper, with regard to the activities of the High Authority, the Assembly, and the Council of Ministers? In other words, what is the distribution of power going to be among those four agencies of the Schuman Plan? In view of the text of the legal instrument, there is room for all possibilities.

I take an example of the second question, and this is probably the most vital of all questions in view of the day-by-day operations of the Community. What is the relation going to be between the agencies of the Coal and Steel Community, on the one hand, and the member governments, on the other? According to the statute, the High Authority as the executive organ of the Coal and Steel Community has primarily investigative and indirect powers. It has almost no direct administrative powers within the territory of the constituent nations. Its main power lies in the field of investment; and here its power is primarily the negative one to withhold investments, loans, and guarantees for loans from recalcitrant member nations. But what if those recalcitrant member nations do not need those loans or can get them elsewhere?

The third question is that of the relationship between the hoped-for community of interests in the spheres of coal and steel and the actual economic, military, and political interests of the individual member nations. Take, for instance, the vital question of Germany, vital here as elsewhere. To what extent will the unfulfilled aspirations of all Germans for the reunification of their country get in the way of the operations of the Schuman Plan? Are the economic interests, in so far as they exist at all—and this is a question which I could not even raise here—of Germany in the Coal and Steel Community strong enough to counteract and even to transcend its unfulfilled national aspirations?

Finally, and this is the most important question of all from the political point of view: What is the relation going to be between the Coal and Steel Community, on the one hand, and Great Britain and, more particularly, the United States, on the other? For here we are face to face with the same fundamental problem which we encountered in the political and military fields before the First and Second World wars. That is to say, the European balance of power cannot be maintained any more by the balancing of Continental forces alone. Great Britain, since 1870 at least, had to support France against Germany, and from the First World War onward there was no possibility of establishing a viable European balance of power without the intervention of the United States. What is the purpose of United States intervention in Europe? Is it to maintain a balance of power in Western Europe within the over-all balance of power between East and West, or is it to maintain the over-all balance of power between East and West regardless of the internal balance of power within the Atlantic community?

It seems from the foregoing considerations of the Coal and Steel Community that an integral part of this attempt at establishing a world-wide balance of power is to create within the Western community, more particularly on the European continent, a viable balance of power between Germany and France. I would submit in conclusion that this Western European unity, this Continental balance of power, cannot be created by preaching the virtues of European federation, but only by the calculated and determined intervention on the part of the United States.

26 *A Positive Approach to a Democratic Ideology*

If the ideological contest between democracy and bolshevism were to be decided by the standards of a seminar in political philosophy, we need have no doubt about the outcome. Unfortunately, what is good and true by the standards of philosophy does not of necessity win out in the political contest of the market place. Our weakness, in Asia as well as in Europe, in the struggle for the minds of men is primarily the result of the confusion of these two standards, the philosophic and the political. Since democracy is superior to bolshevism in the truth which it contains and in the good of which it carries the promise and in part the fulfilment, we tend to believe that by that same token it must also prove itself superior to bolshevism in the political arena. Against this confusion in theory and illusion in practice, four basic principles of ideological warfare must be maintained.

There is a fundamental distinction between the absolute good, which is everywhere the same, and the relative good, which is good only under particular circumstances. To define the former is the job of philosophy; it is for politics to understand, and to make use of, the latter.

There is at the bottom of all political contentions and conflicts an irreducible minimum of psychological traits and aspirations which are the common possession of all mankind. All human beings want to live and, hence, want the things which are necessary for life. All human beings want to be free and, hence, want to have those opportunities for self-expression and self-development which their particular culture considers to be desirable. All human beings seek power and, hence, seek social distinctions, again varying with the particular pattern of their culture, which put them ahead of and above their fellow men.

Upon this psychological foundation, the same for all men, rises an edifice of philosophic valuations, ethical postulates, and political

From the *Proceedings of the Academy of Political Science*, 1951.

aspirations. These, too, might be shared by all men under certain conditions, but actually they are not, except on the verbal level. They might be shared by all if the conditions under which men can satisfy their desire to live, to be free, and to have power were similar all over the world, and if the conditions under which such satisfaction is withheld, and must be striven for, were also similar everywhere. If this were so, the experience, common to all men, of what men seek and of what they are able to obtain would create a community of valuations, postulates, and aspirations which would provide common standards of evaluation and of action.

Actually, however, reality does not correspond to our assumption of similarity of conditions throughout the world. The variations in the standard of living range from mass starvation to abundance; the variations in freedom, from tyranny to democracy, from economic slavery to equality; the variations in power, from extreme inequalities and unbridled one-man rule to wide distribution of power subject to constitutional limitations. This nation enjoys freedom, yet starves; that nation is well fed, but longs for freedom; still another enjoys security of life and individual freedom, but smarts under the rule of autocratic government. In consequence, while philosophically the similarities of standards are considerable throughout the world—most political philosophies agree in their evaluation of the common good, of law, peace, and order, of life, liberty, and the pursuit of happiness—moral judgments and political actions show wide divergencies. The same moral and political concepts take on different meanings in different environments. Justice and democracy come to mean one thing here, something quite different there. A move on the international scene decried by one group as immoral and unjust is praised by another as the opposite. Thus the contrast between the community of psychological traits and elemental aspirations, on the one hand, and the absence of shared experiences, universal moral convictions, and common political aspirations, on the other, point to the fundamental philosophic distinction between the absolute and the relative good.

Not the number and importance of the abstract truths and moral values it contains, but its effectiveness in terms of the immediate satisfaction of popular aspirations determines the success of a political ideology.

The great political ideologies of the past which captured the imagination of men and moved them to political action, such as the ideas of the American and French Revolutions and the slogans of bolshevism and fascism, were successful not because they were true, but because they gave the people to whom they appealed what they were waiting for both in terms of knowledge and in terms of action. That the race theories of the Nazis are totally false no one can doubt. Yet the arguments of reputable anthropologists were completely wasted in their struggle with those theories for dominance over the popular mind. The economic interpretation of imperialism and war is obviously at odds with all the known facts. Yet, as anybody who has tried to teach the truth about these matters will confirm, the popular belief in it is well-nigh ineradicable.

The patent falsity of these theories was irrelevant to their success or failure. What was decisive for their success was their ability to give satisfaction to deeply felt intellectual and political needs. The frustrated authoritarianism of the German people seized upon the race theories as a tool with which to prove to themselves, in spite of all appearances to the contrary, that by nature they were really superior to everybody else and, given the right policies, they would also become superior in fact. In anticipation of that ascendancy of Germany, the race theories made it virtually imperative for the German people to try their superiority out on the minorities within their borders and the inevitable success of the trial seemed to provide experimental proof for the truth of the race theories themselves.

Similarly, the economic interpretation of imperialism and war satisfies deeply felt intellectual and political needs. The popular mind, baffled by the bewildering complexity of international relations in our time, longs for an explanation which is both simple and plausible. The economic interpretation, by providing it, puts the popular mind at rest. What Professor Schumpeter has said of the Marxist theory of imperialism holds generally true: "A series of vital facts of our time seems to be perfectly accounted for. The whole maze of international politics seems to be cleared up by a single powerful stroke of analysis." In the field of political action, the economic theories fulfil a function similar to those performed by the race theories. The economic theory provides in the "warmongers of Wall Street" or the "munitions makers" an easily accessible symbol which political action can use, as it were, for purposes of target practice. In accordance with the theory, measures can be taken "to take the profits out of war" or to restrict commerce with belligerents. With these measures accomplished, imperialism and war seem to have lost their threat, and the popular mind can rest doubly content, knowing what international politics is all about and conscious of having acted in accordance with its knowledge.

If such are the functions which political ideologies perform, it follows that political ideologies, in order to be effective in political warfare, must meet two basic practical requirements. *A political ideology, in order to be effective, must reflect the life experiences of those whom it endeavors to reach.*

Communism has been successful wherever its tenets of social, economic, and political equality appeal to people for whom the removal of inequality has been the most urgent aspiration. Western ideology has succeeded wherever in popular aspirations political liberty has taken precedence over all other needs. Thus communism has largely lost the struggle for the minds of men in Central and Western Europe, and democracy has by and large been defeated in Asia. In Central and Western Europe, the Communist promises of equality could not prevail against the life experiences which the peoples of Central and Western Europe had with the tyranny of the Red Army and the Russian secret police. In those regions communism has succeeded only with those segments of the population in whose life experiences the longing for equality, especially in the economic sphere, has taken precedence over the concern for liberty.

In the other hand, democracy has lost out in Asia because its appeal has been largely divorced from the life experiences of the peoples of Asia. What the peoples of Asia want is freedom from Western imperialism and social justice in terms of economic betterment. What chance is there for democracy to succeed in the ideological struggle as long as democratic ideology is contradicted by the life experiences of the people of Asia? In the minds of the people of Indochina, the appeal to the blessings of democracy and the evils of Russian imperialism cannot prevail over the life experiences which show the citadel of democracy allied with one of the last outposts of Western imperialism. The impotence of a political ideology divorced from the life experiences of the common man is strikingly revealed in a report which appeared on September 30, 1950, in the *Chicago Daily News* under the by-line of Fred Sparks.

The other day I visited a small farmer near Saigon. . . .
Through my interpreter I asked him to tell me what he thought of the Americans coming to Indochina. He said:
"White men help white men. You give guns to help the French kill my people. We want to be rid of all foreigners and the Viet Minh . . . was slowly putting out the French."
I said: "Don't you know there is a white man behind the Viet Minh? Don't you know that Ho Chi Minh takes Russian orders?"
He said: "In Saigon I have seen Americans and I have seen Frenchmen. I have never heard of any white men being with the Viet Minh."

What makes this episode significant is the fact that to a large extent it is representative of Asia's reaction to Western ideologies. Nowhere has this reaction been more drastic and more pregnant with dire consequences for the West than in China, for nowhere has the contrast between ideology and the life experiences of the people been more drastic. The century-old anti-imperialistic record of the United States and the good will it had created in China for the United States were wiped out with one stroke when American weapons were used to kill Chinese and when American planes dropped bombs on the coastal cities of China. As a report in the London *Economist* put it with reference to the air raids on Shanghai:

In the press these raids were represented as being quite as much the work of the "American imperialists" as that of the "reactionary, remnant lackeys" of Taiwan, and while the raids drove out any faith in Chiang which might remain amongst the less educated they no less effectively drove out any faith in America in quarters where it was still harboured.

Here again, the inherent qualities of American ideology in terms of its truth and of the good of which it is the repository were entirely irrelevant for success or failure in the warfare of ideas. What counted and decided the issue was the apparent irrelevance of democratic propaganda in the light of the experiences of the common man. The policies which the United States supported or seemed to support made success in the war of ideas impossible.

Ideological warfare is a mere function of political policy. It can be worse than the policy it is meant to support; it can never be better.

The functions which political policy must fulfil for ideological warfare are threefold. First, it must define clearly its objectives and the methods through which it proposes to attain them. Second, it must determine the popular aspirations of those to whom the ideological appeal is to be made with regard to its objectives and methods. Third, it must determine to what extent political warfare is capable of supporting political policy.

Our ideological weakness in Asia, aside from the other reasons already mentioned, results from the weakness of our political policies. Since we have not been sure of our objectives and of the methods to reach them, our ideological appeal was only too prone to seek refuge from the uncertainties of policy in democratic generalities. Moreover, we are not even quite certain whether we are engaged in a holy crusade, after the model of those we engaged in in the two world wars, to wipe bolshevism from the face of the earth, or whether we are waging a power struggle against the imperialism of the Soviet Union, which uses the ideology of world revolution for the purpose of expanding Russian power. While the speeches of Mr. Acheson are emphatic in stressing the power-political aspects of the struggle with the Soviet Union, the general climate of opinion, private and official, favors the interpretation of the East-West conflict in terms of a democratic crusade. While our China policy, however awkwardly and hesitatingly, seems to subordinate ideological considerations to the calculus of power advantage, our over-all policy in Asia still shows strong traces of counterrevolutionary tendencies for their own sake, and accordingly, our propaganda has been inclined to stress the virtues and truths of democracy and the vices and falsehoods of bolshevism.

It is the same propensity for such moral and philosophic abstractions which has impeded the objective investigation of what other people want. Assured as we are by and large of the protection of our lives from the vicissitudes of death through violence or lack of food and shelter, we are taking the satisfaction of these biological needs for granted. Having taken care in good measure of the protection of life, we concentrate our thoughts and efforts upon the preservation of liberty and the pursuit of happiness. This being naturally so with us, we erect this limited experience, subject to the conditions of time and space, into a universal principle which claims to be valid everywhere and at all times. Thus we assume, at least by implication, that what we are allowed to take for granted all men can take for granted, and that what we are striving for is the object of the aspirations of all mankind. In consequence, since Woodrow Wilson we have made the insistence upon democratic elections everywhere in the world one of the mainstays of our foreign policy.

At the root of this insistence there lie three basic errors. One is the belief, which does not need to detain us here, that democracy and peace are synonymous and, hence, that to establish democracy everywhere is tantamount to making peace secure everywhere. The second error lies in the assumption that democracy is a kind of gadget which is capable of being installed in any political household regardless of the qualifications and preferences of the inhabitants. The historic connection between the development of democratic government and the rise of the middle classes is by implication dismissed as a historic coincidence which can teach us nothing about the limitations of democracy as a universal principle of government. The final error is the conviction that the formal processes of free elections are the earmark of democratic government. Actually, these processes may mean much or little in terms of the actual choices available to the electorate and the actual control exercised by the governed over the government. While there can be no democracy without free elections, free elections can be used for undemocratic or antidemocratic ends. In the last analysis it is the democratic ethos of a people, their philosophy of government and politics, their conception of what is right and wrong, desirable and undesirable, feasible and unfeasible, which determine the function that free elections fulfil in a given society. The similarity of election laws and procedures may or may not connote a similarity of political systems, according to the moral and social context within which those procedures operate. Democratic propaganda, then, is useless in a moral and social context that is indifferent or hostile to democracy. It remains again for policy to create the moral and social conditions receptive to the ideals of democracy.

It is the same disregard for the actual aspirations of human beings and the same predilection for moral and philosophic abstractions which have focused public attention upon piercing the Iron Curtain and bringing "the" truth to the peoples under Russian domination.

Here again, we tend to overlook that in the sphere of political action there is no such thing as one and the same truth for everybody. Even if information and ideas were allowed to move freely over the globe, the triumph of our ideas would by no means be assured. Those who believe that peace and good will among nations are the direct result of the free flow of news and of ideas fail to distinguish between the technical process of transmission and the thing to be transmitted. They deal only with the former and disregard the latter. However, the information and ideas to be transmitted are the reflection of the experiences which have molded the philosophies, ethics, and political conceptions of different peoples. We have seen that there is no identity of experience uniting mankind above the elemental aspirations which are common to all men. Since this is so, the American and the Russian will each consider the same news item from his particular philosophic, moral, and political perspective, and the different perspectives will give the news a different color. The same report on Korea will have a different weight as a newsworthy item, aside from any opinion to be formed about it, in the eyes of different observers, for their perspective is determined by different moral valuations, political interests, and experiences. . . .

Thus, even if we lived in a world actually unified by modern technology with men, news, and ideas moving freely regardless of national boundaries, the chance for democracy to gain the allegiance of the peoples of the world would depend upon political action meeting their aspirations, for, while in default of such political action the minds of men would be capable of communicating with each other without political impediments, they would not meet. Even if the American and the Russian were able to speak to each other, they would speak with different tongues; and if they uttered the same words, those words would signify to them different objects, values, and aspirations. So it is with concepts such as democracy, peace, freedom, security. The disillusion of differently constituted minds communicating the same words, which embody their most firmly held convictions, deepest emotions, and most ardent aspirations, without finding the expected sympathetic response has driven the members of different nations further apart and strengthened their conviction of the incompatibility of their moral values and political interests.

The ability of Western democracy to speak effectively to the peoples of Europe and Asia is dependent upon its ability to establish two different relationships: one between the aspirations of those peoples and the political policies of the West, the other between those policies and their verbal propagation. There are situations where concordance among these three factors can be brought about with relative ease. The waging of political warfare against Nazi Germany in occupied Europe during the Second World War was a relatively simple matter. Popular aspirations were clearly defined, and so were the policies pursued by the United Nations. Both sought the destruction of Nazi Germany, and it was easy to put that aim into words. Similarly, our political and military policies to maintain the territorial status quo in Europe against Russian expansion express the aspirations of the peoples of Western Europe and lend themselves to verbal formulation in terms of the Truman Doctrine, the Marshall Plan, and the North Atlantic pact. Neither in Eastern Europe nor in Asia nor in the Soviet Union itself is the task of political warfare as simple. Two basic dilemmas confront it. One concerns the incompatibility of a certain political policy pursued in one region with the kind of political warfare waged in another. The other dilemma refers to the impossibility of supporting a given political policy by means of political warfare altogether.

The first dilemma is best illustrated by the relations between what is often considered to be the objective of American policy in Eastern Europe and the objective of our political warfare with regard to the Soviet Union. The objective of our policy in Eastern Europe may be defined as the liberation of the peoples of Eastern Europe from Russian domination. The objective of our political warfare with regard to the Soviet Union is to appeal to the Russian people over the head of the Soviet government in terms of our real objectives and thus to force a revision of Soviet policies through the pressure of Russian public opinion. Yet the objective of the liberation of Eastern Europe, especially in so far as Poland and the Baltic states are concerned, runs counter to the centuries-old national aspirations of Russia, regarding which no cleavage between government and people has ever existed. A policy in Eastern Europe which seeks to thwart the aspirations of both the Russian government and the Russian people is bound to cancel out the chances, which otherwise might exist, of separating the Russian people from the Soviet government by means of political warfare. In situations such as these, it is the task of over-all policy to establish a priority of objectives and either to subordinate the objectives of political warfare to those of political policy, or vice versa.

It may be noted parenthetically that the Soviet Union is faced with a similar dilemma in its policies with regard to Poland and Eastern Germany. The recognition of the permanency of the Oder-Neisse frontier is bound to condemn Russian political warfare in Eastern Germany to impotence. Willingness to revise it would have the same effect in Poland. Faced with this dilemma, Soviet policy has decided that, at least for the time being, it is more important for the Soviet Union to maintain and strengthen its political control over Poland by making the Soviet Union appear as the champion of Polish national aspirations than to gain the allegiance of the inhabitants of Eastern Germany by satisfying in some measure their national aspirations.

A striking illustration of the other dilemma is provided by the ideological effect of the American intervention in the Korean War. However justified this intervention has been in terms of international law, political morality, and the long-term interests of the Korean people themselves, its immediate ideological effects have been unfavorable to the United States. Especially in South Korea, where the physical evidence of Russian intervention was not immediately perceptible to the common man, what the Indochinese peasant said to Mr. Sparks has found a widespread echo. While in Pyongyang United Nations troops were enthusiastically received as liberators from the Russians, in devastated Seoul the welcome was rather restrained. What is important in the context of this discussion is the inability of the United States to counteract the ideological liability of that intervention with immediate ideological countermeasures. The appearances of white intervention in the affairs of Asia in the traditional manner of Western imperialism can be refuted at present not by means of political warfare, but only by subsequent political, military, and economic policies which will establish in the life experiences of the Korean people the anti-imperialistic, democratic objectives of American policy. In situations such as these, the immediate answer to the ideological liability of a given political or military policy is not propaganda but policies which will establish the psychological preconditions for successful propaganda.

The struggle for the minds of men, then, is a task of infinite subtlety and complexity. Nothing is easier, more certain of popular support, and also more certain of failure than to approach so intricate a task in the spirit and with the techniques of a Fourth of July oration. The simple philosophy and techniques of the moral crusade are useful and even indispensable for the domestic task of marshaling public opinion behind a given policy; they are but blunt weapons in the struggle of nations for dominance over the minds of men. This is not a struggle between good and evil, truth and falsehood, but of power with power. In such a struggle virtue and truth do not prevail simply upon being communicated. They must be carried upon the steady stream of political policy which makes them both relevant and plausible. To conceive of the ideological task of democracy in the struggle with bolshevism primarily in terms of the technological problem of piercing the Iron Curtain and communicating the eternal verities of democracy to all the world is in large measure to miss the point. Political warfare is but the reflection, in the realm of ideas, of the political and military policies which it seeks to support. It is the mere ideological expression of the objectives and methods of these policies. From the qualities of these policies it draws its strength. With them it wins or fails. To be effective, the call for victory in the struggle for the minds of men must be conceived primarily as a call for political and military policies which have the makings of victory. Here, too, deeds speak louder than words.

27 *The Economics of Foreign Policy*

Foreign policy makes use of the total power of the nation for the defense and promotion of the national interest vis-à-vis other nations. Nine factors go into the making of national power: geography, natural resources, national morale, industrial capacity, military preparedness, population, national character, quality of diplomacy, and the quality of government in general. Of these, three come under the heading of the economic factor: natural resources, industrial capacity, and the quality of government. It is the government that co-ordinates the foreign policy pursued with the available economic resources and that brings the different claims upon these resources into balance with each other.

A nation that is self-sufficient in food has a great advantage over a nation that must import foodstuffs or starve. Thus, the power of Great Britain—and her chances of survival in times of war—has always depended on the Royal Navy's ability to keep open the sea lanes. On the other hand, nations enjoying self-sufficiency in food, such as the United States and the Soviet Union, need not divert their national energies from their primary objectives in order to assure their food supply. They have thus been able to pursue much more forceful and single-minded foreign policies.

What holds true of food is also true of those natural resources which are important for industrial production and, more particularly, for the waging of war. With the increasing mechanization of warfare, national power has become more and more dependent upon the control of raw materials in peace and war. "One drop of oil," said Clemenceau during the First World War, "is worth one drop of our soldiers' blood." It is not by accident that the two most powerful nations today, the United States and the Soviet Union, are most nearly self-sufficient in the raw materials of modern industrial production and that they control at least the access and the sources of those raw materials which they do not themselves possess.

From *Challenge*, February, 1959.

Yet while control of raw materials is an element of national power, it is but a potential source of strength if it is not transformed into industrial capacity. The technology of modern war has made industrial capacity, especially in the field of heavy industry, an indispensable element of national power. Thus the competition among nations for power transforms itself largely into competition for the production of a greater number of more effective implements of war. The quality and productive capacity of the industrial plant, the know-how of the working man, the skill of the engineer, the inventive genius of the scientist, the managerial organization—all these are factors on which the industrial capacity of a nation and, hence, its power in international affairs depend. Thus the great powers are bound to be identical with the leading industrial nations. The spectacular rise of the Soviet Union as a world power, and the aspirations of China to equal and then surpass both the United States and the Soviet Union—these are developments in which industrial capacity plays an indispensable role. It does not follow, however, that economic strength in terms of natural resources and industrial capacity is tantamount to national power. Economic strength is, as it were, the indispensable raw material out of which government must construct the edifice of national power. In order to achieve this, government must perform two different operations. First, it must bring its foreign policy into balance with its economic resources. Second, it must bring the different claims upon these resources into balance with each other.

The economic resources of all nations are limited, and consequently, the means and ends of the foreign policy of all nations are limited by the amount of the available resources. A nation must estimate how far it is able to go in its relations with other nations in view of the available economic resources, and it must choose the ends and means of its foreign policy in the light of that estimate. Its task is completed only when it has distributed wisely the sum total of its economic resources among the different ends and means of its foreign policy. How much ought to be devoted to the armed forces in relation to the foreign aid commitment? How much ought to be allocated to the instruments of atomic war in proportion to conventional weapons? And how should we divide our resources between foreign economic and foreign military aid? What kind of military establishment is the national economy able to support in view of the demands the civilian population makes upon it? How many guns can the economic system provide for the nation, and how many guns and how much butter can it provide for other nations in view of the amount of butter the nation wants and needs for itself?

The United States must make these decisions against the background of a triple challenge: the military challenge of the Soviet bloc, the economic challenge of the Soviet bloc, and the challenge which is presented by the widening gap between the highly developed industrial nations of the West and the underdeveloped masses of Asia, Africa, and Latin America.

The Soviet Union has been explicit in its resolution to prove Marx and Lenin correct in their prophecy that capitalism is doomed. While Marx and Lenin believed that disaster would result from a series of world wars fought primarily among the capitalistic nations themselves, Khrushchev has declared that capitalism will fall because of its inferiority in economic organization and productivity. As he put it to the noted newspaper columnist and author, Walter Lippmann, America enjoys "the last years of its greatness." The Soviet Union is destined to surpass the United States in economic productivity and well-being; and by demonstrating its economic superiority over the United States, it will set an example which the underdeveloped masses of the earth will want to emulate. They will choose the Soviet rather than the American way of life. Furthermore, this economic superiority will enable the Soviet Union to wage full-scale economic war against the United States by taking away its foreign markets and integrating the underdeveloped areas of the world into its economic and political system. Thus, without firing a shot, the Soviet Union will triumph over the United States.

How has the United States responded? Its diplomacy has emphasized the military threat and the military response. Thus it has concentrated throughout the world upon strengthening the existing alliances and concluding as many new ones as possible. Foreign aid, too, has been primarily of a military nature. Only a small fraction of the resources earmarked for foreign aid has been used for economic and technical assistance. Our foreign trade policy has followed the traditional pattern: maximize exports and protect the domestic producer against foreign competition. The subordination of our foreign trade policy to the broader purposes of our political foreign policy, in terms of the challenge of the Soviet Union and of the underdeveloped nations, has been in the nature of sporadic and minor deviations from the traditional pattern. This response has been deficient both in its conception and in the specific policies pursued. The challenge with which the Soviet Union threatens the United States is total, both as to the goal to be attained and the means being employed. The Soviet Union marshals its total economic resources in order to bring about the downfall of the United States. The American response has been for the greater part misdirected and for the remainder halfhearted and piecemeal.

Our diplomacy has been misdirected in its emphasis upon local military arrangements, especially outside Europe, as ends in themselves. The ability of the United States to deter Soviet aggression through its own retaliatory power is indeed the essential minimum requirement of American foreign policy. Yet the concentration upon maintaining and developing local military forces has been useless and even self-defeating in so far as the Soviet challenge has been economic. It has done the United States no good to develop the military forces of, say, an Asian nation which lies outside the effective range of Soviet military power but which is vulnerable to Soviet economic penetration. This misdirected military approach to what is essentially a political and economic problem also tends to distort the distribution of political and economic forces in an irrational manner; it damages the interests of the United States in that it creates political and economic tensions to be exploited by the Soviet Union.

If our military approach is defective, our foreign aid policies suffer from different but no less serious weaknesses. We have not developed a coherent foreign aid policy, subordinating the concrete measures taken in the field of foreign aid to the objectives of both our over-all and local political policies and co-ordinating them with the measures taken in other fields. What is the over-all purpose of our foreign aid? To keep our allies on our side and acquire new ones? To protect uncommitted nations from communism? Or to satisfy the so-called revolution of rising expectations, which is supposed to sweep Asia, Africa, and Latin America? Is it true that all the nations which ask us for aid need it and can use it? To what extent is foreign aid really in the nature of a bribe to foreign governments? And to what extent does it perform the politically useful function of the traditional subsidies that were common in the eighteenth century, especially in British foreign policy? To what extent does it have the function of a stimulus to genuine economic development? A rational foreign aid policy requires empirical answers to these and similar questions. It is the measure of the irrationality of our foreign aid policy that the answers have largely been derived from unexamined popular assumptions of doubtful validity. We have preferred to allocate foreign aid by impulse rather than base it upon a carefully thought-out philosophy which has stood the test of experience.

Our policy of foreign trade shows in still another way the obsolescence of our foreign economic policy. Ideally, foreign trade is carried on by private enterprises for the purpose of private gain. Actually, however, governments have time and again endeavored to use foreign trade as an instrument of national policy. So-called dollar diplomacy is a case in point. It is not true, even though it is widely believed, that private enterprise used the government to further private foreign commercial ventures. Quite to the contrary, the government used private enterprise abroad for the purposes of United States foreign policy. Today, the need for such use has become overwhelming in view of the Communist challenge. Yet the government, shackled by ancient shibboleths and sectional domestic interests, has not dared to develop a policy which would make foreign trade a potent instrument of American foreign policy.

Our foreign economic policy in all its manifestations is deficient in two major and related respects. First, it is in good measure divorced both in conception and execution from the purposes and operations of our foreign political policy. We still regard foreign economic policy, as we did military policy, as a self-sufficient technical entity following its own course according to its own laws, quite independent of extraneous political considerations. Second, hardly anything in our foreign economic policy reflects the total character of the challenge with which the Communist world and the underdeveloped masses confront us. We are not unaware of the existence of that challenge, but we act upon it as though it could be successfully met through a relatively minor effort, with our domestic economic business being carried on as usual. Yet the truth of the matter is that the Soviet bloc subordinates its economic life completely to the purposes of its foreign policy. Are we rich and powerful enough to withstand this total effort, let alone to win out in competition with it, by making only minor and haphazard efforts in response to it? The answer implicit in our foreign economic policy is in the affirmative. Yet it is virtually certain that this is not the right answer.

A sound foreign economic policy must use economic resources as a weapon with which the political interests of the United States are to be defended in competition with the Soviet bloc. In terms of organization, this means that the weapon must be in the hands of the political leaders to be used for political purposes, not in the hands of the economic experts to be used for narrow technical ends. In terms of substance, this means two things. It means that we must apply a political standard both to the purposes and the methods of our foreign aid, and that we must spend more for foreign aid where our political purposes seem to require it and less or nothing where our political goals can be served otherwise. And it means first of all that everywhere and, more particularly, in the field of foreign trade, the public interest in the survival and the safety of the United States must take precedence over private gain.

It would be an illusion to believe that these general principles can be applied to the concrete issues of our foreign economic policy without drastic changes in our domestic economic system or that these changes will not narrow the freedom of private choice. These changes will not be the result of ideological preference, nor can ideological preference be allowed to stand in their way. Faced with an all-out economic challenge to our very existence, we shall have to sacrifice much that is important and much that in the past appeared to us even essential. We must do it for the sake of something that is more important than any other consideration: the survival of the nation itself.

28 *Preface to a Political Theory of Foreign Aid*

Of the seeming and real innovations which the modern age has introduced into the practice of foreign policy, none has proven more baffling to both understanding and action than foreign aid. The very assumption that foreign aid is an instrument of foreign policy is a subject of controversy, for the opinion is widely held that foreign aid is an end in itself, carrying within itself a justification both transcending, and independent of, foreign policy. In this view, foreign aid is the fulfilment of an obligation which the few rich nations have toward the many poor ones. On the other hand, there are many who see no justification for a policy of foreign aid at all. They look at foreign aid as a gigantic boondoggle, a wasteful and indefensible operation which serves neither the interests of the United States nor those of the recipient nations.

The public debate on foreign aid has contributed little to understanding. In the spring of every year, the nation engages in such a debate, carried on almost exclusively in terms of the amount of money to be spent for purposes of foreign aid rather than the substantive purposes which a policy of foreign aid is suposed to serve. The administration tries, as it were, to sell a certain amount of foreign aid to Congress, and Congress refuses to buy that amount. Congress generally appropriates about 10 per cent less than the administration has requested, and the administration spends that amount as it sees fit within the general categories of the appropriation bill. It is only when glaring abuses and inefficiencies are uncovered, as, for instance, in our foreign aid to Laos, that the question of the substance of our foreign aid policy is raised in public, and even then it is raised in the negative terms of remedying the abuses and inefficiencies rather than in the positive terms of what the purposes of our foreign aid policy are supposed to be and what kinds of measures are best calculated to serve these purposes.

From the *American Political Science Review*, June, 1962. Copyright by Public Affairs Conference Center of the University of Chicago–Rand McNally & Co.

It is pointless even to raise the question as to whether or not the United States ought to have a policy of foreign aid. To ask that question is as pointless as to ask whether or not the United States ought to have a foreign political or military policy, for the United States has interests abroad which cannot be supported by military means and which can only in part be appropriately supported by the traditional methods of diplomacy. If foreign aid does not support them, they will not be supported at all. Thus, the question, What kind of policy of foreign aid ought we to have? cannot be evaded. As it has developed in recent years, our policy of foreign aid is fundamentally weak. It has been conceived as a self-sufficient technical enterprise, covering a multitude of disparate objectives and activities, responding haphazardly to all kinds of demands, sound and unsound, unrelated or only by accident related to the political purposes of our foreign policy. The United States has been in the business of foreign aid for more than a decade, but it has yet to develop an intelligible theory of foreign aid that could provide standards of judgment for both the supporters and opponents of a particular measure.

The first prerequisite for the development of a viable philosophy of foreign aid is the recognition of the diversity of policies that go by that name. Six such policies can be distinguished which have only one thing in common: the transfer of money and economic services from one nation to another. They are humanitarian foreign aid, subsistence foreign aid, military foreign aid, bribery, prestige foreign aid, and foreign aid for economic development.

Of these different types of foreign aid, only humanitarian foreign aid is per se non-political. The aid which governments have traditionally extended to each other in case of natural disasters, such as floods, famines, and epidemics, falls in that category. So do the services, especially in the fields of medicine and agriculture, which private organizations, such as churches and foundations, have traditionally provided in Asia, Africa, and Latin America. While humanitarian aid is per se non-political, it can indeed perform a political function when it operates within a political context. The foreign aid private organizations provide will be attributed for better or for worse to their respective governments in so far as humanitarian aid emanating from a foreign country is recognized by the recipient country to perform a political function. Thus the agricultural aid which the Rockefeller Foundation has provided for many years to certain Latin American countries is likely to take on under contemporary conditions a political function which it did not perform previously. The same has been true from the beginning of the work the Ford Foundation has been doing in India. By the same token, humanitarian aid extended by a government may have political effects.

Subsistence foreign aid is extended to governments, such as those of Jordan and Libya, which do not command the resources to maintain minimal public services. The giving nation makes up the deficit in the budget of the recipient nation. Subsistence foreign aid is akin to the humanitarian type in that it seeks to prevent the breakdown of order and the disintegration of organized society itself. It performs the political function of maintaining the status quo. It maintains it without, as a rule, increasing its viability. Where there is a political alternative to an unviable regime, subsistence foreign aid diminishes its chances of materializing.

Bribes proffered by one government to another for political advantage were until the beginning of the nineteenth century an integral part of the armory of diplomacy. No statesman hesitated to acknowledge the giving and accepting of bribes. Thus it was proper and common for a government to pay the foreign minister or ambassador of another country a pension, that is, a bribe. Lord Robert Cecil, the Minister of Elizabeth, received one from Spain. Sir Henry Wotton, British ambassador to Venice in the seventeenth century, accepted one from Savoy while applying for one from Spain. The documents which the French revolutionary government published in 1793 show that France subsidized Austrian statesmen between 1757 and 1769 to the tune of 82,652,479 livres, with the Austrian Chancellor Kaunitz receiving 100,000. Nor was it regarded as any less proper or less usual for a government to compensate foreign statesmen for their co-operation in the conclusion of treaties. In 1716, the French Cardinal Dubois offered the British Minister Stanhope 600,000 livres for an alliance with France. He reported that Stanhope, while not accepting the proposition at that time, "listened graciously without being displeased." After the conclusion of the Treaty of Basel of 1795, by virtue of which Prussia withdrew from the war against France, the Prussian Minister Hardenberg received from the French government valuables worth 30,000 francs and complained of the insignificance of the gift. In 1801, the Margrave of Baden spent 500,000 francs in the form of "diplomatic presents," of which the French Foreign Minister Talleyrand received 150,000. It was originally intended to give him only 100,000, but the amount was increased after it had become known that he had received from Prussia a snuffbox worth 66,000 francs as well as 100,000 francs in cash. The Prussian Ambassador in Paris summed up well the main rule of this game when he reported to his government in 1802: "Experience has taught everybody who is here on diplomatic business that one ought never to give anything before the deal is definitely closed, but it has only proved that the allurement of gain will often work wonders."

Much of what goes by the name of foreign aid today is in the nature of such bribes. The transfer of money and services from one government to another performs here the function of a price paid by the former to the latter for political services rendered or to be rendered by the latter to the former. These bribes differ from the traditional ones, of which we have given examples above, in two respects: they are justified primarily in terms of foreign aid for economic development, and money and services are transferred through elaborate machinery fashioned for genuine economic aid. In consequence, these bribes are a less effective means for the purpose of purchasing political favors than were the traditional ones.

The compulsion of substituting for the traditional businesslike transmission of bribes the pretense and elaborate machinery of foreign aid for economic development results from a climate of opinion which accepts as universally valid the proposition that the highly developed industrial nations have an obligation to transfer money and services to underdeveloped nations for the purpose of economic development. Thus, aside from humanitarian and military foreign aid, the only kind of transfer of money and services which seems to be legitimate is the one made for the purpose of economic development. Economic development has become an ideology by which the transfer of money and services from one government to another is rationalized and justified. However, the present climate of opinion assumes not only that highly developed industrial nations have an obligation to extend foreign aid for economic development to underdeveloped nations, but also that, as a universally valid proposition, economic development can actually be promoted through such transfer of money and services. Thus economic development as an ideology requires machinery that makes plausible the assumption of the efficacy of the transfer of money and services for the purpose of economic development. In contrast to most political ideologies, which operate only on the verbal level and whose effects remain within the realm of ideas, this political ideology, in order to be plausible, requires an elaborate apparatus serving as an instrument for a policy of make-believe. The government of nation A, trying to buy political advantage from the government of nation B for, say, the price of 20 million dollars, not only must pretend, but also must act out in elaborate fashion the pretense, that what it is actually doing is giving aid for economic development to the government of nation B.

This practice of giving bribes as though they were contributions to economic development creates of necessity expectations, in the giver and the recipient, which are bound to be disappointed. Old-fashioned bribery is a straightforward transaction; services are to be rendered at a price, and both sides know what to expect. Bribery disguised as foreign aid for economic development makes of giver and recipient actors in a play which in the end they can no longer distinguish from reality. In consequence, both expect results in terms of economic development which in the nature of things cannot be forthcoming. Thus both are bound to be disappointed, the giver blaming the recipient for his inefficiency and the recipient accusing the giver of stinginess and asking for more. The ideology, taken for reality, gets in the way of the original purpose of the transaction, and neither side believes that it has received what it is entitled to.

Until recently, military aid took the lion's share of the foreign aid programs of the United States. A shift in favor of non-military aid occurred during the 1961 session of Congress when over 2 billion dollars was appropriated for military aid, while the total voted for all the other foreign aid programs amounted to a little over 3 billion dollars. To the latter amount must be added approximately 1 billion dollars from the proceeds of the sale of agricultural commodities for foreign currencies to be used for economic grants and loans to purchasing governments.

Foreign aid for military purposes is a traditional way by which nations buttress their alliances. Rome used to receive tribute from its allies for the military protection it provided. The seventeenth and eighteenth centuries are the classic period of military subsidies, by which Great Britain in particular endeavored to increase the military strength of her continental allies. Glancing through the treaties of alliance of that period, one is struck by the meticulous precision with which obligations to furnish troops, equipment, logistic support, food, money, and the like were defined. The loans which France extended to Russia after the conclusion of the alliance between the two nations in 1894 fall in the same category. This traditional military aid can be understood as a division of labor between two allies who pool their resources, one supplying money, matériel, and training, the other providing primarily manpower.

In contrast to traditional practice, military aid is today not only extended to allies but also to certain uncommitted nations. The military aid the United States has been giving to Yugoslavia is a case in point. The purpose is here not so much military as political. It seeks political advantage in exchange for military aid. It obligates the recipient toward the giver. The latter expects the former to abstain from a political course which might put in jeopardy the continuation of military aid. Military aid is here really in the nature of a bribe.

What appears as military aid may also be actually in the nature of prestige aid, to be discussed below. The provision of jet fighters and other modern weapons for certain underdeveloped nations can obviously perform no genuine military function. It increases the prestige of the recipient nation both at home and abroad. Being in the possession of some of the more spectacular instruments of modern warfare, a nation can at least enjoy the illusion of having become a modern military power.

As bribery appears today in the guise of aid for economic development, so does aid for economic development appear in the guise of military assistance. In the session of 1961, Congress appropriated, for instance, 425 million dollars for economic aid to strategic areas; and it is likely that in the total appropriations for military aid, in excess of 2 billion dollars, other items of economic aid are hidden. This mode of operation results from the reluctance of Congress to vote large amounts for economic aid in contrast to its readiness to vote virtually any amount requested for military purposes. Yet the purposes of aid for economic development are likely to suffer when they are disguised as military assistance, as we saw the purposes of bribery to suffer when disguised as aid for economic development. The military context within which such aid is bound to operate, even though its direct administration be in the hands of the civilian authorities, is likely to deflect such aid from its genuine purposes. More particularly, it strengthens the ever present tendency to subordinate the requirements of aid for economic development to military considerations.

Prestige aid has this in common with modern bribes that its true purpose, too, is concealed by the ostensible purpose of economic development. The unprofitable or idle steel mill, the highway without traffic and leading nowhere, the airline operating with foreign personnel and at a loss but under the flag of the recipient country—these ostensibly serve the purposes of economic development and under different circumstances could do so. Actually, however, they perform no positive economic function. They owe their existence to the penchant, prevalent in many underdeveloped nations, for what might be called "conspicuous industrialization," an industrialization spectacular in producing symbols of, and monuments to, industrial advancement rather than satisfying the objective economic needs of the country. This tendency sheds an illuminating light upon the nature of what is generally referred to as the "revolution of rising expectations."

We are inclined to assume that the revolution of rising expectations, that is, the urgent desire to improve one's lot by means of modern technology and industry, is a well-nigh universal trend in Asia, Africa, and Latin America. Actually, however, this trend is universal only in the sense that virtually all underdeveloped nations want to appear as having achieved industrialization, while only a fraction of the population, and frequently only small elite groups within it, seek the social and economic benefits of industrialization and are willing to take the measures necessary to achieve them. For many of the underdeveloped nations the steel mill, the highway, the airline, the modern weapons, perform a function that is not primarily economic or military but psychological and political. They are sought as symbols and monuments of modernity and power. They perform a function similar to that which the cathedral performed for the medieval city and the feudal castle or the monarch's palace for the absolute state. Nehru is reported to have said, when he showed Chou En-lai a new dam: "It is in these temples that I worship." And the more underdeveloped and less viable a nation is, the greater is likely to be its urge to prove to itself and to the world through the results of prestige aid that it, too, has arrived in the mid-twentieth century.

The advantage for the giver of prestige aid is threefold. He may receive specific political advantages in return for the provision of aid, very much after the model of the advantage received in return for a bribe. The spectacular character of prestige aid establishes a patent relationship between the generosity of the giver and the increased prestige of the recipient. The giver's prestige is enhanced, as it were, by the increase of the recipient's prestige. Finally, prestige aid comes relatively cheap. A limited commitment of resources in the form of a spectacular but economically useless symbol of modernity may bring disproportionate political dividends.

The giver of foreign aid must perform the task of distinguishing between prestige aid and aid for economic development. It is in the nature of prestige aid that it is justified by the prospective recipient in terms of genuine economic development. The prospective giver, unaware of the distinction, is likely to fall into one of two errors. by mistaking prestige aid for aid for economic development, he will either waste human and material resources in support of the latter, while the purpose of prestige aid could have been achieved much more simply and cheaply. Or else he will reject out of hand a request for prestige aid because it cannot be justified in terms of economic development, and may thereby forego political advantages which he could have gained from the provision of the prestige aid requested. The classic example of this error is the American rejection of the Afghan request for paving of the streets of Kabul as economically unsound. It may be noted in passing that the Soviet Union, pursuing a politically oriented policy of foreign aid, paved the streets of Kabul, even though that measure had no bearing upon the economic development of Afghanistan.

None of the types of foreign aid discussed thus far poses theoretical questions of the first magnitude; rather, they raise issues for practical manipulation which can be successfully met by common sense tested by experience. Foreign aid for economic development has been the primary area for theoretical analysis and speculation, which has been mainly of an economic nature. Economic thought, true to its prevailing academic tradition, tends to look at foreign aid as though it were a self-sufficient technical enterprise to be achieved with the instruments, and judged by the standards, of pure economics. And since Western economic development, from the first industrial revolution onward, has been due to the formation of capital and the accumulation of technical knowledge, we have tended to assume that these two factors would by themselves provide the impetus for the economic development of the underdeveloped nations of Asia, Africa, and Latin America. This tendency has been powerfully supported by the spectacular success of the Marshall Plan, conceived and executed as a strictly economic measure for the provision of capital and technological know-how. Yet it is not always recognized that this success was made possible only by the fact that, in contrast to the underdeveloped nations of Asia, Africa, and Latin America, the recipients of Marshall aid were among the leading industrial nations of the world, whose economic systems were but temporarily in disarray.

The popular mind, on the other hand, and, through it, much of the practice of foreign aid have proceeded from certain unexamined assumptions, no less doubtful for being deeply embedded in the American folklore of politics. Thus the popular mind has established correlations between the infusion of capital and technological know-how into a primitive society and economic development, between economic development and social stability, between social stability and democratic institutions, between democratic institutions and a peaceful foreign policy. However attractive and reassuring these correlations may sound to American ears, they are borne out neither by the experiences we have had with our policies of foreign aid nor by general historic experience.

The first of these assumptions implies that underdevelopment is at least primarily the result of lack of capital and technological know-how. Underdevelopment is regarded as a kind of accident or at worst as a kind of deficiency disease, which can be taken care of through the infusion of capital and technological know-how. Yet a nation may suffer from deficiencies, some natural and insuperable, others social and remediable, which no amount of capital and technological know-how supplied from the outside can cure. The poverty of natural resources may be such as to make economic development impossible. Nations such as Jordan, Libya, and Somalia are in all likelihood permanently incapable of economic development for that reason. Many of the nations which are the permanent recipients of subsistence aid are likely to fall in the same category.

A nation may also suffer from human deficiencies which preclude economic development. As there are individuals whose qualities of character and level of intelligence make it impossible for them to take advantage of economic opportunities, so are there nations similarly handicapped. To put it bluntly: as there are bums and beggars, so are there bum and beggar nations. They may be the recipients of charity, but short of a miraculous transformation of their collective intelligence and character, what they receive from the outside is not likely to be used for economic development.

Some nations are deficient in the specific kind of character and intelligence which goes into the making of a modern economic system, but their general qualities of character and level of intelligence qualify them for the necessary transformation. They are, to use a rough analogy, in a medieval stage of cultural development, still awaiting the equivalent of the moral and intellectual revolutions which in the sixteenth and seventeenth centuries created the cultural preconditions for the economic development of the West. Yet we tend to take the existence of these preconditions for granted, forgetting that without the secularization and rationalization of Western thought and society the industrialization of the West would not have been possible.

A civilization such as the Burmese, which deprecates success in this world because it stands in the way of success in the other world, puts a cultural obstacle in the path of industrial development, which foreign aid by itself cannot overcome. Saving—that is, the preservation of capital or goods for future use—has become so integral a part of our economic thought and action that it is hard for us to realize that there are hundreds of millions of people in the under-developed areas of the world who are oblivious of this mode of operation, which is indispensable to economic development. We have come to consider the productive enterprise as a continuum in which the individual owner or manager has a personal stake. Yet in many underdeveloped areas the productive enterprise is regarded primarily as an object for financial exploitation, to be discarded when it has performed its function of bringing the temporary owner a large financial return in the shortest possible time. Foreign aid poured into such a precapitalistic and even prerational mold is not likely to transform the mold, but rather it will be forced by the mold into channels serving the interests of a precapitalistic or prerational society.

The economic interests which stand in the way of foreign aid being used for economic development are typically tied in with the distribution of political power in underdeveloped societies. The ruling groups in these societies derive their political power in good measure from the economic status quo. The ownership and control of arable land, in particular, is in many of the underdeveloped societies the foundation of political power. Land reform and industrialization are in consequence an attack upon the political status quo. In the measure that they are successful, they are bound to affect drastically the distribution of economic and political power. Yet the beneficiaries of both the economic and political status quo are the typical recipients of foreign aid given for the purpose of changing the status quo! Their use of foreign aid for this purpose requires a readiness for self-sacrifice and a sense of social responsibility which few ruling groups have shown throughout history. Foreign aid proffered under such circumstances is likely to fail in its purpose of economic development and, as a bribe to the ruling group, strengthen the economic and political status quo. It is likely to accentuate unsolved social and political problems rather than bring them closer to solution. A team of efficiency experts and public accountants might well have improved the operations of the Al Capone gang; yet by doing so, it would have aggravated the social and political evils which the operations of that gang brought forth.

Preface to a Political Theory of Foreign Aid

Given this likely resistance of the ruling group to economic development, foreign aid requires drastic political change as a precondition for its success. Foreign aid must go hand in hand with political change, either voluntarily induced from within or brought about through pressure from without. The latter alternative faces the giving nation with a dual dilemma. On the one hand, to give foreign aid for economic development without stipulating conditions that maximize the chances for success maximizes the chances for failure. On the other hand, to give aid "with strings" arouses xenophobic suspicions and nationalistic resentments, to be exploited both by the defenders of the status quo and the promoters of Communist revolution. Furthermore, once one has decided upon bringing about political change in opposition to the ruling group, one must identify the alternative group as the instrument of political change. Sometimes, one may have a choice among different alternative groups equally unattractive. Sometimes, and not infrequently, the absence of any alternative group either forces one to create one or else leaves one no choice. Finally, the promotion of drastic social change on the part of the giving nation creates the precondition for economic development, but it also conjures up the specter of uncontrollable revolution.

In many of the underdeveloped nations, peace and order are maintained only through the ruthless use of the monopoly of violence by the ruling group. Determined and skilful foreign intervention may not find it hard to weaken the power of the ruling group or to remove it from power altogether. While it may be able to control events up to this point, that is, to instigate drastic reform and revolution, it may well be unable to control the course of the revolution itself. More particularly, a democratic nation, such as the United States, is greatly handicapped in competing with Communists in the control of revolution. The revolution may start, as did the Cuban revolution, under the democratic auspices of the unorganized masses dedicated to social reform and supported by the United States, and may in the course of its development be taken over by the highly organized and disciplined Communist minority, the only organized and disciplined revolutionary group available.

Successful foreign aid for economic development may have similarly unsettling political results. Economic development, especially by way of industrialization, is likely to disrupt the social fabric of the underdeveloped nation. By creating an urban industrial proletariat, it loosens and destroys the social nexus of family, village, and tribe, in which the individual had found himself secure. And it will not be able, at least not right away, to provide a substitute for this lost social world. The vacuum thus created will be filled by social unrest and political agitation. Furthermore, it is not the downtrodden masses living in a static world of unrelieved misery which are the likely protagonists of revolution, but rather those groups that have begun to rise in the social and economic scale but not enough to satisfy their aroused expectations. Thus, economic development is bound to disturb not only the economic status quo but, through it, the political status quo as well. If the change is drastic enough, the social and political effects of economic development may well amount to a prerevolutionary or revolutionary situation. And while the United States may have started the revolutionary process, it will again be a moot question under whose auspices it will be ended.

The United States faces a number of formidable handicaps in the performance of the task of controlling social and political change in the underdeveloped nations either as a prerequisite for, or a result of, foreign aid for economic development. First of all, the United States is a Western capitalistic nation. It is a conservative power both domestically and internationally, and must so appear particularly to the underdeveloped nations. Both in its civilization and social and economic structure, it belongs to that complex of nations which until recently were able to hold Africa, Latin America, and the outlying areas of Asia in a condition of colonial or semicolonial dependency. It has military alliances with these nations, and while it has generally shunned and even opposed outright colonial policies, it has actively and successfully participated in the semicolonial exploitation of backward nations. Thus the resentment against the former colonial powers attaches also to it, and its policies of foreign aid are frequently suspected as serving in disguise the traditional ends of colonialism.

Furthermore, the United States, by dint of its pluralistic political philosophy and social system, cannot bring to the backward nations of the world a simple message of salvation, supported first by dedicated and disciplined revolutionary minorities and then by totalitarian control. In the nature of things the advantage lies here with the Communist powers. They are, as it were, specialists in exploiting a revolutionary situation, which is bound to cause us embarrassment, for while the Communists are able to direct a revolution into the desired channels through their use of a disciplined minority, we, even if we are convinced that revolution is inevitable and therefore do not oppose it, tend to look with misgivings upon it since we cannot control the direction it will take.

The Communist powers have still another advantage over the United States in that their problems and achievements are more meaningful, at least on the surface, to the underdeveloped nations than are ours. The Soviet Union has achieved, and Communist China attempts to achieve, what the more enlightened underdeveloped nations seek: a drastic increase in the standard of living through rapid industrialization. The Communist powers use totalitarian control as their instrument and Communist doctrine as rationalization and justification. Seeking the same results, the underdeveloped nations cannot help being attracted by the methods which brought these results about elsewhere. In contrast, the slow process, stretching over centuries, through which the nations of the West achieved a high standard of living through industrialization must appeal much less to them. That appeal is lessened even more by the economic processes of the free market and the political processes of liberal democracy through which in large measure Western industrialization was achieved, for these processes require a degree of moral restraint and economic and political sophistication which are largely absent in the underdeveloped nations. The simple and crude methods of totalitarianism must appear to them much more congenial.

Thus we arrive at the disconcerting conclusion that successful foreign aid for economic development can be counterproductive if the social and political goal of the giving nation is the recipient's social and political stability. In some cases at least, the failure of American aid for economic development may have been a blessing in disguise in that it did not disturb a stable status quo whose continuing stability was our main interest. Such aid, intended for economic development, actually performs the function either of a bribe or of prestige aid. Here again, however, these functions are likely to be impaired by disappointed expectations of economic development of the giving and the recipient nation.

It is equally a moot question whether or not successful foreign aid for economic development is conducive to the development of democratic institutions and practices. This is obviously not the place to raise *ex professo* the issue of the relationship between democracy and economic development. But that no necessary relationship exists between the two, recent history has made clear. The most impressive example is the Soviet Union. Its rapid economic development has gone hand in hand with totalitarian government, and a case could well be made for the proposition that the former would have been impossible without the latter. It is more likely than not that where the intellectual and moral preconditions for economic development are lacking in the population at large and are present only in a small elite, as they are in many of the underdeveloped nations, the imposition of the will of that small minority upon the majority of the population is not only a precondition for the start of economic development but also for sustained economic growth.

As concerns the promotion of a peaceful foreign policy, economic development is likely to be counterproductive, provided a political incentive for a belligerent foreign policy is present. The contrary conclusion derives from the popular, yet totally unfounded, assumption that "poor" nations make war on "rich" nations for economic advantage and that rich nations are by definition peaceful because they have what they want. In truth, of course, most wars have been fought not for economic but for political advantage, and, particularly under modern technological conditions, only economically advanced nations are capable of waging modern war. We did not consider the Soviet Union a military threat as long as it was economically underdeveloped; it became such a threat at the very moment its economic development had transformed it into a modern industrial power. Similarly, Communist China today is only a potential military threat by virtue of its economic potential, both of which are likely to be activated by economic development.

Foreign aid for economic development, then, has a very much smaller range of potentially successful operation than is generally believed, and its success depends in good measure not so much upon its soundness in strictly economic terms as upon intellectual, moral, and political preconditions, which are not susceptible to economic manipulation—if they are susceptible to manipulation from the outside at all. Furthermore, the political results of successful foreign aid for economic development may be either unpredictable or counterproductive in terms of the political goals of the giving nation; in any event, they are in large measure uncontrollable. Foreign aid proffered and accepted for purposes of economic development may turn out to be something different from what it was intended to be if it is not oriented toward the political conditions within which it must operate. Most likely, it will turn out to be a bribe or prestige aid, or else a total waste. To do too much may here be as great a risk as to do too little, and "masterly inactivity" may sometimes be the better part of wisdom.

The major conclusions for policy to be drawn from this analysis are three: the requirement of identifying each concrete situation in the light of the six different types of foreign aid and of choosing the quantity and quality of foreign aid appropriate to the situation; the requirement of attuning, within the same concrete situation, different types of foreign aid to each other in view of the over-all goals of foreign policy; and the requirement of dealing with foreign aid as an integral part of political policy.

The task of identifying concrete situations in view of the type of foreign aid appropriate to them is a task for country and area experts to perform. Can this country not survive without foreign aid? Is its government likely to exchange political advantages for economic favors? Would our military interests be served by the strengthening of this nation's military forces? Does this country provide the non-economic preconditions for economic development to be supported by foreign aid? Are our political interests likely to be served by giving this nation foreign aid for purposes of prestige? Can a case be made for foreign aid in order to alleviate human suffering? What kind and quantity of foreign aid is necessary and sufficient to achieve the desired result? To answer these questions correctly demands first of all a thorough and intimate knowledge and understanding of the total situation in a particular country. But it also requires political and economic judgment of a very high order, and it does so in two different areas. On the one hand, it is necessary to anticipate the susceptibility of the country to different kinds of foreign aid and their effects upon the country. On the other hand, when this task has been performed, it is then necessary to select from a great number of possible measures of foreign aid those which are most appropriate to the situation and, hence, most likely to succeed.

In most situations, however, the task is not that simple. Typically, an underdeveloped country will present a number of situations calling for different types of foreign aid to be given simultaneously. One type of foreign aid given without regard for the effects it may have upon another type risks getting in the way of the latter. One of the most conspicuous weaknesses of our past foreign aid policies has been the disregard of the effect different types of foreign aid have upon each other. Bribes given to the ruling group, for instance, are bound to strengthen the political and economic status quo. Military aid is bound to have an impact upon the distribution of political power within the receiving country; it can also have a deleterious effect upon the economic system, for instance, by increasing inflationary pressures. Similarly, the effect of subsistence foreign aid is bound to be the support of the status quo in all its aspects. In so far as the giving nation desires these effects or can afford to be indifferent to them, they obviously do not matter in terms of its over-all objectives. But in so far as the giving nation has embarked upon a policy of foreign aid for economic development which requires changes in the political and economic status quo, the other foreign aid policies are counterproductive in terms of economic development, for they strengthen the very factors which stand in its way.

This problem is particularly acute in the relations between prestige aid and aid for economic development. The giving nation may seek quick political results and use prestige aid for that purpose; yet it may also have an interest in the economic development of the recipient country, the benefits of which are likely to appear only in the distant future. Prestige aid is at best only by accident relevant to economic development; it is more often irrelevant to it, or it may actually impede it. What kind of foreign aid is the giving country to choose? If it chooses a combination of both, it must take care to choose an innocuous kind of prestige aid and to promote economic development in such a way that the benefits are not too long in coming. Afghanistan, as was pointed out earlier, is the classic example of this dilemma. The Soviet Union, by paving the streets of Kabul, chose a kind of prestige aid that is irrelevant to economic development. The United States, by building a hydroelectric dam in a remote part of the country, the very existence of which is unknown to most Afghans and the benefits of which will not appear for years to come, chose economic development.

It follows, then, from the very political orientation of foreign aid that its effect upon the prestige of the giving nation must always be in the minds of the formulators and executors of foreign aid policies. In particular, foreign aid for economic development whose benefits to the recipient country are immediate and patent is a more potent political weapon than foreign aid whose benefits are obscure and lie far in the future. Furthermore, the political effects of foreign aid are lost if its foreign source is not obvious to the recipients; for it is not aid as such or its beneficial results that creates political loyalties on the part of the recipient, but the positive relationship that the mind of the recipient establishes between the aid and its beneficial results, on the one hand, and the political philosophy, the political system, and the political objectives of the giver, on the other. That is to say, if the recipient continues to disapprove of the political philosophy, system, and objectives of the giver, despite the aid he has received, the political effects of the aid are lost. The same is true if he remains unconvinced that the aid received is but a natural, if not invitable, manifestation of the political philosophy, system, and objectives of the giver. Foreign aid remains politically ineffectual as long as the recipient says either "aid is good, but the politics of the giver are bad"; or "aid is good, but the politics of the giver—good, bad, or indifferent—have nothing to do with it." In order to be able to establish a positive psychological relationship between giver and recipient, the procedures through which aid is given, and the subject matter to which it is applied, must lend themselves to the creation of a connection between aid and the politics of the giver which reflects credit upon the latter.

The problem of foreign aid is insoluble if it is considered as a self-sufficient technical enterprise of a primarily economic nature. It is soluble only if it is considered an integral part of the political policies of the giving country, which must be devised in view of the political conditions—and the effects upon the political situation—in the receiving country. In this respect, a policy of foreign aid is no different from diplomatic or military policy or propaganda. They are all weapons in the political armory of the nation. As military policy is too important a matter to be left to the generals, so is foreign aid too important a matter to be left to the economists. The expertise of the economist must analyze certain facts, devise certain means, and perform certain functions of manipulation for foreign aid. Yet the formulation and over-all execution of foreign aid policy is a political function. It must be performed by the political expert.

It follows from the political nature of foreign aid that it is not a science but an art. What that art requires by way of mental predisposition is political sensitivity to the interrelationship among the facts, present and future, and ends and means. The requirements by way of mental activity are twofold. It requires first of all a discriminatory judgment of facts, ends, and means and their effects upon each other. However, an analysis of the situation in the recipient country and, more particularly, its projection into the future and the conclusions from the analysis in terms of policy can only in part be arrived at through rational deduction from ascertainable facts. When all the facts have been ascertained, duly analyzed, and conclusions drawn from them, the final judgments and decisions can be derived only from subtle and sophisticated hunches. The best the formulator and executor of a policy of foreign aid can do is to maximize the chances that his hunches turn out to be right. Here as elsewhere in the formulation and conduct of foreign policy, the intuition of the statesman rather than the knowledge of the expert will carry the day.

29 What Can the United States Do To Strengthen the United Nations?

In order to strengthen the United Nations, the United States must give correct answers to three questions. First, What is the United Nations? Second, What can the United Nations do? Third, How can the United Nations continue to be a part of the aspirations and the policies of America and the free world?

The United Nations is not an alternative to power politics, that is, to the kind of foreign policy which nations have traditionally pursued. Rather it is a new instrument for these traditional policies, a forum on which the old conflicts among nations are fought out, more or less effectively, more or less peacefully, as the case may be. In other words, the United Nations is a club in which all kinds of members can pursue all kinds of policies, a stage on which the drama of international politics is played again in a new setting. The setting is new, but the plot is as old as history.

In order to understand what the United Nations can do, it is necessary to realize that the U.N., as it exists today, is essentially different from what it was intended to be according to its Charter. The Charter bases the United Nations upon the continuing unity of the great powers, which were supposed to be identical with the permanent members of the Security Council. The Charter assumes that unity; it cannot itself create it. The Charter makes the harmonious co-operation of the great powers the very cornerstone of the United Nations and intends the great powers to gather to exercise a limited world government over the rest of the world.

The ever widening rift between East and West has prevented this intention of the Charter from being realized. Not harmony but permanent discord among its most powerful members is the overriding fact which has paralyzed from the very outset the United Nations as a political organization; and the U.N. possesses no instrumentalities of its own to remedy this discord. The remedy to the

From the *Foreign Policy Bulletin*, September 15, 1954.

East-West conflict must be sought in the traditional methods of diplomatic negotiations, accommodation, and compromise. The Charter itself refers at different places to the successful operation of diplomacy as the essential precondition for its own success. There is, then, foreshadowed in the Charter what is obvious from the very structure of international politics and what has become routine procedure in the foreign offices: the implementation of foreign policy by using alternately or simultaneously both the traditional methods of diplomacy and the new procedures of the United Nations.

This frustration of the original intentions of the Charter and the intimate connection between the new instrumentalities of the United Nations and the traditional conflicting interests of the great powers has caused a transformation of the U.N. It is now an organization which performs political functions essentially different from those which the Charter intends it to perform. Within the framework of the Charter a new United Nations has arisen, a child not of the unity of the great powers but of their discord, using not the Security Council but the General Assembly as its main vehicle. It is composed of at least two-thirds of the members of the United Nations, grouped around the United States and the other members of the Western alliance, as its hard core.

This new and living United Nations, which has arisen within the dead, or at best sleeping, body of the old, has become one of the main instruments with which the United States and its allies fight the Cold War. To strengthen the United Nations for that task is as important for the United States as it is to keep the traditional instruments of its diplomacy strong. Yet the United Nations will be strengthened only if it is not burdened with tasks which it was never intended to perform and which, more particularly, it cannot at present perform. To "bypass" the United Nations, then, is not necessarily a vice but may well be a virtue if the traditional methods chosen are more likely to achieve the intended result. Thus the United States must approach the United Nations in a pragmatic spirit, using it for purposes to which its methods seem to be best adapted and refraining from its use if such use would do more harm than good.

However, the strength of the United Nations is, in a still more profound sense, the strength of the United States. In an age dominated by two superpowers and threatened with atomic destruction, a national policy has a chance to prevail only if it defines itself in terms transcending the national interest of a particular nation and comprising the national interests of those nations whose support it seeks. The new United Nations has become a repository of those interests which the United States has in common with the free nations of the world. By defining these interests in terms of the United Nations and channeling the policies serving these interests through the United Nations, the United States will strengthen the free world, the United Nations, and itself.

30 *Is the United Nations in Our National Interest?*

To ask whether the United Nations is in the national interest of the United States is like asking whether diplomatic negotiations or military alliances are in the national interest of the United States. The answer is bound to be that sometimes they are and sometimes they are not. The U.N., seen from the vantage point of the United States, is as much an instrument of American foreign policy as are diplomatic negotiations and alliances, and these instruments must be continuously subjected to the pragmatic test of their usefulness for the national purposes which the United States happens to pursue at the moment. It is no more sensible to approve the U.N. per se as "good" for the United States, or to condemn it as "bad," than it would be to pass such an a priori judgment upon any other instrumentality of United States foreign policy.

While circumstances must determine the usefulness of the United Nations for the United States, the intrinsic capabilities of the organization set limits to the circumstances. Whether to use a knife or a fork depends on circumstances, but the fact that knives and forks are suited only for certain purposes and not for others limits from the outset the choice of circumstances. What, then, are the purposes the U.N. is capable of serving, and what are the circumstances under which the United States might profitably avail itself of its services?

The political purposes which the United Nations is able to serve, by virtue of its Charter and its political dynamics, are four: great-power government, General Assembly government, diplomatic negotiations, and propaganda. The Charter intends the U.N. to be a government of the great powers operating through the Security Council. But because the Cold War destroyed the unity of the great powers upon which this government was predicated, and the Security Council is paralyzed by the Russian veto, the General Assembly, through the "Uniting for Peace" resolution and extensive interpretations of the Charter, has taken over some of the governmental

From the *Foreign Policy Bulletin*, September 15, 1957.

functions the Security Council was supposed to discharge. Aside from performing these formal constitutional functions, the U.N. provides a neutral meeting ground for diplomats to carry on the traditional business of diplomacy. Finally, it offers a platform, visible to the world, on which statesmen can engage in the struggle for the minds of men.

Little need be said, in view of the national interest of the United States, about the first, third, and fourth of these functions. The importance of great power government lies at present in its existence as a legal possibility, of which both the United States and the Soviet Union might avail themselves at some future time with regard, for instance, to the paramount problem confronting both: the supranational control of atomic weapons. The United States has used the United Nations continuously to carry on diplomatic negotiations and propaganda. While one might have sometimes wished it had carried on more of the former and less of the latter, these activities do not raise a fundamental problem for the conduct of American foreign policy.

Such a problem, however, is posed by the second function: government by the General Assembly. During the first decade of the United Nations, it was the United States which benefited from that government because the United States could muster the necessary two-thirds majority in support of the policies it wished to carry out through the instrumentality of the General Assembly. The culmination of this period was the U.N. collective action in support of United States intervention in the Korean War. The admission of twenty-odd new members to the U.N. has drastically altered this distribution of voting strength. The United States and its allies can no longer rely on a two-thirds majority to support their policies, while the combined Afro-Asian and Soviet blocs can. In consequence, the relationship between the national interest of the United States and U.N. measures taken through the General Assembly has been reversed. The United States now faces the risk that such measures will run counter to its interests. Its best chance to protect its interests no longer lies in marshaling a two-thirds majority to their support, but rather in preventing such a majority from forming against them.

Consequently, the United States will in the future have to use considerable discrimination in deciding whether or not it serves its interests to have the General Assembly deal with a certain issue. It was exactly this lack of discrimination, strengthened by the popular tendency to assume for the processes of the United Nations a kind of natural superiority over national policies, which some observers found objectionable in the policies which the United States pursued during the Suez crisis of November, 1956. This tendency, while always wrong intellectually, was politically tolerable as long as the U.N. was likely to be a weapon in the hands of the United States rather than in those of its enemies. With that relationship reversed, a discriminating and unemotional intelligence is more necessary than ever in our approach to the United Nations.

31 *Threat to—and Hope for—the United Nations*

The United Nations is in crisis. Will it survive? The diseases from which it suffers are both congenital and acquired. The congenital disease is the insoluble contradiction between national sovereignty and an effective international organization. Its acquired debilities are the lack of political cohesion among the new nations and the hostility of the Soviet Union.

The U.N. has actually been threatened from its inception by the insistence of its members upon the preservation of their national sovereignty. National sovereignty demands that the governments of individual countries decide for themselves the domestic and international issues that concern them. An international organization, in order to be effective, requires a transfer of that power of ultimate decision, at least in certain matters, from the national to an international authority. The U.N. has tried to overcome this conflict by a kind of compromise. On the one hand, it stipulates the "sovereign equality" of all its members; on the other, it intends the Security Council to be an international government of the great powers.

In practice, however, the U.N. has never operated according to the intentions of its Charter. Its members, great and small, have tried to use it for the defense and promotion of their own interests and have bypassed it if their interests seemed to require it. Among the great powers, the Soviet Union and Gaullist France in particular have insisted upon the precedence of their interests and decisions over those of the U.N. The Soviet veto has paralyzed the Security Council, and when the Soviet Union proposed the "troika" system as a substitute for a single Secretary General, its purpose was nothing else than the injection of the principle of national sovereignty into the day-by-day operations of the Secretariat.

The paralysis of the Security Council led to the ascendancy of the General Assembly as the politically dominant agency of the U.N. Yet the increase in the U.N.'s membership in the past six years,

From the *New York Times Magazine*, October 29, 1961.

from the original 51 members to 101, has drastically changed the distribution of voting power in the General Assembly and has caused a paralysis similar to that in the Security Council. That increase has given the nations belonging to the so-called Afro-Asian bloc a key position within the Assembly. The Afro-Asian bloc comprises nearly half the membership of the U.N. Thus, if it were to vote in unison, it could exercise a veto on any resolutions adverse to its interests or else, by joining either the American or the Soviet bloc, become the core of a working two-thirds majority. In reality, however, the Afro-Asian bloc has but rarely voted as a unit; its vote has typically been split, with some members voting with the Western bloc, others with the Soviet, and a very considerable number abstaining. Consequently, in the matter of the ability of the U.N. to function politically through the General Assembly, the Afro-Asian bloc has thus far performed a negative function. By splintering its vote, it has strengthened the power of the Western and Soviet blocs to oppose the will of a simple majority with the veto of more than one-third of the membership. As a result, the Assembly has been incapable of passing resolutions calling for any action more decisive than investigations and good offices. At best, it has charged the Secretary General with the execution of policies defined in the vaguest terms, such as the restoration of peace and order in the Congo.

The impotence of the Assembly gives the Soviet Union the opportunity to launch a frontal attack against the U.N. as an effective international organization. It did so by attacking the late Mr. Hammarskjold personally and by trying to divest the office of the Secretary General of all power. The eminence which the office of the Secretary General gained in recent years is intimately related to the impotence of the General Assembly, just as the responsibility for action which the Assembly has taken on is intimately related to the impotence of the Security Council. Charged with responsibilities which either the Security Council or the Assembly should have performed but could not, the Secretary General became the initiator and executor of policies only tenuously related to the expressed will of the Charter and the collective organs of the U.N. He became the exponent of a conception of the U.N. as "a dynamic instrument of governments," to quote Mr. Hammarskjold's last annual report. In that capacity he was bound to come into conflict with the Soviet Union.

This conflict was inevitable because the long-term objectives of Soviet foreign policy are irreconcilable with the fundamental principles of the U.N. A political international organization such as the U.N. is necessarily identified with the defense of a particular status quo, to be changed only by peaceful and lawful means. The Soviet Union, on the other hand, is the great imperialistic power of our time, which seeks the radical transformation of the status quo by whatever means at hand. Thus the U.N. has been a stumbling block in the path of the Soviet Union's march toward world domination, both during its first decade when Western influence prevailed and under the stewardship of Mr. Hammarskjold. It was not surprising that the Soviet Union would attack Mr. Hammarskjold as it had attacked his predecessor, Trygve Lie.

However, the Soviet Union has today at its disposal two new weapons which allow it to attack not only the Secretary General personally but also his office and, through it, the U.N. itself as "a dynamic instrument of governments." One weapon is the new distribution of votes in the General Assembly, which gives the Soviet Union at the very least a chance to prevent the formation of a hostile two-thirds majority. The other and more potent weapon is the actual power of the Soviet Union. Fifteen and even ten years ago, the power which the U.N. could muster in defense of the status quo, with American power as its backbone was superior to the power of the Soviet Union. Today the forces of imperialism and of the status quo are more nearly in balance.

What the Soviet Union aims at is not so much to succeed to the predominance of Western influence, or to be able to use the U.N. for its own purposes, as to destroy the usefulness of the U.N. altogether. Soviet proposals for the reform of the Secretariat were designed to serve that purpose.

These are the dangers that today threaten the very existence of the U.N. as a working political organization. What are the factors of strength which stand in the way of these threats? They are essentially four: the past successes of the U.N., the interest of the new nations in survival, the interest of the United States and its allies in protecting and strengthening international order, and the interest of all nations in avoiding a nuclear war.

In spite of its weaknesses, the U.N. can boast of a number of successes, admittedly of minor significance, which testify both to its ability to act and to the desire of most or all of its members to have it act now and then. From 1947 to 1949 the U.N. aided effectively in the transition of Indonesia from colonial status to independence without a prolonged war. It contributed to the settlement of the Palestine war of 1948. It shortened the hostilities and helped in the pacification of the Egyptian-Israeli frontier in the Suez crisis of 1956. It participated in the defense of South Korea from 1950 to 1953. In 1948, it arranged for the emancipation of Libya, Somalia, and Eritrea from colonial status. In 1958, when Lebanon's independence seemed to be threatened from without, it sent observers. And it is currently engaged in what has turned out to be its most ambitious undertaking: the restoration of peace and order in the Congo.

The U.N., through its demonstrated ability to act in behalf of small nations, has become the natural ally of the new members composing the Afro-Asian bloc. Many of those nations are deficient in one or another of the prerequisites of statehood. They lack political, military, or economic viability. These deficiencies threaten them with anarchy. All of them, to a greater or lesser degree, are threatened by the new imperialism of the Soviet Union and Communist China. All are therefore in need of support from a source which cannot be suspected of colonialism, old or new. The U.N. is the only such source available to them. If it cannot support and defend them, many of the new nations will have no defense and support at all, or they will have them only at the price of their independence.

The United States and its allies have a vital interest in an effective U.N. for the same reason that the Soviet Union has an interest in destroying it. The U.N. is an obstacle, weak in actual performance but endowed with untried and intangible potentialities, that stands in the way of the Communist bloc. The United States and its allies are committed to the containment of that bloc. They want what the U.N. must want: the preservation and strengthening of international law and order and, more particularly, the protection of the territorial status quo from violent change. In that respect, the interests of the U.N. and of the United States and its allies coincide. Thus the latter cannot help defending and trying to strengthen the former as an effective organization. The U.N. is their natural ally, too.

However, there is an interest that all nations, big and small, Communist and non-Communist, have in common: the avoidance of a nuclear war. That interest overrides all the other purely national interests that oppose or support the U.N. The United Nations was created in 1945 for the purpose of ridding the world of the scourge of war, which then still meant conventional war. When the chips are down and the world faces the likelihood of self-destruction through nuclear war, desperate nations may well turn to the U.N. as a last resort for mediation, for a face-saving formula. And that contingency cannot be far from the minds of statesmen today.

In view of these divergent factors, what are the U.N.'s chances for surviving its present crisis? The answer to that question depends upon the qualities of the new Secretary General and upon the ability of the new nations to act in unison. It should not be forgotten that the active role the U.N. was able to play in recent years was predominantly due to the wisdom, skill, courage, and dedication of one man—Mr. Hammarskjold. By reason of his extraordinary qualities, he became the prime minister of the U.N., able to conceal for the time being the inherent impotence of its collective organs. Had an average man been chosen Secretary General in 1953, the U.N. might well have sunk into impotence right then and there. Thus its new Secretary General must have the courage and the skill of a Dag Hammarskjold.

The U.N. is confronted with another challenge, more important in the long run. That challenge is the fashioning of a new two-thirds majority in the General Assembly. The nucleus of such a majority is bound to be the new nations of Africa and Asia. Its purpose must be the avoidance of a nuclear war and the peaceful development of these nations in opposition to any latter-day imperialism. If the new members can accomplish this task, they will give the U.N. a new lease on life. By doing this, they will have taken a big step toward assuring their own survival. They will also have demonstrated to all the world that they have come of age politically.

Once the U.N. has thus recovered its ability to act, it can make three major contributions to the prevention of a nuclear war. It can limit the scope and shorten the duration of a local war, as it did in

Indonesia, the Congo, and twice in Palestine. For the great powers, it can provide opportunities for compromises and for face-saving formulas, those which enable two parties to a conflict to retreat from extreme positions without appearing to do so. Finally, and most important, it will have the opportunity to point the world in the direction of replacing national sovereignty with supranational decisions and institutions, for the fundamental argument in favor of the United Nations is the incompatibility of national sovereignty with the destructive potentialities of the nuclear age. Whether the U.N. will live up to that challenge or follow its predecessors into impotence will in good measure be decided by the current General Assembly.

32 *An Approach to the Summit*

The President of the United States visited Bonn, London, and Paris last August. The Premier of the Soviet Union and the Prime Minister of Italy visited the United States in September. The Chancellor of West Germany visited London in November and Paris in December. The Italian Prime Minister visited London in December. The President of the United States visited eleven nations in Asia, Africa, and Europe in December. A Western summit meeting took place in Paris in December. The President of Italy will visit the Soviet Union in January. The Soviet Premier will visit France in March. The President of France will visit London, Washington, and Ottawa in April. The President of the United States will visit the Soviet Union in May or June. And there will be an East-West summit meeting in April or May. What is the purpose of these constant movements of heads of state and prime ministers? What have they achieved thus far, and what are they likely to achieve? The declared purpose of all these travels is the improvement of the international climate and thereby, the strengthening of the foundations of peace. There can of course be no doubt that the international climate has in good measure been improved. To what extent this improvement has also increased the chances of preserving peace is moot; but this is the decisive question.

It must be noted at once that none of the substantive issues which have threatened world peace in the past have been affected at all by the visits that have taken place, and are not likely to be affected by most of those that will take place. More than a year has elapsed since Soviet Premier Nikita Khrushchev raised the issue of Berlin in the most acute form, but despite all the visits and diplomatic exchanges no common ground has been found on which the Soviet Union and the West could meet, nor has there even been developed a common Western policy. On the very question as to whether Berlin is a negotiable issue at all from the Western point of view, there

From the *New Leader*, January 4, 1960.

is no agreement between the United States and Great Britain, on the one hand, and France and West Germany, on the other.

Yet while summit and near-summit meetings have left the substantive issues threatening the peace of the world as they found them, the climate of opinion has changed. It has changed in the West because we tend to attribute to summit meetings per se a positive value, as though a summit meeting, regardless of what it achieves, is a good in itself. This positive attitude constitutes a complete reversal of the negative attitude which we have taken until recently not only toward summit meetings, but toward negotiations with the Soviet Union on any level. Both attitudes, I submit, are irrational.

There is nothing intrinsically good or bad in negotiations either at the summit or at a lower level. Negotiations are a means to an end. Under certain conditions, it is wise to negotiate; under others, it will do neither good nor harm; and under others still, negotiations will impair your cause. The wisdom of negotiations depends on three fundamental factors: the relative power position of the prospective negotiators, the susceptibility of the outstanding issues to a negotiated settlement, and the substantive policies to be pursued through negotiations. Ten years ago I argued against the mystique of not negotiating with the Soviet Union and especially against equating negotiations with appeasement. At that time I cited former Secretary of State Dean Acheson and Sir Winston Churchill in support of the proposition that the time was then ripe for a negotiated settlement.

Among the many speeches—more than forty—in which Sir Winston urged a negotiated settlement, those of January 23 and December 19, 1948, were especially noteworthy. In the former he said: "I will only venture now to say that there seems to me to be very real danger in going on drifting too long. I believe that the best chance of preventing a war is to bring matters to a head and come to a settlement with the Soviet Government before it is too late. This would imply that the Western democracies, who should, of course, seek unity among themselves at the earliest moment, would take the initiative in asking the Soviet for a settlement. . . . We may be absolutely sure that the present situation cannot last. . . . There are very grave dangers . . . in letting everything run on and pile up until something happens, and it passes, all of a sudden, out of your control." In the other speech he stated: "Finally, I wish to say one word . . . about the greatest topic of all which overhangs our minds, our relations with Soviet Russia. I have frequently advised that we should endeavor to reach a settlement with Russia on fundamental, outstanding questions before they have the atomic bomb as well as the Americans. I believe that in this resides the best hope of avoiding a third world war." I also cited Acheson's statement of February 12, 1950, that only those agreements are useful which "record an existing situation of fact . . . so it has been our basic policy to build situations which will extend the area of possible agreement, that is, to create strength instead of the weakness which exists in many quarters."

If Acheson and Churchill were right ten years ago, as I still believe they were, they are right now. Yet the application of their principles to the present situation must lead to the conclusion that since the beginning of the Cold War there has not been a worse moment for a negotiated settlement with the Soviet Union than the present. The Soviet press has pointed out correctly that we are no longer negotiating from a position of strength, which is another way of saying that we are negotiating from weakness, and it has congratulated us upon this reversal of our position, as it might well do in view of Soviet interests. The issues which by their very nature lent themselves to a negotiated settlement ten years ago are, with one exception, now less susceptible to such a settlement than they were then. And if we have a foreign policy—beyond the preservation of the status quo and of peace—whose objectives we intend to further through negotiations, the public is not aware of it.

It is significant that we have embarked upon the policy of summit meetings not because we felt strong enough to support our policies with promises and threats sufficient to induce the other side to make concessions, but because we were frightened by the power of the other side and by the uses to which it might put that power. The radical reversal, which has undoubtedly occurred in our attitude toward relations with the Soviet Union, is the direct result of the Khrushchev ultimatum of November, 1958. Khrushchev frightened us, and so we invited him to come here and set the sequence of summit and near-summit meetings into motion.

As we have embarked upon summit meetings out of a feeling of weakness, so shall we meet at the different summits and near-summits in a position of weakness; for now we are beginning to reap—and alas, we are seeing only the beginning of it—the fruits of a military policy which defines the resources of the nation not in terms of what the nation needs to survive and to succeed, but in terms of what it can afford in view of the overriding goal of a balanced budget. Thus we have concentrated the national effort upon an all-out atomic capability, mistaking what must remain one of the indispensable foundation stones of foreign policy for its day-by-day instrument.

Since the use of such a capability is manifestly suicidal and is plausible only as an act either of desperation or miscalculation, the threat to use it in support of a negotiating position is both insufficient and inadvisable. If you sit down at the negotiating table having nothing to threaten with but the H-bomb, the other side will either not take you seriously or else take you only too seriously. In the former case, you will negotiate from utter weakness; in the other, you will provoke your destruction. Thus it is exactly because we are strong only in the most irrational and least flexible weapon of modern war that we are negotiating from weakness and not from strength.

But what can we negotiate about, either from weakness or from strength? What are the issues which by their very nature lend themselves to a negotiated settlement? Not all issues outstanding between the United States and the U.S.S.R. are, in terms of their objective nature, susceptible to a negotiated settlement. Their nature is in good measure determined by the conflicting objectives of the nations concerned. This being so, it must be said—however paradoxical this may sound at first hearing—that the over-all relations between the United States and the U.S.S.R. were more susceptible to a negotiated settlement in the Stalinist period of Soviet foreign policy than they are now. For Stalin's objectives were limited; they were by and large identical with the traditional objectives of Russian imperialism. They could be pinpointed on a map and dealt with one by one. The methods of Stalinist foreign policy were also by and large in the tradition of Russian power politics. They consisted of military threats, diplomatic pressure, and subversion at the service of both.

Khrushchev's foreign policy departs radically from both the objectives and methods of his predecessor. His objectives are as unlimited as Lenin's were, and his methods are unorthodox both in Leninist and Stalinist terms. Khrushchev revives the universalism of Lenin in that he seeks the communization of the whole world. His main instrument is the prestige of the Soviet Union as the most powerful, most productive, and technologically most advanced nation on earth, which will establish its ascendancy by example, subversion, aid and trade. With Stalin it might have been possible to negotiate a settlement of some of the outstanding issues; for since his objectives were essentially limited and his methods essentially orthodox, there was room for maneuver, mutual concessions, and the give-and-take of compromise. But what can you talk about with a statesman whose declared objective is to bury you? What negotiable middle ground is there between your desire to stay alive and the other fellow's desire to put you six feet under? Shall we settle on three feet only? Obviously the fundamental issue which Khrushchev's new foreign policy poses is in its very nature not susceptible to negotiation. The very issue posed by Khrushchev allows of only two possible settlements: victory or defeat. Either we stay alive, or we perish.

Among the specific issues, only three seem a priori to be capable of a negotiated settlement: the interchange of ideas and persons, the modalities of the Western presence in Berlin, and atomic disarmament. Of these three issues, the first is by far the easiest to deal with; it is also politically the least consequential. It is being handled successfully through normal diplomatic channels and certainly requires no spectacular summit meetings for its continued improvement. That improvement is the result of increased Soviet self-confidence. The Soviet Government is no longer, and no longer needs to be, afraid of allowing foreigners and its own citizens to compare conditions in the U.S.S.R. with those in other countries. However, the increased exchanges of ideas and persons are irrelevant to the overall political relations between the United States and the Soviet Union and the overriding issue of war and peace itself. For even if ideas and persons were to be exchanged between the two countries on a massive scale, we would still be faced with the issue of whether

Khrushchev will actually bury us—that is to say, whether we will survive the competition with the Soviet Union.

The modalities of the Western presence in Berlin, in contrast to the Western right to be there, can be negotiated about. It should not be impossible to devise a formula which will give the Soviet Union a certain satisfaction without impairing the title to the Western presence. The danger is considerable, however, that, seduced by the virtue of negotiations per se and compelled by our military weakness, we shall step by step—first imperceptibly, then drastically—retreat from the substance of our position in Berlin. Spectacular meetings at the summit, inevitably arranged and conducted with an eye to the electorate at home, are more likely than not to produce grandiose but vague formulas which the weaker and less prudent party will eventually have reason to regret.

The outcome of the atomic disarmament negotiations, presently concentrating on the cessation of atomic tests, will provide ultimate proof as to whether a negotiated agreement with the Soviet Union can be reached on any outstanding issue. For nowhere else is the community of interests between the United States and the U.S.S.R. so perfectly clear or the problems to be settled by negotiations so narrowly defined. If the two countries cannot agree on the cessation of atomic tests, it is hard to see how they will be able to agree on anything else. Yet a negotiated settlement, at the summit or elsewhere, of this issue is up against a difficulty which goes to the substance of American foreign policy. It is a matter of record that the United States government is divided within itself over the desirability of reaching agreement on the cessation of atomic tests. The Defense Department and the Atomic Energy Commission have consistently supported the continuation of atomic tests, and the State Department has been in favor of an agreement to stop them. While the State Department seems to have been weakening in its support of what appears to be official American policy, the policy conflict within the government has never been authoritatively resolved. The President has committed himself in words to a policy seeking cessation, while leaving the implementation of the policy to the warring departments. And since obviously there can be no perfection in arrangements for the control and enforcement of such an agreement but only a weighing of different risks, the departments hostile to such an agreement have been able to sabotage it by calling for perfection where the search for perfection must be tantamount to no agreement at all. Summit meetings may temporarily conceal but they cannot cure this disease.

While in the field of atomic disarmament we are handicapped by an unresolved policy conflict within the government, we are handicapped in the other fields of foreign policy by the absence of a substantive policy altogether. What are we after in Europe, Africa, and Asia? What are we seeking to achieve, say, in Eastern Europe? In one word, what are we going to talk about in all those meetings at the summit and near-summit? What objectives are we going to pursue and what policies are we going to put to the test at those meetings? There is no positive answer to these questions beyond the preservation of the status quo by whatever policy requires the least effort and expenditure.

Such negative and sterile policies do not need the spectacular demonstrations of summit meetings; the ordinary diplomatic procedures are perfectly sufficient to carry them through. But in a sense, these summit meetings perform a dual function within the context of such negative and sterile policies. On the one hand, they create the illusion of initiative in foreign policy where there is only the initiative to travel. They create the illusion of substantive action where there is nothing but the bodily movements of statesmen. In other words, summit meetings, instead of being an instrument of substantive foreign policy, become a substitute for it. They become part and parcel of the public relations, the histrionic, the make-believe approach to foreign policy, with which we are so well acquainted. On the other hand, the policy of summit meetings, being the outgrowth of political and military weakness, provides through its very existence a justification for that weakness; for if it were true that mutual visits have by themselves improved United States–U.S.S.R. relations and that a multiplication of such visits and summit meetings were bound to improve them still more, we might indeed relax our efforts, since tensions have already been relaxed through the experience and expectation of summit meetings. This argument, tempting at home, threatens to become irresistible among our allies. Two examples of this trend toward neutralism and accommodation with the Soviet Union have only recently come to my attention. Under the impact of the policy of summit meetings, the Italian Christian Democratic party is split over the attitude the government, of which it is the mainstay, should take toward the Soviet Union. One of the most influential conservative newspapers of Japan has put to me a number of questions to be answered for its New Year's edition. One of the questions reads: Since the Cold War is about to come to an end, why does Japan need a security treaty with the United States?

In truth, if the policy of summit meetings were not an act of escape born of heedless despair but part of a well thought-out new foreign policy, it would require more of a national effort—moral, intellectual, material—rather than less; for in order to be prepared to negotiate seriously with the Soviet Union on the outstanding issues that threaten the peace of the world, we would have to marshal all our present strength and increase it drastically in support of our negotiating position. To negotiate at the summit with a feeble head, an unclenched fist, and an empty holster is tantamount to one of two alternatives deplorable in different ways: Either we shall negotiate from weakness and, hence, give up what we ought to defend, or else we will only go through the act of negotiating without negotiating at all and, in consequence, will only slide farther down the slope toward all-destructive war.

THE RESTORATION

OF FOREIGN

POLICY

The Specific Issues

33 *The World Situation*

It would be rash indeed to assume that the world is moving definitely in the direction of relaxing East-West tensions. What one can assume with confidence is that the nature of the tensions is in the process of changing. While the possibility of armed conflicts, global or local, cannot be completely ruled out, it is obvious in view of both the interests of the Soviet Union and Khrushchev's new foreign policy that the East-West conflict is likely to take the form of competition through example, propaganda, aid, and trade for gaining the allegiance of the uncommitted nations and of some vacillating allies on either side.

It seems to me that at present only three issues outstanding between the United States and the Soviet Union are susceptible of a negotiated settlement: the exchange of ideas and persons, the Berlin issue, and disarmament. Of these issues, the exchange of ideas and persons is most easily negotiable, but it is also of least importance from a political point of view. A good beginning has already been made in this respect, and more can be expected in the future. But even if there were complete movement of ideas and persons between East and West the question would still remain open as to who shall control Eastern Europe and whether or not the whole world will go Communist and Khrushchev will bury us. The substance of the Berlin issue is not susceptible of a negotiated settlement, but its modalities are. There can obviously be no compromise between the Russian position telling the West to get out of Berlin and the Western resolution to stay in Berlin. But if they want to, the statesmen concerned ought to be able to find a formula which would give the Soviet Union a measure of satisfaction in terms of prestige while leaving the core of the Western position in Berlin intact. The problem of disarmament is focused at present on the cessation of atomic tests. This issue has a very great symbolic importance, for the interests of the Soviet Union and the United States obviously coincide

Answers to questions posed by *Sekai*, Tokyo, January, 1960.

in so far as the international control of nuclear weapons is concerned. Furthermore, the cessation of nuclear tests constitutes a relatively simple and limited technical problem. If the United States and the Soviet Union can reach agreement on this issue and make the agreement work, they will have taken an enormous symbolic step toward more important measures in the field of disarmament. If they cannot agree on this simple and limited issue it is difficult to visualize any other of the outstanding issues on which they could agree.

As pointed out already, the new nations of Asia and Africa and the established nations of Latin America are likely to provide the battleground for the great competitive contest between East and West. Considering the intrinsic weakness of most of these nations, I would suspect that they will provide opportunities for this competition rather than play an independent part in it. In other words, their fate will be determined in good measure by other nations rather than by themselves. The West is aware of this paramount issue and is in the process of developing policies designed to meet it.

It is of course not impossible that in certain respects the economic systems of the United States and the Soviet Union will come to resemble each other more closely as time goes on. To what extent they will come to resemble each other politically and ideologically is a moot question. If they should come to resemble each other in these respects, the ideological conflict would simply lose its substance, and two gigantic mass societies would then compete for power throughout the world.

I do not believe that the United States can at present take any initiative for the improvement of the relations with Communist China. For a decade, I have consistently maintained the position that the recognition of Communist China ought for the United States to be a matter of expediency and not of principle, and I would have welcomed such recognition ten years ago. In view of the present Chinese attitude, I cannot see what useful purpose recognition would serve, even if it were possible. In order to understand this argument, one needs only to take a look at the position in which the Western nations which have actually recognized Communist China find themselves. It has been quite useless and even embarrassing from their point of view.

The division of Korea and Vietnam is a function of the over-all balance of power in Asia. Like the division of Germany, it is indicative of the fact that neither the West nor the East is capable of uniting these countries on its own terms. It seems to me that nothing can be done to unite these countries as long as the present stalemate between East and West prevails.

The question of the alliance between Japan and the United States is of course of a most delicate nature. In order to answer that question adequately, it is necessary not to start from what one would like to happen but from what is attainable under the circumstances. There is of course no country in the world which would not like to be neutral in a nuclear war. For some nations it may not be a priori impossible to remain neutral in such a war; for other nations it is manifestly impossible. Neutrality is not primarily a matter of choice but of the objective conditions of a nation's existence. Sweden and Switzerland could remain neutral in the two World Wars because the interest of the belligerents to see their neutrality maintained outweighed their interest in seeing their neutrality destroyed. There can be no doubt in anybody's mind that Japan vis-à-vis East and West is not in the same position in which Sweden and Switzerland found themselves vis-à-vis the belligerents of the two world wars. Japan is today again, potentially if not actually, the most powerful nation of Asia. Anybody who travels through Asia with an open mind must be impressed with the superior dynamism, ability, and potential power of Japan. The United States has only one interest with regard to Japan: to withhold that power from Communist China and the Soviet Union. In other words, if the United States could be confident that the Soviet Union and Communist China would allow a disarmed and neutral Japan to remain neutral, the United States would be delighted to underwrite the neutrality of Japan and take in its stride whatever temporary military disadvantages the neutrality of Japan would entail for itself.

But it ought to be perfectly obvious that Communist China at least is not interested in the neutrality of Japan. Its interests must militate strongly against such a benevolent attitude; for if China could add to its enormous manpower the industrial potential and technological ability of Japan it could make itself in a relatively short period of time the most powerful nation on earth. In other words, what China must want today is exactly what Japan wanted twenty years ago: to create a great combination of Chinese quantity and Japanese quality, which might well inherit the earth. What has changed are only the auspices. Twenty years ago it was Japan who wanted to use the manpower and resources of China for the purposes of its imperialism. Today and, more particularly, tomorrow it will be Chinese imperialism which will seek to exploit the human and material resources of Japan for its purposes. The neutrality of Japan would open the door to Chinese imperialism and would make it possible for China to transform Japan into a Chinese colony. Only the alliance with the United States stands in the way of these designs.

That this is not mere speculation is obvious from the policies which China is pursuing vis-à-vis India. Here is a genuinely neutralist nation, a nation which has refused to enter into any military commitments with the West. The Communist government of China has regarded this lack of military commitments as a kind of standing invitation to push India around and to pursue its territorial objectives on the mainland of Asia at India's expense. Considering how much more attractive Japan must be for Chinese imperialism than is India, it is not difficult to imagine what would happen if Japan were as militarily uncommitted as India is today.

The question which Japan faces today is therefore not whether or not it can escape the risks implicit in the objective conditions of its existence but whether it would minimize those risks by retreating into a neutral position. It must weigh the risks of neutralism against the risks of association with the United States. It would of course be unrealistic to maintain that Japan does not run risks by being associated with the United States. But, as I have tried to point out, I think it can be argued convincingly that neutralism would directly jeopardize the very survival of Japan as an independent nation. This being so, the real question before Japan is how it can minimize the risks of its association with the United States.

I have always regarded the dispersal of atomic weapons into the hands of any number of nations as a catastrophic development for both the two superpowers and the other nations as well. An independent nuclear deterrent in the hands of a nation such as Great Britain and France seems to me to be a self-defeating absurdity. Japan is, in terms of all-out nuclear war, very much in the position of Great Britain. It is an unmovable target which can be obliterated by a few well-placed H-bombs. It can have no defense of its own against this mortal threat but must be defended against it by the only nation which has the power to do so, the United States. Yet, while Japan cannot defend itself against a nuclear attack by nuclear weapons of its own, it ought to be able to defend itself against a conventional attack with conventional forces. How large these forces ought to be, how they ought to be composed and under whose auspices they ought to operate are technical questions which I do not feel competent to answer. However, I am prepared to state that Professor Sakamoto's idea of a combined Japanese-United Nations force or of a Japanese force under United Nations auspices strikes me as original and worthy of serious exploration.

34 *Prospect for a New Foreign Policy*

Exactly eight years ago, I sat down to write an article explaining why great things could be expected from Messrs. Eisenhower and Dulles in the conduct of American foreign policy. On paper, the estimate was reasonable. The President-elect enjoyed enough prestige to marshal popular support for any foreign policy he might have chosen, from unilateral disarmament to preventive war. The new Secretary of State was uniquely prepared, and appeared to be eminently qualified, for the position: Dulles' *War or Peace*, published in 1950, was as sound a statement of the principles of American foreign policy as could then be found. Yet before I was able to finish the article, certain depressing indications of what the new foreign policy was likely to be had already appeared. The article was never finished, and the history of the last eight years has shown how mistaken my original estimate was.

These sobering reminiscences provide an appropriate background for evaluating the prospects of American foreign policy under the new administration. On paper, again, Rusk, Bowles, Stevenson, and Harriman each looks at least as good as Dulles ever did, and Mr. Kennedy's *The Strategy of Peace* is as sound a statement of the requirements of American foreign policy for the sixties as was Mr. Dulles' book for the fifties. The foreign policy of the United States has probably never been entrusted to so high-powered a team, every member of which is qualified, in his own particular way, to be secretary of state. Nevertheless, while personal excellence in those who make and carry it out is indispensable for a sound foreign policy, it does not assure a successful one. The new men must work within old circumstances, domestic and international, and the circumstances will put their excellence to the test. Regardless of their convictions and intentions, they are the prisoners of the past—of established institutions, policies, and habits of mind. They may at best be able to gain a little freedom of movement by loosening some

From *Commentary*, February, 1961.

chains, but they cannot break down walls. Whatever they may have hopefully counseled or planned or worked for when they were not in office, once they assume office, they are in prison, and their ability to do what they would like to do depends only in part upon themselves.

Eisenhower and Herter have left to Kennedy and Rusk a heritage much inferior to that bequeathed by Truman and Acheson to the Eisenhower administration. At the beginning of 1953, the foreign policy of the United States was still a going concern. Brilliantly conceived in the spring of 1947 to counter the threat of Stalin's imperialism, it was still serviceable five years later, even though its weaknesses had by then become clear. Those weaknesses were in part owing to inherent misconceptions, such as the nature of the military role of NATO and the German contribution supposedly indispensable to it; and in part they stemmed from such new circumstances as the changes in the balance of world military power and the awakening of Asia. (The persistence of the issues of our foreign policy is indicated, I think, by the chapter headings in a book of mine published in 1951: one reads "The Precarious State of the Atlantic Alliance"; another, "The Struggle for Asia as a Struggle for the Minds of Men.")

It was the great failing of Dulles that he subordinated the requirements of a sound foreign policy to the demands of domestic politics; in consequence, he was compelled to accentuate the weaknesses of the foreign policy he had inherited while at the same time resisting its adaptation to new conditions. When Dulles assumed office, he resolved that what had happened to Mr. Acheson would not happen to him. Mr. Acheson, the architect of a sound and successful foreign policy, found himself deserted by public opinion, and, more particularly, by congressional opinion, and hence was handicapped in the conduct of his policy. Dulles made it his first order of business to secure for his person and policies the support of the Congress and of public opinion at large; in this endeavor, he was eminently successful. But as a result something happened to him that had never happened to Mr. Acheson: he became the prisoner of a public opinion—in good measure created by his own words and deeds—which limited his freedom of action to a foreign policy conceived in the image of a world-wide Maginot line around the Russo-Chinese em-

pire, manned by invincible American military might and its stead-
fast allies. However popular that policy was, it proved unsuccessful
outside Europe. A military policy which vacillates between the im-
plausible threat of "massive retaliation," on the one hand, and ineffectual response, on the other, is incapable in the long run of containing the military expansion of communism. And so far as the
acute threat of Communist political expansion through "competitive
coexistence" is concerned, the policy yields not only an irrelevant
response but actual ammunition for the enemy. Meanwhile, with the
United States embarked upon an essentially futile, and even self-
defeating, foreign policy, the world situation has changed in at least
four important respects.

The Soviet Union, of course, now ranks with the United States
as an atomic power. And if the present trend continues, an indefinite
number of nations will have acquired atomic weapons within the
next decade. Second, the countries of Western Europe and Japan,
having recovered their economic strength, are now in the process
of building up their military and political strength as well. China,
above all, is likely to become a first-rate power: it need only add to
its enormous population and territory the achievements of modern
technology. Third, the emancipation of the colonial and semicolonial
peoples of the world has entered its last stage in Africa and has begun in Latin America. Finally, both the Soviet Union and (to a lesser
extent at the moment) China have embarked upon a new expansionist foreign policy; it is no longer based so much upon a combination of the infallibility of Marxist prophesies and open military
pressure as upon the achievements, actual and potential, of the Communist system.

The task of the new administration, if it hopes for success in cop-
ing with the changed world situation, lies in rethinking and re-
fashioning American foreign policy in five major areas: the relations
with our allies, the relations with the uncommitted nations, the relation between domestic politics and foreign policy, the relations with
the Communist bloc, and, finally, the supranational control of atomic power.

The several alliances of which the United States is a member owe
their existence to two different factors: the need in which our European allies, as well as our former enemies, found themselves after

the Second World War to have American economic, military, and political support; and the United States objective of containing by military means the Soviet Union and Communist China in the Middle East and Asia. In recent years, the foundations for the first type of alliance have changed radically; whereas the foundations for the second type were weak from the very outset. The economic recovery of the nations of Western Europe and the former enemies has made them less dependent upon American support than they once were. As a consequence, they have at times been able to pursue their own narrower interests regardless of—indeed, to the detriment of— the common interests of the alliance. The Kennedy administration must find a new foundation for these alliances, one which reflects more faithfully the present underlying community of interests of the major nations of the non-Communist world. These alliances were primarily conceived in military terms. They must now be given an economic, political, and cultural content as well. The transformation of the Cold War into what is now called "competitive coexistence" has revealed the essential unsoundness of the policy of military containment as extended to Asia and the Middle East. For the conflict between East and West has taken on more and more the aspects of a struggle for the minds of men, especially in the uncommitted nations of Asia, Africa, and Latin America—a struggle to be fought with the weapons of prestige, subversion, political pressure, foreign aid, and foreign trade. Military alliances—in any contest for men's minds—are likely to be at best of minor importance and at worst a political handicap.

If the United States is to wage this struggle for the minds of men with any chance of success, the Kennedy administration must devise a new grand strategy. Two fundamental reforms are called for: the integration of all the factors involved in the struggle for the single purpose of maintaining and expanding the influence of the non-Communist world, and the adaptation of these various factors to the local conditions prevailing in any one country. In particular, the Kennedy administration must develop, and act upon, a coherent philosophy of foreign aid and foreign trade.

The uncommitted nations confront the Kennedy administration also with a problem in political organization. Many of the new nations owe their existence to mere accidents of colonial history and are therefore not likely to become viable political, economic, and military units within the boundaries they now occupy. This being the case, they present a standing invitation for a new imperialism to establish a new order where the old colonial order has disappeared; alternatively, they are threatened with anarchy, into which the rest of the world might well be sucked. This enormously complex problem will test the political creativity and determination of the new administration.

It is obvious that the domestic policies pursued by the United States, especially in the field of race relations, are bound to have a direct influence upon our ability to wage the struggle for the minds of men with any chance of success. The new administration needs to be fully aware of this influence in its conduct of domestic policies. Where it cannot entirely control these policies, it must at least give moral support to the positions which confrom most closely to the best traditions of America. Throughout the better part of American history, our foreign policy drew strength and its attractiveness to other nations from the character of our domestic politics. The American experiment in government and social organization was intended from the very outset—and was received by other nations as being so intended—not only for America but for the world. It was meant as a model for other nations to emulate. The new administration has the duty to restore that meaning.

The ultimate outcome of these new policies, which we must look to the Kennedy administration to undertake, will depend upon the kind of relations which are established with the Communist bloc; for, if in the course of the successful pursuit of these policies, our relations with the U.S.S.R. and Communist China should further deteriorate, our very success might in the end turn out to be self-defeating in so far as it would bring closer the probability of a third world war fought with atomic weapons. Thus the Kennedy administration must achieve the supreme task of statesmanship of successfully waging the competitive struggle with the Communist bloc without at the same time increasing the risk of war. The first precondition for minimizing that risk is the stabilization of the present territorial frontiers between the Western world and the Communist bloc. The second precondition is the maintenance and, if need be, the restoration of the Western atomic deterrent. The risk of war will diminish only in the measure that the points of conflict which might ignite a war can be reduced, at the same time that deterrence against the starting of a war is strengthened.

Finally, even if the Kennedy administration should be successful in the pursuit of all these policies, the United States and the world will still be confronted with a mortal danger: the spread of atomic weapons to an indefinite number of nations. This danger we can cope with only in co-operation with the other great nations of the world. The prospect of such a spread is bound to become a reality unless the present trend is reversed; if the trend continues, it is likely to cause unprecedented anarchy which will finally be beyond the control of the big powers. To bring nuclear weapons under supranational control is indeed the overriding task of the age. History is likely to judge the Kennedy administration by its approach to this task and its success in accomplishing it.

Nevertheless, even if the new administration were to devise sound policies for the five areas I have mentioned, their success would in good measure depend upon factors, such as the policies of other nations, over which the government of the United States has no control. It would also depend upon the ability of the American government to put the policies, once decided upon, into actual operation. This problem is peculiar to the United States, stemming from our constitutional arrangements and political system. The problem arises in four different areas of policy formation: in the relations between the President and the Secretary of State; between the Secretary and the Department of State; between the President and Secretary of State, on the one hand, and other executive departments, on the other; and, finally, between the President and Secretary of State, on the one hand, and Congress and public opinion at large, on the other.

The President is ultimately responsible for the conduct of American foreign policy, and the Secretary of State is supposed to be his main aide in the discharge of that responsibility. In reality, the relations between the President and the Secretary of State have conformed to this constitutional intent only when the President was in effect his own Secretary of State and used the titular head of the State Department as a mere instrument, as in the Roosevelt-Stettinius relations; or if the President and Secretary were continuously of one mind, as in the case of Truman and Acheson. Otherwise, the President has either bypassed the Secretary of State, as Roosevelt did with Hull, or given him a free hand, normally ratifying his decisions, as Eisenhower did with Dulles. When both the President and the Secretary of State have had their strong and different convictions about foreign policy, conflict has more often than not been the result. Within the State Department, the chance of conflict is always present, and conflict has frequently materialized when the Secretary's subordinates have had strong policy preferences of their own. The relations between Hull and Sumner Welles and the independent and contradictory policies pursued in the thirties by Ambassador Kennedy in London and Ambassador Dodd in Berlin come to mind. That problem is superimposed upon the ever present task of fashioning a bureaucracy, set in its ways, into a pliable instrument of a new policy.

The new Secretary of State faces a slow-moving, if not recalcitrant, department. He and the President must also impose their new foreign policy upon other departments of the executive branch which may be committed to a different policy. The official Far Eastern policy of the United States, for example—for all practical purposes, the policy of two Chinas—not only is being obstructed by the government of Taiwan but has also been opposed in practice by certain groups within the State and Defense Departments. The official policy of the United States concerning the cessation of atomic tests has been openly challenged in word and deed by the Atomic Energy Commission. The new administration, which must soon make crucial decisions on this latter problem, minimizes its chances for successful negotiations—slim as they are in view of the objective nature of the issue and Russian attitudes—if it is unable to commit its own agencies to a common position.

Finally, it is obvious that the government of the United States can only go as far in its conduct of foreign policy as Congress and public opinion at large permit. The task of combining sound foreign policies with popular support is always difficult, and the temptation to sacrifice the former to the latter is always great and at times has proved irresistible. The foreign policies upon which the new administration must embark are not only new in that they differ from those which have been pursued up till now. They are also startling in that they run counter to cherished popular preconceptions. The international developments of the last eight years have transformed these preconceptions into illusions; neither the words nor the deeds of our government took cognizance of those developments. The new administration, in order to marshal public opinion behind its new foreign policies, must first of all restore a sense of reality to the American people.

The demands which these tasks make upon the courage, wisdom, and ability of the Kennedy administration are superhuman, in view of which the prospects for a wholly successful American foreign policy are of necessity less bright than is suggested by the contrast between the personal and intellectual qualities of the new team and those of its predecessor. Whoever expects spectacular changes is likely to be disappointed. We others will be grateful to the Kennedy administration if it can give American foreign policy a new spirit and awareness and a consistent movement in the right direction.

35 _Kennedy's Foreign Policy: Failure and Challenge_

After five months in office, the Kennedy administration cannot boast of anything that can be called a success in foreign policy. But it has registered two glaring defeats: the Cuban disaster and the Communist conquest of Laos. Consequently, there is a general disenchantment with the administration. The Republican opposition is naturally, and one might say professionally, disenchanted and advocates "strong action" after the model of what President Eisenhower did in Lebanon and Guatemala. The Democrats are disenchanted because all that was wrong with United States foreign policy has not been set right since January 20, as they thought it would be. Most significant, the administration is disenchanted with itself; it has come to recognize that intelligence and initiative are not enough to vouchsafe success in foreign policy. Quite a number of Hamlets must have walked the battlements of the White House in recent nights, debating with themselves the relation between thought and action.

Two strands can be distinguished in this negative attitude toward the administration's foreign policy: One is rooted in the psychology of the public, the other stems from actual deficiencies of Kennedy's policy. We all share to some degree the ineradicable tendency to expect immediately from a new administration all the achievements which we hoped for in vain from its predecessor. We expect dramatic and spectacular reversals of fortune. These expectations are bound to be disappointed. However unwise and unsuccessful the preceding administration may have been, and however wise the new one may be, the very vices and failures of its predecessor put strict limits upon the administration's freedom of action.

An even more important consideration is the policies of other nations that limit a new administration's freedom of action. As long as Khrushchev insists upon a Soviet veto on the political decisions of international organizations, the disarmament policies of the Ken-

From the _New Leader,_ July 3, 1961.

nedy administration must remain a dead letter. As long as President de Gaulle seeks an independent position for France within Europe and an independent position for Europe, under French leadership, within the Atlantic alliance, it will remain impossible for the Kennedy administration to do what it wants to do, e.g., to strengthen the Atlantic alliance.

Furthermore, in so far as a new administration has the freedom to start new policies and makes use of it, the results of those new policies are not likely to be visible at once. The Kennedy administration, for example, has embarked upon a new policy of foreign aid, derived from what appears to be a sound philosophy of the conditions and purposes of foreign aid. It will take some time for this new policy to filter down through the ranks of the officials in the field, if it ever does. Most of these officials have operated on certain primitive assumptions, deeply ingrained in the folklore of American politics, about the relations between foreign aid and economic development, economic development and social stability, social stability and democracy, democracy and a peaceful foreign policy. They are not likely to have been selected for their political sophistication and manipulative skills. Yet even after they have learned how to translate the new philosophy into effective action, it may take years for the results of the new policy to show.

Our disenchantment is also nourished by the nature of the tasks which it has fallen to the Kennedy administration to perform. One of these tasks is the liquidation of overextended commitments. That is to say, the United States, if it does not want to risk war in the defense of indefensible and at best non-essential positions, must retreat from these positions. It has already retreated from Laos and has been trying, at this writing unsuccessfully, to obtain the cooperation of the Communist powers in covering up that retreat. It may soon be faced with a similar choice in South Vietnam.

But the American people are utterly unprepared for these retreats. As concerns American power vis-à-vis the power of other nations, they are living in a dream world which antedates the atomic age, especially in its bipolar quality. In that dream world the United States need only use its strength to get what it wants. It is the misfortune of the Kennedy administration that it has assumed office at a moment when the veil which had hidden an obstreperous and dangerous world from the eyes of America has worn thin enough to show at least some of the contours of a disturbing reality. The reassuring slogans which for eight long years we had taken to describe reality have now started to clash openly with the facts of life. Since nobody in authority has yet told the American people what the facts of life are, the Kennedy administration is widely suspected of weakness in the face of Communist aggression because it is not living up to the slogans it has not dared repudiate. The people are disenchanted with the Kennedy administration for its failure to do what it was expected to do but was incapable of doing in view of the objective circumstances. What is worthy of blame here is the people's judgment, not the government's actions.

However, the administration is also being blamed deservedly for failures of commission and omission. Its outstanding failure of commission is, of course, the invasion of Cuba. What has shocked our sensibilities was not so much that the administration tried to intervene in Cuba by force of arms or that the intervention failed; but we were shocked by the manner in which it failed. It is that manner, the incredible folly of the whole thing, that points to actual weaknesses in the administration's conduct of foreign policy. These weaknesses are conceptual, organizational, and intellectual.

In Cuba, as elsewhere, the administration has operated with an outdated concept of revolution. When it staged the invasion of Cuba, it thought the Cuban people would rise up against Fidel Castro. It assumed that the Castro revolution was not a genuine popular revolution or, if it once had been, it was no longer. The people, it was reasoned, are anti-Communist by nature and if they live under a pro-Communist government, it must be under duress. Thus the overthrow of the Communist governments of Russia and China has been predicted and expected time and again. And when countries such as Laos and Cuba go Communist, or are in danger of doing so, as is South Vietnam, it can only be through foreign intervention and not through popular consent. All that is needed, then, is military intervention to free an unwilling people from Communist domination. Since the Communists are gaining control through guerrilla warfare, we must reply in kind. The administration is therefore emphasizing what it calls "paramilitary operations."

But the modern totalitarian regimes, Fascist and Communist, have not been imposed by a tyrannical minority upon an unwilling population. While the Franco regime came to power on the bayonets of Nazi Germany and the satellite regimes of Eastern Europe came to power on the bayonets of the Red Army, the modern totalitarian regimes have come to power and maintained their rule with the support of populations willing to sacrifice individual freedom and self-government, actual or potential, for order and what they consider to be social justice. Such regimes cannot be overthrown by counterrevolutionary invasions, but only by the vision of a realizable social order superior to the status quo.

Where guerrilla warfare is an instrument of foreign invasion, as it was in Greece and Malaya, it can indeed be countered in kind. But where guerrilla warfare is to some extent the spearhead of popular revolution, as it was in Cuba and is today in South Vietnam, counter-guerrilla warfare, operating in hostile territory without a popular base, must fail. The administration, by seeming to look to counter-guerrilla warfare as its main answer to Communist revolution, falls into the trap of assuming that what works well for the Communists must work equally well for us, if only we make the effort to imitate it.

Both the Cuban invasion and the official sanction of the prisoner-tractor deal point up another real weakness of the administration's foreign policy: the process of policy formation. President Kennedy has made a conscious effort to avoid his predecessor's isolation from both relevant information and effective control. To that purpose, he has done away with the committee system of governing, at least on the top level, and has surrounded himself with a number of individual advisers, in different degrees brilliant, knowledgeable, and experienced. These advisers, operating as equals, are supposed to present the President with a variety of individual views and recommendations from which he can choose. This concept of presidential government has considerable merit compared with the committee system which it is intended to replace, but it is not likely to work in practice. The successive presentation of views and recommendations by isolated individuals is no substitute for the dialectic confrontation of such views and recommendations in a group which can put differing opinions to the test of empirical verification and logical analysis. Also, in a contest among equals for the President's ear those with offices in the White House are likely to be more equal than those with offices, say, in Foggy Bottom. And those who are supposed to have a monopoly of at least some of the *arcana imperii,* such as officials of the Central Intelligence Agency and the Pentagon, are likely to have an advantage over those who can boast of nothing more than intelligence with a small *i.* This system also tends to separate the men of ideas from the men of facts and gives an inevitable advantage to brilliant presentation unchecked by practical experience. Thus the President, when he had to make a decision on Laos, was compelled by the objective requirements of government to restore the National Security Council to its original function as the President's principal adviser on issues of national security.

This equalitarian diffusion of the advisory function raises another issue: the role of the intellectual in the process of policy formation. We all smile in memory of what was once a maxim of our government: that a man who knows how to run General Motors knows by definition how to run the Department of Defense, and that a man who has met a payroll must also be capable of meeting the requirements of government. It is, however, not self-evident that a man who knows how to run a university is thereby qualified to run the foreign policy of the United States, and that an intellectual who knows how to lecture and write books knows by definition also how to make foreign policy.

The intellectual does not need to have, and is frequently devoid of, that quality which is indispensable in the statesman—practical wisdom. It is possible to be very intelligent without being very wise, or for that matter, without being wise at all, which is another way of saying that one can be very intelligent and very foolish at the same time. Woodrow Wilson was a brilliant intellectual without, at the very least, the full measure of wisdom. Harry Truman had practical wisdom without being an intellectual. Two qualities are essential in the statesman which are not necessarily present in the intellectual: a sense of limits—limits of knowledge, of judgment, of successful action—and a commitment to a grand design born of a sense of purpose which neutralizes the doubts engendered by the awareness of limits. The intellectual is rather sure of himself, satisfied with himself, and out for the next little triumph in his little world. In the world of the intellectual, ideas meet with ideas, and anything goes that is presented cleverly and with assurance. In the political world, ideas meet with facts which make mincemeat of the wrong ideas and throw the pieces in the ashcan of history. To stand one's ground in this battle of ideas which will determine the course of history is a different matter, requiring different qualities of mind and character, from that innocuous and frequently irrelevant pastime which we call pretentiously the academic dialogue.

Perhaps it is not by accident that an administration whose style is to an exceptional degree determined by intellectuals speaks a great deal about purpose but appears to lack a sense of direction, and calls upon the people for sacrifices without being able to tell them what to do. Here indeed is the administration's failure of omission. And it is first of all the President's failure. When the President finally spoke in positive terms about the national purpose, he and his advisers could think of nothing better than being first in sending a man to the moon, a patent publicity device which an unexcited public took in its stride. It is also another instance of that trap of imitating the Russians and playing the game according to their rules. And whenever the President called for sacrifices, he said hardly anything of substance, but he said it in beautiful prose.

The quandary of the administration in knowing that it must give American foreign policy a new direction and instil it with a new purpose without knowing how to go about it stems from the contrast between the nature of the tasks before it and the quality of its thinking about them. The administration has found to its dismay that it has even less freedom of action than it thought it had when it assumed office. The negotiations on the cessation of atomic tests are at dead end. Consequently, the chances for disarmament are virtually nil. The positions on Berlin appear irreconcilable. The Atlantic alliance remains in disarray. Our positions in Asia are deteriorating. This being so, the administration is naturally tempted to reconcile itself to the inevitable and to put its stakes upon the unabated continuation of the nuclear armaments race, hoping for the best but knowing in the back of its collective mind the inevitability of the worst. It is the easiest policy to pursue, it is bound to be popular, but it cannot fail to lead to disaster. Here the administration is offered a great opportunity to put its brain power to work on a task of constructive statesmanship. It must try to break out of the sterile patterns of past policies and put forward proposals which equal in boldness the novelty of our tasks and the urgency of the dangers that face us. The tasks of greatest urgency are Berlin, the supranational control of nuclear power and, intertwined with the latter, the revitalization of the Atlantic alliance.

If the administration were to embark upon these and other tasks with sufficient boldness, it could not doubt the kind of sacrifices it must ask of the American people. They are sacrifices not primarily of money or of toil but of long-held, cherished convictions which have turned out to be illusions. The President must set an example to the American people by offering popular illusions on the altar of the truth. This task is politically risky in the short run, but in the long run it is the precondition both for the restoration of the vigor of our national life and for the renewal of our foreign policy.

Our awareness of the administration's failure to perform this task is perhaps the deepest source of our disenchantment. We have been told and we know that there is something fundamentally wrong with our national life and our foreign policy; yet the administration seems to think and certainly acts on the assumption that traditional remedies will cure our ills. What gives us pause is the discrepancy between the actual foreign policies pursued and the kind of thinking which apparently goes into them, on the one hand, and what we have been led to believe about our condition and what we know to be true. History will judge the Kennedy administration on how well it meets the challenge of bringing its thought and action up to the level of that truth.

36 *What the Big Two Can, and Can't, Negotiate*

In disputes between nations, as between individuals, some issues are susceptible of negotiated settlements through bargaining and compromise, and some are not. The two women who came before King Solomon, each claiming the baby as her own, raised an issue which in its very nature could not be settled through negotiations. The issue itself called for all or nothing, and the wise King, by giving the appearance of treating it as though it could be settled by a compromise, demonstrated that it could not. The possibility of settling an issue through negotiations, then, depends only in part upon the intentions and skill of the negotiators. The limits within which the negotiators can usefully operate are circumscribed by the objective nature of the outstanding issues. Only in so far as the conflicting interests from which these issues have arisen can be reconciled is there a chance for negotiations to succeed. If these interests are incompatible—so that what one side wants the other cannot concede even in part—no amount of talk will make either party yield.

What, then, are the issues outstanding between the United States and the Soviet Union, and to what extent do they lend themselves to a negotiated settlement, assuming that one can be reached with the agreement of our allies?

First, let us dispose of the catch phrase "settling the Cold War." The momentous issue of the Cold War, transcending all others in importance and intractability, cannot be negotiated out of existence. It arises from the challenge which communism has flung in the face of the West and from the West's response to it. This challenge and that response concern the future political and social organization of the world. Communism is convinced that it will inherit the world after it has buried us, and we refuse to be buried or to concede the inheritance. All foreign policies of the Soviet Union serve the ultimate end of assuring the triumph of communism over the Western

From the *New York Times Magazine*, September 20, 1959.

way of life (as all Western foreign policies seek to forestall that triumph), and as long as the Soviet Union believes in the inevitable world-wide triumph of its cause, it cannot stop promoting it. That belief will not yield to a negotiated settlement, but only, as we shall see, to the inescapable logic of facts.

We tried in vain to dispose of one of the manifestations of that belief by negotiating in 1933 an agreement with the Soviet Union to stop subversion in the United States. But the Soviet Union has not stopped subversion, either here or wherever else Communist parties will do its bidding, for subversion is one of the means by which the inexorable process of history, culminating in the communization of the world, is to be pushed forward. Yet if the Cold War is bound to go on and on, are there any areas in which we can lessen tensions through negotiations? There are five that seem to me at least not impossible. Let us consider them in turn:

Of the issues which might be settled through negotiations, that of the Iron Curtain appears to be the easiest to deal with. The systematic impediments to the free flow of persons and ideas have been imposed by the Soviet Union primarily for domestic reasons. A terrorist regime, patently inferior to the West in all the essentials of political, economic, and social life, had to shun all contacts which might have provoked invidious comparisons. With the passing of the Stalinist era and the rise of Russian self-confidence nourished by actual achievements, the Soviet Union has opened its gates to a modest degree to Western persons and ideas, and the United States has responded in kind. Nothing of an objective nature stands in the way of the United States and the Soviet Union's agreeing upon the exchange of persons and ideas on an ever larger scale. As long as the Soviet Union maintains its totalitarian control of the mass media of communications, it will be able to neutralize the potential effects of such exchanges upon the minds of its citizens. It must be remembered that such exchanges, while they may be desirable in themselves, are irrelevant to the peaceful settlement of the political issues which separate the two nations. Even if every adult American and Russian were to visit the other's country and learn the other's language and understand each other perfectly, the question as to whether the world is fated to be transformed by communism would still divide the United States and the Soviet Union.

The issue of Europe and Berlin is contained in the question, Where ought the western boundaries of the Soviet empire to be? The Soviet Union has consistently claimed that they ought to be where they are today, following by and large the line of military demarcation fixed at the end of the Second World War. The United States has as consistently claimed that the line was only provisional and that Soviet political and military control ought to be confined to the territory of the Soviet Union. The Western presence in Berlin is for both the United States and the Soviet Union the tangible symbol of this unresolved issue, for the presence of Western troops in Berlin challenges—as a matter of spectacular fact—the permanence of the division of Germany upon which the Soviet claim to the permanence of the western frontiers of its empire is based. It is because of the symbolic significance of West Berlin that neither side has been willing to yield an inch on the status of the city.

Yet a chance does exist for negotiations to succeed, provided the discussion can be moved from the realm of political theology to the world of political and military facts, for the controversy over the western boundaries of the Soviet empire has already been settled in the world of these facts. The Soviet Union cannot extend these boundaries westward, and the United States will not push them back toward the east. If proof for the latter proposition were needed, American abstention during the Hungarian uprising of 1956 provided it. Why, then, must Mr. Khrushchev, as did Stalin before him, reopen an issue which the facts of life have settled? Why must he get excited over our "Captive Nations Week," as though he did not know that a nation which relies for the attainment of an objective upon nothing but divine intervention induced by organized prayer does not expect to attain that objective by political or military means? Perhaps he really does not know of our politicians' tendency, to quote Theodore Roosevelt, "to treat elocution as a substitute for action, to rely upon high-sounding words unbacked by deeds," to combine "the loose tongue and the unready hand." If he does not know he ought to be told. But he ought also to be told—even though he ought to know it by now—that when we speak as a nation we mean what we say. While we shall continue to hope and pray for a retraction of the Soviet empire without doing anything about it, we shall prevent its expansion at the risk of war. If the United States and the Soviet Union can recognize the political and military facts of life in theory, as they have in their policies, they ought to be able to find a formula for accepting—at least by implication—the status quo: acceptance of the Western presence in Berlin by the Soviet Union, of the division of Germany by the United States, both, as it were, until further notice, which both sides would expect to be very long in coming.

Messrs. Mikoyan, Koslov, and Khrushchev have laid the greatest stress upon the issue of trade. They have evoked memories of Cobden and Bright, the leaders of the Manchester liberals of a century ago, as well as of our own Secretary of State Cordell Hull, with their praises of what foreign trade can do for private profits and international peace. But the Russian leaders are not liberals. They want foreign trade, and they want it very badly, because they need it to implement their domestic and foreign political and military policies. Mr. Khrushchev has staked his personal rule upon his ability to make the Soviet Union surpass the United States in economic productivity. That productivity, as an example and in the form of foreign aid and trade, will be the weapon with which the Soviet Union means to conquer the world, and it would, of course, be delighted if it could induce the United States to lend a helping hand.

The United States has shown a spectacular lack of interest in trade with the Soviet Union for exactly the same reason that the Soviet Union is so vitally interested in trade with the United States. Since the Soviet Union, in view of its economic organization and objectives, cannot help but use foreign trade as a political weapon, the United States must use it so, too. It can do so the more easily since trade with the Soviet Union has been economically insignificant—amounting in 1958 to less than half of 1 per cent of its total foreign trade—and such trade is unlikely to become significant even if the United States should abolish some or all of its statutory restrictions, for the Soviet Union wants to buy from the United States much more than it can expect to sell, so that it would have to finance American imports either with gold or through massive credits. This one-sidedness of the possible American-Soviet trade pattern is accentuated by the fact that the United States already obtains from other sources the commodities which the Soviet Union could sell.

Yet it is exactly because trade between the United States and the

Soviet Union poses an issue which is not primarily economic but political that it could be affected by a political agreement. An American concession in the form of increased trade might be a proper price for a Russian guarantee of the status quo in Berlin, especially since it could be enlarged, decreased, or canceled altogether, as circumstances might require. Foreign trade is by its very nature a most flexible instrument of foreign policy and can be a most potent one, provided one side has a much greater interest in trading than the other. The use of foreign trade in the Russian manner—that is, as a political instrument rather than in an economic context—offers the United States a bargaining power of which it has not even begun to take advantage.

What holds true of trade applies to disarmament. Disarmament as a general proposition, divorced from a settlement of the political conflicts which have caused the armaments race, is as futile as its attraction seems to be ineradicable. Disarmament has proved viable, however, when it either has followed a political settlement or was negotiated as an integral part of one. Why do the United States and the Soviet Union oppose each other in Europe, poised for mutual destruction? Because they are afraid that if they were not so poised, the other side might try to change the status quo in its favor by force of arms. As long as that mutual fear persists, neither side can afford to disarm. In so far as a political settlement would create confidence in the stability of the status quo, the United States and the Soviet Union would be at least in a state of mind to consider seriously the possibility of disarmament, either in the form of disengagement or otherwise.

The cessation of atomic tests is important less in itself than as a symbol. It is essentially a test case which will show whether there is any issue, however technically limited and however strongly supported by common interest, on whose settlement the United States and the Soviet Union can agree. That common interest is the common fear of atomic destruction, the danger of which is inherent in the atomic armaments race and is enormously increased by the impending dispersal of atomic weapons into the hands of any number of governments. On rational grounds, that common fear ought to outweigh even the fear of each other. The ability of the United States and the Soviet Union at least to face together this issue of nuclear power, on whose settlement their physical survival so manifestly depends, will provide a proof of their ability to negotiate in earnest on anything.

Two other great world issues which confront the Soviet Union and the United States are—at least at present—a priori incapable of negotiated settlement. They are the Middle East and Asia. The reason they cannot be settled between the United States and the Soviet Union is that neither we nor the Russians have much of anything with which to bargain.

Before the Iraqi revolution of last year, when Soviet and Western spheres of interest in the Middle East were still defined with some degree of precision, the possibility of a negotiated settlement, which the Soviet Union had repeatedly proposed, could not have been automatically excluded. It must be excluded now, for with political alignments in the Middle East completely in flux, the United States and the Soviet Union have nothing to dispose of because they have nothing to control: the West no longer controls Iraq, nor does the Soviet Union exert the same influence over Egypt it once did. The Middle East has thus reverted to the state of the uncommitted nations: the object of competition between the United States and the Soviet Union. While the United States and the Soviet Union might agree upon the rules of the competition—excluding, for instance, resort to open violence—they can have nothing to say to each other about the direction in which the Middle East should move.

The same general observation applies to the unsettled issues of Asia. Even if the United States and the Soviet Union saw eye to eye on how to settle the issues of Formosa, the offshore islands, Korea, Vietnam, and Laos, they could settle nothing between themselves; for it is Communist China, not the Soviet Union, which is the principal antagonist of the United States in Asia, and it has become obvious that the Soviet Union cannot speak for a Communist China ominously growing in power and ambition, when the latter's interests are at stake.

How will awareness of these momentous issues affect the prospect of negotiations? As the common fear of atomic destruction ought to neutralize the United States' and Russia's fear of each other, so they ought to be brought closer together by the common fear of a China which may well be on its way to becoming the most powerful nation on earth; for a China with a centrally controlled population of, say, 800 million in possession of the instruments of modern technology would be vastly superior in power to either the United States or the Soviet Union. A China with such prospects in mind must have a vital interest in seeing its two nearest competitors embroiled with each other, and by the same token the United States and the Soviet Union must have a vital interest in not getting so embroiled. The mood of hostility and suspicion with which the United States and the Soviet Union approach each other ought to be tempered by the awareness of this new configuration whose vague outlines have just begun to appear on the horizon. With that mood tempered, it ought to be easier for them to envisage settlements of the issues which in themselves are negotiable.

The mood of hostility and suspicion, however, is more than just a subjective state of mind. It reflects, on our side, the total challenge of communism and, on the Russian side, the Communist conviction that a capitalism defeated in peaceful contest for the world might resort to a war of desperation. While their common anxiety over the potential threat of China must draw the two sides closer together, mutual fear and suspicion must pull them farther apart. Obviously, that mood cannot be negotiated away, nor ought it to be dispelled by pleasant formulas while the facts from which it springs remain unchanged. It ought to yield only to facts that disprove it.

And so we end where we began. Certain issues outstanding between the United States and the Soviet Union are negotiable in themselves, but their settlement is impeded by the mutual fear and suspicion of two antagonistic political and social systems. The Cold War is a cancer, feeding the unsettled issues as it is fed by them. That vicious circle can be broken only in the realm of facts, through making a beginning with the settlement of a concrete issue. Of the issues susceptible to a negotiated settlement, the Iron Curtain is both the most promising and the least important politically. Trade is the most tempting, but dangerous politically and militarily. Disarmament must await the beginning of a political settlement. Berlin in the short run and the cessation of atomic tests in the long run are the most urgent issues. By virtue of their urgency, they ought to be settled now, and, by virtue of their intrinsic nature, they can be settled now.

If these two politically potent issues were settled, the result would not be an end to the Cold War, but it could mean a beginning of its transformation. The Cold War threatens to become hot because the unsolved political issues serve as a tangible focus upon which the fears and suspicions of the Cold War can concentrate, seeking release in armed conflict. Remove that focus by settling the political issues, and the Cold War is deprived of its tangible object, and there is no longer anything to fight about. Fear and suspicion there would still be, but of a different sort. They would be fear and suspicion of ourselves rather than of the other fellow. We would fear lest our vision and ingenuity were not equal to the task upon whose achievement the fate of the world depends. We would suspect that we might not possess the determination and courage the task required, for the Cold War would then have become completely what it has always been primarily: a contest between two conceptions of man, two principles of social and political organization, two visions of mankind's future. That contest cannot be settled by the give-and-take of negotiations. It will be settled, after negotiations have done their work on the political plane, by the nobler and weightier act of performance. Which system will prove capable of meeting basic human aspirations for itself and for mankind? Only when the answer to that question will have been given by the facts of life will the Cold War be settled.

37 *The Problem of Berlin*

Premier Khrushchev did not raise the issue of Berlin in November, 1958, and again in June, 1961, for purposes of propaganda or to meet demands from China or from within the Kremlin. He raised it as a means to the ends of Soviet policy. As concerns Germany, the Soviet Union pursues three ends: the removal of Berlin as a provocative reminder of Communist weakness, the separation of West Germany from the Western camp, and the stabilization of the territorial status quo.

The main objective of Soviet foreign policy in Europe since the Second World War has been the stabilization of the western frontiers of the Soviet empire. Stalin conceived of the postwar world as two gigantic spheres of influence controlled by the Soviet Union and the United States. He viewed the 1945 line of military demarcation which divides Germany as the definitive boundary line between the two spheres. Stalin made numerous proposals to that effect, both directly and through neutral and satellite diplomats. The United States has consistently refused even to consider such proposals. It has always maintained the provisional character both of the line of military demarcation between East and West and of the eastern boundary of Germany in the form of the Oder-Neisse line. It has been committed to the unification of Germany, which, if achieved on Western terms, would necessarily move the western frontiers of the Soviet empire father east, at least to the Oder-Neisse line if not beyond.

Paradoxical as it may seem, Khrushchev has called into question the status quo of Berlin because he seeks the stabilization of the territorial status quo of Europe, and the United States is committed to the defense of the status quo of Berlin because it refuses to acknowledge the territorial status quo of Europe as definitive. The German issue finds its symbolic manifestation in the issue of Berlin, and by raising the latter, Khrushchev has by implication raised the

From the *Washington Post*, July 2, 1961.

former. The Western presence in Berlin—the former capital of a once-united Germany and the potential capital of a reunited Germany—symbolizes the provisional character of the division of Germany. The abandonment of Berlin by the West would symbolize the definitive character of that division. By raising the issue of Berlin in an acute and threatening form, Khrushchev tries to force the West to recognize what it has refused to recognize for sixteen years, i.e., the definitive character of the division of Europe. The issue Khrushchev has raised is, then, the fundamental issue of who shall rule what and whether what is ruled by the Soviet Union now shall be ruled by it in perpetuity, its rule being recognized as legitimate by the West. This is the issue from which the Cold War arose and which has divided the United States and the Soviet Union ever since. It is the stuff of which hot wars are made as well.

It is in accord with his long-term purpose of stabilizing the territorial status quo that Khrushchev has not raised the Berlin issue directly but, as it were, as a by-product of recognition of the East German government. It is true that he has told the Western powers, as Stalin did in the form of the Berlin blockade, "Get out!" But how does he propose to get them out? He plans to do it by replacing the occupation statute upon which the Western presence in Berlin rests with a peace treaty with the East German government. Thus he can tell the Western powers, "Whatever rights you are going to have in Berlin you must negotiate with the East German government, to which we are transferring our control over the access to Berlin."

Khrushchev is a much more subtle and ingenious adversary than Stalin was. He tries to make it appear that what is at stake is not the freedom of West Berlin and the freedom of Western access to it but only a change in the legal title which would leave the substance of the present rights intact. In truth, of course, the freedom of West Berlin—an island in a Red sea—and of the Western access to it derives not from a legal document but from the Western military presence in West Berlin. West Berlin has remained free because an attack upon its freedom would be tantamount to an attack upon the Western military establishment in West Berlin, and the Western powers have been able to supply their troops in West Berlin because interference with these supplies would in the long run be impossible without a direct military confrontation. The Soviet Union has been anxious to avoid such a direct military confrontation in Germany and elsewhere and has sought its objectives rather by indirection, especially through the interposition of proxies. The attempt to interpose the East German government between the Soviet Union and the West is a typical example of that technique. Yet the application of that technique to Germany tends to jeopardize the main goal of Soviet policy: the stabilization of the territorial status quo, especially in the face of West German rearmament, for it raises an issue of the utmost gravity for all concerned: the possibility of a German civil war. Here is, indeed, the Achilles heel of Khrushchev's German policy.

Khrushchev appears to be genuinely afraid of a West German army, equipped with nuclear weapons, as the instrument of a West German policy which would recognize neither the existence of the East German government nor the legitimacy of the Oder-Neisse line. For this reason, he wants to bring the issue of the territorial status quo in Europe to a head before the West German army is equipped with nuclear weapons. On the other hand, when it comes to the preservation of peace, he trusts the East Germans no more than he does the West Germans, and while he may feel for Chancellor Adenauer a grudging admiration, he can hardly feel for his hapless East German stooges anything else but that contempt to which Stalin used to give vent in unguarded moments. He cannot but loathe the idea of seeing two German governments, each ineffectually controlled by its respective allies, oppose each other over undefined frontiers. It is this specter which has made him hesitate to bring the Berlin issue to a head ever since he raised it first in a seemingly peremptory form in November, 1958.

Khrushchev, then, is faced with a dilemma: he seeks the stabilization of the territorial status quo in Europe, for he fears the threat to peace stemming from instability in the heart of Europe. Yet the means he has chosen to achieve his end threaten to create an instability much greater and less controllable than the one he tries to remove. This dilemma provides the Western powers with an opportunity for constructive statesmanship. However, they are handicapped by a dilemma of their own.

The Western position must rest upon a threefold foundation: the Western right to be in Berlin is not subject to negotiations; the territorial status quo in Europe is not subject to change for the foreseeable future; a shift of West German allegiance from the West to the East is not compatible with Western security. The Western right to be in Berlin cannot be subject to negotiations because the very willingness to negotiate about it implies a denial of that right. . . . Yet while the substance of the Western right to be in Berlin is not negotiable, the modalities of that presence indeed are. Since the Western presence in Berlin has been primarily symbolic to begin with, it is susceptible to manipulation as long as its symbolic character remains intact.

That the territorial status quo in Europe cannot be changed in the foreseeable future, that for the time being Germany will remain divided and the Oder-Neisse line will remain its eastern frontier, is admitted by all concerned in the privacy of their offices and is loudly proclaimed by Khrushchev. "We proceed from the premise," he said in his June 15, 1961, television speech, "that the peace treaty with Germany will put a seal on what has already been established by the Potsdam Agreement. Indeed, the governments of the Western powers obviously understand, too, how senseless it would be to raise now the question of revising Germany's boundaries. Their representatives have often told us about this during our conversations. A simple operation, it seems—to put a seal on what already exists."

It is at this point that the Western dilemma comes into play. Khrushchev can afford to say bluntly what the statesmen of the West, those of Germany included, can only whisper among themselves because, with regard to the German question, the Soviet Union holds an enormous advantage over the West. The Soviet Union has it in its power to unify Germany and move the frontiers of Germany eastward whenever it wishes. It only needs to withdraw its support from the East German government and divide Poland with Germany again for the fifth time in two centuries. What the Soviet Union would ask of a united and restored Germany in return would not necessarily be its communization but as a minimum the transfer of its support from the West to the East.

West Germany has joined the Western camp because it mistrusts the ultimate objectives of the Soviet Union and has confidence in the aims and power of the West. If the West were to speak of the frontiers of Germany as Khrushchev has spoken, West Germany would have nothing to choose between East and West in terms of verbal commitments, and in terms of the ability to give West Germany what it wants, the advantage would remain with the Soviet Union. West Germany would then be tempted to strike a bargain with the Soviet Union, and Khrushchev has indeed voiced the expectation that sooner or later this will happen. Thus it is for the sake of the very same prize—the allegiance of West Germany—that Khrushchev wants the West to recognize the territorial status quo in Europe, and the West cannot accede to that demand.

What, then, can the West do? It can do essentially three things. First, it can try to negotiate over the modalities of its presence in West Berlin with whoever effectively controls the lines of communications. Its aim must be the preservation of the symbolic significance of that presence while not insisting upon its more provocative aspects. Second, it can try to exploit Khrushchev's dilemma. Mindful of the fact that President de Gaulle has come out in favor of recognition of the Oder-Neisse line as the permanent eastern frontier of Germany, it can try to contribute to the stabilization of the territorial status quo in Europe without increasing the danger of a German civil war. Finally, in doing this, the West must try to avoid being caught in its own dilemma. Whatever it contributes to the stabilization of the territorial status quo must be compatible with its verbal commitment to the unification of Germany. It must somehow manage to bridge the gap between what it has so often declared it will do in Germany and what it can do.

It is obvious that these tasks are enormously difficult to achieve and require for their achievement qualities of statesmanship, both daring and wise, which are harder to come by and less certain of popularity in the short run than that verbal bravery which the crowd is ever ready to applaud. However, if those qualities are not forthcoming, the West will be faced with two equally unacceptable choices: retreat, or fight a war on behalf of the freedom of West Berlin which will destroy West Berlin and its freedom as well.

38 *The End of an Illusion*

A great historian has said that history should make us not clever for one day but wise forever. In the life of nations, as in the life of individuals, a great crisis can be a boon if it reveals in the contours of the abyss the stark and simple outlines of the eternal verities which men and nations neglect only at their peril. The Berlin crisis, if we come out of it alive, can teach us some lessons about the nature of foreign policy. One of them is the short-term convenience and long-term perniciousness of basing foreign policy on pleasant illusions rather than the unpalatable truth. Thus we may well look back to the Berlin crisis in gratitude for the insight it has given us not into the evil intentions of Khrushchev but into the errors of our own ways. And we may face with greater confidence, and handle with greater competence, the crises of the future—which are as sure to follow Berlin as night follows day—if we understand and remember the lessons of Berlin.

It is hardly open to doubt that a negotiated settlement of the Berlin issue will result in an appreciable weakening of the Western position. This weakening will not be due to the lack of steadfastness of purpose and of diplomatic skill of the representatives of the West. Rather it will be due to the fact that the objective distribution of interests and power with regard to Berlin makes such an outcome inevitable. That distribution has always favored the Soviet Union, and the drastic change in the distribution of nuclear power which has occurred during the last decade has increased the Russian advantage—so Khrushchev seems to think—decisively. The effectiveness of the legal arrangements safeguarding the Western position in Berlin and the symbolic function which Berlin was supposed to perform as the prospective capital of a united Germany were predicated upon a distribution of power decisively favoring the West. That distribution was always unfavorable to the West locally, and it has now turned against the West in the world arena.

From *Commentary*, November, 1961.

It is no exaggeration to say that the fate of Berlin and all of Germany was decided on the battlefields of the Second World War and not by the war and postwar agreements which have borne most of the blame. Both Churchill and Stalin knew what Roosevelt should have known—that in war and peace possession is the better part of the law. This is another way of saying that the kind of peace settlement you will be able to obtain after the conclusion of the war will in good measure be determined by the kind of military strategy you are willing and able to pursue during the war. The ability of the Soviet Union to conquer all of Eastern and most of Central Europe established the ability of the Soviet Union to control the conquered territories politically. The location of the Western garrisons in West Berlin deep inside Soviet-controlled territory put those garrisons at the mercy of the Soviet Union. It has been our great illusion both with regard to the Berlin issue and the German problem as a whole to think and act on the assumption that, in the absence of extraordinary diplomatic trumps, the facts of military power established by a victorious war could be changed by anything but another victorious war and, more particularly, that these facts would yield to a legal arrangement based on the assumption that they did not exist.

The Yalta agreements in particular were an attempt, doomed to failure from the outset, to maintain a modicum of Western influence in the nations of Eastern Europe which the Red Army had conquered. That influence was to be maintained through the instrument of free, democratic elections. Yet in view of the fear and hatred with which most of Eastern Europe had traditionally reacted to the colossus from the East, free elections in Eastern Europe could be considered by the Soviet Union only as a weapon with which first to limit, and then to destroy, Soviet control. Thus it was utopian to expect that the Soviet Union would jeopardize its conquests in order to make good on a legal promise to a competitor who had lost his ability to enforce such a promise on the battlefields of the Second World War.

Our German policy derives from an identical illusion. It has assumed that the line of military demarcation which was established in 1945 dividing Germany into Soviet and Western zones of occupation, and the Oder-Neisse line marking the frontier between Germany and Poland, were provisional administrative boundaries. The

329

permanent delimitation of the German-Polish frontier would have to await a peace treaty, and the division of Germany would have to yield to unification based upon free elections. It is of course a foregone conclusion that free elections in East Germany would bring Soviet control to an end, just as free elections in, say, Poland would mean the end of Soviet control there.

The Soviet Union could not be expected to agree to the dismantling of its European empire without either being faced with an irresistible threat—which the West was unwilling to make—or receiving a proportionate advantage from the West—which it was not in the West's power to offer. Similarly, the rectification of the Oder-Neisse line in favor of Germany could only be envisaged in consequence of a radical change in the distribution of power in Eastern and Central Europe which the West was unable to bring about by peaceful means.

The liberation of Eastern Europe and the unification of Germany on Western terms could have been accomplished only by a victorious war. However, the United States shrank from the risk of war even when it possessed a monopoly of nuclear weapons and when the issue was not to liberate a nation of Eastern Europe but to support a liberation already accomplished, as in the case of the Hungarian revolution of 1956. Thus the West has never had a policy with regard to Eastern Europe and Germany. Its declared aims could not be achieved through the means it was willing to use. Between the words pronounced and the actions contemplated there has been a gap which could remain invisible only so long as the West was not compelled to square its actions with its words, or vice versa. It is the historic significance of Khrushchev's initiative that it now forces the West to face two alternatives, dangerous in different ways: eating its words and thereby endangering its relations with West Germany, or else risking military action and thereby endangering its very existence.

The chancelleries of the Western nations, that of Bonn included, have of course not been unaware that it is impossible to unify Germany on Western terms and to push the German-Polish frontier eastward without exerting well-nigh irresistible diplomatic or military pressure, or both, upon the Soviet Union. Why, then, have they for fifteen years refused, in the historic words of General Clay spoken in Berlin on September 22, 1961, "to accept reality" and instead disguised an illusion in the trappings of a policy? The answer to that question is twofold. The illusion of our German policy was a by-product of a more fundamental illusion about the nature of foreign policy itself. It was as a protection against having to face that fundamental illusion that we have clung to the illusion of our German policy. That fundamental illusion soothes our collective ego, and it is much more pleasant than the reality which it has superseded. Furthermore, it has been the most important ingredient of the cement that joins West Germany to the Western alliance.

Our leaders saw in the Yalta Conference not the futile attempt it was to undo with words the actual expansion of Russian power, but the beginning of a new and noble chapter in the history of international relations. As President Roosevelt put it in his report to Congress on the Yalta Conference:

> The Crimean Conference . . . spells the end of the system of unilateral action and exclusive alliances and spheres of influence and balances of power and all the other expedients which have been tried for centuries —and have failed.
>
> We propose to substitute for all these a universal organization in which all peace-loving nations will finally have a chance to join.

To blame Soviet malevolence for the disappointment of that expectation was easier than to seek the cause of the disappointment in one's own faulty thinking about foreign policy. By continuing to insist upon the fulfilment of unfulfillable stipulations, such as free elections, one could maintain the conviction of having been right all along while accusing the adversary of having been consistently at fault. This picture of the postwar world had the additional advantage of not calling for any initiative or coherent action; it actually precluded both. Thus it gave us the satisfying illusion of having a policy without our incurring any of the risks and liabilities which a policy entails.

While this illusion had but a negative impact on American policy in that it seemed to make the search for a policy superfluous, it had a decisive, positive effect upon the orientation of the foreign policy of West Germany. We induced West Germany to join NATO and make herself the strongest European member of the Western alliance with the argument that this was the road to unification and to the rectification of the Oder-Neisse line. What all the governments concerned knew to be no more than a verbal commitment and a substitute for a policy, the mass of West German opinion took as a solemn undertaking to be followed sooner or later by action. The inability of the West to react to Khrushchev's initiative in a way that squared with its verbal commitments has suddenly brought home to West Germany opinion the illusory character of what it thought was a policy of unification and revision of the eastern frontiers; for since neither objective is attainable without the co-operation of the Soviet Union, which is of course not forthcoming, the West is now forced to admit, at least by implication, that it has no way of achieving the objectives for the sake of which West Germany joined the Western alliance.

This is a dangerous admission to make, for it removes the main rationale for the Western orientation of West Germany and by the same token suggests the possibility of a quite different orientation. The West is incapable of unifying Germany and revising its eastern frontiers through its own initiative, short of a victorious war. But the Soviet Union is not so incapable. As I pointed out more than ten years ago:

> Only the Soviet Union has it in its power to satisfy the irreducible minimum of German aspirations: the unification of Germany. Nobody will doubt that the Soviet Union would not hesitate to throw the Communists of Eastern Germany overboard if it could buy with so insignificant a sacrifice the neutrality, if not the support, of a unified German nation. Looking at the international scene through the distorting lenses of ideological animosity, we tend to forget that other nations are much less likely than we are to subordinate their perennial national interests to emotions, and that neither the Germans nor the Russians are likely to take the issue of communism as seriously as we do. The mutual support of, first, Prussia, then Germany, and Russia in challenging the rest of Europe is older than the issue of communism. A tradition of two centuries testifies to its persistence. If Stalin was able to come to an understanding with Hitler—which Hitler, not Stalin, destroyed, and much to Stalin's regret—he can be expected to deal with whoever may succeed Hitler as the head of a united Germany, on terms advantageous to both and surely for Germany less disadvantageous than to serve as the battleground in the initial stages of a third world war.
>
> Furthermore, only the Soviet Union is capable of satisfying to whatever extent it wishes a probable objective of a united Germany which ranks second only to unification itself: the rectification of Germany's

eastern frontiers. The Soviet Union has championed the territorial aggrandizement of Czechoslovakia and, more particularly, of Poland at the expense of Germany for reasons of power politics. There is no stronger cement sealing the alliance between the Soviet Union and its two strongest neighbors to the west than the latters' dependence upon Russian protection for their new frontiers. What ties Czechoslovakia and Poland to the Russian chariot is not national sympathy nor is it the affinity of political ideologies. It is the overwhelming power of the Soviet Union, which in its own interest must defend the western frontiers of these two satellites against a Germany allied with the West. However, if the Soviet Union could advance the western limits of its sphere of influence from the Order-Neisse line and the Elbe to the Rhine by winning a united Germany over to its side, what reason would there be for the Soviet Union to protect the new frontiers of Czechoslovakia and Poland against a friendly Germany, especially if the friendship of that Germany could be bought by the surrender of these frontiers? Faced with a choice between the potent enmity or sullen indifference of a resentful Germany and the hapless enmity of its abandoned satellites, Stalin would not hesitate to do what the tsars did time and again, and what he himself did once before: sacrifice the interests of Poland on the altar of Russo-German friendship.[1]

What Stalin would have done Khrushchev will do if the opportunity presents itself. By substituting illusions for facts and verbal commitments for policies, we have brought that opportunity appreciably closer. Thus the iceman cometh to nations, as he does to men.

[1] *In Defense of the National Interest* (New York: Alfred A. Knopf, Inc., 1951), pp. 196–97.

39 *Neutralism*

Neutralism, the desire not to be aligned with either side in the Cold War, is today a most persuasive trend in world politics. Virtually all the new nations of Africa and Asia have openly espoused it and made it their official policy. Moreover, as a popular movement, more or less articulate, the trend is strong even in the nations which belong to one or the other of the two blocs. Nations such as England, France, West Germany, and Japan, who were masters of their own fate only yesterday, resent being wedded for better or for worse to the United States. While their governments remain committed to the alliance with the United States, large masses of their peoples wish they were not so committed. That such tendencies are not limited to this side of the Iron Curtain was clearly revealed by the Polish revolt of 1956, which at least temporarily increased the freedom of maneuver of the Polish government on the international scene, and by the Hungarian revolution of the same year, which produced the Nagy government's declaration of neutrality between East and West.

This world-wide trend toward neutralism has baffled the United States. On the one hand, challenged by a communism which seeks the dominion of the world and is convinced that it will attain it, the United States has a vital interest in seeing as many nations as possible share its way of life and support its point of view. On the other hand, it is not lost upon the United States that many nations refuse to do either, and prefer to steer an independent course between East and West. The United States has thus far not been able to reconcile these contradictory attitudes in a consistent foreign policy and has moved from the extreme of blanket disapproval of neutralism to the other extreme of blanket approval.

John Foster Dulles expressed the then prevailing mood when, in a speech on June 9, 1956, he defined neutrality as the pretense "that a nation can best gain safety for itself by being indifferent to the

From the *New York Times Magazine*, August 27, 1961.

fate of others. This has increasingly become an obsolete conception and, except under very exceptional circumstances, it is an immoral and short-sighted conception." More recently, American opinion has tended to go to the other pole of finding virtue in neutralism because it avoids at least the vice of alignment with the Soviet bloc. "We do not urge," said President Eisenhower to fifteen African leaders on October 14, 1960—"indeed, we do not desire—that you should belong to one camp or the other. You cannot afford to waste your money which is needed to build the hospitals, the schools, the roads that your people need—you cannot afford to put that money into costly armaments."

The new foreign policy of the United States, as it is now being fashioned by a new administration, should first of all recognize that the term "neutralism" covers four different situations which require different American responses. Neutralism may mean escapism, pure and simple; it may mean political non-commitment; it may mean moral indifference. And it may mean surreptitious alignment with the Soviet bloc.

The escapist variety of neutralism is popular in the formerly great powers of Western Europe and in Japan. Large masses within these nations long for a detached position which would restore to their nations the ability to pursue an independent foreign policy and minimize their exposure to atomic destruction. This type of neutralism expresses a popular mood but is repelled by the awful risks which the atomic age imposes upon nations of the second rank, and by such nations' impotence in the face of these risks. But could those nations not escape these risks and at the same time restore their freedom of action if they were to loosen their ties with the United States? A majority of delegates to last year's conference of the British Labor party thought so. They went on record in favor of the unilateral nuclear disarmament of Great Britain. And many outside the Labor party share their desire to be done with American bases on British soil.

The second form of neutralism, political non-commitment, is the official policy of most of the new nations of Asia and Africa. As such, it is a matter of self-interest based upon three facts of the new nations' existence. First, most of these countries owe their independence to national revolutions. Second, they are unstable. Third, they need a maximum of foreign aid with a minimum of political strings. A political commitment of the new nations to one or the other bloc would run counter to the interests derived from these facts. They feel they could not join the Western bloc, of which their former colonial overlord is a member, without endangering their national revolutions, and they could not join the Communist bloc without running the risk of their national revolutions being taken over by communism. In view of their weakness, most of them could not join either bloc without being reduced to satellites—that is, colonies by a different name. And by remaining uncommitted and threatening to commit themselves to the other side (or to collapse), they play upon the fears of both sides in order to gain maximum advantages.

This type of neutralism has at times tried to go beyond mere political non-commitment and create a positive political force—a neutralist "third force" pursuing a common policy. The declaration of Bandung of April, 1955, the meeting of Nasser, Nehru, and Tito of July, 1956, and the recent attempt of a number of African nations to pursue a common policy in the Congo are cases in point. Yet while some of these nations have been able to act in unison with regard to certain specific problems, all attempts to commit them to common policies on the basis of their neutralism have failed; for what unites them is but one—negative—fact: the desire not to commit themselves to either bloc. Beyond that, their foreign policies are determined by the same conflicting ambitions and interests as are those of older nations. It is indicative of this essentially negative character of neutralism that in the General Assembly of the United Nations the neutralist nations, in spite of commanding a majority of the votes, have been unable to substitute for the policies of the two blocs a common policy of their own, but have generally split three ways: a minority voting with either bloc and the majority abstaining.

Neutralism as political non-commitment, joined to the attempt to pursue an independent foreign policy, is most typically represented by Nasser's United Arab Republic. While leaning on the Soviet bloc without definitely committing himself to it, Nasser has been trying to establish under Egyptian leadership a three-circle empire composed of the Arab world, all Islamic nations, and the new nations of

Africa. Yet, while at times the Arab League and more recently the so-called Casablanca nations—Ghana, Guinea, Mali, and Morocco—have followed Nasser's lead in their verbal declarations, Nasser has been much less successful in committing his neutralist associates to common policies under Egypt's leadership.

The third type of neutralism, moral indifference, refuses to take sides in the ideological struggle between East and West. More particularly, it refuses to pass moral judgment upon the policies of either side. It sees that struggle as a contest for power between two blocs and social systems which are both morally defective in different ways. "A plague on both your houses" is about as far as it is willing to go by way of moral commitment. The neutralism of moral indifference has found its most eminent champion in Nehru of India. (However, it is worthy of note that Nehru's moral indifference has had a way of decreasing as the political interests of India are directly affected, as in the case of Tibet and China.) The neutralism of moral indifference is not uncommon in England and France, and Poland and Hungary.

Finally, the pseudo neutralism marking alignment with the Soviet bloc is a by-product of drastic changes in the world balance of power favoring that bloc. These changes are forcing the United States to retreat from certain exposed positions. The agreement to "neutralize" such a position, of which of course Laos is the prime contemporary example, has nothing to do with genuine neutralization. It amounts to nothing more than a façade behind which Soviet influence prevails. It performs no genuine function in terms of neutralism. Its only function is to spare the sensibilities of the West in the face of a defeat.

Neutralism has been growing in recent years due to four factors which have transformed the international scene. First, many of the nations who fifteen years ago had to ally themselves with the United States for the sake of survival have regained their economic strength and political stability. For them to remain within the American orbit can at least appear to be again a matter of choice rather than of necessity. Second, in view of the emergence of the Soviet Union as a nuclear power of the first rank, alliance with the United States strikes some as no longer an asset, but a liability. While in case of a nuclear war no nation is safe from nuclear destruction, the risk is increased almost to the point of certainty for the allies of the nuclear powers. Or, to put it the other way around, there may be a slightly better chance for a nation not so allied to escape nuclear destruction. Third, the "new look" of Soviet foreign policy seeks to strengthen neutralist tendencies throughout the world by proclaiming "peaceful coexistence" for all nations as an alternative to the Cold War. It threatens the allies of the United States with atomic destruction and holds out the promise of disarmament, foreign trade, and foreign aid to those who keep at least a neutralist course between the two blocs. Finally, the acceptability of this alternative is considerably enhanced by the competition between the United States and the Soviet Union for the privilege of supplying aid to the uncommitted nations. This competition offers the uncommitted nations the advantages, and exempts them from the liabilities, of belonging to either bloc. What more can such a nation hope for than to have the best of both worlds without belonging to either?

This is obviously not a heroic attitude. But in our disparagement of neutralism we have refrained from asking: Does it make sense from the point of view of the neutralists? This is the only politically relevant question, because nations align themselves with other nations or refuse to do so in view of their interests rather than on the basis of some abstract moral standard. And in view of their interests, the answer is bound to be yes. A nation such as the United Arab Republic, which pursues a neutralist policy by playing the United States against the Soviet Union or vice versa, obviously is better off politically, militarily, and economically than if it were to commit itself fully to one or the other side; for thus it is able to use the support it receives from both sides rather than being used for the purposes of one side. Similarly, a nation such as India, considering its unsolved ethnic, cultural, and economic problems, might fear for its very existence if it were to join one or the other bloc. Most of the new, weak nations of Africa, if they were to exchange their neutralist position for one of alignment, would risk being reduced to a new colonial status.

As for Japan and the nations of Western Europe, why should they not search for an escape from the liabilities of the nuclear age, since we are searching for such an escape ourselves? In truth, we are all—Americans, Englishmen, Japanese—neutralists in the escapist sense, for we all seek and hope for a way out of the awful dilemma of the nuclear age. The difference is only that we Americans, by virtue of our deeper involvement and paramount responsibility, know better than some of our friends how futile it is to try to opt out of a commitment to which there is no viable alternative.

The three genuine types of neutralism call for varied American reactions. To the escapist variety we ought to bring human sympathy and understanding. Yet we shall respond to it most effectively when we pursue policies clearly calculated to minimize, if not eliminate, the risk of atomic destruction. To the neutralism of moral indifference our most effective answer similarly lies in our deeds. We shall deprive this type of neutralism of its plausibility if our policies at home and abroad clearly establish a moral posture not only different from, but also superior to, that of the Communist world. However, it is neutralism as political non-commitment which presents our foreign policy with its really creative opportunity. President Kennedy recognized this when, in his interview with John Fischer on December 9, 1959, he called neutralism "inevitable" and "the great trend." He continued:

During the immediate years ahead this is likely to be an increasing trend in Africa and probably also in Latin America. In Asia, however, there may be some movement away from a wholly uncommitted neutralism as a result of the growing awareness of the Chinese threat. The desire to be independent and free carries with it the desire not to become engaged as a satellite of the Soviet Union or too closely allied to the United States.

We have to live with that, and if neutrality is the result of a concentration on internal problems, raising the standard of living of the people and so on, particularly in the underdeveloped countries, I would accept that. It's part of our own history for over a hundred years. We should look with friendship upon those people who want to beat the problems that almost overwhelm them, and wish to concentrate their energies on doing that, and do not want to become associated as the tail of our kite.

However, it is not enough that we have left behind unqualified opposition to neutralism, of which the indiscriminate search for allies—the collector's approach to alliances—was a logical consequence. Having recognized that political non-commitment is the only policy many of the new nations can afford to pursue, we must find a positive relationship to them. A number of uncommitted nations are weak, and their weakness together with the Balkanization of vast areas of the globe, especially of Africa, has greatly increased the sources of disorder. That Balkanization runs counter to the technological requirements of the age, which call for political units larger than even the traditional nation-states of Europe. What is required is a "new order" to replace the defunct order of empire. Communism offers such a "new order," adapted to the wants of neutralism, for it appears to seek only an implicit kind of alignment without formal explicit commitment. We have tended to counter this Communist attempt at establishing a "new order" among the uncommitted nations by offering them protection against communism. Yet while these nations need such protection, they refuse to recognize that need, for they fear that if they did they would be drawn into the Cold War on the side of the West. For them the paramount issue is not communism, but colonialism. The invocation of anticommunism pure and simple, then, is self-defeating as an American policy toward the uncommitted nations.

What we need is a positive alternative to, rather than a negative polemic against, the Communist "new order." It goes without saying that the "new order" to be promoted and supported by the United States must be unequivocally anticolonialist and must meet the material aspirations and requirements of the uncommitted nations. Yet that "new order" must also be a political order which has room for all kinds and degrees of political non-commitment. The uncommitted nations may well incline toward one or the other side in their moral preferences, political sympathies, economic interests, and even limited military support. The reconciliation of these different shades of neutralism with the interests of the United States, without compelling the neutralists to enter into an explicit commitment, will put the statesmanship of the Kennedy administration to its supreme test.

Even so, resentment against Western power is likely to persist among neutralist nations and with it the tendency to play off the East against the West. To counteract this, it will avail the United States little to try to curry favor with the neutralists by trimming its policies to their preferences; neutralism feeds on this kind of weakness. Rather, we must pursue clearly defined, strongly executed, and ably presented policies to a successful conclusion, thereby demonstrating to all concerned that we know what we are about and that it does not pay to cross us. Only so will we gain the respect of the neutralists and have a chance to win their support as well. And we might well remind the neutralist nations—at appropriate occasions, and tactfully but firmly—that their neutralism is but a function of the power of the United States. Were the United States not committed to containing the Communist bloc, neutralism could not exist as a policy and would at best survive as an impotent desire and a vain hope. Neutralism, like peaceful coexistence, is for the Soviet Union but a stepping stone toward communization. A nation can afford to be neutralist, not because this is what the Soviet Union wants it to be, but because the power of the Soviet Union is not sufficient to absorb it into the Soviet bloc. For neutralism in the Cold War, like neutrality in a shooting war, depends upon the balance of power. It is a luxury which certain nations can afford because the power of one antagonist cancels out the power of the other.

40 *The Political Problems of Polyethnic States*

The peace and order of the state rests on a dual foundation: the disinclination of the citizens to disturb peace and order and their inability to do so if they should be so inclined. Groups within a state are unable to disturb peace and order if the power of the government cannot be challenged. They are unwilling to do so under two conditions. They must have a loyalty to the state as a whole which surpasses their loyalty to any part of it, and they must expect from the state at least an approximation to justice through the partial satisfaction of their aspirations. Overwhelming power, suprasectional loyalties, expectation of justice—those are the cornerstones of peace and order within the state.

As long as loyalty to the state was defined primarily in dynastic terms and justice primarily in religious ones, the polyethnic composition of a state did not affect its cohesion. It was only when these traditional principles of integration were replaced by national ones, defined in linguistic, ethnic, or historic terms, that polyethnic composition became an important factor in the integration of the state. It became a factor of disintegration for the old dynastic states and for the colonial empires and the principle of integration for the new nation-states.

Tension between nationalism as a sectional focus of loyalty and a dynastic or imperial focus is, of course, existential. Whether or not this inevitable tension will develop into open conflict depends upon the intensity of the respective loyalties and, more particularly, upon the measure of justice which an ethnic group expects from the central government. It also depends upon the reputation for unchallengeable power the central government enjoys. In the measure that this reputation is unimpaired, only desperation will move an ethnic group to challenge the central government; and in the measure that

Paper presented at the Fifth World Congress of the International Political Science Association, September, 1961.

this reputation is justified by actual performance, the ethnic group will either be cowed into submission or extinguished altogether.

It is only when the reputation for unchallengeable power has been impaired that the existential tension between nationalism and the central government has a chance to become acute as actual or potential conflict. It is only then that conflicting loyalties and disappointed expectations of justice have a chance to generate political and military conflicts which have international repercussions. The dissolution of the French colonial empire exemplifies the interconnection of these different factors. France emerged from the Second World War with its reputation for unchallengeable power impaired in the eyes of its colonial subjects by virtue of its defeat in Europe and, more particularly, at the hands of the Japanese. The fact that a European power had been defeated—and drastically so—by an Asian one gave the latent conflict or loyalties and frustrated expectations of justice of the people of Indochina a sharp political and military edge; for the Japanese victories made it plausible for the Indochinese to believe that they, too, could win victories over the French.

Yet while the process of disintegration was in full swing in Indochina, it was but in its beginnings in North Africa, and especially in Algeria. Many leaders of the Algerian insurrection fought with the French army in Indochina. For, while Indochina was in full revolt, many North Africans thought that they could reconcile loyalty to the ethnic group with loyalty to France and expected justice from France for their national aspirations. It was only when France was being defeated in Indochina and had disappointed the North African expectations of justice that the disintegrating forces took hold.

A polyethnic state may disintegrate into its polyethnic components because of its inherent centrifugal tendencies. That is to say, while its breakup is bound to have an impact upon international relations, it is not primarily due to their influence. The dissolution of the Asian and African empires of Great Britain and of the African empire of France is of this kind. In the other hand, disintegration may be a mere function of international factors. This is the case when an ethnic group within a polyethnic state is being used by another state on behalf of the latter's interests against the polyethnic one. Nazi Germany used in that way German minorities throughout the world for the spread of German influence and the establishment of German rule on the ruins of polyethnic states. The destruction of Czechoslovakia is the classic example of this technique.

This technique is, of course, greatly facilitated by ethnic affinity between the group within the polyethnic state and the hostile power. For here it is not only the conflict of loyalties between the ethnic group and the central government of the polyethnic state that plays a part, but also the fact that the loyalty of the ethnic group is centered upon the hostile power. The conflict is here in fact between the central government of the polyethnic state and the hostile power for which the ethnic group holds an advance position. The interests of the hostile power and the ethnic group are identical.

The same relationship between a hostile power and a group within a polyethnic state can also exist without ethnic affinity. The hostile power may support any such group that accepts this support, both pursuing the negative purpose of weakening the polyethnic state, however different their own positive purposes may be. The support which the European subjects of the Ottoman Empire received in their struggle for independence from European nations exemplifies this situation. It is also exemplified by the support different ethnic groups within the Congo have received from different European powers. The conflict of loyalties remains here within the polyethnic state, playing between the group seeking independence and the central government. The result of the successful struggle for independence is "balkanization," that is, the dissolution of the polyethnic state into component groups rather than the formation of a new large-scale political unit based on ethnic affinity.

The polyethnic state is, then, under modern conditions an unstable political unit which tends to disintegrate under the impact of nationalism or foreign intervention. It presents a standing invitation for new imperialisms to fashion new polyethnic states from the fragments of the old ones. These disintegrating tendencies are held in check by new concentrations of unchallengeable power and by new loyalties and expectations of justice overriding the ethnic ones. The new polyethnic states which were formed out of the fragments of the dynastic and colonial empires must maintain themselves by the same techniques to which these empires owe their existence and which finally failed them. Thus the polyethnic state of Pakistan

344

maintains a precarious existence only through the overwhelming power exercised by a military dictatorship and the overriding loyalty to a common religion. Similarly, the Soviet Union maintains itself as a polyethnic state through the unchallengeable power of "democratic centralism" and the overriding loyalty to communism.

The future of the new polyethnic states, especially those of Africa, will depend upon their ability to develop a central power, common loyalties, and a common expectation of justice—strong enough to keep centrifugal tendencies in check. In the measure that they will be incapable of developing common loyalties and expectations of justice, they are bound to emphasize unchallengeable power which will then take the form of tyranny or totalitarianism. Even this desperate remedy, however, may not save them from new imperialisms which may either spring up in their midst or conquer from without.

In consequence of the dissolution of the colonial empires, polyethnic states have proliferated in our time. Their polyethnic character is in good measure the result of colonial boundaries drawn either by the accidents of discovery and control or according to the principle of compensation between rival colonial powers. These new polyethnic states are threatened in their existence by two paradoxes. On the one hand, they owe their existence to the principle of nationalism; by virtue of that principle, they freed themselves from colonial rule. Yet that self-same principle now threatens their existence as polyethnic states. For the principle of national self-determination which the polyethnic colony invoked against the colonial power, the several ethnic components now invoke against the new polyethnic state.

The other paradox that threatens the new polyethnic state results from the contradiction between the triumph of a nationalism unqualified by any other principle of order, on the one hand, and technological developments which have rendered nationalism obsolete as a principle of political organization, on the other. The actual political organization which corresponds to nationalism as a principle of political organization is, of course, the nation-state. Yet the new polyethnic states, too, owe their existence to the same principle of nationalism, and what we shall say about the obsolescence of the nation-state applies to them as well.

The justification of the nation-state, as of all political organization, is its ability to perform the functions for the sake of which political organization exists. The most elementary of these functions is the common defense of the life of the citizens and of the values of the civilization in which they live. A political organization which is no longer able to defend these values and even puts them in jeopardy must yield, either through peaceful transformation or violent destruction, to one capable of that defense. Thus, under the impact of the invention of gunpowder and of the first industrial revolution, the feudal order had to yield to the dynastic order and the nation-state. Under the technological conditions of the pre-atomic age, the stronger nation-states could, as it were, erect a wall behind which their citizens could live secure and the weak nation-states were similarly protected by the operation of the balance of power which added the resources of the strong to those of the weak. Thus, under normal conditions, no nation-state was able to make more than marginal inroads upon the life and civilization of its neighbors.

The modern technologies of communication, transportation, industrial production, and arms have completely destroyed this protective function of the nation-state. Yet the age which has seen the nation-state become obsolete witnesses the emergence of a multitude of new states fashioned from the fragments of the colonial empires. The number of sovereign states has approximately doubled since the First World War. Many of these new states would not have been viable political, military, and economic entities even in the heyday of the nation-state, deficient as they are in the essential prerequisites of nationhood. They could not have fed, administered, and defended themselves then; nor can they now. The disorder and threats to peace which the dissolution, first, of the Turkish and, then, of the Austro-Hungarian and western part of the Russian empires brought in its wake are being spread, in the name of nationalism, to ever wider areas of Africa and Asia. In our age, even the infinitely stronger nation-states of Europe are no longer viable political, military, and economic entities, but must submit either to the support or the conquest of the two remaining nations of the first rank, which are significantly not nation-states in the traditional sense but continental states. The tragedy of Hungary and the collapse of

346

the British and French intervention in Egypt in November, 1956, demonstrated in different ways both the continuing emotional strength of national aspirations and the political and military weakness of the nation-state. Is it then reasonable to expect that these new nations, some of them so artificial as to be even lacking the ethnic and historic foundations of nationhood, will be able to create a viable order among themselves and with their more powerful neighbors?

How can these new polyethnic states be saved from the twin evils of anarchy and a new imperialism? The principle of nationalism to which they owe their existence and which remains their main justification and principle of action carries within itself a tendency toward anarchy. Hence, it must be replaced by a supranational principle capable of maintaining order and achieving a measure of justice both among the polyethnic components of the new states and among the polyethnic states themselves. It is a moot question, which cannot be answered by theory, whether this new principle of order will develop from the policies of the United Nations or regional groupings or whether it will be imposed by the benevolent intervention of outside powers. However, it must be clear from a theoretical analysis of the forces which created them, and which now maintain and threaten them, that the new polyethnic states are faced with three alternatives: anarchy, a new imperialism, a new supranational principle of order neutralizing the anarchic tendencies which are inherent in the principle of nationalism.

41 *Polycentrism*

The split in the Communist camp, made manifest by the 22d Congress of the Soviet Communist party, is another stepping stone in the process of repudiation to which Marxist doctrine has been subjected by historic experience almost since its inception.

Marxism assumes that conflicts among nations are a mere by-product of the inner contradictions of capitalism, projected onto the international scene and bound to disappear with the disappearance of the class society itself. It further assumes that the international solidarity of the proletariat will supersede the proletarian's loyalty to the nation to which he happens to belong: If the proletarian must choose between the interests of the international proletariat and the interests of his nation, he will choose the former over the latter. Thus, before the First World War it was a matter of principle for the Marxist parties of Europe never to vote a cent for military appropriations. These assumptions suffered their first blow in 1914, when the proletarians of Europe killed each other on behalf of their respective nations, instead of either sitting on their hands or rising in unison against their capitalistic exploiters. They suffered their second blow at the end of the War, when the world proletariat did not come to the aid of the Bolshevist revolution in Russia by starting proletarian revolutions in their respective countries, particularly in the most advanced industrial nations where the proletarian revolution should have started in the first place.

Obviously, the readiness of a particular proletariat to revolt depends upon historic conditions peculiar to its national environment rather than upon the stage of its development as a class in Marxist terms. The Stalinist development of socialism in one country put the pragmatic seal upon this historic experience.

The Marxist assumption that the international solidarity of the proletariat supersedes national interests and loyalties is now in the

From the *New Leader*, March 19, 1962.

process of suffering its third great refutation. That process started with the rise of Titoism in the late 1940's. While Titoism could be dismissed as an isolated minor aberration, the continuing and ever more acute conflict between the Soviet Union and China cannot be disposed of so simply. Nor can it be explained by the Marxist doctrine of the different stages of Socialist development in different countries. We are now witnessing the reassertion of national interests by individual nations, in the face of the doctrinaire assumption of the international solidarity of Communist societies.

The divergent national interests of the Soviet Union and China have come to the fore in three different areas. (1) The Soviet Union has attained a degree of power, especially in the form of prestige, which allows it to believe that the ultimate triumph of communism throughout the world will be achieved by peaceful means. Under present conditions, China cannot expect to attain its immediate international objectives in the Far East and Southeast Asia by peaceful means. This difference in belligerence is accentuated by the greater vulnerability of Russia to nuclear destruction as compared with China. Hence, the different attitudes of Moscow and Peking toward the question of war. (2) Having completed the Stalinist phase of forced economic development, the Soviet Union can afford—or may even be pressed by its domestic public opinion—to seek a relaxation of international tensions. China, threatened by the hazards of the first violent phase of forced economic development, needs international tensions, as did Stalin in his time, to justify repression at home. (3) The Soviet attempt to manage Chinese economic development through Russian experts, on the model of Soviet management of the Eastern European economies, called forth a reaction through which the national autonomy of China reasserted itself against the prospect of being made a Russian satellite.

This last source of conflict is also a source of light illuminating the probable pattern of the future. Those of us who believe in the continuing monolithic character of the Communist camp are victims of a Marxist illusion, which the Marxists themselves, by dint of historic experience and political necessity, are in the process of throwing overboard. The national interest triumphs again over doctrinaire assumptions and ideological affinities, as it has done before under similar circumstances (for example, Richelieu's policies during

349

the religious wars and Talleyrand's policies during the Napoleonic Wars). The monolithic character of the Communist camp, derived from identical social conditions and interests and based upon ideological affinities, has always been an illusion, engendered by the Red Army's conquest of Eastern Europe and by the dependence of Communist parties throughout the world upon Soviet support. Where neither of these situations prevails, as in Yugoslavia and China, Russia has not been able to impose its will upon the domestic and foreign policies of Communist nations. And it is indeed possible, if not likely, that indigenous political developments elsewhere will bring to power Communist governments which, at the very least, will not be necessarily subservient to either the Soviet Union or China.

The United States will increase the likelihood of subservience to the extent that its foreign policy proceeds from the obsolete assumption of the solidarity of the Communist camp. By treating a Communist government as though it were a priori a mere extension of Russian or Chinese power, it increases the chances of that Communist government having no alternative but to become exactly that. Such a policy is of course much simpler to execute abroad and much easier to defend at home than the alternative policy of judging and treating each case on its merits—that is, in terms of the interests and power involved—which are bound to vary from country to country. But such a policy is also self-defeating. It is in the nature of a self-fulfilling prophecy. It gives the appearance of reality to an assumption which history has repudiated three times in the last half-century.

42 *Asia: The American Algeria*

Two great illusions have obscured for France the true nature of the Algerian problem. Their persistence has depleted the resources of France, contributed to the political and moral disintegration of France, and brought the nation to the verge of civil war. One illusion sees in Algeria just another French province, as integral a part of France as any other. The other illusion holds that the Algerian rebellion can be stamped out by military means. The illusory character of these beliefs is obvious to the outsider, but not to many intelligent Frenchmen. Nations, like men, need illusions to sustain them in their relations with themselves and their fellows, and most of the illusions are in the nature of foibles and, hence, do little harm. However, there are other illusions, such as the French ones about Algeria, which obscure a vital complex of a nation's concerns and confound its thoughts, corrupt its judgments, and misdirect its actions. They are the stuff catastrophe is made of.

It is not only France which suffers from illusions of this kind. America has them, too. What has happened in Laos allows us a glimpse into the nature of some of them. And it is probably the most dangerous of our illusions which the events in Laos have brought to the fore.

It is tempting to look at the Laotian debacle as an isolated instance of misfortune from which we must extricate ourselves as painlessly as possible. Thus we are relieved of the necessity to search in ourselves for the causes of our misfortune, to revise our ideas in the light of the facts of experience, and to adapt our actions to the objective conditions. In truth, what has happened in Laos is not a self-contained local defeat which must be regretted but can be forgotten; rather, it is the first and for the moment localized symptom of a disorder in our minds which, if it is not cured, is bound to bring forth more serious symptoms and will in the end bring us to the verge of a national catastrophe of one sort or another. The disorder

From *Commentary*, July, 1961.

consists in two illusory but strongly held beliefs: that the Communist threat outside Europe can be countered by military means, and that the Sino-Soviet empire can be contained within its present limits by surrounding its non-European periphery with local military strongholds.

The policy of containment was eminently successful in the area to which it was originally applied, that is, Europe. It was this success which led to its transformation into a general principle of American foreign policy. What has worked so well in Europe was expected to work as well at the periphery of the Sino-Soviet empire in Asia. It did not work as well. It could not have worked as well because containment as a general principle of policy derives from a dual misunderstanding. It misunderstands what made containment successful in Europe, and it misunderstands the nature of the threat containment is supposed to meet outside Europe. The Soviet Union has never been contained in Europe by the military forces which NATO could muster in Europe itself. That the Soviet Union was or could be so contained has been one of the abiding illusions which have confounded the policies of NATO. The Soviet Union has been contained by one thing and one thing alone: the nuclear power of the United States and the plausibility of its use.

The United States built its containment policy outside Europe upon the mistaken assumption that as local forces were containing the Soviet Union in Europe, so local forces could contain communism outside Europe. Thus the United States embarked upon a policy, for which John Foster Dulles bears the primary responsibility, of collecting allies and clients wherever it could find them at the periphery of the Sino-Soviet empire in order to build up their conventional military forces. Laos is part of that collection. However, military power—nuclear or conventional—is incapable of containing communism outside Europe; for the primary threat communism presents outside Europe is not military but consists in political penetration and subversion and the use of foreign aid and trade as instruments of an expansionist foreign policy. The build-up of local conventional forces is not only useless but counterproductive as an answer to this threat. Laos is a case in point.

When the Indochina war ended in 1954, the two northeastern provinces of Laos bordering on North Vietnam were under the control of the Communist Pathet Lao. The Geneva conference of the same year envisioned Laos as a neutral state with the Pathet Lao being incorporated into the royal army. That army was to be trained by the French. When the French pulled out, they were replaced by 'American military personnel in civilian clothes. This personnel tried to create a "modern" Laotian army. Its effort was supported by a total of $310 million in foreign aid. The infusion of such an amount of money into a poor economy, whose annual consumptive capacity was estimated at $24 million at the most, thoroughly corrupted the Laotian elite and created the very conditions of conspicuous consumption, demoralization, and popular dissatisfaction upon which communism feeds. In a country whose main economic problem is agriculture, we spent in 1960 somewhat more than half a million dollars for agricultural aid! The administration of our economic aid to Laos has been marked by inefficiency, incompetence, and large-scale corruption on the part of our officials and American contractors. The June 16, 1959, report on United States Aid Operations in Laos by the subcommittee of the House of Representatives Committee on Government Operations reads like a detective story peopled by crooks and misfits against whom a very few honest and competent men never had a chance.

Despite this American policy which blindly played into the hands of the Communists, the design which the Geneva conference of 1954 had developed for Laos remained, however precariously, intact. The country remained for all practical purposes divided between the Pathet Lao and the royal government under Prince Souvanna Phouma. The relations between these two groups ranged from sporadic fighting to friendly co-operation. The high point of friendly co-operation was reached in 1958 when the Pathet Lao joined the royal government. At this point the tenuous fabric of Laotian politics came apart. The United States withdrew its aid from the new government and brought about its downfall. It shifted its support from Prince Souvanna Phouma, whose policies had been pro-Western in fact and neutralist in aspiration, to a succession of inefficient and unpopular governments whose main claim to American support was their vociferous professions of anticommunism and their attempts to suppress the Pathet Lao by violent means. The shift was in the main engineered by the CIA and opposed both by

353

the State Department and even some of the CIA's own agents in the field. The shift resulted in a polarization of Laotian politics between anti-Communists and pro-Communists. Pro-Western neutralists, such as Prince Souvanna Phouma, apolitical patriots, such as Captain Kong Le (who in 1960 staged a successful coup against the royal government), and all politically conscious elements not committed to the royal government were now branded as pro-Communists and most of them became so in fact.

The attempt to replace a covertly pro-Western government with one which was openly so and had at its disposal an army trained and led by Americans called forth a drastic reaction from the outside. While the clashes between the royal government and the Pathet Lao had been perfunctory and of a local nature up to 1960, the Pathet Lao now staged what amounted to a strategic offensive whose obvious goal was the conquest of Laos and the overthrow of the royal government. And while up to 1959 the Communist powers reacted with considerable restraint to the attempts to destroy the Pathet Lao and transform Laos into a Western military outpost, both North Vietnam and the Soviet Union now started in earnest to provide the Pathet Lao with supplies and technicians. As these lines are being written (early June, 1961), the Communist domination of Laos is virtually a foregone conclusion.

What has happened in Laos has happened before and will happen again—in more important places and with more serious consequences —unless the underlying disorder in our thinking is removed. It happened before in China when we put our bets upon the most inefficient, corrupt, and unpopular group (hence the one most unlikely to succeed), allowed a one-time promising moderate group to fall by the wayside, and thereby actively promoted the polarization of Chinese politics between anti-Communists and Communists, which led to the latter's victory. The same pattern has emerged in South Vietnam and is in the process of emerging in Spain. In both countries, we have identified ourselves with a regime that suppresses the opposition and equates it with communism. In consequence, the popular aspirations for change tend to flow into Communist channels. The opposition tends to live up to the Communist reputation bestowed upon it by the powers that be, and the same polarization of political life which we have noticed in Laos and in China in the last stages of civil war is taking place in South Vietnam and Spain.

The United States, of course, no longer has any freedom of action once this polarization takes place. Yet it bears the responsibility of having contributed actively, if not decisively, to that polarization by supporting those groups whose anticommunism seemed to be the most reliable and effective because they appeared to be most firmly committed to the defense of the status quo and most ruthless in that defense. Emphasis upon military aid is the appropriate practical concomitant of this conception of the political problem, and since military force is the last resort of decaying regimes, military aid becomes also a practical necessity.

The emphasis upon military aid is still further supported by the assumption that a revolutionary situation, likely to lead to civil war, in a country close to the periphery of the Sino-Soviet empire, was bound to be caused by Communist military intervention. Thus when the Laotian military disorders flared up in 1959 and 1960, our government assumed, and acted upon the assumption, that North Vietnamese units had entered Laos in force. This assumption, fostered by the royal government for obvious reasons, proved to be without foundation.

This emphasis upon military aid, to the detriment of economic assistance, is being nourished from still another root: the absence of a plausible and workable philosophy of economic aid. To improve the lot of the Laotian peasant—the main economic problem of Laos —through economic aid from the outside requires a subtle understanding of alien economic conditions and a delicacy in social and political manipulation far beyond the ken of most of the administrators of foreign aid we have sent to Laos. It also requires awareness of the political context within which economic aid is supposed to operate. Where that context is blurred, as it has been in recent years in Laos, foreign aid loses its sense of direction. Considering these and other complexities of economic aid, it is infinitely simpler intellectually and more satisfying practically to concentrate upon the military sector. Any army can be expanded, trained, and supplied, and you can show the taxpayer by way of tangible results what he has got for his money. If the army is too big for the population to support, if its training is unsuited to the terrain in which it is likely to operate, if its build-up is politically counterproductive—all of which apply to the results of our military aid in Laos—Congress and the public at large are not likely to be aware of it.

A policy of military containment outside Europe is self-defeating in that it is a powerful factor in the expansion of what it intends to contain. Yet, while in Europe our policy of containment has thus far not been put to the test because of the plausibility of the American atomic deterrent, it has been tested in Asia. It has worked unmistakably only in Korea, albeit at the cost of war, and for the time being in the straits of Taiwan. In Indochina it did not work before 1945, nor does it work now. It is exactly this mixture of success and failure in the short run and the prospect of failure in the long run that threatens the United States with a catastrophe of one sort or another.

In the short run, the inner weakness of our position in the territories of our Asian allies and clients has brought about the virtual loss of Laos, it acutely endangers South Vietnam, and threatens Iran; it may threaten other nations tomorrow. The administration has reconciled itself to the loss of Laos. Is it going to reconcile itself tomorrow to the loss of South Vietnam and the day after to that of Iran? If it does, it is likely to face a storm of indignation at home, and only a very courageous and farsighted President will be willing to face it. If the administration does not reconcile itself to further territorial losses to the Communists, it will be compelled to embark upon a policy of military intervention which can only have inconclusive results at best. Furthermore, in so far as that intervention takes place at the periphery of the Chinese empire, it is predicated upon the continuing military weakness of Communist China.

What contains China today is not the military power that the United States can muster in Laos, Thailand, South Vietnam, or Taiwan; what contains China is its own weakness. However, that weakness is likely to be replaced in the not too distant future by a strength which will make Communist China the foremost military power in Asia. When that moment comes, the policy of peripheral containment will be put to its crucial test and will face the United States on the grand scale with the choice between retreat and war—a choice which has faced us already on a very limited scale in Laos. That war will not be a jungle war but an all-out nuclear war. Once China has become militarily strong, it will be contained—if it can be contained at all—as is the Soviet Union today in Europe, only by the plausibility of the American nuclear deterrent. How great is that plausibility likely to be ? And even if the Chinese government should consider it to be fully persuasive, how will it assess the damage it might suffer as over against that of the United States? It is upon calculations such as these, implicit in the policy of containment in Asia, that not only the success of that particular policy but the very fate of the United States may well depend.

It is disturbing that a policy which has such fateful implications is being pursued without an obvious regard for these implications. Some—myself included—have heard very influential and otherwise intelligent men, military and civilian, express opinions about our policy toward Communist China which, in their bland disregard of obvious facts and likely developments, were no less at odds with reality than the opinions of French generals and politicians who believe in the possibility of keeping Algeria French by military means. The very folly of trying to transform Laos into an American military stronghold at the borders of China without anticipating a reaction from across the border points to a collective loss of the sense of reality.

Nor is that loss limited to officials of the government. The great mass of our people live in virtually total ignorance of the realities of the situation in Asia. Here looms the prospect of another catastrophe. The popular assessment of America's position in the world is about ten years behind the times. The standards of judgment of the American people stem from the pre-atomic age and that short-lived period when the United States had an atomic monopoly. Nobody in authority has told us how radically the bipolarity of nuclear weapons has affected the position of the United States and how the further proliferation of nuclear weapons is likely to affect it, to what extent the commitments of the United States are out of tune with its power, and what changes in our thinking and actions are necessary to cope with the new conditions. How will the American people react when they come face to face with the facts of life, not by way of a reasoned and authoritative presentation, but through the unintelligible and, hence, misinterpreted experience of piecemeal reverses? The memory of McCarthyism should give us warning; and so should the political and moral devastation which France is

357

suffering in consequence of its Algerian illusions. Yet as France owes its awakening from these illusions to the insight and courage of one man, so must America rely upon the mind and character of one man to awaken it from its Asian illusions. The President has a sacred duty to think deeply about these matters and, regardless of political risk, to speak with frankness.

43 *The China Policy of the United States*

In order to understand the policy of the United States toward China it is necessary to go back to the Chinese civil war. It is at this point that the confusion over the real issue obscured the thinking and frustrated the policies of the United States. When it became obvious that the Nationalist regime was unable to cope with the revolutionary situation even if supported by American arms and advice, only two courses, which General Wedemeyer's report of 1947 clearly envisaged, were logically open to American policy. One was military intervention on such a scale as to be sufficient not only to crush the Communist armies but also to keep discontent permanently in check. Military intervention of this kind would have entailed military and political commitments of incalculable magnitude. This course of action was rejected by the framers of the United States' foreign policy on the advice of, among others, the then Secretary of State, George Marshall. The other course of action was predicated on the assumption that the triumph of the Communist revolution in China was inevitable. It would then have been incumbent upon American policy to reconcile itself to the inevitable—as policy, being the art of the possible, frequently must— and to exploit whatever potentialities there were for the promotion of American interests; for while Chinese communism is the ideological ally of Moscow, its rise to power owes little to Russia, nor will it need to rely on Russian support to maintain itself in power.

This fundamental difference between Chinese communism and the Communist regimes of Eastern Europe, which would not have come to power nor could have stayed in power without Russian support, allows the Communist government of China a freedom of action in international affairs which the Communist governments of Eastern Europe almost completely lack. Consequently, the Communist government of China can, if it chooses, pursue a course in foreign policy which is determined not by the interests of the Soviet

From the *China Quarterly*, May, 1962.

Union expressed in orders from Moscow but by the traditional interests of China. These interests may or may not coincide with the interests of the Soviet Union, and Chinese and Russian policies may or may not be parallel.

It must be remembered that the traditional objectives of Russia in the Far East have more often than not been at odds with the traditional objectives of China. Furthermore, and more importantly, the Soviet Union cannot look with equanimity on the economic and military development of Communist China; for if Communist China should add to its enormous superiority in manpower the achievements of modern technology under the firm political direction of the Chinese Communist party, it would then become of necessity the most powerful nation on earth, overshadowing by far the Soviet Union. The rulers of the Kremlin, considering the opposition they face at home and their uncertain relations with the satellites of Eastern Europe, must also fear—and probably already have reason to fear—the influence which China can exert in the struggle for power within the ruling group of the Soviet Union and in the struggle for a certain measure of independence which the satellite nations are waging against Moscow. Whether there will be further coincidence or divergence of Russian and Chinese interests and policies will depend in good measure upon the policies of the non-Communist nations.

There was the chance for the United States to pursue a policy which, although difficult to explain to the general public and necessarily devoid of spectacular short-run successes, offered the only chance, granted the inevitability of the Communist domination of China, to further the traditional American interest of maintaining the balance of power in Asia. The United States chose neither of the two courses open to it, or rather, it chose both of them, pursuing them sometimes simultaneously, sometimes alternately, but always half-heartedly and without consistency. During the civil war the United States intervened on the side of the Nationalists but limited its commitments in matériel and men so strictly as to preclude any chance of success. Simultaneously, the United States tried to bring about a coalition between the Nationalists and Communists which, if it had succeeded, would, of necessity, have led to the absorption of the former by the latter.

360

General Marshall's attempt in 1946 to end the civil war by forming a coalition government of Communists and Nationalists partook of the same underestimation of Nationalist weakness which underlay all of American policy in the immediate postwar years and compounded it by misunderstanding the character of Chinese communism. It was grounded in two false assumptions. One was that the Chinese Communists were really agrarian reformers at heart using Marxist slogans without believing them. The other was a misplaced faith in the Nationalist regime as an efficient and reliable machine of government. Actually it had become impossible at that stage to do business with Chiang Kai-shek with any expectation of future efficient and honest performance, and it was to misunderstand completely the nature of communism, as it manifests itself in China and elsewhere, to disregard its necessary aspirations for total power as a means to realize the truth of Marxism.

After the end of the civil war, the United States continued this essentially contradictory and indecisive policy. Under the impact of the Chinese intervention in the Korean War and influenced by domestic politics, the United States drifted into a policy of counter-revolution per se. That is to say, the United States has refused to recognize the Communist regime as the legitimate government of China and has denied its right to represent China in the United Nations. On the other hand, the United States has continued to recognize the Chiang Kai-shek regime of Formosa as the only authentic voice of all China. The United States has given it political, economic, moral, and military support, assuring its very existence through the commitment of the armed forces of the United States. The United States has countenanced small-scale operations of the Chiang Kai-shek forces against the Chinese mainland and has given its active military support to the Nationalist defense of the offshore islands.

The result of this policy has been inconclusive in terms of the very assumptions upon which that policy is based; for while that policy has strengthened the Nationalist forces on Formosa, that policy being the very precondition for their survival, it has done virtually nothing to weaken the Communist domination of the Chinese mainland. Thus, on the one hand, the United States refuses to recognize that the Chinese Communists are here to stay, and on the

361

other hand, it has done nothing to dislodge that regime by counter-revolutionary measures. The United States has done nothing effective because there is nothing it can do short of an all-out war against China which it fears will degenerate into an all-out world war destroying the United States and its enemies. This policy has had one positive result: it has kept Formosa out of the hands of the Communists. It has had two major negative results: it has isolated the United States completely from its allies, and it has lost the United States the support of public opinion throughout the world. The Chinese Communists have not been slow to exploit the difficult position in which the United States finds itself today by virtue of its own policy.

While the United States has tried to extricate itself from the impasse of its Far Eastern policy, the Chinese Communists have refused to lend a helping hand. From their point of view it is much more advantageous to let the United States remain entangled in a web of self-created contradictions, unable to advance or retreat, than to co-operate with the United States in the search for a compromise settlement. The Chinese Communists are aware of the difficult American position, and they also know that time is on their side, for the balance of military power is bound to tilt more and more toward the Chinese side. Communist China will become an independent military factor in world politics, and the world-wide opposition to American policy toward China will grow stronger as America's military position grows weaker. Thus, paradoxically enough, the main issue is today no longer whether or not the United States wants to recognize Communist China. The issue is, rather, whether Communist China wants to be recognized by the United States, and obviously it does not want to be recognized if it has to pay the price of recognizing the status quo in the Formosa Strait.

What is the rationale of the Far Eastern policy of the United States which has led to such unfortunate results? That policy is based upon two fundamental assumptions: first, the use of force as an instrument of national policy cannot be countenanced anywhere in the world; and second, the policy of containment can be successfully applied to the Far East. The first assumption derives from the fear that the use of violence, however limited, may leap by stages to the use of nuclear weapons and to the destruction of civilization itself. A policy derived from this assumption, however, requires the existence of a status quo which is reasonably acceptable to all concerned and therefore does not offer an incentive for change by violent means. This condition does not prevail at present in the Far East. The other assumption holds that the threat that confronts the United States around the world is primarily military in nature and therefore must be countered primarily by military means. The policy of military containment, eminently successful in Europe where it originated, must then be applied around the world. The correctness of this assumption is subject to very serious doubt. What threatens the United States in Asia is not primarily military aggression but political aggression and, more particularly, a slow and insidious shift of the allegiance of hundreds of millions of people to Russian and Chinese communism. To try to stem this tide by military means is likely not only to be useless but also to be self-defeating. Furthermore, even if the threat emanating from Communist China were primarily of a military nature, the United States' military policy in the Far East would be inadequate.

The balance of military power between Communist China and the United States is quite different from that between the United States and the Soviet Union in Europe. The Soviet Union has thus far been deterred by the retaliatory nuclear power of the United States; but can China, in its particular position and with its particular tactics, be so deterred? In terms of conventional war, a strong China is as superior to southeast Asia as the United States is to Central America. Southeast Asia has been the traditional sphere of influence of a strong China. In order to deny that region to China, peripheral military measures will not suffice. Whoever wants to contain a strong China must strike at the center of that power. The United States has never been willing, and for good reasons, to contemplate such a strike. Thus the United States has been caught in a contradiction between what it wants to achieve and the measures it is willing and able to apply in order to achieve it. Only a radical revision of the very assumptions upon which its China policy is based will extricate it from that contradiction.

The chances that the government of the United States will take the initiative in revising its China policy are virtually nil. A considerable number of high officials are aware of the facts of life in the Far East, yet quite a number, especially in the military establishment, are not. Furthermore, and most importantly, public opinion has been conditioned for more than a decade to support a negative policy toward China, unaware of the risks, expecting at worst an indefinite continuation of the status quo and at best some kind of miracle which will make the Chinese Communists go away. The present policy could only be reversed through the President's initiative, requiring a combination of political insight and courage that has not been forthcoming in the past and cannot be expected in the foreseeable future.

More likely than not, then, the China policy of the United States will be changed not by a deliberate act of statesmanship, but under the impact of irresistible pressures from without. One of these pressures is likely to emanate from the United Nations; the other, from the growing military power of China. The United States cannot but yield to the former; the latter will confront it with the painful alternative of retreat or war. Wise policy would anticipate these alternatives and try to avoid them by creating conditions opening up different and more favorable alternatives. It would explore the degree of the Chinese Communists' present weakness and, if it should appear promising, exploit it politically, militarily, and economically. On the other hand, it would assess the likelihood of future Chinese strength and would, before it became acute, prepare positions designed to withstand it with a minimum of risk. To do nothing and wait for something to happen and then react by improvisation is the very opposite of rational policy; it is tantamount to its abdication. It sacrifices reason and interest upon the altar of a domestic political peace which in the nature of things is bound to be precarious and temporary.

44 *Vietnam: Another Korea?*

The involvement of the United States in the Vietnamese war poses acutely two fundamental issues with which the foreign policy of the United States has tried to come to terms elsewhere and which it is likely to have to face in Vietnam and elsewhere in an even more acute form. These issues are the unqualified support we are extending to regimes whose political weakness compels us in the end to commit ourselves militarily beyond what our national interest would require, and the peripheral containment of Communist China. In order to understand the nature of these issues, as they pose themselves in Vietnam, it is first necessary to take a look at the history of our involvement with the affairs of Vietnam.

That history has been determined by a number of paradoxes. The war which France fought in Indochina until the Geneva agreement ended it in 1954 was for her essentially a colonial war, no different than the wars that France and Spain had fought in Africa in the 1920's. For the great majority of the Vietnamese, on the other hand, the war was a war for national liberation. However, for the United States and Communist China, without whose intervention the Indochina war would have taken on a different character and might well have had a different outcome, the war had nothing to do with national liberation or colonialism. As far as Communist China was concerned the war was an attempt to extend the area of influence and domination of communism. For the United States, too, the main issue of the war was the expansion of communism. Certainly the United States did not support France for the purpose of maintaining French power in Indochina. The United States looked at the Indochina war as part and parcel of its over-all strategy of containing communism throughout the world.

Yet while the interests of the United States were directly affected by the outcome of the Indochina war, the United States

From *Commentary*, May, 1962.

intervened in that war only to the extent of supporting the French war effort. It did not intervene directly in the war, nor did it participate actively in the Geneva settlement. On the one hand, the United States realized that the war was lost for the West, short of the intervention of the United States. On the other hand, it did not see fit—recovering, as it was, from the trauma of the Korean War just ended—to intervene actively in that war, to take over the military burden which France had shouldered so long, with such enormous liabilities and such lack of success. While the United States is committed to the containment of communism everywhere in the world, this commitment is obviously subject to qualifications; the limited involvement of the United States in the Indochina war and its passivity during the Geneva negotiations are cases in point.

The Geneva Conference ratified the military defeat of France and the political bankruptcy of its policy in Indochina. This defeat and bankruptcy being complete, one must ask oneself why it was that the Geneva Conference was held in the first place. From a strictly military point of view, the Vietminh could have marched south and forced the French to evacuate. Why, then, did the Communists agree to hold a conference? Why did the Soviet Union, in fact, emphasize at the Berlin conference of 1954 the necessity for such a conference? And why was it that at the conference itself the Communist powers, for the sake of agreement, made important concessions to the West? The Communists went into the conference proposing the fourteenth parallel as the dividing line between North and South Vietnam, and they retreated to the seventeenth parallel. They wanted elections six months after the armistice, and they conceded two years.

We have heard much of negotiating from strength. Certainly at Geneva in 1954, the Communists had strength. Yet they conducted the negotiations in the spirit of compromise, and the political settlement to which they agreed was much more advantageous to the West than was warranted by the actual military situation. It would certainly be absurd to suggest that it was magnanimity which induced the Communists to make these concessions, or that it was simply for the sake of an agreement per se that they were made. It seems to me that a consideration of the reasons why those concessions were made—why there was a conference to begin with, with a

366

compromise agreement to terminate it—will give us an inkling of the place that South Vietnam has today in the over-all world situation, particularly from the point of view of the United States and its interests.

First of all, Communist China pursues in Asia an over-all military and political objective which parallels the objective of the Soviet Union in Europe. It is to remove the power of the United States from the continent of Asia; for American power on the continent of Asia, especially in the form of military strong points, constitutes a permanent challenge to the power of Communist China on that continent. A continuation of the Indochina war, ending foreseeably with a complete military disaster for France, might still have led to the active participation of the United States and established it as a military power within the traditional sphere of influence of China. Second, what the Communists conceded at Geneva both they and many Western observers viewed as only temporary concessions. It was then generally believed that South Vietnam was doomed; that Mr. Diem was the creation of the United States, pulled out of a hat by desperate American officials; that he would be unable to master the chaos then prevailing in South Vietnam; and that elections, whenever held, would give an overwhelming majority to the Communists. Thus the Communists expected, and in view of the facts then available, had a right to expect, that sooner or later South Vietnam would fall to them. Third, the Vietminh wanted to take over the Red River delta intact rather than to have to conquer it. Finally, and perhaps most important, the Soviet Union had just embarked upon its new policy of transforming the Cold War of position into a Cold War of maneuver, which was to be decided not in southeast Asia but Europe. At that time, France occupied a key position in the over-all struggle for power in Europe. Its attitude was decisive for the success of the European Defense Community. By making a concession to France, by not humiliating France to the limit of its ability, the Soviet Union must have hoped to prevent France from ratifying EDC. For whatever reasons, France did not ratify EDC, and in that measure the expectations of the Soviet Union were justified.

However, the expectations of friend and foe alike, which anticipated the absorption of South Vietnam in the Communist orbit as inevitable, were belied by the vigor and success with which South Vietnam set about creating a new state from the ruins of a French colony. The vigor and at least temporary success of this seemingly hopeless experiment were due to three factors: American support, the qualities of the Vietnamese people, especially of the refugees from the north, and the personality of President Diem.

The United States, once the danger of its getting involved in another Korean-type war had passed, recovered its ability to correlate its commitments to the objective of its foreign policy. That objective being the containment of communism, the United States embarked upon a concerted policy of political, military, and economic assistance to President Diem's regime. Without that assistance, President Diem could not have achieved his initial successes. Yet these successes owe a great deal also to the extraordinary qualities of the Vietnamese people. Anybody who has traveled in Asia with his eyes open, beholding the different degrees of decay and backwardness, must have been impressed with the vitality and intelligence of the Vietnamese people. For instance, the order, vigor, and productivity of the refugee camps were monuments to these qualities. These qualities of the Vietnamese people and American aid needed the fulcrum of President Diem's extraordinary personality in order to become effective as raw material in the building of a temporary political order in South Vietnam. In order to explain the impact, for good and evil, of that personality upon the situation in South Vietnam, I don't think I can do any better than quote from the report I published in the *Washington Post* of February 26, 1956:

. . . The first impression of lofty impracticality is belied by the concrete achievements of President Diem. In little more than a year Diem has gotten rid of the Emperor and made himself President; he has established his control over the army; he has purged the police of the gangster element; he has pushed back, and in part eliminated, the independent power of the religious sects and of the Communists; and he has thus been able to establish something approaching efficient administration in a considerable part of the territory of Vietnam. He has done so entirely by totalitarian means.

Of the eleven parties opposing Diem, only two splinter groups, the Socialist and Republican parties, dare operate in the open. The others, of which the Communist party, called Vietcong, is the most important, work underground or else are engaged in open rebellion. Freedom of the press does not exist. When recently a bomb was thrown onto the stage of a Saigon theatre, blowing off the legs of the foremost actor of Vietnam, the press was not allowed to print the news. On the other hand, on December 12 of last year these two news items appeared in the Saigon press:

> On Dec. 9 the Second district police arrested NGUYEN DUY HINH, editor of the now-closed daily paper DAN DEN. HINH has been under investigation for several months for various dishonest acts committed against several persons.

> The only incident during the meeting [of newspaper owners and writers] was the throwing out of Mr. PHAM VAN THU, owner of the now-closed weekly paper CAI TAG. As he rose to speak in defense of his position, the majority protested and demanded his expulsion. THU was unanimously blamed for serving the Vietcong and Colonialist cause.

This repression is not limited to newspapers. Almost daily the newspapers report the shooting of some rebels or Communists. But nobody knows how many people are shot every day by the armed forces of the regime and under what circumstances. There have been popular trials of suspected subversives in the villages with the death sentence executed on the spot. When one tries to engage private persons in political conversation, one meets a furtive glance and silence.

Nor are the positive—puritanical and ideological—elements of totalitarianism missing. Diem has embarked upon a successful "Anti-Loose Living" campaign which has transformed Saigon, the former Paris of Southeast Asia, into the dullest of French colonial towns. A most intricate and elaborate system of propaganda and control has just been instituted in the villages. In its essence it is a cell system the lowest unit of which is composed of the representatives of five families. Each representative is responsible for the performance of a particular function, such as education, security, tax collection, on which he reports, and is reported on, to a higher unit. I have seen the organization charts of this "five houses" system. If it works, hardly anything a Vietnamese peasant does will remain unobserved, uncontrolled, and unreported.

Considering the enormity of the task which confronts Diem, it would certainly be ill-advised to be squeamish about some of the methods he has used. However, if he should try to establish a totalitarian regime in permanence rather than as an emergency measure, he will have given his people little to choose between the totalitarianism of the North and his own.

It was obvious to me then, and I told President Diem so to his displeasure, that these policies would inevitably lead to a bipolarization of politics in South Vietnam. Supported by an oligarchy whose interests were tied to the regime, he would have to govern a politically frustrated and, hence, indifferent population, while the Communist underground would provide the only organized opportunity for political opposition. By equating all opposition with communism, he would force the popular aspirations for change into Communist channels. This is what happened. Having to choose between President Diem's personal totalitarianism and the totalitarianism of communism, which at least can justify itself by a forward-looking philosophy, the Vietnamese people at best abstain from choosing and at worst choose communism.

The extent of popular disaffection with the Diem regime is not known to American public opinion, which, following the example of the government, prefers to think of the problem of South Vietnam in terms of Communist aggression versus the defense of freedom. This disaffection is particularly widespread among those classes which are the natural supporters of a democratic regime or else its indispensable allies, such as business and professional men, university teachers and students, civil servants, and army officers. It is particularly strong among the refugees from the north, who, after becoming refugees from Communist totalitarianism, are disappointed and embittered at the recognition of having exchanged one totalitarianism for another. Their disaffection extends to the Kennedy administration from which they expected support for their aspirations. It is significant and bodes ill for the future of the regime that the intensity of disaffection increases with the degree of education and political sophistication. The attitude of the great mass of the peasants, on the other hand, is marked by indifference to the ideological positions of either side. They tend to look at Diem as a kind of American puppet, the successor to Bao Dai, the French puppet, and at the Americans as the successors to French colonial rule. Communism means nothing to them one way or other. What interests them and determines their attitude is the benefits and disadvantages to be expected from either side. Thus they will submit to, and co-operate with, whoever happens to exercise authority at a particular time, and prisoners will join the other side almost as a matter of course, only to rejoin their former friends if the fortunes of guerilla war should change.

How has American policy tried to cope with this situation? It has done so by two simple expedients, which have recommended themselves here as elsewhere exactly because of their simplicity: support for the domestic political status quo and military defense against the foreign enemy. Both policies are simple, as compared with the alternatives, in terms of the intellectual effort to be expended and the short-term political risks to be taken. But they also contradict each other in that the domestic political status quo is the greatest single impediment to successful military defense, short of commitments in men and matériel on the part of the United States out of all proportion to the American interests at stake. Nothing can be simpler than to see in President Diem's regime the only viable anti-Communist government of South Vietnam, which therefore must be supported come what may, despite one's misgivings about its philosophy and policies. Nothing can be simpler than to reduce the political and military instability of South Vietnam to the result of Communist aggression from without, to be countered by military action. But the very simplicity of these conceptions distorts a complex reality, and in consequence, policies based upon such misconceptions are bound to be unsuccessful or can be made successful only at disproportionate costs and at inordinate risks.

If it was obvious to a casual observer like myself in 1955, it could not have been lost upon the experts six years later, that the main source of the political and military instability of South Vietnam must be sought in the very status quo which our policy is committed to maintain. If South Vietnam had a government which could count upon the loyalty of its civil service and armed forces and the support of the peasants, guerillas would not be able to control whole provinces and penetrate to the very outskirts of the capital. Guerilla warfare is a political problem before it is a military one. Both in Malaya and Greece, military action against the guerillas remained ineffective until drastic political reforms removed the causes for popular indifference and hostility. The case of Greece is particularly instructive in this respect, for here the United States in the late forties had to cope with a situation not dissimilar to that which confronts it today in South Vietnam. The United States was able to restore peace and order in Greece through a co-ordinated political, economic, and military campaign which required the commitment of limited American resources because it gave priority to political and economic reforms. The arguments advanced then on behalf of the inevitability of the existing political and economic status quo were as specious in the case of Greece as they are now in the case of South Vietnam.

The argument that there is no alternative to Diem is in the nature of a self-fulfilling prophecy. There appears to be no alternative to Diem only because we have placed all our bets on him. Six years ago, I was impressed with both the number and quality of public figures who took a passionate and intelligent interest in establishing a free and decent political order in South Vietnam. It is, of course, impossible to say from a distance whether such men are still available today. But certainly the United States could, if it had a mind to, find a general who could take over the reigns of government and through whom the United States could effect the necessary political, economic, and social reforms.

The United States has two alternative policies to choose from: political reforms as a precondition for the restoration of peace and order in South Vietnam or purely military means. The former policy requires the elimination of Diem, and demands of American officials in the field great manipulative skills and exposes them to considerable short-term political risks, while it is likely to require of the United States but a limited military commitment. On the highest level at least, the government of the United States seems to have recognized the need for such political reforms, but there is no indication that this intellectual recognition has been transformed into effective political action in Saigon. Thus we have been forced to choose, half-heartedly and almost by default, the other alternative of a purely military solution.

This policy is a legacy from the Dulles era. It was then widely held that the acquisition by a Communist power of any piece of territory, regardless of its size and location, was a calamity which signaled the beginning of the end of the Free World. Vietnam, for instance, was considered to be the "cork in the bottle," the "first in a row of dominoes"; if it fell, all of Indochina would fall, too. In fact, of course, North Vietnam went Communist, but South Vietnam did not; nor did the other states of Indochina. This unexpectedly favorable outcome of the Indochina war provides empirical proof for the proposition that Communist territorial gains can be localized and can affect the interests of the United States adversely in differing degrees.

The misconception that each Communist territorial gain constitutes for the United States a calamity of the first magnitude has as its corollary the proposition that the United States must commit its military power to the defense of any territory that might be threatened by Communist subversion or aggression. The indiscriminate policy of alliances, offering our military support to whatever nation was willing to accept it (i.e., SEATO and the Eisenhower Doctrine), reflects that conviction. However, when the chips were down we were fortunately capable of distinguishing among interests which did not require any American military commitment at all, those which required a limited military commitment, and those which might require an all-out military commitment. Thus we did not intervene in the Indochina war, risking thereby, and reconciling ourselves to, the loss of all of Vietnam to the Communists. We did not commit our military strength to the liberation of the countries of Eastern Europe, of Cuba and Tibet. We were very careful in limiting the Korean War; and it was Mr. Dulles himself, the most consistent proponent of a militarily oriented foreign policy, who liquidated the Korean War on the basis of the *status quo ante bellum*.

It is therefore incumbent upon the government of the United States to determine with all possible precision the extent of the American interest in South Vietnam. The extent of our military commitment must depend upon that political determination. Is South Vietnam as important to us, or more or less so, than Korea or Cuba? Or is it as important as Berlin? The answer to political questions such as these must determine the extent of our military commitment. Once South Vietnam is assigned its place in the hierarchy of American interests throughout the world, the government of the United States can profitably raise the question of a diplomatic solution to the problem of South Vietnam. Such a solution could be envisaged after the model of the diplomatic solution of the Geneva agreement of 1954, to which South Vietnam after all owes its very existence as an independent state. The United States is not the only country that has interests in Vietnam and elsewhere. So do the Soviet Union and Communist China, and so do our allies. The possibility of a negotiated settlement within the context of the over-all interests of the major interested parties is certainly worth exploring, and it is an open question whether the chances for such a settlement are greater now than they would be at the conclusion of a drawn-out, inconclusive war.

A purely military policy is popular with the officials in the field because it frees them from the burden of political manipulation, to which they are unaccustomed and from which they shy almost instinctively away because of the political risks involved. It is also popular with large segments of the American people because it promises a clear-cut solution to an irksome problem in the form of victory. Yet in truth, this purely military policy is fraught with enormous risks and dangers for the United States, for it raises acutely the fundamental issue of our Asian policy: the peripheral containment of Communist China by military means. It conjures up the possibility, if not the likelihood, of a repetition of the Korean War, perhaps even more drawn-out and less conclusive in its results than that war was. It should not be forgotten that, fought under much more favorable political conditions, the guerilla war in Greece lasted five years and the one in Malaya twelve.

It is an illusion to think that Communist China is being contained today by the military power which the United States can bring to bear locally in Laos, Thailand, South Vietnam, or Taiwan, or that it has thus been contained in the past. Communist China has it in its power to increase the challenges locally with little cost to itself and thereby force the United States to increase its military commitments far beyond its own. It will stop, as it has stopped in the past, at the point where the escalation of American conventional military commitments conjures up the possibility of an all-out war initiated by the United States. It is at that point that containment becomes effective. In other words, what contains Communist China is its over-all weakness vis-à-vis the United States. Yet barring a catastrophe within Communist China, this weakness is likely to be replaced in the foreseeable future by a strength which will make Communist China the foremost military power in Asia. It is from the perspective of this actual source of the containment of Communist China and of the prospect of China's future military strength

374

that the present military policy of the United States in South Vietnam must be viewed.

If the present primarily military approach is persisted in, we are likely to be drawn ever more deeply into a Korean-type war, fought under political and military conditions much more unfavorable than those that prevailed in Korea and in the world a decade ago. Such a war cannot be won quickly, if it can be won at all, and may well last, like its Greek and Malayan counterparts, five or ten years, perhaps only to end again in a stalemate as did the Korean War. Aside from the military risks to which it will give rise in view of the distribution of military power which exists today and is likely to exist five or ten years hence, such a war is bound to have a profound impact upon the political health of the nation. McCarthyism and the change in the political complexion of the nation which the elections of 1952 brought about resulted directly from the frustrations of the Korean War. The American people are bound to be at least as deeply affected by the frustrations of a Vietnamese war.

The present primarily military approach has been undertaken without sufficient regard for its own military implications and its likely impact upon American politics at home and the American position in the world. The only viable alternative to that approach is the subordination of our military commitments to, and thereby their limitation by, our political objectives in South Vietnam. These objectives must be defined as the restoration of a viable political order, which constitutes the only effective defense against Communist subversion. It is obvious that such a political order can be established only through American intervention. It would be infantile to argue against such a policy on the grounds that it is intervention; for if we had not intervened consistently since 1954 in the affairs of South Vietnam, Mr. Diem would not be its President today and South Vietnam itself would not exist. The choices before us are not between intervention and non-intervention, but between an intervention which serves our political interests and thereby limits our military commitments and an intervention which supports to the bitter end the powers-that-be, even if their policies, by being counterproductive, jeopardize the interests of the United States.

EPILOGUE

45 *The President*

"It is the extraordinary isolation imposed upon the President," wrote Woodrow Wilson in 1908, "that makes the character and opportunity of his office so extraordinary." That isolation is the inevitable result of the great responsibility and power of the President's office. He is the chief executive, the commander in chief of the armed forces, the leader of the nation, and the head of his party. Our constitutional and political system culminates in this one man. What he does or does not do will determine the fate of his party and of the nation. Wilson continued:

Let him once win the admiration and confidence of the country, and no other single force can withstand him, no combination of forces will easily overpower him. His position takes the imagination of the country. He is the representative of no constituency, but of the whole people. When he speaks in his true character, he speaks for no special interest. If he rightly interpret the national thought and boldly insist upon it, he is irresistible; and the country never feels the zest of action so much as when its President is of such insight and caliber. Its instinct is for unified action, and it craves a single leader.

To be President, then, means of necessity to be lonely, to carry what Dean Rusk has recently called an "almost unbearable responsibility" and to wield almost superhuman power. The man who becomes President on January 20, 1961, will sit behind a massive desk in the south arc of an oval room of noble classical proportions and austere decor, located in the west wing of the White House. Hundreds of officials and personal aides will enter this room to advise and assist him; foreign statesmen and diplomats will come and go; members of Congress will confer with him; civic delegations will chat and leave through the French doors to be photographed with him in the rose garden. Yet this variety of his human contacts and his crowded appointment schedule only serve to underline the "extraordinary isolation" in which the President of the United States

From the *New York Times Magazine*, November 13, 1960.

must spend the most important hours of his tenure—the hours of decision.

Lincoln has given us the classic account of Presidential loneliness, both terrifying and ennobling. After he had decided to issue a proclamation emancipating the slaves, he called a meeting of his Cabinet for September 22, 1862, and addressed it in these terms:

> I have got you together to hear what I have written down. I do not wish your advice about the main matter, for that I have determined by myself. . . .
> I know very well that many others might in this matter, as in others, do better than I can; and if I was satisfied that the public confidence was more fully possessed by any one of them than by me, and knew of any constitutional way in which he could be put in my place, he should have it. I would gladly yield it to him. But though I believe I have not so much of the confidence of the people as I had some time since, I do not know that, all things considered, any other person has more; and, however this may be, there is no way in which I can have any other man put where I am. I am here; I must do the best I can, and bear the responsibility of taking the course which I feel I ought to take.

Of Woodrow Wilson's lonely ordeal during the last three weeks of March, 1917, we have Ray Stannard Baker's and Frank I. Cobb's accounts. "For about ten days," reports Baker, "he remained almost constantly in his room: he saw few visitors: he wrote scarcely a dozen indispensable letters. . . . Even after he had completed his message on April 1st, the doubts that besieged him were all but overwhelming. Feeling, apparently, that he must talk them out with someone, as he could not talk even with the members of his Cabinet, he sent for Frank I. Cobb, of The New York World." Here is Cobb's account of the meeting:

> I'd never seen him so worn down. He looked as if hadn't slept, and he said he hadn't. He said he was probably going before Congress the next day to ask a declaration of war, and he'd never been so uncertain about anything in his life as about that decision. For nights, he said, he'd been lying awake going over the whole situation. . . .
> "I think I know what war means," he said, and he added that if there were any possibility of avoiding war he wanted to try it. "What else can I do?" he asked. "Is there anything else I can do?"

President Truman has written of his decision to drop the atomic bomb:

I gave careful thought to what my advisers had counseled. I wanted to weigh all the possibilities and implications. Here was the most powerful weapon of destruction ever devised and perhaps it was more than that.

Conscious of how great a responsibility had been placed on me, I suggested to Secretary Stimson that we give Japan a warning in advance by sending Japan an ultimatum to surrender. . . . I then agreed to the use of the atomic bomb if Japan did not yield.

I had reached a decision after long and careful thought. It was not an easy decision to make. I did not like the weapon. But I had no qualms if in the long run millions of lives could be saved.

This is then the President's great burden—the burden of loneliness in the hour of decision. There is much talk of another burden, overwork, and many proposals have been made for lightening the President's load. But the crux of the problem is not quantitative but qualitative—the need to aid and sustain the President in those lonely moments of decision.

Quantitatively, the President's burden has been greatly relieved. When the "Report of the President's Committee on Administrative Management," known as the Brownlow Report, stated in 1937 in an often-quoted phrase, "The President needs help," it had the work load in mind. The recommendations of the Brownlow Report were in good measure implemented. Today, two types of institutions assist the President directly in the performance of his functions: (1) the White House staff and (2) the agencies combined in the Executive Office of the President, such as the Council of Economic Advisers, the National Security Council, and the Central Intelligence Agency.

It has been much commented upon that during Mr. Eisenhower's major illnesses, which incapacitated him for considerable periods, the Presidency functioned very much as it did before and after. The Cabinet and the National Security Council deliberated under the chairmanship of the vice-president. The Department of State conducted the foreign policy of the United States. The Bureau of the Budget made decisions of high policy by allocating or withholding funds. And the routine of the White House was hardly affected. In brief, the Presidency operates with so high a degree of administrative efficiency that it operates even without the President.

The Presidency has been transformed into a depersonalized administrative machine, very much in the manner of a modern corporation. The men and women who make up this bureaucratic apparatus do what the President is supposed to do and once did, but can no longer do. They stand between him and the government departments transmitting information, problems, and proposed solutions to him, and requests and decisions from him. They have lightened his work load enormously. They have in good measure replaced him.

But by curing the ailment of overwork we have—paradoxically enough—aggravated the ailment of isolation. The President has been cut off from direct and full contact with the great issues which he alone must decide by layers upon layers of agencies and interagency committees. Thus, as a rule, he is presented not with an issue in all its complexity and controversiality, but with a dehydrated condensation and a solution which satisfies no one entirely but hurts nobody too much and, hence, is acceptable to all and susceptible of Presidential approval. The alternative solution may never even come to the President's attention. It has been said, for example, that when President Eisenhower chose the Vanguard over the Redstone as the missile for space exploration, he actually confirmed a choice made on lower levels without being aware of the relative merits of the two missiles.

The danger that the President will see the great issues he must decide through the eyes of his immediate subordinates is always present. It is aggravated if some of these subordinates have strong policy preferences of their own or seek to shield the President from controversy. It would be made still worse by the suggestions which have been made recently for further reorganization of the executive branch—for the establishment of an executive vice-president, or a number of them, or of a new Office of Executive Management—widening still more the gap that separates the President from the great issues.

The real problem is to enable the President to govern intelligently and decisively. In this he needs help. Where can he get it? In order to perform the supreme task of his office, the President needs three qualities: knowledge, power, purpose. Knowledge he must obtain from others; power he must wield with the aid of others; the purpose he must supply himself.

First, the President must have knowledge of the issues which require initiative on his part and of the alternative policies designed to meet them. If the President were to make it a rule—it is now but the exception—that no draft of a decision be submitted to him without an alternative where such exists, if he would hold an individual official responsible for correct and complete information in a particular field, and if he were to seek out areas of controversy and expose himself to their pressures, he would have taken the first steps toward the restoration of his power to govern.

The President must also draw upon informal sources of information and might well consult with groups of experts, official or private, of differing points of view, which in a sense would duplicate the alternative solutions of the pending issue. If this should make for a degree of administrative untidiness, let us accept it as the price we must pay for Presidential leadership.

Once the President has rendered his decision, he must make sure that it is executed. Here his knowledge and the exercise of his power blend. All modern Presidents have expressed their frustration on this count. Marriner Eccles, the former chairman of the Federal Reserve Board, has given this much-quoted account of Franklin D. Roosevelt's reaction:

> The Treasury is so large and far-flung in its practices that I find it is almost impossible to get the action and results I want—even with Henry [Morgenthau] there. But the Treasury is not to be compared with the State Department. You should go through the experience of trying to get any changes in the thinking, policy and action of the career diplomats and then you'd know what a real problem was.
>
> But the Treasury and the State Department put together are nothing compared with the Na-a-vy. The Admirals are really something to cope with—and I should know. To change anything in the Na-a-vy is like punching a feather bed. You punch it with your right and you punch it with your left until you are finally exhausted, and then you find the damn bed just as it was before you started punching.

Professor Richard E. Neustadt, of Columbia University, reports similar reactions by Presidents Truman and Eisenhower. "He'll sit here," he quotes Truman, referring to President-elect Eisenhower, "and he'll say, 'Do this! Do that!' *And nothing will happen.*" Neustadt quotes an aide of Eisenhower as having remarked to him in 1958: "The President still feels that when he's decided something, that *ought* to be the end of it . . . and when it bounces back undone or done wrong, he tends to react with shocked surprise." What Jonathan Daniels, a former aide to Franklin D. Roosevelt, has observed applies to others besides the members of the Cabinet:

Half of a President's suggestions, which theoretically carry the weight of orders, can be safely forgotten by a Cabinet member. And if the President asks about a suggestion a second time, he can be told that it is being investigated. If he asks a third time, a wise Cabinet officer will give him at least part of what he suggests. But only occasionally, except about the most important matters, do Presidents ever get around to asking three times.

The help the President needs for the task of making his decisions stick, he must essentially provide himself. He can make his will prevail within the executive branch to the extent that he is willing and able to employ the power of his office and of his person, for, as chief executive, the President is the politician-in-chief of the nation. In order to see his decisions put into action by his subordinates, he can and must promise and threaten, reward and punish. He needs assistance in the exercise of this power, but he cannot delegate its substance to a vice-president or "first secretary" without risking either its dissipation or its abuse.

There is no remedy outside himself for the heaviest burden—loneliness. When he makes one of the great decisions which Presidents have to make, he is alone with himself and with history. But there is a compensation, for from that loneliness, calling forth the ultimate reserves of his mind and soul, springs the President's greatness. Let us beware lest, by hemming him in with still another batch of assistants or managers, we impair the source of that greatness.

Index

Topics, if not indicated otherwise, refer primarily to the United States.